Radical
Innocence

Radical Innocence

A CRITICAL STUDY OF THE

Hollywood Ten

Bernard F. Dick

THE UNIVERSITY PRESS OF KENTUCKY

Scholarly publisher for the Commonwealth,
serving Bellarmine College, Berea College, Centre
College of Kentucky, Eastern Kentucky University,
The Filson Club, Georgetown College, Kentucky
Historical Society, Kentucky State University,
Morehead State University, Murray State University,
Northern Kentucky University, Transylvania University,
University of Kentucky, University of Louisville,
and Western Kentuky University.

Editorial and Sales Offices: Lexington, Kentucky 40506-0336

Library of Congress Cataloging-in-Publication Data
Dick, Bernard F.
　　Radical innocence : a critical study of the Hollywood Ten /
　　Bernard F. Dick.
　　———p.　cm.
　　Bibliography: p.
　　Includes index.
　　ISBN 0-8131-1660-0
　　1. Screenwriters—United States—Biography.　2. Motion picture
producers and directors—United States—Biography.　3. Motion
picture plays—History and criticism.　4. American literature—20th
century—History and criticism.　5. Motion picture industry—
California—Los Angeles.　6. Blacklisting of authors—California—
Los Angeles.　7. Hollywood (Los Angeles, Calif.)—Biography.
　8. Los Angeles (Calif.)—Biography.　I. Title.
PN1998.2.D5　1988
812'.03'09—dc19　　　　　　　　　　　　　　　　88-17366

This book is printed on acid-free paper meeting
the requirements of the American National Standard
for Permanence of Paper for Printed Library Materials. ⊖

Contents

115120

For Louis Harris

Acknowledgments

This book could not have been written without the cooperation of the following: Michael Cole; Irwin Danels; Samuel Gill, archivist, Margaret Herrick Library; the late John Hall, West Coast manager, RKO Pictures; Vernon Harbin; Ian McLellan Hunter; Judith Katz, Mary McMahon, and Laila Rogers of the Fairleigh Dickinson University Library staff (Teaneck-Hackensack campus); Peter Kells; Kristine L. Krueger, National Film Information Service; Robert Knutson, head, Archives of Performing Arts, University of Southern California; Ring Lardner, Jr.; Lynne Larsen; Audrée Malkin, head, Theatre Arts Library, University of California at Los Angeles; Karen Morley; Martin Nocente; Herbert S. Nusbaum, attorney, MGM; Sadie Ornitz; Kit Parker of Kit Parker Films; Arnold Pickelney, film distributor; Allan Scott; Joan Scott; Geoffrey Wexler, reference archivist, State Historical Society of Wisconsin.

I am grateful to Fairleigh Dickinson University for granting me release time to complete my research and above all to my wife, Katherine M. Restaino, for forgoing vacation time to rummage through files whose contents often provoked tears.

Introduction

On Monday 20 October 1947 at 10:30 A.M. in the packed Caucus Room of the Old House Office Building in Washington, D.C., amid the whirring of newsreel cameras and the popping of flashbulbs, the House Committee on Un-American Activities (HUAC) formally began hearings about alleged Communist infiltration of the motion picture industry. On Thursday 30 October at 3:00 P.M. the hearings ended, although it was clear from the concluding remarks of Chairman J. Parnell Thomas that the topic was far from exhausted: "The hearing today concludes the first phase of the committee's investigation of communism in the motion-picture industry. While we have heard 39 witnesses, there are many more to be heard. . . . I want to emphasize that the committee is not adjourning sine die, but will resume hearings as soon as possible. The committee hearings for the past 2 weeks have clearly shown the need for this investigation."[1]

Of these thirty-nine witnesses, ten were recommended for and eventually received contempt citations for refusing to answer what, in a rare moment of levity, Thomas called "the $64 question," also known as the "Are-you-now-or-have-you-ever-been" question; it followed the $32 question about their guild membership, which they also declined to answer. How ten men came to be called the Hollywood Ten is sufficiently well known from their own accounts and the works of others, the most authoritative of which is Larry Ceplair and Steven Englund's study.[2] But because the individuality of ten human beings vanished with the imposition of a label, the circumstances under which they acquired a collective identity merit a brief summary.

By the third week of September 1947, forty-three members of the Hollywood community had received subpoenas requiring them to appear before HUAC the following month.[3] Some might have been surprised; most probably were not. The October hearings, to use a Hollywood cliché, had been many years in the making; they were the culmination of a series of events harking back to the screenwriters' wars of the 1930s, which ended in what was perceived as a victory for the left when the Screen Writers Guild (SWG) became the writers' official bargaining agent.[4] The extreme right saw the unionization of writers as the first step toward the left's domination of the screen: hence the notion that the SWG was Communist-infested.

The Motion Picture Alliance for the Preservation of American Ideals, founded in 1944, had similar concerns. Its purpose, as member James K. McGuinness told HUAC on 22 October 1947, was "to combat what we regard as a growing menace within our own industry of Communists and to some degree Fascists, and to preserve . . . the screen in its loyalty to the free America which gave it birth" (136). The Motion Picture Alliance also served another purpose: it provided HUAC with witnesses willing to testify about Communism in Hollywood when the committee came to Los Angeles in May 1947 to conduct closed hearings on the subject about which it would hold open hearings in Washington five months later. It was not coincidental that of those subpoenaed the following September, eleven were members of the Motion Picture Alliance—including its first president and vice-president, Sam Wood and Walt Disney respectively.

Our film capital, like our nation's capital, is essentially a small town. Both Hollywood and Washington thrive on gossip; both insist upon a certain amount of privacy (closed sets, closed hearings), but leaks are inevitable and often deliberate. No set can really be closed; if it were, no film could ever be made. Similarly, during the second week of May 1947 only a newcomer to Hollywood would not have known that HUAC was ensconced at the Biltmore Hotel listening to Sam Wood, Richard Arlen, Adolphe Menjou, Lela Rogers, and ten others divulge the names of real, suspected, or imaginary Communists. The "closed" hearings even made the front page of the New York Times (15 May 1947), which reported the testimony of Robert Taylor that he was prevented from entering the Navy until he had finished Song of Russia, and of Lela Rogers (Ginger's mother), who named Dalton Trumbo and Clifford Odets as Communists. As a result of the May hearings, HUAC had little difficulty compiling a list of witnesses for October. Like the Spanish Civil War, which was the dress rehearsal for World War II, HUAC's May run-through was a preview of October when many of the same witnesses returned under subpoena to repeat, augment, or embellish what they had disclosed in May.

The subpoenaed were a combination of recognizable names and faces (Robert Taylor, Gary Cooper, Robert Montgomery, Ronald Reagan, George Murphy), recognizable names alone (Jack Warner, Walt Disney), and names or faces that even film stalwarts would have had difficulty placing (McGuinness, Howard Rushmore). It is customary to think of the witnesses as "friendly" and "unfriendly" because they had been designated as such before the October hearings; "friendly" was a term Thomas used at the end of the May hearings for the cooperative witnesses; "unfriendly" was applied by the Red-baiting Hollywood Reporter to nineteen who openly expressed their opposition to HUAC and thus became known as the Hollywood Nineteen or the Unfriendly Nineteen.

The nineteen were a curious mix of screenwriters (Alvah Bessie, Lester Cole, Richard Collins, Gordon Kahn, Howard Koch, Ring Lardner, Jr., John Howard Lawson, Albert Maltz, Samuel Ornitz, Waldo Salt, and Dalton Trumbo); directors (Edward Dmytryk, Lewis Milestone, and Irving Pichel); writer-directors (Herbert Biberman and Robert Rossen); a writer-producer (Adrian Scott); a playwright (Bertolt Brecht), and an actor (Larry Parks). In 1947 the only name familiar to the average moviegoer would have been that of Larry Parks, whose ability to capture Al Jolson's mannerisms and lip-synch his songs in *The Jolson Story* (1946) is still a marvel of verisimilitude.

Why these particular men (interestingly, they *were* all males) were subpoenaed has never been satisfactorily explained, apart from the fact that HUAC had acquired enough information about them to know where they stood politically. Even Ceplair and Englund can only conjecture, noting that most of the nineteen were or had been Communists; most were or had been writers and therefore—to HUAC—constituted a conduit through which Communist propaganda reached the screen; all had been pro-Soviet and, with the exception of Richard Collins, had not been in the service during World War II.

However, the same could be said of other Hollywood radicals; Thomas did claim to have seventy-nine names. If a military record is the sine qua non of patriotism, it would have been impossible for the medically disqualified Lardner and the overage Lawson, Ornitz, Milestone, and Pichel to acquire one. Being pro-Soviet after June 1941 was hardly a crime; Douglas MacArthur went so far as to pin the hopes of civilization on the Soviet Union's ability to crush Hitler's armies. If Howard Koch, who was not even a Communist, could be subpoenaed because the voluble Jack Warner mentioned him in the same context as Communist writers and because Koch had written the screenplay of *Mission to Moscow* (1943)—which Warner made at President Roosevelt's request—then Casey Robinson should have been subpoenaed for writing the screenplay of the equally pro-Soviet *Days of Glory* (1944). (Robinson, however, had no worries; apart from being apolitical, he was also a member of the executive committee of the Motion Picture Alliance.)

There was no limit to HUAC's inconsistencies. If the friendly witnesses included women (Ayn Rand, Lela Rogers), why was "the other side" (HUAC's term), all male? The committee had enough information on Lillian Hellman and Karen Morley to subpoena them in September 1947—and did so in 1952; why not in 1947? Why did a committee so publicity-hungry that it had a camera rehearsal on 18

October come up with what *Variety* would term a cast of relative unknowns? How much less tedious the hearings would have been if the "other side" had included Elia Kazan (who might have turned informant then instead of waiting until 1952), John Garfield, Dashiell Hammett, Hellman, Morley, and Dorothy Parker.

Even the way the subpoenas were issued shows that the committee had only the vaguest idea of how to stage the most significant session in its history to that point. Whether or not HUAC planned to hear the friendly and unfriendly witnesses separately is uncertain, although that is roughly what happened. The subpoenas sent to the unfriendly witnesses all specified an appearance date of 23 October; those sent to friendly witnesses gave no date at all with the exception of Eric Johnston (20 October), Oliver Carlson and Howard Rushmore (22 October), and Robert Montgomery (23 October). As it happened, Montgomery did testify on 23 October, but the unfriendly witnesses did not; apparently realizing its error, HUAC sent telegrams to the unfriendlies, informing them that they would be called the week of 27 October. By the week before the hearings, HUAC had at least decided that the friendlies would precede the unfriendlies and that each group would be given a week, although the latter was shortchanged by a day.

It would have made sense to begin with Eric Johnston, president of the Motion Picture Association of America, but on reflection Thomas must have realized that Johnston would be obliged to defend the industry he represented. It would be better to start with someone safe, a known quantity. And who was safer than Jack Warner, who had appeared in May and could be counted on to name names indiscriminately? Since another and greater studio head, Louis B. Mayer of MGM, was also in attendance on 20 October, he was the logical next witness—but one demonstration of logic, however calculating, was sufficient, and so Warner was followed by a director (Sam Wood); the director by the head of the biggest studio in Hollywood (Mayer); the studio head by a writer (Ayn Rand); the writer by an actor (Adolphe Menjou); the actor by two more writers (John Charles Moffitt and Rupert Hughes); the writers by a film executive (James J. McGuinness); the executive by one of Hollywood's biggest male stars (Robert Taylor); the star by an ex-Communist (Howard Rushmore); the ex-Communist by three more writers (Morrie Ryskind, Fred Niblo, Jr., and Richard Macaulay); the writers by four actors (Robert Montgomery, George Murphy, Ronald Reagan, Gary Cooper); the actors by Ginger Rogers's mother (Lela Rogers); Ginger's mother by a political scientist (Oliver Carlson); the political scientist by Walt Disney. That the maker of *Fantasia* (1940) should close out the week was a fitting commentary on five days of fantasy that, if filmed, could best have been rendered as an animated cartoon.

On Friday, Chairman Thomas announced that the second week of hearings would begin on 27 October with Eric Johnston, labor leader Roy Brewer, John Howard Lawson, Dalton Trumbo, Alvah Bessie, and Emmet Lavery. That order, however, vanished over the weekend. Expecting to be third, Lawson discovered at 10:20 A.M. that he was first, thus becoming the first of the unfriendlies and consequently the first of the Hollywood Ten. Trumbo and Bessie, along with the unannounced Maltz, were called on 28 October; Trumbo was first, even though at the close of the previous day's hearings Chairman Thomas had said Brewer would be.

As Ceplair and Englund have observed, HUAC never explained the order in which the unfriendly witnesses were called. It is commonly thought to have been determined by the amount of evidence collected, but the actual order—Lawson (27 October); Trumbo, Maltz, Bessie (28 October); Ornitz, Biberman, Dmytryk, Scott (29 October); Lardner, Cole, Brecht (30 October)—does not bear out such a belief. Nor does the fact that Clifford Odets was never called, even though HUAC claimed to have a "voluminous record" (231) on him. After the witnesses had testified, Louis B. Russell, HUAC investigator and former FBI agent, presented his evidence of Communist affiliations, which was then incorporated into the minutes. Russell admitted to having fifteen single-spaced pages on Maltz, as opposed to nine on Lawson. Maltz, then, should have been first—a fact HUAC remembered a month later when it was time to win Congressional approval for the contempt citations: on 24 November, at a session of the House of Representatives, Maltz was the first to be voted on, the fifteen pages being offered as proof.

As the first of the Ten, Lawson was not the ideal witness, although Maltz would not have been much better. Lawson could not conceal his contempt for the committee; that, combined with his hauteur, led to his inadvertently answering the SWG membership question. He insisted that HUAC had no right to ask it, but when his anger got the better of him, he admitted it was common knowledge that he was not only a member but also the Guild's first president.

For some inexplicable reason Lardner was to have testified sixth, after Ornitz, but since he had not been given a specific date, he decided to remain in his hotel room on 29 October and listen to the hearings on the radio. Naturally, he was surprised to hear his name called.[5] Because of Lardner's absence, Biberman, who was to have followed Lardner, instead followed Ornitz; yet as the transcript shows, Russell had more evidence on Biberman (nineteen affiliations) than he did on Lardner (twelve). After Biberman had so exasperated the committee that Thomas muttered, "Take him away," chief investigator Stripling had no idea who was next. Thomas asked who was present; hearing that

Edward Dmytryk was there but that Adrian Scott was absent that morning with laryngitis, Thomas looked for someone else. The reason was obvious: the director and producer of RKO's *Crossfire* were considered a team and had to testify consecutively. "How about Mr. Lavery?" Thomas inquired (418). Emmet Lavery had been scheduled for 27 October when only Lawson and Johnston had testified. Since he was in attendance, he was called on 29 October.

For all it mattered, Lavery could have testified at any time; the prominent Catholic layman, playwright, screenwriter, lawyer, and current SWG president answered both the $32 and $64 questions. He could hardly deny membership in the organization he headed, and he did not wait for the question of questions: "Let me break the suspense immediately and tell you that I am not a Communist. I never have been. I don't intend to be" (442). This came as a relief to HUAC since, during the first week, Warner had mentioned him in the same breath with other Communists, Rupert Hughes accused him of being at least a fellow traveler, and John Charles Moffitt had claimed that he used the Communist tactic of alerting Americans to the danger of the A-bomb. Thomas even admitted that he thought Lavery belonged to "the other side" (422), which explains why he was scheduled in the second week.

By the afternoon of 29 October, Lardner was still in his hotel room, much to Thomas's annoyance. But Scott had recovered from his laryngitis, so Dmytryk and he became the next witnesses. If the amount of evidence had really been the determining factor in the order of testimony, Adrian Scott, on whom all Russell could produce was a single paragraph, would surely have been last. But as Thersites exclaimed in *Troilus and Cressida* (II.iii), "all the argument is a cuckold and a whore." Scott had to testify with Dmytryk because *Crossfire*'s assault on anti-Semitism was considered Communist, the argument being that only Communists would make a film in which the anti-Semitic killer is a deranged ex-GI.

If the director and producer of *Crossfire* were summoned, why not the writer, especially since HUAC insisted that the script is "the principal medium through which Communists have sought to inject their propaganda" (225)? The reason is that the writer, John Paxton, was not a Communist, nor was there any evidence he had ever been one. Since RKO was Dmytryk and Scott's home studio, and since RKO's head of production, Dore Schary (also a *Crossfire* enthusiast), was present, Schary followed Scott. Like Lavery, he had been scheduled for the second week because HUAC was uncertain of his sympathies; he was, after all, a liberal. While Schary told HUAC what it wanted to hear—"I am not a Communist. I never have been a Communist" (472)—he stopped short of saying he would fire Dmytryk and Scott for being

Communists. This is more than Louis B. Mayer had done when asked if he would employ Cole and Trumbo after seeing their Party cards. "No, sir" (73) was Mayer's unequivocal reply. Similarly, when Johnston was asked if he thought John Howard Lawson had any place in the industry, he had answered unhesitatingly: "If all of the evidence here is proven to be true, I would not employ Mr. Lawson because I would not employ any proven or admitted Communist because they are just a disruptive force and I don't want them around" (323). The blacklist had begun, with the blessing of the president of the Motion Picture Association of America.

On Thursday 30 October, which turned out to be the last day of the hearings, the committee finally got around to Ring Lardner, Jr., who should have been sixth and was now ninth. After Lardner was dismissed for the same reason as the others, Lester Cole testified, and for as short a time. That Cole, who entitled his autobiography *Hollywood Red*, should have been tenth, thus becoming the last of the Hollywood Ten, does not speak well of Russell's research. As Morrie Ryskind said on 22 October when asked about Cole, "Well, if Lester Cole isn't a Communist, I don't think Mahatma Gandhi is an Indian" (187).

Of the nineteen, only eleven were called; the eleventh was Bertolt Brecht. Ostensibly, HUAC could have made a better choice. Brecht had only been in the United States since 1941, and his connection with the film industry was tenuous at most. His sole screen credit was the story of *Hangmen Also Die* (1943); thus he could not even be asked if he were a member of the Screen Writers Guild. But HUAC wanted Brecht for a reason as devious as the one that required Dmytryk and Scott to testify in tandem. On 24 September composer Hanns Eisler, Brecht's friend and fellow émigré, had been interrogated by the committee and treated more shabbily than any of the unfriendlies. Eisler, who had written the music for Brecht's *Measures Taken*, *The Mother*, and *Galileo*, had also written the music for *Hangmen Also Die* and several RKO films, including *None but the Lonely Heart* (1944), which Lela Rogers considered Communistic. It was therefore not out of character for Stripling to ask Dore Schary if Brecht worked at RKO (although it certainly revealed Stripling's ignorance of the medium he was investigating). Again the argument is a whore: if Brecht knew Eisler, and if Eisler wrote the music for a film to which Brecht contributed the story, and if Eisler is a Communist, *ergo*, so is Brecht. Brecht, however, made the argument a cuckold by answering the $64 question: "I was not a member or am not a member of any Communist party" (94). Since his syntax was ambiguous (perhaps, it has been suggested, because *he* was), the question was rephrased: "Your answer is, then, that you have never been a member of the Communist party?" "That is correct," Brecht replied. A model witness, Brecht left the stand—and the country—with HUAC's thanks.

By Wednesday it had been obvious that Thomas was trying to speed up the proceedings, perhaps influenced by an unfavorable press and a general loss of interest but probably not by the appearance in Washington of the Committee for the First Amendment (even though it included such luminaries as Danny Kaye, Humphrey Bogart, and Lauren Bacall). In any case, HUAC had ten victims and could now deliver an ultimatum to Hollywood: "It is not necessary for the Chair to emphasize the harm which the motion-picture industry suffers from the presence within its ranks of known Communists who do not have the best interests of the United States at heart. The industry should set about immediately to clean its own house and not wait for public opinion to force it to do so" (552).

Within less than a month the industry responded with the Waldorf Statement (25 November 1947) according to which it would "forthwith discharge without compensation and . . . not re-employ any of the Ten, until such time as he is acquitted, or has purged himself of contempt and declared under oath that he is not a Communist." By 5 December the Ten had been formally indicted for contempt. Lawson and Trumbo, the first two to be called, were tried and convicted in the spring of 1948. After two years of petitions, briefs, and appeals, the Ten were all serving their sentences by 1950.

Since HUAC portrayed the Ten as a cadre, the belief persists that they were film's equivalent of the Chicago Eight or the Catonsville Nine. Yet nothing is further from the truth. They did not come to a particular place for a particular purpose, nor did they have a common aesthetic; they represented different talents within the industry as well as different traditions within the arts. If Lardner had been in attendance on 29 October, if Scott had not had laryngitis, if the hearings had continued through Friday (when Waldo Salt and at least one other witness were scheduled), there would have been more than ten; if HUAC had called all of the seventy-nine on its list in 1947, the terms Hollywood Nineteen and Hollywood Ten would not exist.

What the unfriendly witnesses had in common, apart from left-wing sympathies that ran the gamut from Stalinism to populism, was the stand they took against answering HUAC's questions. Basically, they had two alternatives: to take the Fifth or the First Amendment. Rather than take the Fifth (which during the next decade evolved into such a joke that one could take the Diminished Fifth) they agreed after considerable discussion to take the First on the grounds that the investigation was a violation of their freedom of expression. The Fifth, on the other hand, would suggest that the desire to avoid self-incrimination stemmed from having done something wrong; that having been Communists—or, in the case of the few who were not (Koch, Milestone, Pichel), of having been fellow travelers or sympathizers— was un-American or subversive.

Moreover, answering one question made a witness liable to further questioning. The two questions HUAC posed, as to membership in the Screen Writers Guild (in Dmytryk's case, the Screen Directors Guild) and membership in the Communist Party, were really one double-edged question because HUAC had the notion that the SWG was teeming with Communists. The unfriendly witnesses thought the question about Guild membership impertinent and irrelevant; HUAC could easily have examined the masthead of SWG stationery or read the Guild's magazine to know who the officers and members were. The unfriendly witnesses chose to respect the tradition sacred to trade unionism of not revealing the names of Guild members, including their own—not because public knowledge of their membership would imperil their jobs (even though SWG was founded over studio opposition) but because HUAC had no authority to inquire into trade-union affiliations. Inquiring about membership in a political party is also an invasion of privacy: Congress cannot investigate what it cannot legislate; unable to legislate one's politics, theoretically, Congress should not be able to investigate them. While Brecht seems to have betrayed the First Amendment stand, he feared that as a foreigner he would not be protected by the First Amendment—but then, neither were ten Americans.

By taking the Fifth, the Ten might at least have avoided jail; however, when a committee is bent on scapegoating, no position is entirely secure. Their First Amendment stand gave the Ten a group identity, yet that stand was completely unrelated to their work in the film industry or to their abilities. It was a legal strategy, and not one that was easily adopted. Once labeled, the Ten might have thought their designation had some publicity value; it was easy to remember, like The Three B's. But while no one would consider Bach, Beethoven, and Brahms identical, the public perceived the Ten as the human equivalent of a single-cell organism. They were not; they neither inspired a movement nor invented a genre whose characteristics can be neatly summarized for students, yet they have a label as meaningless as "pre-Romantic." It should always be remembered that before there were ten, there were nineteen; and before there were nineteen, there were seventy-nine.

The story of the Hollywood Ten has been told in many forms, by themselves and others, in memoirs, histories, essays, and novels that are cited in the chapters of this book. There is no need, then, to continue with a story whose inherent drama and fascination have overshadowed something of far greater significance: the work of the Ten—their fiction, nonfiction, plays, poetry, criticism, pamphlets, and of course films. Before they became casualties of the Cold War, the Ten were craftsmen in an industry; some had achieved a measure of success in other genres before coming to Hollywood. *Radical Innocence* is the first critical assessment of the Ten's work; as Ceplair and Englund argue, critics have treated the Ten with the same indifference they experienced during their years on the blacklist. For more than forty years, they have also been stigmatized by Billy Wilder's quip "Of the unfriendly Ten, only two had any talent; the other eight were just unfriendly." Whether Wilder was right or wrong, only an examination of their writings, screenplays, and films can show. But to accomplish this task, the focus must be shifted from the Ten's politics to their work to see whether that work either suffered from or has been eclipsed by their politics.

A phrase in *All's Well That Ends Well* (IV.iii) aptly describes the Ten: "a mingled yarn." Since strands can vary in length and texture, and range in color from neutral to vermillion, the yarn must be disentangled and the strands separated. This method at least acknowledges individuality, although it does not resolve the insoluble art versus politics dilemma. These ten individuals acquired a political conscience and were then persecuted because that conscience was formed by the wrong politics, as determined by a committee whose chairman was convicted of embezzlement a year after the first session concluded and was sent to the same prison—Danbury Federal Correctional Institution—where two of the Ten were serving their sentences. Whatever art the Ten were still capable of producing was hindered, curtailed, and in some instances terminated in 1947 by a committee's attempt to investigate an area over which it had no jurisdiction. No one—not even Tacitus, who professed to write history without wrath and partisanship (*sine ira ac studio*)—can be dispassionate about a subject that continues to arouse the strongest of passions. Interest in the Ten will end when interest in injustice ends.

Having been denied justice by their country, the Ten are entitled to it from the critic. One way of achieving this end, and the one employed in *Radical Innocence*, is to give each his own chapter, beginning with those whose Hollywood careers either ended in 1947 or never returned to what they had been (Ornitz, Cole, Lawson, Biberman, Maltz, Bessie, Scott) and concluding with those who survived the blacklist by recanting (Dmytryk) or selling their work on the black market until the miasma lifted (Lardner, Trumbo). This method at least discourages hierarchical arrangements and Procrustean categories; it is less manipulative than the Scale of Excellence that ranks individuals from superfluous to superior or, as in the Sarris system, from Pantheon to Miscellaneous. It is also one way of saying that before ten men were subsumed under the rubric of the Hollywood Ten, they existed as individuals.

1 SAMUEL ORNITZ
Mazel Tov! to the World

John Howard Lawson may have been the ideologue of the Ten, Herbert Biberman the organizer, and Ring Lardner, Jr., the wit; but Samuel Badisch Ornitz was the patriarch. Although Ornitz would have preferred Lawson's title, Dalton Trumbo's description of him as "a man of immense dignity, sincerity and learning"[1] is more suited to a gifted storyteller, a champion of human rights, and one of the few residents of Los Angeles who could claim to read the daily *New York Times*.

Like most of the Ten, Ornitz came from the middle class; although he was born on New York's Hester Street, where the proletariat and the bourgeoisie intermingle, the Ornitzes, who were wool merchants, lived comparatively well. Samuel attended the Henry Street School; at ten, he underwent a political transformation, moving gradually to the left until at twelve he was a confirmed Socialist, mounting his soapbox on Lower East Side streets and haranguing passersby. After two years at City College he knew that his commitment to the underprivileged would not be realized by sitting in a classroom. Hence he became a social worker, a profession to which he devoted the next twelve years of his life, from 1908 to 1920, working for the New York Prison Association (where he also did penological research) and at the Brooklyn Society for the Prevention of Cruelty to Children. Ornitz's love of children remained with him throughout his life, manifesting itself in much of what he wrote, particularly in a children's book, *Round the World with Jocko the Great* (1925), and his last screenplay, *China's Little Devils* (1945).

As Ornitz became increasingly more intent on improving society, he started moving in radical circles that included left-wing theater companies. On 7 May 1919 the People's Playhouse on East 15th Street presented an evening of "three proletarian plays at proletarian prices" (fifty cents) that included Don Orno's *Deficit*. Samuel Ornitz, activist, was on the brink of a new career, writing under a pseudonym that conjures up a dashing man of letters in a cape and top hat instead of the associate superintendent of the Brooklyn Society for the Prevention of Cruelty to Children. Ornitz's first published work appeared under the same pseudonym; *The Sock: A Play of Protest*[2] protests the left's eternal bane, economic inequity, in a Dostoevskian setting where the characters speak in solemn epigrams ("Conscience is the pall with which the church stifles the soul"). Since the mercenary landlady in *The Sock* (so titled because that is where she keeps her money) is modeled after the pawnbroker in *Crime and Punishment*, the hero must be modeled after Raskolnikov; if that is the case, he must kill the landlady. However, since Raskolnikov was not a Socialist, he had no humanitarian motive for murder; Ornitz's hero does: to send a tubercular poet to a sanitarium ("I destroyed an ugly, strangling weed to preserve a beautiful plant").

Ornitz would write more plays, only one of which would be produced. Still, his first appearance in print, even in a pamphlet that cost a quarter, demonstrated that it was possible to be both a writer and a radical. His next work was a novel, one of the most famous in American Jewish literature: *Haunch Paunch and Jowl* (1923). Subtitled *An Anonymous Autobiography*, it is part disguised memoir, part fictionalized life. Ornitz's turn-of-the-century boyhood is narrated by an alter ego, Meyer Hirsch, but when the boy becomes a man, Ornitz and his persona part company, as do memoir and fiction: while Meyer Hirsch turned to law, Samuel Ornitz turned to writing. The book, then, is an account of what might have happened if Ornitz had betrayed his convictions and developed into a politico like Meyer, caricatured in cartoons for his ever expanding waistline and pendulous cheeks—his haunch, paunch, and jowl.

A novel whose gaslight quaintness masks the sadness of hopes betrayed and dreams unrealized, *Haunch Paunch and Jowl* has an unsettling effect; at first, one wishes Ornitz had been as ruthlessly ambitious as Meyer and pursued a career in fiction instead of succumbing to the blandishments of Hollywood—where, instead of making his fortune, he became a full-time antifascist and a part-time screenwriter. *Haunch Paunch and Jowl* reveals a writer, perhaps not of depth but certainly of substance, who is able to sketch a milieu in strong, decisive lines, leaving the remaining details to the reader's imagination. Ornitz's was a careful style, made up of words interlocking in epithetic combinations and phrases evocative of the rotogravure era: prostitutes are "available to the scanty purses of boys"; a singer is "desperately painted beyond her magnificent years."[3] This is a time of street lamps burning orange in the winter night, teenage soapboxers, potatoes roasting in milk cans, and rathskellers where Irish tunes are sung with Jewish inflections.

As Meyer moves into adolescence, he becomes an atheist, leaving the *cheder* for the law courts and hustling clients for whiskey lawyers until he becomes a lawyer himself. He gains in weight what he loses in principles, supporting capital at the expense of labor at one time;

strengthening labor by subverting capital at another. Ornitz, writing in his early thirties, is looking back at the types he encountered in his youth—sweatshop owners, Socialists, anarchists, unionists; the Hester Street Jews and the uptown German-Jewish barons with their contempt for their Lower East Side co-religionists; and the Jews who preferred to be known as God's scapegoats rather than God's chosen— and wondering into what category he would have fallen had he not embraced radical politics and the muse simultaneously. While Ornitz favors assimilation in this book, it is with the Socialist Avrum, who would solve the problem of Jewish clannishness—and nationalism in general—through a classless society, that his sympathies lie: "But it will be different when the workers of America become a racial identity. Then they will see each other as brothers, in sympathy, comradeship and understanding, as Americans all. Meanwhile we must keep at them to learn, to rise above their clannishness, and mean aspirations; stop the sporadic struggles and unite as one. When we break down the class lines, the snobbery of nationalism, replace it with a commonality of spirit, then labor in its dignity and knowledge will share equally with capital the good things of the earth."[4]

It was probably on the basis of this and similar speeches in *Haunch Paunch and Jowl*, one of which attributes anti-Semitism to extreme Jewishness, that the *Encyclopedia Judaica* dismissed Ornitz as "a professed atheist [who] saw no virtues in Jewish immigrant life and wished to end Jewish isolation by a policy of downright assimilation."[5] As a Socialist, Ornitz could not believe in a chosen people; since his goal was a classless society, he naturally favored assimilation over parochialism. Yet he did see virtues in immigrant life, as some of his later work shows.

That Ornitz's second novel was for children is not surprising; having worked with them for twelve years, he knew the sort of book that would appeal to them. He also kept a file on child abuse and planned a book showing "what we do to children in the name of protecting them."[6] While he never lived to write that book, he could have, and from a child's point of view. In *Round the World with Jocko the Great*, a charming tale of a monkey who becomes an international circus attraction, Ornitz neither condescends to children nor allegorizes for them. As he knew, there is a distinction between propaganda and entertainment. The moral to be drawn and the lessons to be learned from *Jocko* are so traditional that they can be found in any grade school primer: "Warriors conquer for a moment . . . but a song, or an idea lives forever"; "Wars nearly never decide things one way or another."[7]

Ornitz teaches as he entertains, subtly undermining received ideas and popular misconceptions. Jocko weeps at man's inhumanity when he attends a bullfight in Madrid; a Martian complains of the identification of his planet with the Roman god of war when in fact Martians war only against disease and ignorance; a stork champions the bat who is discriminated against because it is not favored by folklore. The book is most impressive, however, not in its Aesopic wisdom but in its vivid turns of phrase (the earth's burned surface is compared to the skin of a baked apple), playful descriptions (scholarly frogs, grasshoppers playing on their fiddle legs), and unforced allusions (Jocko visits Westminster Abbey where Browning's Pippa "passes" by; at Dickens's house he is greeted by Tiny Tim).

At the end, Ornitz promises a sequel, but his next novel was not for children. *A Yankee Passional: The Biography of a Synthetic Self* (1927) is his only non-Jewish novel; still, it reflects his preoccupation with the ethnic and religious conflicts he witnessed on the Lower East Side. Here the milieu is Irish-Catholic but no less provincial than that of *Haunch Paunch and Jowl*, as one of the characters emphasizes: "It is well to remember the Irish-Catholic is like no other Catholic people in the world. Religious oppression has made us racial religionists, like the Jews."[8]

A Yankee Passional is the most populous of Ornitz's novels; it is a sprawling narrative that, only as it nears the end, begins telescoping events and summarizing years with a speed quite different from the gingerly pace set in the first chapter. Whatever its faults, the book suggests that had Ornitz continued to pursue fiction, he could have become a respected novelist, probably a successful one as well. He had a gift many popular writers lack: a sense of the poetic in both life and language. Irish doctors and ex–hooch dancers here speak not only colorfully but also poetically and rhythmically, in multiple images and compound epithets ("sweetseducing humility," "warmbreath fire," "shamefear") that go beyond archaism into folk poetry.

The inspiration for the main character, Daniel Matthews, was Father Isaac Hecker, founder of the Paulist Fathers. Although Father Hecker died two years before Ornitz was born, Ornitz grew up hearing about him; the Heckers had at one time also lived on Hester Street. Given his interest in religion, Ornitz may well have read the early biographies of Father Hecker by Walter Elliott or Henry D. Sedgwick, Jr.; he might even have read Hecker's own *Aspirations of Nature* and *Questions of the Soul*. Certainly he knew of the priest's concern for the rights of workers, his interest in social justice, and his introduction through Orestes Brownson to the communal life of Brook Farm.

In *A Yankee Passional*, Daniel Matthews is a Maine woods primitive in search of the peace that passeth understanding; ultimately he finds it in Catholicism, though he stops short of becoming a priest. His sanctity makes him a surrogate son to childless men, a fantasy lover to unfulfilled women, and an inspiration to youths in need of a model of masculine purity. To embody such ideas in characters who are still believable—particularly characters alien to the author's own religious background—is a mark of Ornitz's awareness of Catholicism's other side, which is not so much dark as crepuscular; those recesses of the Catholic psyche which, if suddenly illuminated, blur into grayness. Ornitz does not merely depict the mutual antagonism of Catholic and Protestant and their history of retaliatory persecution; he dramatizes that strange correlation between sex, guilt, and chastity which, though not peculiarly Irish, is much in evidence in Irish literature. Those like Liam, the alcoholic doctor, who enjoy sex find no joy in it; those like Daniel who could find joy in it forswear it because of the guilt it brings.

Ornitz's best writing appears in the lyrical exchanges between Dan and Mame, the carnival dancer-poet. Torn between flesh and spirit, Dan exclaims: "Mame, I prayed for the peace of purity. Always your warm-breathed face came between me and God. Then a great light divided the cloud and made a clearing for the stars. I then knew if I could face you with pure eyes, I could see God through you." Mame replies simply, "It's better for you to burn out your fire in me" (90)— which, of course, he cannot do. Ornitz also poeticizes Dan's relationship with Liam, who feels a homoerotic but not homosexual attraction to Dan, warning him against men who would mistake gentleness for effeminacy, yet at the same time wanting that gentleness for himself. Liam's love of Dan illustrates a uniquely spiritual form of male bonding: males who are attracted to each other because of the presence or absence of the feminine in themselves. To Liam, sex is an escape from the reality of professional failure and thus no different from alcohol or morphine; what under ordinary circumstances he would have sought in a woman, he seeks in Dan, who becomes his anima.

Despite its overwhelmingly Catholic atmosphere, A Yankee Passional is not a Catholic novel in the same sense as Graham Greene's The Power and the Glory or Walker Percy's The Moviegoer. Ornitz's main purpose in writing it is made evident by the denouement: at the outbreak of World War I an interventionist monsignor burns Dan's appeal to the Pope to make pacifism an article of faith. Catholic Machiavellianism, then, is the peg on which Ornitz has hung his plot; the life of Father Hecker is only an exemplary subtext, a point of reference. The story of Daniel Matthews is not an edifying biography like that of Father Hecker, the Yankee Paul, but a Yankee passional, a book of sufferings culminating in Dan's death in the Maine woods, victim of the elements and right-wing extremists. Dan is Ornitz's recreation of what Isaac Hecker might have been if he had never become a priest and if he had been living at the time of World War I. Yet both Isaac Hecker and Dan Matthews had a faith that Samuel Ornitz could never embrace, because it had no name: they believed in both God and humankind;

Ornitz, only in the latter. What Ornitz admired in both was the purity of
their commitment, a state oblivious to the tugs of the flesh and the call
of ideology. While Ornitz wrote eloquently of Dan's spiritual goals,
they could never be his. Socialism became, to use the novel's subtitle,
Ornitz's synthetic self; it was also the tegument of his real self, the
novelist. While his involvement in left-wing politics sustained him
through two of the worst periods in twentieth-century history, the
Great Depression and World War II, it also made him less of a writer:
"1929 saw the crash and the rise of Hitler and fascism. To write novels
seemed as puerile as they were profitless. I wrote pictures and barn-
stormed against fascism."[9]

Not until his career in Hollywood was over did he return to fiction
and allow the creative self to reemerge. In *Bride of the Sabbath* (1951),
Ornitz recalls the Lower East Side with a magnanimity that is at the
same time gently critical of its insularity. Ornitz's Jews are magnifi-
cently unassimilated; although he himself believed in assimilation, he
portrays them with such compassion and humor that in admiring them
one is almost tempted to admire their parochialism, which is founded
on faith so strong one is ashamed not to share it. The world of *Bride of
the Sabbath* is one of religion based on fear as well as love; of households
dominated by the extremes of a grandmother who believes in silver
wine cups for Seders and a Marxist uncle who believes in Comrade
Jesus; of Jews who try to pass for Christians by kissing a crucifix; of
Yids and Micks, *rebbes* and ministers, sweatshop workers and pushcart
peddlers—in short, the world of the ghetto opens miraculously at the
author's bidding.

Although Ornitz considered himself an atheist, he still wrote about
the Sabbath with the veneration of an awestruck child. The sabbath he
describes is observed by unassimilated Jews, who feel it more deeply
than their coreligionists uptown; it is a special Sabbath, a ghetto
Sabbath, made holy by the cessation of activity and transfigured by
love. Whenever Ornitz describes the holy days, it is with reverence—
the reverence not of a believer but of a witness to a sanctified moment.
What he remembers and evokes so eloquently is the purity of the ritual.
He recalls the grace with which women braid their hair into a crown
covered with a white handkerchief; the sculpting movement of their
hands encircling their necks with coral; the finishing touch of a paisley
shawl thrown around their shoulders. These are memories unsullied
by adult cynicism, the true destroyer of innocence.

"Innocent," in fact, is an apt description of *Bride of the Sabbath*; it is
also innocence that keeps it from being a true novel. Ornitz is so eager
to capture each moment in its pristine state that he creates a series of
vignettes, as delicately strung as the coral encircling a woman's neck,
making the novel a series of poetic hand movements. But once the

chain of coral has fallen decorously over the breast, the portrait is complete; likewise, the other images, conjured up and exquisitely rendered, pass into pictures. The book is more a reminiscence than a novel, a storyteller's meditation on the past rather than reminiscence reshaped as narrative.

It is understandable that Ornitz was admired in Hollywood as a storyteller. The beginning of *Bride of the Sabbath* is typical: an anecdote expands into a vignette with a punch line. Baba, the grandmother of Saul Kramer, the main character, spots a man smoking on the street as the Sabbath approaches; slapping the cigarette out of his mouth, she mutters, "For this Columbus discovered America?" The man, who is not even Jewish, cries, "Hell, I can't hit a woman"; instead, he crosses the street and knocks down a Jew.

Occasionally, the novelist interrupts the storyteller; it is at such moments that one knows Ornitz never achieved as much in fiction as he might have. While *Bride of the Sabbath* purports to be Saul Kramer's story, it is dominated by the character of Baba as so many *Bildungsromans* are haunted by secondary figures (Magwitch in *Great Expectations*, Mrs. Morel in *Sons and Lovers*) who are already formed and therefore possess a depth the protagonist has not yet reached. For all Baba's faults, such as her perpetuation of a scapegoat mentality in teaching her grandson to expect persecution from the *goyim*, she remains an individual rather than a type of the unassimilated Jew. One cannot help smiling at some of her ways, which include spitting three times at the mention of Christ's name. Even her death, poignant as it is, is an event not lacking in humor. Knowing she will die before Saul's bar mitzvah, she asks him to recite his speech and expires during the recitation at the very moment a Salvation Army band passes by singing "Onward, Christian Soldiers."

What Baba was at her best never leaves Saul. Although there will no longer be Seders with macaroons and hazelnuts and unleavened bread spread with goose fat, there will still be the family unity the Seder symbolizes, even after Saul's family becomes not merely his own but the human race. He never really breaks with his past. Because of his exposure to the polyglot of the Lower East Side, he becomes an interpreter in the parole division, then a researcher and a psychiatric social worker, hoping to alleviate the plight of the mentally ill, who are treated worse than convicts. Finally, Saul receives the highest compliment that can be paid to a white liberal: a black lawyer insists that Saul has some black in him because he does not "think white."

Neither Saul nor his creator thought white. While Ornitz moved from Judaism to atheism, Saul made a detour into Christianity, which had fascinated him ever since he saw his first crucifix and identified with the suffering Christ. However, what attracted Saul was not orthodox Christianity but a Tolstoyan variety that was actually closer to Baba's religion. For him, life is bearable when grief and joy are considered kindred emotions; tragedy is endurable if the irony in it can be found. Saul marries a Roman Catholic, who, after losing a child, becomes so obsessed with religion that she enters a convent. Saul grew up hearing the Sabbath spoken of as God's bride; by marrying a Catholic, he takes on a new Sabbath and a new bride, who leaves him to become the bride of Christ.

After seeing his wife for the last time, Saul walks into the December night, brightened by the lights of Christmas. Raising his arm too quickly, he accidentally breaks his glasses and instinctively cries, "*mazel tov*," as he did as a child whenever anything broke. To shout "*mazel tov*" in time of grief, to find hope in loss and to understand that sorrow is the other side of joy—this is Ornitz's benediction. *Bride of the Sabbath* begins as a reminiscence and ends as a prayer, with the author imparting his blessing to the reader: "And [Saul] walked away with his head high and his spirit exalted. And he found himself shouting to the river and the night, and to the bridge above him and the Navy Yard across the river, and to the ghetto he was approaching and the nunnery he was now passing, 'Mazel Tov, Mazel Tov, Mazel Tov,' his pledge to rebuild his temple on these ruins and at the same time his felicitation of the bride he had led to espouse Christ—Mazel Tov!"[10]

Nature did not bestow the same blessing on Samuel Ornitz: he was in poor health when he was writing *Bride of the Sabbath* and in prison when he read the galleys; he died of cancer six years after it was published. At least he had the satisfaction of seeing it climb to tenth place on the best-seller list. But it may have given him the greatest satisfaction to know that his last published words were *mazel tov*!

Once Ornitz began writing for the screen, he was unable to exercise his gift for evoking time and place. Still, this was his choice; after *A Yankee Passional* he decided to become a professional antifascist, supporting himself by writing for a new medium that initially had scarcely interested him. In 1928 he sold two original stories to Paramount: "Tong War," which was filmed as *Chinatown Nights* (1929), an early talkie produced by William Wellman; and "The Case of Lena Smith," filmed under the same title by Josef von Sternberg. Once Ornitz realized he could get some of his favorite subjects on the screen—*The Case of Lena Smith* (1929) dealt with the exploitation of a peasant girl by her social superiors—he started taking screenwriting more seriously.

Although Ornitz shared credit on *Hell's Highway* (RKO, 1932) with two other writers, it was he who wrote the original story, "Liberty Road," on which the film was based.[11] "Liberty Road" had its origin in fact: the death of a Florida prison camp inmate from confinement in a sweat box. Having just returned from Kentucky, where at the invitation of Theodore Dreiser he was part of a delegation investigating the exploitation of workers in the Harlan County coalfields, Ornitz was eager to expose inhumanity wherever it existed.

Because *Hell's Highway* opened shortly before *I Am a Fugitive from a Chain Gang* (1932), to which it bears some resemblance, it never attracted the attention it might have otherwise; yet it is even more condemnatory of prison brutality than *Chain Gang*, which is chiefly about World War I's forgotten men who turned to crime because they had no jobs. Still, the film was moderately successful, and Ornitz went on to write another for RKO, *Secrets of the French Police* (1932), an interesting case of self-plagiarism. The credits were to read: "Based on 'Secrets of the Sureté' by Ashton Wolfe and *The Lost Empress* by Samuel Ornitz," the latter supposedly a novel about Anastasia, the (so-called) last of the Romanovs. RKO's legal department debated the matter, concluding that since the studio did not own the rights to the novel, the work could not be cited in the credits.[12]

There were no rights because the book was unpublished. What Ornitz had done was to combine part of his unpublished novel with the ninth and tenth cases of Wolfe's series in the *American Weekly*. At first glance, the Anastasia story seems to bear no relationship to a film in which a mad sculptor embalms models so realistically that they look like statues, and a deformed criminal drugs and mesmerizes celebrities to steal their jewels. Ornitz forged the relationship by making the madman a white Russian who preys on Parisian models in order to embalm them in formaldehyde and kidnaps a flower girl who is an Anastasia look-a-like. If there is an implicit attack on Czarist Russia in the film, as Ornitz intended, it was lost amid these lurid trappings.

Ornitz wrote two more films for RKO, *Men of America* (1932) and *One Man's Journey* (1933). The latter is important for two reasons having nothing to do with the film itself: one is that it was remade six years later with a slightly improved script by Dalton Trumbo; the other is that the career of the main character, a small-town doctor "who has labored without glory and profit" (as the opening title proclaims), parallels that of Paul Christian, the hero of RKO's Dr. Christian series. Since the first two films in the series were, in part, the work of Ring Lardner, Jr., it is not inconceivable that Lardner was as influenced by Ornitz's earlier film as he was by the *Dr. Christian* radio series that debuted on CBS in 1937. Like Paul Christian, Eli Watt of *One Man's Journey* accepts payment in produce, battles epidemics, defends squatters' rights, and realizes that the gulf between the affluent and the needy can be bridged by a stronger commitment to social justice. The difference is that while Paul Christian did not go unheralded, Eli Watt was acknowledged only at the end of his career for possessing the one quality that modern medicine, for all its advances, had not acquired: the wisdom of the human heart.

One Man's Journey was Ornitz's last film for RKO; he returned there briefly in the early 1940s for projects that were never completed, but he was never meant to stay long at any one studio. Ornitz did not understand that scripts written for stars must be tailored to the image of star and studio. In 1935 he tried unsuccessfully to interest David O. Selznick and others in a script about a cache of Russian diamonds that ends up in Manchuria, where merchants, card sharpers, adventurers, spies, and smugglers vie for them. To suggest William Powell and Myrna Loy for his diamonds film because they had costarred in MGM's *The Thin Man* (1934), or to propose a vehicle for Joan Crawford in which she would progress from ex-convict to couturière, is to misunderstand the nature of the screen persona.

In the 1930s Ornitz was so preoccupied with fascism that he frequently went abroad to learn firsthand about the situation in Europe. Thinking that New York was ready for an antifascist comedy with social overtones—a tall order for any playwright—Ornitz returned to the theater, where his career had begun. *Geraniums in My Window*, coauthored with Vera Caspary (a lifetime friend), ran on Broadway for a scant twenty-seven performances in the fall of 1934.[13] The play showed exactly where Ornitz's interests lay—not in the drama as an art form but in the drama as a forum for attacking fascism ("You've Hitlerized our existence"), glorifying the New Deal (with a New Deal employment agency), and elevating the proletariat (with a plot about a millionaire writer posing as an illiterate dishwasher to learn the language of the people). The hero's philosophy of writing reverses the eighteenth century's notion of illiteracy, which meant ignorance of Latin and Greek. To the hero, it is not to know the vernacular: "What if I can read Euripides in the original? If I don't know the language, and the people, of my own time, I *am* illiterate."

The stage was not a natural medium for Ornitz; it brought out the orator in him. It took the novel, his real metier, to bring out the storyteller. Still, Ornitz persisted in writing plays. The magazine *New Masses* (3 April 1934) published *In New Kentucky*, which was inspired by his investigative trip to Harlan County. Ornitz's characters are not crackerbarrel types but strikers and bosses enacting the perennial we/them agon. *In New Kentucky* reminds one of what drama must have been like when Thespis arrived on the scene: a loose alliance of rudimentary scenes and crude litanies. Naturally, the strike ends in tragedy for the strikers, who bury their dead to the music of "The Battle Hymn of the Republic," known to touch the heart regardless of context. While the dialogue uses the phonetic vernacular ("jest," "ol'," "thar," "shet"), the stage directions are written in the kind of poetic prose at which Ornitz excelled: a face is like parched earth; a funeral procession winds like a locomotive up a mountain; eyes shine like sapphires surrounded by grime. If *In New Kentucky* attests to anything, it is to Ornitz's abilities as a novelist whose forays into drama were strictly diversions.

Screenwriting was a compromise, but it gave him an outlet for his crusading spirit; though he had to entertain, he could preach if the theme warranted it, and that, he said, justified working in film. *Three Kids and a Queen* (Universal, 1935) enabled him to argue that ghetto scrappers are basically decent, since even the dowager they "kidnap" is humanized by the experience. In *Little Orphan Annie* (Paramount, 1938), which he coauthored with Budd Schulberg, the heroine from the comics becomes the saint of the proletariat, saving Chinese men from racists and reading immigrants the Declaration of Independence as well as the story of Robin Hood, whom she presents as a folk hero. At the end, with the help of some prize money, the neighborhood forms a Robin Hood Mutual Aid Society.

Although *Army Girl* (Republic, 1938) was a military romance with Madge Evans and Preston Foster, Ornitz was at least able to frame it within a mildly pacifist context: in the next war, which was imminent, machines can do the fighting so the men can stay at home—a hope that was dashed the following year. A better illustration of Ornitz's pacifism is *The Man Who Reclaimed His Head* (Universal, 1935), which gave him his best opportunity in the 1930s to indulge one of his favorite theories: the World War I conspiracy. It was hardly a liability to have as his collaborator Jean Bart, who wrote the original play: a melodramatic *Major Barbara*, with the disillusioned protagonist as a liberal writer rather than a member of the Salvation Army. Naturally, Ornitz was sympathetic to Bart's thesis that the greed of industrialists precipitated World War I.

The Man Who Reclaimed His Head is a pacifist tract disguised as a mystery that begins with a man's seeking out a lawyer to explain to him how he has reclaimed his head; when the contents of his hatbox elicit a gasp from the lawyer, one knows that the title is not merely symbolic. Paul Verin (played by Claude Rains) is a radical journalist duped by an unprincipled publisher into writing for an ostensibly pacifist newspaper. When a munitions cartel dangles a newspaper chain before the publisher, he does an about-face, committing the paper to endorsing rearmament and, with the assassination at Sarajevo, to justifying war.

One scene is as chilling as the conference table sequence in *Dr. Strangelove* (1964). In what is clearly the left's idea of a warmongers' summit, the members of the cartel plan their strategy on board a yacht. They agree to pool patents, ship arms to the belligerents through neutral Switzerland, and protect iron and coal fields from being bombed;

since patriotism is expensive, they hope to prolong the war for at least five years.

Verin joins the army; learning that the publisher has been courting his wife in his absence, he returns to Paris to reclaim his "head"—by decapitating the publisher. In his haste to board the Paris train, Verin collides with two nuns, causing their rosaries and his saber to fall at the same time. The juxtaposition of the objects gives religious sanction to the beheading accomplished by the saber, now blessed by the beads. If the imagery does not convince, the fade-out line does: "You're not the accused; you're the accuser," the lawyer decides.

The studio with which Ornitz had the longest association was Republic, which was always looking for cheap talent. The scripts he turned out there were a cut above the typical 1930s Republic products: westerns, thrillers, serials. Ornitz wrote scripts not for Gene Autry or Bob Steele but for Alison Skipworth, Walter Abel, Frieda Inescort, Heather Angel, and Madge Evans. His first assignment was *Follow Your Heart* (1936), a collaboration with Lester Cole and Nathanael West. The script seems to have been more Ornitz than Cole or West, judging from the plot, which celebrates a madcap musical family and contains some shrewd satire of grand opera. Unlike Cole, Ornitz knew music, as he showed in *Fatal Lady* (Paramount, 1936), in which an opera singer's lovers keep dying mysteriously; he had also incorporated Beethoven's Fifth Symphony into *One Man's Journey* and Wagner's *Tristan und Isolde* into *The Man Who Reclaimed His Head*, where the second-act love duet inspires an attempted seduction. In *Follow Your Heart* there is a hilarious parody of the *Lucia di Lammermoor* sextet, with music provided by the sound of popping lids, hissing kettles, spoons tapping on glass, and French bread shredded on a grater.

Republic's occasional musicals tended to resemble the austerity budget on which they were made, but *Follow Your Heart* was something of an exception: it had a comparatively elaborate finale, as did *The Hit Parade* (1937), which Ornitz coauthored with Bradford Ropes. *Follow Your Heart* did not lend itself to social commentary, however; *The Hit Parade*, Republic's attempt to capitalize on the success of the NBC radio show, did. A radio station can be a social microcosm when its star attraction, an ex-debutante who sings the classics but disdains pop, is replaced by her working-class opposite.

Films such as *The Hit Parade, Portia on Trial, Two Wise Maids, It Could Happen to You* (all 1937), and *Three Faces West* (1940)—all Republic productions—gave Ornitz ample opportunity to do what he did best: tell interesting stories and teach lessons ranging from simple justice to antifascism. In *Portia on Trial* a female lawyer pleads for mercy for a boy who "never had a chance to be anything but a gunman's stooge, growing up as he did on the garbage heap of neglected childhood"—a view shared by Ornitz after twelve years of working with delinquents. In *Two Wise Maids* (1937) Ornitz returned to the Lower East Side of ethnic malapropisms ("Let him who is without sin pitch the first ball") and teachers forced to retire because their ways are at variance with modern pedagogy. One such teacher is considered old-fashioned because she believes in rehabilitating children so they will not be sent to reform school. Her somewhat unorthodox methods include taking over a city street for a playground. When she asks a police officer, "Has it occurred to you, Sergeant, that treating children like criminals is liable to make them into criminals?" she is crystallizing Ornitz's philosophy of education in a single sentence.

Republic, oddly enough, was one of the first studios to take a position on Nazism, albeit not an especially strong one; in *Range Defenders* (1937)—a Three Mesquiteers western—the villains were black-shirted, and one sported a Hitlerian mustache. While the major studios feared the loss of the German market and the alienation of German-Americans (it was considered daring of Warner Brothers to make *Confessions of a Nazi Spy* in 1939), Republic was always trying to inject topical elements into its films—without necessarily exploring those elements. In the same year as *Range Defenders*, Republic released *It Could Happen to You*, with a script by Nathanael West and Ornitz, based on a story by West. The film shows no more insight into fascism than most Hollywood movies; the title was meant to suggest Sinclair Lewis's *It Can't Happen Here*, and after seeing the film, one can only conclude that not only could it *not* happen to anyone; it could not happen here or anywhere. A young man, adopted by an immigrant whose natural son is a lawyer, dreams of opening a school for immigrants like his adoptive father—whom he accidentally kills in a robbery attempt to get the money for his institution. A Nazi agent, knowing of his involvement, forces him to turn the school into a center for fascism where Nietzsche is taught and where the students, most of whom are illegal aliens, are compelled to pay hush money to avoid deportation. To compound absurdity with irony, the dead man's lawyer son ends up defending his adoptive brother who, although acquitted, commits suicide by jumping from a roof. Such films makes fascism seem less a political horror than a bad dream whose traumas vanish with the dawn.

Ornitz's next attack on Nazism was more effective because it had a narrative rather than a nightmare behind it. *Three Faces West* (1940), his last Republic film, is also his most memorable. That John Wayne starred in it explains, in part, its frequent appearance on television and its availability on videocassette. Since the script was the product of three writers—the poet Joseph Moncure March, the playwright F. Hugh Herbert, and Ornitz—isolating specific contributions is difficult.

One can say, however, that it is very much a novelist's film: the action is not fragmented but encapsulated within chapterlike episodes. It is also a reply to the novel *The Grapes of Wrath*, which had been published the previous year. In *Three Faces West*, when dust storms force the farmers off their land, they set out not for California—which is dismissed as "a state of fruit pickers"—but for Oregon. The implication is that if John Steinbeck's Okies had set their sights on the Northwest, they would have found the golden apple instead of the grapes of wrath.

Three Faces West, while modestly produced, is unusually intelligent for a Poverty Row film. Parallels are established between refugees and pioneers, and authoritarianism is equated with fascism when an outbreak of lawlessness imperils democracy. For a film that is partly the work of a Communist, it contains a curious reference to the Soviet Union. The heroine's fiancé, who once risked his life so that she and her father could flee Austria, becomes a Nazi and flees from Austria to the Soviet Union—not to escape Nazism but rather, as he puts it vaguely, "on business." It is hard to imagine what business an Austrian Nazi would have in the Soviet Union on the eve of Germany's invasion of Poland unless it was in conjunction with the Hitler-Stalin nonaggression pact. If one of the writers was trying to point out the synonymy of fascism and Communism, it certainly was not Ornitz, who defended the pact and whose disenchantment with the Soviet Union did not begin until 1953.

Ornitz did not receive another screen credit until four years later, when Columbia's Harry Cohn hired him for *They Live in Fear* (1944). Cohn had a soft spot for radicals, perhaps because of his pre-mogul days as a song plugger, trolley car conductor, and pool hustler. He even offered Lillian Hellman a million-dollar, eight-year contract in 1947 that would have allowed her to write and produce four films of her choice, provided she would sign a loyalty oath—which she refused to do. Cohn's hiring of Ornitz, then, was typical, just as *They Live in Fear* was typical Ornitz—and, by 1944, dated—antifascism. By then there was no shock value in Hitler youths interning at Dachau, where they beat Jews to death with shovels.

Perhaps the real reason for Ornitz's paucity of screen credits in the 1940s, boom years for other writers, was his inability to adapt to the screenplay requirements of the war; his interest was less in World War II than in the forces that caused it, and he was not comfortable weaving a script around a battle or writing moist romances about GIs and the girls they leave behind.

Significantly, Ornitz's last film was about children; it was also a personal statement. While the 1940s abounded in resistance films, only in *China's Little Devils* (1945) was the resistance entirely organized and carried out by children. The picture contains its share of Yellow

Peril propaganda (including the ubiquitous mark of the Japanese impe-
rialist, horn-rimmed glasses) but concentrates on the plight of children
in war. It presents the Little Devils not as waifs but as heroes who
emulate American commandos, ambushing Japanese patrols, at one
point using one of their own as decoy.

Unlike many of his comrades who loathed Chiang Kai-shek's
China because Chiang was such a militant anti-Communist, Ornitz
made the Chinese worthy allies who practice the ultimate form of
democracy: the right to choose death. When a Chinese couple is
sentenced to be hanged for harboring a Flying Tiger pilot, they ask
their children if they wish to share their fate; the children reply in the
affirmative. One cannot help thinking of the united stand the Hollywood Ten took later and of Ornitz's words of encouragement in 1947:
"Let us at least be as brave as the people we write about."

In the best World War II movies there are moments that occasion a
respectful silence. In *China's Little Devils* it is the scene in which an
American missionary tells a Chinese orphan that he cannot abandon
his pacifism because America is at war; the orphan—referring to the
ten-year period between Japan's invasion of Manchuria and Pearl
Harbor—quietly replies, "I've been at war all my life." With the orphan's death, the missionary's pacifism is suspended for the duration.

Little Devils is a thoughtful film, but it typifies everything that went
wrong with Ornitz's career. Like Rose in *Gypsy*, he was born too soon
and started too late; his last film was written too late and released too
soon—too soon after V-J Day. It was reviewed in *Daily Variety* in April
1945, yet for some reason Monogram did not release it until the fall,
when the film languished amid the jubilation over the end of the war.
Anyone who saw it probably agreed with the *Los Angeles Examiner* (26
Sept. 1945) that its "powerful message of fight or bow to evil does not
lose its punch now that the Japs have been defeated." But the message
was heard by only a few.

Filmographies list Ornitz's last screen credit as an adaptation: Fox's
Circumstantial Evidence (1945).[14] This is not quite correct. *Circumstantial
Evidence* began life in 1938 as an original story by Robert Meltzer, "The
Postman Walks Alone," in which a widower accidentally causes the
death of a misanthropic baker and is convicted of murder on circumstantial evidence. A postman sets the wheels of justice in motion by
devising a plan to make the witnesses, who swore they had seen a
murder, admit they were wrong. Darryl F. Zanuck liked the "wrong
man" angle and commissioned Sam Duncan and Nat Ferber to work up
a treatment, which they did under the title "Tomorrow." The writers
had apparently seen more than their share of Warner Brothers social
consciousness films: "Tomorrow" made the widower an embittered
World War I veteran who, after returning to civilian life, becomes a

unionist and is accused of killing a strikebreaker; thanks to a group of boys who reenact the incident to prove the death accidental, the widower is acquitted. Zanuck called the treatment a "great cyclone of good stuff" but "too much" of it. "Simplify—eliminate—set on straighforward line and follow," he urged.

In January 1939, Ornitz entered the picture. For one who had spent the previous three years on Poverty Row, the opportunity to work at Fox was the realization of a long-concealed wish. No doubt it was Ornitz's sensitive portrayal of children and the flair for courtroom melodrama that he revealed (and critics noted) in *Portia on Trial* that brought him to Zanuck's attention.

"Tomorrow" appealed to Ornitz, as did the prospect of working for Zanuck, whom he was eager to please. On 25 January 1939 he presented a treatment that drew on his own experiences in juvenile court. Zanuck, unimpressed, gave Ornitz ten days to come up with a better treatment; Ornitz complied in six. Zanuck was still dissatisfied, scrawling on the front page, "tries to tell too much—high stuff—all propaganda—reduce to simple heart drama—not national issue."[15] Zanuck wanted Ornitz to eliminate the father's World War I background and any reference to the rehabilitation of delinquents; he also expected a better motive for the accidental killing, suggesting that it might stem from the local curmudgeon's taking a bat away from the boy.

This time, Ornitz took the full ten days to make revisions, using Zanuck's suggestion about the bat and most of his others as well. Zanuck was pleased with the result, deeming it "far superior to anything we have had up to date on the subject." Although there was still too much propaganda ("keep philosophies out of it"), "Mr. Ornitz is to go to work on a First Draft Continuity."[16]

By 5 April 1939, Ornitz had a first-draft continuity ready: a 150-page script in the usual screenplay format with each shot numbered and identified in terms of place and time. The script makes it clear that Ornitz was both in and out of his element. He could write courtroom scenes and devise a dramatic prison break because this material he understood; but to remove what Zanuck didn't want was tantamount to removing part of himself, and he had little to give of the humor Zanuck did want—at least in this kind of plot. The real problem was that the usually astute Zanuck had no confidence in the script; he penciled over the 16 February 1939 revised treatment: "Load with melodrama—guts—and sock comedy, enough to hide the plot, to blanket all goody goody stuff—cover sentiment and Boy Scout hoke—with melo and gags. This is the only chance."

As the script progressed, the postman, who in the original story was a major character, yielded to the children. Ornitz could no more identify with the postman than he could with Zanuck's conception of filmmaking; he could only identify with the children. As much as he tried to create a plausible existence for the postman, he could not. In the last script, he has the man's wife awakening her husband with, "Did you meet me in your dreams, tootsie-woo?"

By June 1939, Ornitz had no connection with the film, but Zanuck had not given up. Over the next few years several writers tried their hand at "The Postman Walks Alone/Tomorrow," including Milton Sperling and Harold Buchman. The final script, written by Robert Meltzer, who also received sole screenplay credit, resulted in one of Fox's shortest films: a sixty-eight-minute programmer. But Ornitz deserved more than adaptation credit for *Circumstantial Evidence*; he had created a script with the same plot points that appear in the film: the town misanthrope who confiscates a boy's possession, the witnesses, the conviction, the children's restaging of the incident, and the climax in which the father attempts to escape and returns to prison before his absence is discovered.

Such are the vagaries of a collaborative medium. Despite his predilection for the communal, Ornitz did his best work alone, as his novels attest.

2 LESTER COLE
Hollywood Red

Lester Cole arrived in Hollywood about the same time as Samuel Ornitz, both receiving their first screenplay credits in 1932. Cole's Hollywood years are better documented because they have been recounted in his autobigraphy. As Hollywood autobiographies go, *Hollywood Red* (1981) is one of the better examples of a genre that has always been suspect. Cole's at least throws some light on his screenwriting, particularly on the script of which he is proudest: *The Romance of Rosy Ridge* (1947). However, the focus of *Hollywood Red* is, as it should be, on the subject's transformation from a high school dropout to a screenwriter who, in the critical fall of 1947, was on the verge of signing a two-year contract with MGM calling for $1,250 a week for the first year, $1,500 a week for the second. In some respects, Cole's life explains the kind of scripts he did best: tough, gritty melodramas celebrating life's ironies, triumphs, and disasters. That he could write so well about criminals, the oppressed, the poor, and the maligned is partly the result of the Socialist politics he inherited from his Polish-born father, and partly the result of a humanitarianism that may have been nurtured but was not created by the camaraderie he found in the Communist Party—Cole's surrogate parent until he died in 1985, two months after covering the International Film Festival in Moscow for *People's World*.

What Cole shares with other left-wing writers, especially some of the Depression playwrights, is an interest in the criminal, because miscarriages of justice are readily seen in sentences that fail to consider extenuating social or environmental circumstances. His first screenwriting credit was for the anthology film *If I Had a Million* (1932), in which he was one of eighteen writers for a picture that had seven directors and consisted of eight episodes, all revolving about people who receive a million dollars from a supposedly dying plutocrat.[1] Cole's contribution, known as the "Death Cell Episode," went through several revisions. His first script was overwritten, with the prisoners giving out a collective wail when Wallace is electrocuted and the camera craning up "with glimpses of the men clutching the bars of their cells." The second was an improvement, stressing irony over melodrama: although Wallace is the recipient of the millionaire's largess, it does not save him from the electric chair. The final script dispensed with histrionics but kept the irony intact.

Throughout the 1930s Cole's affinity for plots about lower socio-economic types precluded his moving in the rarefied circles of writers of sophisticated comedy, costume drama, or women's films. His name was synonymous with two-fisted melodrama. Since he had his own conception of people and their needs, he interpreted "popular" in the broadest sense as something geared to general audiences, straightfor-ward, unembellished by intellectual trappings. If the plot warranted a soupçon of social consciousness, he added it; if not, he served it plain.

Because Cole understood the masses, he worked either at studios that specialized in the mass product (Universal, Republic) or on B films at such major studios as Paramount. In 1933, two years before Twen-tieth Century–Fox was formed, Cole came to the moribund Fox Film Corporation to work on a minor Charlie Chan movie, *Charlie Chan's Greatest Case* (1933), and the gold rush melodrama *Wild Gold* (1934). In *Pursued* (1934), also a Fox release, he took a hackneyed story involving an heir to a plantation, a villainous sea captain, and a tart with a heart of gold and gave it some verve—which was more than the team of screenwriters who had been trying to adapt the *Saturday Evening Post* story since 1930 had been able to do.

Cole also come to the rescue of *Sleepers East* (1934), on which at one point even Oscar Levant had worked.[2] *Sleepers East* was Fox's attempt to cash in on the success of *Grand Hotel* (1932), this time with characters on a train. Because the character that most interested Cole was Lena, an alcoholic hooker, he opened up the plot so that Lena returns home to discover that her mother, unable to locate the daughter who left for New York to become an actress, has died. In addition to humanizing a stereotype, Cole also juggled six stories but made Lena's the one the others encircled.

Because of his flair for virile melodrama, Cole stayed on at the newly formed Twentieth Century–Fox for one more film, *Under Pres-sure* (1935),[3] a "two guys" movie harking back to the prototype, *What Price Glory?* (1926), which had featured Edmund Lowe and Victor McLaglen as the battling buddies; eight years later the two were ready to team up again. The genesis of the picture is interesting for what it reveals about screenplay preparation at a new studio where even a minor property required a host of writers to make it filmable—an understandable situation if one remembers that Darryl F. Zanuck, vice-president in charge of production, began as a writer of pulp fiction and frequently wrote scripts under such pseudonyms as Melville Cross-man, Mark Canfield, and Gregory Rogers.

Between June and December 1934, when Cole became involved in the script, Borden Chase (who coauthored the novel on which it is based), Jack Kirkland, Howard Young, and Philip Dunne had labored on it. Although Cole ended up sharing credit with Chase and Noel Pierce, it is clear from the Cole-Pierce drafts that both writers made major improvements on the original, which was little more than the story of two rival sandhogs. They introduced a newspaper woman, Pat—not a newshound of the Rosalind Russell–Claudette Colbert school—who decides to write a human interest story celebrating the "grimy giants who brave the hazards of the high air." Having acquired some spunk, thanks to Cole and Pierce, Pat can then marry one of the giants.

Although there is no way of knowing who wrote the opening title of *Under Pressure*, it certainly displays a proud lack of nuance which would have met with Cole's approval: "Sand Hogs—Tunnel Builders—Under Rivers and through Mountains. Always Rivals but Always Pals. Men Sapped by High Temperatures—Crippled by High Pressures—Giants at Work and Giants at Play—A Short Life at Top Speed." Some of the dialogue also has Cole's aphoristic punch. When a cocky fighter is piqued that a sandhog receives more attention than he, the sandhog replies: "You live on phony fights and hot air. We live on compressed air, and sometimes it kills us."

What Cole had to offer Hollywood in the 1930s was a sense of plot, a social conscience, a talent for creating a reasonably authentic urban milieu peopled by the proletariat, politicos, prostitutes, and criminals, and particularly an ability to tighten the plot screws so that even when the twists go counterclockwise, the bolts never loosen. And so Cole went from film to film, providing the story, the adaptation, the screenplay, or the co-screenplay.

Moving from Fox to Republic[4] was a demotion, but Cole knew he would be fired from Fox when he could not provide the studio with a script for its newest star, Shirley Temple; moreover, his active role in the formation of the Screen Writers Guild made him politically suspect, so he was willing to take a pay cut to keep working at his trade. His first script for Republic, *Hitch Hike Lady* (1935), featured Alison Skipworth, a superb character actress who had appeared with W.C. Fields in the "Rollo and the Roadhogs" episode of *If I Had a Million*. It is the old story of the big mistake: a mother, assuming the San Quentin from which her son writes to her is a ranch, decides to visit him. For the plot to make sense, the mother can have no idea of what or where San Quentin is; thus Cole makes her British. Hitchhiking, immortalized as well as legitimized in *It Happened One Night* (1934), is the way the mother travels across the country.

The mode of transportation determined the genre: road movie, comedy. The genre, in turn, called for certain character types and conventions: con artists (lovable), migrants, an ingenue who takes a shower in an auto court (à la *It Happened One Night*), a running gag ("Rancho San Quentin"), and a happy ending with a double-twist denouement. In the end the son's sentence is commuted—as well it should be, since it has been excessive and therefore unjust, as Cole intended to show: eight years for robbing a grocery store.

Once ensconced at Republic, Cole made it possible for Samuel Ornitz and Nathanael West to work there. Cole had met West at Fox a few years earlier through his brother-in-law, S.J. Perelman. Disconsolate over Columbia's failure to film his novel *A Cool Million*, West eagerly accepted Republic's offer of $200 a week in January 1936; by the end of 1937 he was making $350. In 1936 the three men collaborated on *Follow Your Heart*, which seems to have been more Ornitz than Cole or West; perhaps Cole's contribution was the addition of blacks to the "Magnolias in the Moonlight" finale.

The Affairs of Cappy Ricks (1937), the second of the Cappy Ricks films, was the kind of script Cole did best; qualities that he personally admired—loyalty, cooperation, and respect for workers—served as a means of resolving the plot. The title character, an eccentric part-owner of a shipping company, returns from a two-year voyage to discover that his business has not only been automated but is about to be swallowed up by a conglomerate. To teach the technocrats a lesson, he takes them on a cruise that ends up on a desert island, where the technocrats cannot survive because, unlike Cappy, they cannot construct living quarters. Cappy now has an opportunity (which Cole must have relished) to denounce their capitalist ways. To prove the superiority of man to machine, Cappy arranges for the rescue ship, supposedly a model of automation, to malfunction. Cole uses the Robinson Crusoe premise to prove a point that other 1930s films (*State Fair; Our Daily Bread; The Life of Jimmy Dolan; The Trail of the Lonesome Pine*) were also making: a return to nature makes humans realize that they must cooperate in order to survive.

Cole's best script for Republic, coauthored with Nathanael West, was *The President's Mystery* (1936), which was more political than anything the studio had previously made. There is probably more of Cole than West in the script. It is a variation on the return-to-nature theme, but with a twist: the return is accompanied by a change of identity. An idealistic attorney, tired of being a cog in a political machine, fakes a suicide, takes a new name, and heads upstate to help a failing cannery. While the film abounds in speeches about the dangers of monopolies and the sacredness of property rights, it applies the communal philosophy of *Our Daily Bread* to the cannery, which the plucky heroine hopes to reorganize as a cooperative where "everyone would share in the work and the profits." Rarely has Socialism been so openly endorsed on the screen, and in a Republic movie, no less.

Generally Cole knew how far he could go with his politics; in *The President's Mystery* he goes the limit. Yet Cole could never have known that by socializing the plot he was unwittingly putting his finger on Socialism's main flaw. When the railroad prevents the cooperative from transporting its goods, the workers storm the cannery shouting, "Everybody works, everybody shares, the food belongs to us and nobody's going to stop us." The anarchy, while frighteningly real, is short-lived; still, it reveals the canker in the rose; the utopian belief that public control of the means of production results in the absence of want is, as the economy of eastern Europe has shown, untrue. Fortunately, the farmers come to the rescue with their trucks. This is not Socialism; it is humanitarianism.

Cole was pleased with the script, which succeeds in accommodating an unusually large number of plot devices: assumed identity, little man vs. big business, political activism, a false murder charge, feigned suicide—the last deriving from *Frankenstein* (1932). The attorney substitutes a cadaver, purchased from a hospital attendant, for himself. Dr. Frankenstein would have approved of the scheme, although he would have seen no reason to pay for a corpse.

Cole always maintained that if the blacklist had not occurred, he would have moved into producing and then into directing. He often wrote shooting scripts, not just screenplays; *The President's Mystery* is such a script, specifying camera angles and types of shots. For the car crash suicide he wanted low shots, so that only the legs of the cadaver would be shown. The rest of the sequence consisted of a montage of kerosene splashed on the car, the flick of a cigarette lighter, a sudden burst of flame, a hand turning on the ignition, a car crashing into a rail and disappearing into a ravine. Cole knew how to visualize action; unfortunately, he never had a chance to get behind the camera.

In 1937 Cole moved from Republic to Universal—a step up—where he spent the next three years but wrote only two scripts of any significance; it may have been the right milieu, but it posed no challenge. In the late 1930s Universal melodramas were, for the most part, quickies about government agents, parolees, racketeers, blackmailers, the wrongly accused, women duped by gangsters, undercover cops posing as criminals, and the poor masquerading as the rich. Since Cole had written similar scripts, he recycled old devices and motifs. In *The Man in Blue* (1937), which even the critics regarded as a heredity versus environment film, the orphan son of a criminal is befriended by the policeman who killed his father. The blonde of *Some Blondes Are Dangerous* (1938) is an actress who marries a prizefighter to boost her career. The crime in *The Crime of Dr. Hallet* (1938) is self-infection with a serum to prove its worthlessness; when Dr. Hallet dies from his experiment, his guilt-ridden associates continue his research and save Mrs. Hallet's life. *Midnight Intruder* (1938) is an assumed-identity film with a penniless pair masquerading as dilettantes.

Since the "wrong man" movie was a Universal staple, Cole was in his element, providing the studio with four such films in two years: in *The Jury's Secret* (1938) one of the jurors on a homicide case is really the killer (though his murder of an opponent of flood control legislation, according to Cole's politics, would make him innocent); *Secrets of a Nurse* (1938) is a last-mile movie in which an innocent victim is saved from the electric chair; *The Big Guy* (1939) featured Jackie Cooper as a boy who almost goes to the chair for a murder actually committed by the prison warden; in *The Invisible Man Returns* (1940) Vincent Price becomes invisible to unmask the real killer.

Of Cole's ten Universal screenplays, two are worth discussing in some detail: *Sinners in Paradise* (1938) and *The House of Seven Gables* (1940). Although *Sinners in Paradise* involved two other writers and was directed by the underrated James Whale—who elevated *Frankenstein* (1932) and *Bride of Frankenstein* (1935) from the threshold of horror to the height of gothic—it is still very much a Cole film. Despite its B-movie aura, which even Whale could not dispel, *Sinners* is a political tract—naive, utopian, but undeniably sincere, with Cole accomplishing what he was only partially able to do in *The Affairs of Cappy Ricks*: write a proletarian desert island movie. The characters are a cut above the usual island castaways. Nine survivors of a plane crash—a mother, a windbag senator, a hooker, a hood, a flight attendant, an heiress, a nurse, and two gunrunners peddling ammunition to an unspecified country that is obviously Japan—are tossed up on an island whose sole inhabitants are a doctor fleeing a murder rap and his Chinese factotum. In 1938, references to the gathering storm were rare in movies, yet Cole managed to insert allusions to the "trouble in China" and the "tense" European situation.

Cole's aim was more political than historical, however. Once the nine discover they are "all in the same boat," they prove, perhaps too patly, that the most heterogeneous of groups can keep the boat from sinking if they apply the principle of division of labor. Everyone learns from the experience; the humble are exalted; the exalted, humbled; and most find a mate in the bargain. The heiress, whose Detroit plant is plagued by strikes, decides to aid the workers; the nurse and the doctor pair off; the hooker and the gangster, in what appears to be a deliberate reply to the money-as-panacea philosophy of *If I Had a Million*, burn thousand-dollar bills because money is worthless in the earthly paradise.

When Universal decided to film *The House of Seven Gables* (the movie title omits the second "the"), Harold Greene had already done the adaptation. No doubt it was Greene who changed the relationships between the characters: Clifford and Judge Pyncheon, cousins in Hawthorne's novel, are brothers in the film on the supposition that rivalry is more dramatic and false allegations more shocking between brothers. Hepzibah and Clifford Pyncheon are no longer siblings but cousins—distant ones, so they can marry at the end. (This is perhaps not entirely inappropriate; Hawthorne's Hepzibah seems to ·harbor feelings for her brother that are midway between maternal and conjugal.)

Once Cole was given the adaptation, he was able to fashion a screenplay that was true to the spirit, if not the letter, of the original. Hawthorne's narrative, which traces the fate of six generations over two centuries, is considerably simplified. In keeping with his politics, Cole portrayed the Pyncheons as a dynasty of frauds and traitors who supported the British during the Revolution and engaged in shady land deals. A curse lies on the family because a Colonel Pyncheon expropriated the land of Matthew Maule; "God will give him blood to drink," Maule's last utterance, is a prophecy that has been fulfilled by a common manner of death: pulmonary hemorrhage or, as Cole calls it, "high blood pressure and thin-veined aristocracy," the capitalist affliction.

Only Clifford Pyncheon, whom the Judge falsely accuses of causing their father's death, is pure of heart. Cole took Hawthorne's portrait of Clifford even further, making him an idealist, a Yankee Quixote who is at times too quixotic. Perhaps in 1940 audiences did not smirk at Clifford's fantasy about leaving Massachusetts for New York, a city of "laughing, struggling, working people" (a Cole line if there ever was one); today, one can only smile at such naiveté—Clifford's as well as Cole's. In the clash between corruption and innocence, Cole was quite specific about the kind of corruption: the slave trading motif is his addition. Whenever he could, he tried to work blacks into the script or at least acknowledge their existence.

In the novel, Holgrave, the daguerrotypist and Maule's descendant, has no given name; Cole makes him his ancestor's namesake: Matthew. Holgrave must be a Maule so that the novel can end with the marriage of a Pyncheon (Phoebe) to a Maule (Holgrave), symbolizing the amalgamation of the Old World and New, of Europe and America. Cole did not radicalize Hawthorne's plot; he only brought to the surface what Hawthorne implied. Hawthorne's Holgrave is something of a social reformer who, by twenty-two, has done everything from teaching school to peddling cologne; he has also spent several months with the Fourierists, who practiced communal living. Cole raised Hawthorne's character from liberal to radical.

In the novel Holgrave meets with distinctly progressive types, but Hawthorne never specifies the nature of their meetings. Cole does: they were meetings of an abolitionist society whose purpose was to help blacks escape on the Underground Railroad. With Holgrave a radical and Clifford a utopian, the characters can be doubles—cellmates, in fact. Clifford is imprisoned for his father's alleged murder; Holgrave, for inciting a riot. No sooner does Holgrave enter the cell than he declares, "The prison hasn't been built that can stifle mankind's cry for freedom." While the voice is unmistakably Cole's, it would surely have had Hawthorne's sanction, as would Holgrave's admonition to Hepzibah that she must "contribute toward the struggle of mankind." If this sounds like Marxist propaganda, one should recall that Holgrave says something similar in the novel. When Hepzibah opens a shop, thereby reverting to working-class status, and tells Holgrave that she still considers herself a lady, Holgrave replies that in the New World, there are no ladies and gentlemen—terms that imply privilege—but men and women.

Cole realized that once the antislavery theme had been introduced, it would have to continue to the end, in which the Judge dies, as do all the Pyncheons, from a hemorrhage. Hawthorne is vague about the circumstances, but Cole cannot afford to be vague; if Holgrave is an abolitionist and the Pyncheons are slave traders, it is only logical that slavery would have something to do with the Judge's death. Hence, confronted by a mob of angry abolitionists whose funds he has appropriated to purchase the services of a slave runner, the Judge dies the Pyncheon death, enabling Clifford to marry Hepzibah, Holgrave to marry Phoebe, and the House of the Seven Gables to be sold.

In terms of Hollywood's approach to the classics, the film version of *The House of Seven Gables* is a compromise between slavish fidelity to the text and total disregard for it. Cole understood the novel; he also understood how to streamline it for a mass audience. His work on the film, however, did not compensate for three lucrative but uncreative years at Universal, during which he had acquired the reputation of a B-movie screenwriter and script doctor; it was on the basis of that reputation that Paramount hired him in 1941.

His first assignment was a quasi-horror film, *Among the Living* (1941),[5] based on an original story he had written with Brian Marlow. Horror at Paramount was not the same as, say, horror at Universal; Paramount did not favor synthetic creations like Frankenstein's monster, victims of metamorphosis like the Wolf Man, creatures of the time warp like the Mummy, or the reincarnated like Dracula; it preferred to generate *frissons* instead of mere shivers. After Paramount's success with *Dr. Cyclops* (1940), starring Albert Dekker as the mad scientist, the studio cast Dekker in the dual role of twins, one deranged, the other sane. What sets *Among the Living* apart from the conventional horror film is an intelligence that has merited it an entry in the encyclopedia of film noir where, generically, it does not belong.[6] It does belong, however, in a discussion of Lester Cole and Paramount Pictures; its well-documented production history throws considerable light on the way a studio, on the eve of Pearl Harbor, responded to a script that was crypto-leftist and openly antifascist.

First, Cole did a script that included, not unexpectedly, blacks, slum scenes, and an unusual plot twist: the mad brother Paul, who is presumably dead, is really alive; an idealistic doctor forged a death certificate in return for a clinic "for everyone regardless of race, creed or color." After killing his victims, Paul leaves them with their hands pressed to their ears; he grew up watching his mother cover her ears when she was abused by her German-born, proto-Nazi husband. Paul the psychopath may be a killer, but Paul the humanitarian hopes to improve conditions in the town by reopening the mills and providing "food for [the workers'] children, installments on their furniture."

This was hardly the kind of script Paramount wanted; the comments written on it by associate producer Colbert Clark are revealing: "The explanation here can be edited; the phony fascism might be dropped." Once Garrett Fort became coscreenwriter and the editing began, the fascism vanished. Paul has no redeeming features; there is no free clinic for the doctor, no polio epidemic, no veiled allusions to Nazism. *Among the Living* became a twin-brothers movie—better than most but focusing primarily on what happens when one twin is mistaken for the other.

Since Cole was known as a script doctor, his next assignment was *Pacific Blackout* (1942), based on a story called "Air Raid" that had been kicking around Paramount for four years.[7] The first writer assigned to it was the distinguished Donald Ogden Stewart. A recent convert to the radical left, Stewart had given the script the full antifascist treatment, complete with a blazing Foreword ("Half the world already faced death, and destruction rained upon it from the air") and footage of the bombing of Barcelona and Nanking. During a defense drill an official asks a Spanish woman, "Have your children received drill instruction?" The woman replies, "I don't think, sir, that will be necessary; they lived in Barcelona."

Chastened somewhat by his experience with *Among the Living*, Cole eliminated the Spanish mother when he took over the script in the summer of 1941, yet he could not resist the opportunity for some premature antifascism. Since *Pacific Blackout* was a civil defense film,

Cole made the defense expert a Nazi, never identifying him as such but giving him a Third Reich sound-alike name: Ronnel. Cole also created a Dr. Strangelove atmosphere; although the raid is supposedly a test, one of the planes is equipped with real bombs. Nothing happens, of course, and as a cop says at the end, "It's all over."

With America's entry into the war, characters could be as anti-Nazi as the writer wished, and Cole went the limit. His next film for Paramount was *Night Plane from Chungking* (1942),[8] an airborne *Grand Hotel* with an international passenger list.

More than diversity of characterization, the film needed the up-to-the-minute accuracy mandated by Pearl Harbor, the rapid turn of events in the Pacific, and the increasing hatred of the Japanese at home. In 1942, accuracy was difficult to achieve; accordingly, Cole accepted the notion that spies were everywhere and made a Dutch minister a Japanese agent. The minister's exposure is accompanied by Cole invective typical of the left's lofty logic. The assumption is that anyone working for the enemy is as brutal as the enemy; when the enemy is Japan, the capacity for brutality is unequaled.

Faulty comparisons and unfounded inferences abound in World War II movies. In *Night Plane*, when the Japanese agent wants to negotiate, the flier replies: "I'm negotiating—for the millions of kids you've starved and mutilated, for the helpless old people and women you've tortured in China and Russia and all over Europe." Exactly what the Japanese had done to Europeans is never explained. Similarly, in *Sahara* (1943), written for the most part by John Howard Lawson, Humphrey Bogart compares his stand in the desert to Dunkirk and Stalingrad, arguing that just as the British and the Soviets gave the democracies time to mobilize, so too did he and his ragtag detachment. Actually, the detachment has nowhere else to go; while the Battling Bastards of Bataan could boast of engaging in a holding action, the detachment in *Sahara* does not even know what, or for whom, it is holding.

When Paramount asked Cole to adapt Stefan Heym's *Hostages* (1942), Cole was elated at the prospect of adapting the novel of an author whose vision he shared and whose portrayal of the Nazi take-over of Czechoslovakia moved him deeply. Because he identified with the subject matter, he tended either to sentimentalize or sensationalize it. Frank Butler, who eventually received coscreenplay credit, had to curb Cole's anti-Nazism, which had exceeded even the sky-high 1940s limit. Butler reminded Cole, who had a German lieutenant commit suicide when his wife is sent to a breeding camp, that married women were not sent to breeding camps. When Cole had the heroine blanch at a German's touch, Butler politely informed him that the Czechs "are living with these people and this isn't their first encounter." When

Cole had the heroine speak like La Pasionaria, Butler reprimanded him for making her sound "like a heroine in a cheap melodrama."

It is evident from the number of drafts and the nature of the revisions that *Hostages* gave Cole more trouble than any of his previous films.[9] He had unusual difficulty devising an opening. He planned a fade-in on the destruction of Lidice, with a lone dog silhouetted against a sky streaked with smoke. The camera would track from the dog to a bullet-scarred wall, panning down to a skein of bodies; a swing dissolve would show a Nazi putting up a poster reading, "This is Lidice! The People of Prague take warning." When the Nazi left, partisans would replace the poster with one of their own. The actual film opens with a replacement of posters but not about Lidice and without the dog and the charred ruins. It took several drafts to remove the excess, but the result was worth it, and the plot pegs were still Cole's. *Hostages* is a moving portrayal of a people under siege that makes few audience concessions.

Cole's best World War II script is *None Shall Escape* (1944), one of the few assignments in which he encountered no studio interference. More important, he was able to confront an issue that he had implied but had not yet dramatized: the plight of the Jews under the Nazis. The film's strongest scene occurs when Jews from the Polish town of Litzbark are ordered to assemble at the railroad station for deportation to what is presumably a labor camp (the time is late 1939) but what the post-Auschwitz viewer, who equates cattle cars and a summons in the night with the Holocaust, would consider a death camp. As a Party member, a Russophile, and a Jew whose father had emigrated to America from a town not unlike Litzbark, Cole intended the connection. He had read such accounts as Ilya Ehrenberg's in the Soviet Embassy's *Information Bulletin* (22 July 1943) in which eyewitnesses testified to the gassing of the Jews in portable vans and recounted their experiences in camps intended not just for the internment of political prisoners but for the systematic annihilation of a race.

When *None Shall Escape* was released in early 1944, few realized how prophetic it was, not just in the proleptic reference to death camps but also in the frame narrative involving a tribunal for the prosecution of war criminals. Cole had assumed that the war in Europe would soon be over; actually, it continued for more than a year after the film was released. Still, his instincts were correct, even though the trials would be held at Nuremberg rather than Warsaw.

The deportation sequence in *None Shall Escape* played a significant role in Cole's life, not because of his prescience but because of the speech the rabbi delivers to his people as they are about to enter the cattle cars; it is an appeal to resist, phrased in the idiom of the class struggle: "Let us prepare ourselves to face this supreme moment in our lives. This is our last journey. It doesn't matter if it's long or short. For centuries we have sought only peace. We have tried to take our place honestly, decently, alongside of all mankind, to help make a better world, a world in which all people would live as free neighbors. We have hoped and prayed, but now we see hope was not enough. What good has it done us to submit? Submission brought us rare moments when we were tolerated—tolerated! Is there any greater degradation than to be tolerated? To be permitted to exist? We have submitted too long. If we want equality, we must take our place along with all other oppressed peoples. . . . By our actions we will be remembered. It is our last free choice, our moment in history. I say to you, let us choose to fight, here, now." The rebellion ends with a railroad platform strewn with corpses; the shadow of a cruciform signpost extends the length of the platform.

At the time of the HUAC hearings, a story circulated that Cole had written a college film in which a football coach gave his team a peptalk ending with La Pasionaria's famous maxim: "It is far better to die on your feet than live as slaves on your knees." Although the story persisted and even appeared in Cole's *New York Times* obituary,[10] the closest Cole had ever come to writing a college film was *Winter Carnival* (1939), for which he shared credit with Maurice Rapf and Budd Schulberg (who, as Dartmouth alumni, knew more about the setting than Cole). But no such sentiment is expressed in *Winter Carnival*. The line does appear in *The Spirit of Culver* (1939), written in part by Cole's close friend Nathanael West; the setting is a military academy where "an upper-class boy . . . states that 'sometimes it is better to die on your feet than live on your knees'."[11] In a time of transferred guilt, West's quotation of one of the most radical left-wing apothegms was imputed to Cole—and since West had died in 1940 and *The Spirit of Culver* was only a memory, HUAC felt no need to verify the charge. Cole did not help matters by claiming in his autobiography that he did have the rabbi utter La Pasionaria's words in *None Shall Escape*. Perhaps he had intended to use them; nevertheless, they appear neither in the final script nor in the film. Interestingly, HUAC was ignorant of both the film and the rabbi's speech, perhaps because the committee preferred dialogue of telegraphic brevity.

Cole, who had worked at Warner's briefly in 1940 on a forgettable Errol Flynn mystery, *Footsteps in the Dark* (1941), returned to that studio in 1944, probably through the efforts of Alvah Bessie, who had arrived the previous year and whose original story "Objective, Burma!" was about to be filmed. Cole was assigned to the screenplay, and despite Bessie's displeasure with the film, which he considered inferior to his story, *Objective, Burma!* (1945) is among the more mythic World War II movies, reworking one of the oldest archetypes in literature: the return. What was to have been a simple mission results in a nightmarish odyssey as paratroopers are stranded in the jungle when the absence of a landing field prevents their plane from setting down; the platoon must journey through the jungle to a hilltop to await rescue. The action moves in an ascending arc with the anabasis becoming an ascent to Golgotha; once the men arrive at the desolate hilltop, they think their journey has been in vain. Only a *deus ex machina* can help them; to keep the film from ending on a note of despair, Cole arranged for a supply plane to land.

In 1944 Cole also wrote *Blood on the Sun* (1945) for William Cagney Productions as a vehicle for William's brother James. Though not the film by which James Cagney will be best remembered, it is certainly one that his fans cherish, as evidenced by its frequent television airings and its videocassette sales. The plot hinges on a spurious document known as the Tanaka Plan, long believed to have been a blueprint for world conquest formulated by Baron Giichi Tanaka, Japanese prime minister from 1927 to 1929. The Plan never existed, yet just a few years earlier Frank Capra's *Prelude to War* (1942), the first of the *Why We Fight* series, had insisted that it did. In *Blood on the Sun* historical accuracy is no more an issue than is Shakespeare's geography in *A Winter's Tale* or chronometry in *Julius Caesar*. As Aristotle noted, it is far worse to draw a hind inartistically than not to know it has no horns. *Blood on the Sun* is a tangy, colorful espionage tale that is no more improbable than most specimens of the genre.

The film is a throwback to Cole's melodramas of the 1930s but better written, because it was starring an Academy Award winner who had his own ideas about it. Cole wanted the story to end with the newsman (Cagney) and the Eurasian agent (Sylvia Sidney) spiriting the Tanaka Plan out of Tokyo and taking it to the League of Nations in Geneva, where they discover that it has already been put into operation with Japan's invasion of Manchuria.[12] But such an ending would have been anticlimactic in June 1945 when the movie was scheduled for release. Apart from the fact that V-J Day would make such a film an artifact, there was an even more important factor to consider: the implication that the League, in catering to Chiang Kai-shek's anti-Communism, was indirectly responsible for leaving Japanese imperialism unchecked in the early 1930s. While not an icon on the order of MacArthur, the Generalissimo and his wife always drew applause from World War II audiences when they appeared on the screen in a newsreel. To cast doubt on Chiang's integrity would verge on the sacrilegious.

Unknown to Cole, the Cagneys commissioned Nathaniel Curtis to rewrite the ending, for which Curtis received an "additional dialogue" credit. It must have been a quick decision because the publicity director had already sent out a plot summary including everything but the climax, noting "Finish to come." By spring 1945, the finish had come. In the film, Cagney delivers the fadeout line, which sounds quintessentially Cole: when a Japanese assassin, whom Cagney succeeds in overpowering, admonishes him to forgive his enemies, Cagney replies, "The United States Government doesn't settle for a deal. Sure, forgive your enemies but first get even." Cole disclaimed responsibility for the ending; nevertheless, the line "The United States Government doesn't settle for a deal" does appear in the *Screen Romances* (June 1945) synopsis, where sole screenplay credit is given to Cole. Perhaps Curtis, thinking the line too good to discard, felt it could serve as the penultimate statement, leading into the zinger. If so, he was right; the two-line speech does work. Cole tossed off a short piece for the *Hollywood Quarterly* (forerunner of *Film Quarterly*) castigating the Cagneys for their pusillanimity, but the industry paid no attention; what mattered was that *Blood on the Sun* was a commercial success. If it had not been known before, it was clear that Lester Cole's films made money.

In 1946—a bonanza year for the industry, and for the Ten, the year of plenty before the famine—Cole received a call from Jack Cummings, Louis B. Mayer's nephew: MGM, the Tiffany of studios, wanted his services. At forty-one, Cole found himself at the studio that boasted of having more stars than there are in the heavens; he also found himself revising George Bruce's script for the nonswimming Esther Williams vehicle that introduced Ricardo Montalban to American audiences. *Fiesta* (1947) led to two more MGM assignments, one of which was for Robert Taylor, who had shown a slight flair for melodrama in *Undercurrent* (1946), where he was cast against type as a murderer; in *High Wall* (1947) Taylor was another of Cole's "wrong men," falsely accused of murdering his wife and staging a car crash to make her death look accidental. Although Cole shared screenplay credit with Sidney Boehm, *High Wall* is very much a Cole script, and Taylor was so pleased that he wanted more films from Cole; he soon changed his mind when the witch-hunt began. On 22 October 1947, appearing before HUAC as a friendly witness and asked whether he knew any Communist writers, Taylor replied: "I know one gentleman employed at the studio at which I am employed, Mr. Lester Cole, who is reputedly a Communist."[13]

The Romance of Rosy Ridge, Cole's best MGM script and one of which he is deservedly proud (he quotes liberally from it in his autobiography), is a post–Civil War story set in the border state of Missouri; it recalls *The Birth of a Nation* (1915), with friends finding themselves on opposite sides. Cole wrote the screenplay in dialect, as he often did when the setting or the characters called for it. Although the film is based on a novel by Mackinlay Kantor, who thought Cole had taken too many liberties with his book (to which Cole replied that he had made it dramatic), it is closer in spirit to William Saroyan's *Human Comedy* (1943).

Cole made Rosy Ridge an antebellum workers' paradise that had been plagued since the war's end with "barn burnin' and hate burnin', 'stead of tradin' labor like they used to." Into this postlapsarian world comes a schoolteacher, eager to restore Rosy Ridge to what it was before the war polarized it; the villagers, however, are interested only in knowing on which side he fought. Cole managed to generate some suspense in what was originally a static idyll by allowing a series of revelations to culminate in the unmasking of the villain, an opportunist who caused divisiveness so that families would move and he could buy up their land. The teacher has come to Rosy Ridge to do what Ben McBean would have done if he had lived: help his father gather the harvest. In language of dramatic simplicity, the teacher recounts how he and Ben met and became friends, even though the teacher was a Yankee and Ben the son of a Yankee-hating father. When they reached a bifurcating road, one spur going north, the other south, the teacher asked Ben, "We're goin' the same way, aren't we?" They went north.

When the teacher explains why he fought for the Union, it is clear that he is talking not about the Civil War but about a more recent one: "We fought because we believed it didn't make any difference in this country what color a man's skin was, and here we are not six months later, a-battlin' over what color his pants are. If you don't put a stop to it, a-fore long you'll be a-killin' over how long your neighbor's nose is." A 1947 audience would have picked up the reference to nose size, which was hardly an issue in the War between the States but frequently did determine who lived or died in the war just concluded.

Even after Cole had received his HUAC subpoena, Louis B. Mayer renewed his contract at MGM because he wanted to keep a good writer. Yet Mayer had no choice but to abide by the Waldorf Statement of 25 November 1947—an industry creation like self-censorship—which declared that the Ten were unemployable until they recanted. The Waldorf Statement ended Cole's tenure at MGM; it also virtually ended his screenwriting career.

Like all discriminatory actions, the blacklist had no consistency; for Dalton Trumbo, it ended in 1960; for Ring Lardner, Jr., it ended in 1964; for Lester Cole it never ended at all. Even in 1965 his name could not be used on *Born Free* (1965); the screenplay is attributed to "Gerald L.C. Copley."[14] In *Hollywood Red* Cole recalls that after it was known that he was Copley, he was deluged with script offers—for animal films. He was not interested; the saga of Elsa was enough. Another name under which Cole wrote was J. Redmond Prior, which he used for an original screen story that he sold to Warner's and that became the basis of *Chain*

Lightning (1950). Cole's presence can be felt in the story line, which—like Arthur Miller's *All My Sons*—attributes shoddy aircraft to greed for government contracts.

Cole's gift for plot construction should have guaranteed him work in television, but he was barred from that medium also. He managed to coauthor one teleplay, *The Pied Piper of Hamelin* (1957), though from the absence of any writers' names, it appears to have been self-authored. Alvah Bessie and Albert Maltz were able to publish fiction; Cole tried his hand at stage plays but with little success. However, once film study became a respectable academic discipline, Cole—who had not even finished high school—found part-time positions teaching screenwriting first at eastern universities and then, in the mid-1960s, at San Francisco State University, where he so endeared himself to his students that on the last day of class they arrived wearing "I Love Lester" T-shirts. His death on 15 August 1985 attracted more attention than might have been expected: the *New York Times* published a lengthy obituary, and the Pacific Archives in Berkeley held a memorial service at which Harry Bridges, Lou Harris (former Paramount publicist and a longtime friend), and Jack Cummings (who had brought him to MGM) spoke, and clips from Cole's films were shown.

Lester Cole died a Stalinist, yet his generosity and commitment to humankind were not qualities acquired by politics or ideology.

3 JOHN HOWARD LAWSON
Hollywood Commissar

John Howard Lawson came to Hollywood for the first time in 1928, shortly before Ornitz and Cole arrived. Unlike his comrades, however, Lawson had already built a reputation: five of his plays had been produced in New York.

Lawson also differs from most of the Ten in having been the subject of doctoral dissertations, one of which has been published.[1] This is not surprising; although his plays have not been revived, they are historically important. Spanning a fourteen-year period from 1923 (*Roger Bloomer*) to 1937 (*Marching Song*), they illustrate the transition from the expressionism of the 1920s to the social drama of the 1930s; they also mirror Lawson's own evolution from expressionist to political playwright, as well as from Marxist neophyte to hard-line Communist. In his early plays, Lawson was torn between Communism as a political philosophy and Communism as a panacea; in his expressionist phase he was more social than political, more liberal than Marxist, more imaginative than didactic.

It was inevitable that the first theatrical form that attracted Lawson was expressionism, as practiced by the German playwrights who portrayed as a nightmare a society that exploits, depersonalizes, and corrupts. *Roger Bloomer*, sometimes called the first American expressionist drama (it preceded Elmer Rice's *Adding Machine* by almost three weeks), is less extreme in its expressionism than, say, Georg Kaiser's *From Morn to Midnight* (1912), with which Lawson was clearly familiar. Unlike many expressionist works, *Roger Bloomer* is not so much nonlinear as antilinear. Understandably, it is linked with *The Adding Machine* because, like Rice's play, it is accessible expressionism; the atmosphere is far less threatening or hallucinogenic than that of Eugene O'Neill's *Emperor Jones* or *The Hairy Ape*. *Roger Bloomer* might even be called modified expressionism: it has the basic features—short scenes that flow into each other, sometimes giving the impression of concurrent action; aphoristic dialogue that barely avoids being apocalyptic; fragmented plot; half-formed thoughts and unfinished sentences that resemble the non sequiturs of a dream; a phantasmagoric ending like that of *From Morn to Midnight* and especially Frank Wedekind's *Spring's Awakening* (1891)—without the exaggeration.

Roger Bloomer is a midwestern Candide who leaves Iowa for New York—"our granite mother," as he calls it—in the archetypal quest for selfhood. His purity leaves him impervious to New York's blandishments, but Louise, his beloved, is less fortunate. Torn between maintaining her virtue and succumbing to her employer's advances, she finds the tension too difficult to bear; after stealing some bonds, Louise commits suicide, not for fear of being detected but so that Lawson can bring her back at the end as a shade—the "virgin harlot," the merging of the blessed damozel and the chthonic mother.

While *Roger Bloomer's* final scene is the least satisfying part of the play, it does reveal Lawson's knowledge of the arts (which became even more apparent in the following decade with the publication of his *Theory and Technique of Playwriting*). The ghosts of Wedekind, Kaiser, Stravinsky's *Rite of Spring*, and Aeschylus hover in the background: Stravinsky in the rituals of rebirth; Aeschylus in the crones who speak of themselves as "older than time," like the Furies in *The Eumenides*. Although the language occasionally flowers into pretentiousness, a reading of *Roger Bloomer* leaves no doubt that one is in the presence of a promising playwright who, unfortunately, never fulfilled his promise. Perhaps one reason is that he could not dismiss the sound of "marching people singing a new song,"[2] which Louise hears at the end but which Lawson would not hear in its entirety for more than a decade.

It certainly was not audible in his next play, *Processional* (1925). In this dazzling recreation of Aristophanic comedy a serious situation, a West Virginia strike, is treated like a running gag in a vaudeville show. The characters, who are enslaved to their names (Dynamite Jim, Boob, Dago Joe), include slow-witted blacks, whining Jews, and comic-strip Communists.[3]

Processional is the wedding of drama and pop art, theater and burlesque, stichomythic dialogue and jazz rhythm; it recalls Aristophanes' deceptively anarchic structure where a weighty subject is debated, lampooned, and ultimately resolved, often with a total disregard for verisimilitude, logic, and history. In *Lysistrata* a sex strike is shown to be ineffective, yet it succeeds in averting war between Athens and Sparta; the utopia in *The Birds* attracts so many undesirables that it must be termed a failure, yet Aristophanes makes it seem a success. Similarly, the strike in *Processional*, which should have ended in the defeat of the workers, is resolved by a magnanimous management.

Comedy has always seemed closer to the sleeping than the waking state; what transpires in comedy is often lunatic, best appreciated by those whose eyelids are bedewed with magic. In Aristophanes there is an intentionally dreamlike atmosphere, a carryover from the *komos* or revel band that awakened dignitaries with rowdy verses sung at their window. *Processional's* controlled shapelessness suggests the form out of which Old Comedy, as distinct from the classically constructed comedies of Menander, evolved. Lawson treats the strike as Aristophanes treated the Peloponnesian War—as a dream fantasy; it is peopled by proletarian and vaudeville types, speaking dialogue that in the post-*Godot* era is absurdist.

While *Processional* has an absurdist looseness, it is, like the best absurdist drama, not haphazardly constructed. In *Theory and Practice of Playwriting* Lawson notes that plays such as Sidney Howard's *Yellow Jack* contain scenes that have their own beginning-middle-end; such scenes are microcosmic of the whole through their concentric arrangement of the episodes. Lawson achieved the same effect in *Processional* by giving each episode its distinctive quality: tragic, surreal, absurdist, satiric. In the fourth act a jazz trial and a jazz marriage play off each other contrapuntally. The Klan tries Sadie Cohen, the local jazz baby, for her waywardness. At the trial a chorus behaves as outrageously as Aristophanes' frogs or wasps, rhyming whatever it hears: to "outrageous" it answers with "contagious." When Sadie laments how her father "sighed an' he cried an' he pretty near died," the chorus responds, "For the loss of her honor and pride. Shame." Picking up on "shame," Sadie exclaims, "I ain't ashamed—I'm glad. I'm the glad girl." The jazz wedding of Sadie and Dynamite Jim is the Aristophanic *gamos* or marriage feast that provides the sexual reconciliation toward which the phallic songs, the precursors of Old Comedy, tended. Lawson, however, goes one step further; if the play is a dream fantasy, the resolution must be equally fantastic: management concedes to the strikers' demands.

Although *Processional* has political overtones, it avoids a militant stance; rather, it relies on the same kind of unreality one finds in burlesque skits like "Floogle Street" and "Crazy House." By pushing literalism to the limit, burlesque demolishes denotation, making it laughable. On one level, *Processional* is about a strike; on another level, it depicts the strike as a cartoon. Lawson was still uncertain as to how far to the left he cared to go.

He did not go far in his next two plays. *Nirvana* (1926), a satire on the meaning-of-life quest, ran for eight performances. *Loud Speaker* (1927), produced by New Playwrights, of which Lawson was a founding member, was more fortunate; it ran for forty-two.

Loud Speaker is more surreal than expressionistic. The plot is virtually nonexistent; if the play is about anything, it is about a gubernatorial candidate who is elected by revealing, rather than concealing, his thoughts. While the surrealism, which is really antic expressionism, is intermittently amusing, the play as a whole is not, because

Lawson makes uninspired use of traditional comic devices: puns (adore/a door, prostrated/prostituted), bedroom farce (the scantily clad ex-mistress emerging as wife and husband are about to reconcile), ethnic zaniness (a delegation of Harlem blacks who bring down the first-act curtain with a dance), and insult trading:

Johnnie. I knew a girl once used to write me letters starting "Big Man."
Clare. She must have been a midget.
Johnnie. On the contrary, she was a fat lady with the circus, and she conceived a
    hopeless passion for me.
Clare. Naturally, any passion for you would be hopeless.[4]

Joseph Wood Krutch, who wrote the introduction to the published text, defended *Loud Speaker* by comparing Lawson's cartoon characters to those of the commedia dell'arte; the vamp, the flapper, the shrew, and the politician are stock characters, and the plot to which Lawson assigns them is synthetic, made of up strains from various traditions. The political satire harks back to the revels that gave birth to Aristophanic comedy. The *komos* lampooned politicians, and *Loud Speaker* is a politician's nightmare: figures from his past suddenly emerge; his persona drops like a top banana's pants; and mayhem reigns like Mardi Gras royalty. One thinks of Falstaff at Hearns Oak, or the haunting of Malvolio, but in a far less creative context. *Loud Speaker* is more like a collegiate hazing ceremony, devised by a literate English major who sees to it that the audience comes in for its share of (good-natured) baiting for its bourgeois values.

The constructivist setting with platforms and stairs, which Lawson specified and Mordecai Gorelick provided, created an atmosphere of simultaneous action. The onstage jazz band further diminished verisimilitude, along with the mannequins representing politicians. But Lawson's inability to handle political satire except surrealistically bears out Krutch's comparison. The commedia dell'arte needed an artist like Molière to individualize its types.

Lawson was still too much a student of theater, as his second work for New Playwrights showed. It is not surprising that Malcolm Goldstein found reading *The International* (1928) an exasperating experience;[5] the play is not so much to be read as to be visualized. It is a political cartoon that lies somewhere between a silent serial like *The Perils of Pauline* and Brechtian epic theater. It has a story but no plot, only a series of episodes in which David Fitch (an *engagé* Roger Bloomer but equally naive), who is eager "to do one of two things . . . see the working class . . . or see the world," chooses the latter, goes to Asia where he encounters Communist revolutionaries, and after a host of madcap adventures in the tradition of the cliffhangers, meets his death in New York during a revolution.

While *The International* has the speeded-up action of a serial, it is also an attempt at Gordon Craig's total theater in which song, dance, word, and image intermingle; a semitransparent backdrop that functions as a map of the world was inspired by Erwin Piscator's use of projections and film; the Dionysian choruses and ritual action again show the influence of *The Rite of Spring*. Lawson has brought rhyming dialogue to a higher level than in *Processional*; the blues-inspired rhythm grows incantatory, litany-like:

Madam Miau. [*Chanting softly.*] Sing for him, sing for a rich man, 'Cause he's
  richer than God.
Second Chorus. [*Softly.*] Yellow gold for a yellow girl's love.
Madam Miau. Fallin' on her body like rain from above.
Second Chorus. Fallin' in showers
  Like rain on the flowers
  Where it does the most good!
Madam Miau. Nights of pleasure . . .
Second Chorus. Fallin' like rain . . .
Madam Miau. Nights without hope . . .
Second Chorus. Nights of pain . . .
Madam Miau. Nights of unholy holiday . . .
Second Chorus. Unholy . . . unclean . . . unholy . . . [6]

Yet *The International* is also a personal play; it was Lawson's attempt to formulate a question he would eventually have to answer: what side, exactly, was he on? The play endorses revolution, but the revolutionary characters are the figures of absurdist farce, and the revolution itself is a failure. Cartels are willing to wage wars to get Asian oil and to crush attempts to prevent their getting it. Whatever Lawson was in 1928, he was not a radical. Still, that year is significant: it marks the end of his theatrical experimentation and the beginning of his screenwriting career.

Unlike Albert Maltz, who became a screenwriter when his playwriting days were over, Lawson was still a working dramatist when he received an offer from MGM. New Playwrights was moribund, however, and his financial situation was bleak. While he may have ennobled his motives for going west ("gaining cinematic knowledge which would be invaluable for future work in either drama or film")[7], the offer had come at the right time.

Lawson was an unusually adaptable writer and versatile enough to survive in Hollywood. Although he had not practiced linear narration in his experimental plays, he could do it, as he would have to in writing for film. Yet his experiments in expressionism also stood him in good stead. He knew how to write laconic, even telegraphic dialogue. He also knew how to cut from one action to another; he had done it repeatedly in *The International*, as well as switching from one continent to another.

Lawson's first assignment at MGM was to write not a script but a sound sequence for the Greta Garbo film *Flesh and the Devil*, which had been shot as a silent but—after the success of Warner Brothers' *Don Juan* (1926) and *The Jazz Singer* (1927)—would need something in the way of the aural for re-release. Lawson's expressionistic sequence was rejected, but Irving Thalberg—MGM's production head—was impressed with him as a man of ideas, and that was sufficient to keep him on the payroll.

When Cecil B. DeMille came to MGM in 1928, the name of John Howard Lawson was not unknown to him. He had seen *Processional* and wanted Lawson to model the character of the miner in *Dynamite* (1928), DeMille's first sound film, on Dynamite Jim. As early as *Roger Bloomer*, Lawson had discovered a story peg strong enough to support an indefinite variety of plots: boy/girl, rendered not so much in romantic as in social terms. Its most extreme form is the bipolar rich/poor: rich Roger/poor Louise of *Roger Bloomer* and similarly, in his films, heiress/miner (*Dynamite*), adventuress/peasant (*Blockade*), and femme fatale/thief (*Algiers*). A less extreme form is working-class/middle- or upper-class: middle-class Sadie/working-class Jim of *Processional* and in his films, millionaire/model (*Our Blushing Brides*) and working girl/wealthy rake (*Bachelor Apartment*). Lawson had his hook, or what he would prefer to call a "root-idea" that could branch out in enough directions to create a varied system.

Thus *Dynamite* was no problem; it was heiress meets proletarian. However, DeMille's current inamorata, Jeanie MacPherson, was given story credit for it, which so infuriated Lawson that he protested to DeMille; he received an apology but only the minor satisfaction of a dialogue credit.[8] The credit allocation for *Our Blushing Brides* (1930) also displeased Lawson, who had to share screenplay credit with Bess Meredyth. For all practical purposes, Lawson was finished with MGM by 1930; although he returned for six months in 1932, nothing he wrote during that period was filmed.

Not surprisingly, he moved on to RKO where he was delighted to learn that he could do his writing away from the studio. William LeBaron, a former writer and RKO's first head of production (whom Selznick would replace), had only a title for him: "Bachelor Apartment." Lawson knew the plot could go either of two ways: a blue-collar hero attracts wealthy women, or a wealthy hero attracts working girls. Lawson chose the latter: swinger meets middle-class girl who has come to New York to locate her pleasure-loving sister. In a way, *Bachelor Apartment* (1931) is the precursor of *The Tender Trap* (1955), with women dropping into the bachelor flat to look for their shoes or change their rain-drenched clothes. Lawson was hardly in his element; the humor is at best strained. Moreover, history repeated itself: Lawson received only story credit for *Bachelor Apartment*, despite his insistence that it was his script. He returned to RKO only after his play *Success Story* had been purchased by the studio. Although he had to share screenplay credit for the film version, called *Success at Any Price* (1934), the movie was at least billed as an adaptation of his most successful Broadway play (121 performances).

Lawson could probably not have written *Success Story* if he had not first written the beginning-middle-end scripts required in Hollywood. When he returned to the stage in 1932 after a four-year absence, he was able to give theatergoers an old-fashioned gangster melodrama with social overtones. *Success Story* traces the rise of Sol Ginsberg from East Side radical to copywriter, ad agency owner—and murder victim. In the course of his rise and fall he throws over his childhood sweetheart, Sarah, then supplants his boss and marries his boss's mistress, Agnes. When Sarah kills him, it is really the alter ego executing the will of the ego; having betrayed his religion and his politics, Sol seeks release in death. Since Sarah has, in effect, carried out Sol's wishes, Agnes considers the murder a suicide and agrees to a coverup.

Because the Production Code stipulated that crime must not pay, and because Depression moviegoers were not necessarily Depression theatergoers, the play could not be filmed as written. Therefore, the plot was reworked for audiences that preferred Anglo-Saxon names, spiritual regeneration, and a happy ending. Sol Ginsberg becomes Joe Martin, who dreams he has committed suicide but has only suffered a heart attack while scaling the ladder of success.

At the beginning of the 1930s, Lawson was as torn between art and commercialism as he was between liberalism and radicalism. Realizing that art for its own sake leads to oblivion, and loss of integrity to remorse, he tried to reconcile dramaturgy and conscience by writing about victors and victims instead of heroes and villains. The victors survive by renouncing capitalism, as Sarah does in *Success Story;* the victims succumb to its lure or fall beneath its weight, like Sol, who climbs to the top of the executive ladder only to discover there is no place to go but down. While Albert Maltz would have made Sol irredeemable, Lawson refuses to damn him; instead, he portrays him as a would-be militant whose humanity shortcircuited, like that of Charles Foster Kane (*Citizen Kane*), who yearned to be a champion of the people but became a champion of himself.

After *Success Story* Lawson sought real success, but theatrical fame was never to be his. He best understood two types of people: those who might have been radicals under less economically demoralizing circumstances but instead became losers and outcasts; and those who could curl up alone on a bourgeois sofa but would rather share it with a proletarian, even though there would never be enough room. As Harold Clurman commented, Lawson was so much a product of his times that "he is often entangled in the same contradictions he has tried to describe."[9]

In 1934—a watershed year for Lawson—he began formulating his theories of the drama; he embraced Communism; and on 20 and 22 March two of his plays opened on Broadway—*The Pure in Heart*, which ran for seven performances, and *Gentlewoman*, which lasted for twelve. The main characters of *The Pure in Heart* are programmed for failure. That Annabel Sparks falls in love and dies with Larry Goshen, a two-time loser, is not fortuitous; she is as much a victim of *amour fatale* as she is of a depressed economy that encourages deadly dreams. In its chronological compression, *The Pure in Heart* resembles a screenplay; writing for the screen taught Lawson to collapse time instead of atomizing it and to write realistic dialogue. After striving to reproduce the raw licks of jazz in prose, Lawson decided to invigorate stage dialogue by duplicating the unforced rhythms of discourse and the metaphors that give it color. Annabel and Larry speak in images of reckless romanticism; although they would like to "dance a rhumba all over hell" (109), they must settle for the "long trip" into the "fog."

If, in their self-destructiveness, Annabel and Larry anticipate Lorna and Joe of Clifford Odets's *Golden Boy*, it is because life has given them no other choice but to court death. As divided beings, they are doubles, reflecting each other's unfulfilled yearnings. Although Larry is a murderer, he still seeks a better world "where people could be happy . . . build things, work without stealing, love without going crazy" (108). When Annabel insists there is no such place, Larry replies, "You couldn't find it, maybe you could build it." Denied a chance to achieve their conscious goals, the lovers yield to their unconscious, which beckons them to a fogbound world where "you just float around . . . you melt" and where "there's no minutes and no hours" (106)—in short, eternity.

Odets may well have been thinking of *The Pure in Heart* when he was writing *Golden Boy* (1937). Lorna yearns for "some city where poverty's no shame—where music is no crime!—where there's no war in the streets—where a man is glad to be himself, to live and make his woman herself!" That city, however, is the city of the dead; to reach it, one travels in a death car: "We'll drive through the night. When you mow down the night with headlights, nobody gets you. You're on top of the world then—nobody laughs! That's it—speed! We're off the earth—unconnected!"[10] As Joe and Lorna proceed to "burn up the night," they are heading for the same destination that Annabel and Larry reached earlier.

While *The Pure in Heart* was a sociological melodrama with a Freudian slant, *Gentlewoman* was a drawing room drama with social overtones, like S.N. Behrman's *Biography* (1932). In fact, Lawson's heroine, Gwyn Ballantine—his finest female creation—seems to be the playwright's answer to Behrman's Marion Froude, who is a liberal but an uncommitted one. Marion cannot choose between a radical and a right-wing lover; Gwyn can. Since the characters in *Gentlewoman* are, as the title suggests, more urbane than those of *The Pure in Heart*, they speak in the language of the drawing room, which Lawson reproduces quite accurately without sounding like a second-rate Philip Barry. From the standpoint of dialogue, both plays were closer to traditional stage idiom than anything Lawson had written. The plays themselves, as Harold Clurman intimates in his foreword to *With a Reckless Preface*, are more significant than their undeservedly brief runs imply. What the critics failed to realize was that Lawson had recreated a drawing room sensibility only to undermine it by making an elegant setting a forum for questions that the privileged were unlikely to consider: "Can *we* remake the world? Can we create a decent standard of living? Can we preserve peace?" (126).

Gentlewoman's civilized tone was lost on Mike Gold, who chastized Lawson in the pages of *New Masses* (10 April 1934), calling him a "bourgeois Hamlet" because of his political indecisiveness and accusing him of squandering his talent on inferior plays and scripts. The 17 April issue of *New Masses* contained Lawson's reply; adopting an almost penitential air (which he would later expect of others), he asked his critic to be patient with him, promising to answer the question "Where do I belong in the warring world of the two classes?"[11] The answer was forthcoming that year: in the Party. Politically, he was now a radical, though as a playwright and screenwriter he would have to couch his radicalism within traditional dramatic and cinematic forms. In the year that he became a Communist, his politics and poetics merged into a coherent vision of theater which was basically left-wing Aristotelianism.

Lawson's theory of drama, as expressed in *Theory and Technique of Playwriting* (1936), is based on the classical model of an action—or what Lawson preferred to call "a system of actions"—that undergoes various permutations and shifts of balance until, through conflict and crisis, a resolution is reached, restoring the system to a state of equilibrium and the play to a state of organic wholeness. His concept of dramatic form differs little from Aristotle's; Lawson would emend the Aristotelian idea of drama as the imitation of human beings in action to read "action of a social nature." The dramatic structure he favors is the Aristotelian beginning-middle-end, cast in the Hegelian mold of thesis/antithesis/ synthesis—by no means an alien configuration. Any system, whether Aristotelian or Marxist, that is based on the counterbalancing and resolution of forces views the result as teleological: events move toward an end, whether it is the classless society or the culmination of a dramatic action.

Once Lawson had formulated his theory of drama and envisioned a play as having a shape and a structure, he could then reconcile it with his politics, which required a similar clarity of vision. In *Marching Song* (1937) his politics and poetics merge in what is, structurally, his best play. The "root-idea" is a strike that generates a conflict not—as usual— between labor and management but between the workers themselves. Thus Lawson places the lesser force concentrically within the greater. A lack of unanimity within the ranks produces another element he favors: suspense. Will Pete inform to get his job and house back? Although Pete does not inform, his display of integrity does not resolve the action. Within the play's bipolar structure is another tension: Pete's racism. Because Lucky is black, Pete refuses to call him "Brother John-son," dubbing him "Brother Blackbird" instead. If Pete is to grow in understanding, Lucky must become more militant, disassociating him-self from the apathetic blacks of his youth.

The conflict in *Marching Song* is social; the denouement, revolu-tionary. The play is an excellent illustration of self-applied theory. The action is a series of forces, each affecting the other and causing tempo-rary imbalances until, through realignment of characters and goals, order is restored. The climax does not bring about the restoration of order; to Lawson, the climax is just the concrete realization of the theme in terms of an event and may result in a new set of forces which themselves require balancing. The climax of *Marching Song* occurs when the workers paralyze the city by shutting off the electric power. That action does nothing but plunge the city into darkness, but what comes out of the action is a coalition of black and white, of Lucky and Pete. With the people supplying the power that the city has lost, Lucky sings the marching song, which confidently proclaims that "step by step the longest march can be won."

Lawson's approach to dramatic construction was transferable to the screen: his was the kind of stage and film Marxism that could be diluted into humanitarianism, depending on which direction the winds of politics were blowing. When Walter Wanger approached him to take over the script of the Spanish Civil War movie that became *Blockade* (1938), Lawson thought they might be blowing from the left.[12] Wanger was well known in the industry as a liberal: that is, someone who was willing to tackle controversial subjects without necessarily treating them controversially. Wanger's original choice was Clifford Odets, who had demonstrated his ability to deal with nebulous wars in *The General Died at Dawn* (1936). However, by the time he was writing his Spanish Civil War script, which he called "The River Is Blue," Odets had lost interest in the party and had become less of a radical.

When Lawson took over, he chose as his "root-idea" the blockade of Bilbao by Franco's forces in April 1937, but he had to observe the Breen Office mandate that the sides not be identified. By being intentionally vague about the conflict but not about its effect on the Spanish people, Lawson was really taking a position. It required very little— only a knowledge of current events and a passing acquaintance with classic cinema—to appreciate the way he defused a political plot without depoliticizing it. He merely converted his Marxism into empathy, specifically for the people of Bilbao—called Castelmare in the movie— who not only awaken to the sound of war but also find themselves victims of a blockade.

As a playwright, Lawson knew that turbulence should be preceded by tranquillity if it is to have any impact. Thus *Blockade* opens in the Spanish countryside where a shepherd pipes and his friend Marco (Henry Fonda), an Iberian Tom Joad, eulogizes mother earth. Having inherited Odets's script, which like *The General Died at Dawn*, paired a proletarian with a blonde Venus, Lawson had no difficulty translating the relationship into his favorite plot device: the upper-class/working-class agon. Here, the agon is a clash—or crash—as Norma drives right into the shepherd's cart. The collision sets off a series of plot imbalances which, in Lawson, are not corrected until the resolution; in 1938 it could not be the resolution of the still-raging Spanish Civil War but only the resolution of the film based on it.

Historically, the British merchant ship *Seven Seas Spray* broke the blockade when it arrived at Bilbao on 20 April 1937 with 3,500 tons of food. Lawson's handling of the incident illustrates his capacity for reconciling his Marxism with classic plot construction. The unnamed anticipated relief ship is torpedoed, but its sinking is a Loyalist ruse as well as a screenwriter's ploy: the ship is a decoy, intended as such both by the (unidentified) Loyalists and Lawson, who uses it as mystery writers use false clues and red herrings. When the real ship, appropriately called *Fortuna*, arrives, Lawson the writer yields to Lawson the Russophile. The episode is unmistakable homage to Sergei Eisenstein's *Potemkin* (1925), notably the scene in which the people of Odessa welcome and bring provisions to the mutinous sailors of the battleship. In both films, the sailors pack the quarterdeck, waving and raising their caps; in both films there is an alliance of sailors and civilians.

Lawson winds up *Blockade* as quickly as Euripides concludes his plays: after a (Loyalist) general exposes a (Nationalist) fifth columnist masquerading as a patriot and then tells Marco to find some peace, Henry Fonda looks straight into the camera and delivers a peroration with which no one can argue because it is on the side of the angels: "Peace? Where can you find it? Our country has been turned into a battlefield. There is no safety for old people and children. Women can't keep their families safe in their houses; they can't be safe in their own fields. Churches, schools, and hospitals are targets. It's not war; war is between soldiers. It's murder, murder of innocent people. There's no sense to it. The world can stop it. Where's the conscience of the world?" Lawson does not even have to identify the Loyalists as such to arouse sympathy for their cause. Since the situation is both general (people fighting for their republic) and particular (the blockade of Bilbao), *Blockade* was able to be both a spy melodrama and a political film. That it was booked into Radio City Music Hall is a testament to Lawson's success in combining two genres without letting either one lose autonomy.

Lawson began writing *Algiers* (1938), his next film for Wanger, immediately after *Blockade*, thereby acquiring two screenplay credits in the same year. Since *Algiers* was an English remake of Julien Duvivier's *Pepe Le Moko* (1937), Lawson could not radically alter the plot, but the adaptation posed no problem; it was another poor boy/rich girl melodrama—except that boy does not get girl, because Pepe is a jewel thief with a past and Gaby is a bejeweled amoureuse who lives in the present. Despite its exotic setting, *Algiers* is very much a 1930s film. Lawson was able to widen the socioeconomic gulf between Pepe and Gaby so that Pepe resembles a slum dweller and Gaby a penthouse mistress; together, they recall Gimpty and Kay in Sidney Kinglsey's *Dead End* (1935). Pepe is confined to the Casbah, a network of alleyways, terraces, and roofs that affords anonymity and easy access to any part of the quarter. The Casbah, however, is a ghetto, a slum of the hopeless; when Pepe attempts to leave it, he is betrayed by a jealous mistress, who is as much a victim of her environment as he is.

Lawson's opportunity to write a real tenement film came when Samuel Goldwyn hired him for *They Shall Have Music* (1939), a hybrid of *Dead End, One Third of a Nation* (1939), and *Babes in Arms* (1939): in short, a Great Depression children's crusade with a happy ending. In order to acquire enough money to live by themselves on an East River barge, a group of children give sidewalk concerts outside Carnegie Hall. A Jascha Heifetz recital so affects their leader that he becomes a student at a financially troubled music school which he saves from closing—with the aid of Heifetz, whose appearance is all anyone seems to remember about the film.

Lawson's interests tended to be radial rather than parallel: they

derived from a common source, the human condition, but then di-
verged in myriad directions—theater, film, politics, unionism, criticism, antifascism. As the decade ended with a world war, Lawson's
commitment to antifascism made the Anti-Nazi League more important than Twentieth Century-Fox. *Earthbound* (1940) a Zanuck remake,
is a melodramatic fantasy in which the ghost of a philandering husband directs his wife to extract a confession from the woman who
murdered him. Asked to do the screenplay, Lawson planned a pacifist
Topper set during World War I, with "people going about customary
tasks, wearing gas masks [and] two lovers parting on a street corner,
trying to say goodbye, unable to take off their masks."[13] Not surprisingly, Zanuck vetoed the wartime background and the gas mask
farewell.

Lawson fared better with another Fox remake, *Four Sons* (1940).
The 1928 original dramatized the plight of a German mother who loses
three of her sons in World War I. John Ford directed the film expres-
sionistically, with shadows and black cats portending death, and his
Four Sons still retains much of its original power. The same cannot be
said of the remake, whose World War I setting Zanuck wanted to retain
until the outbreak of World War II convinced him that the action had to
be contemporary and the locale shifted from Bavaria to the Sudetenland.

Lawson worked out a chronology that would cover the period from
1934 to 1939, thus including the main events leading up to the war. He
also wanted to demythologize the annexation of the Sudetenland, and
historically, he was on solid ground: "In 1938," a popular history of the
period explains, "Hitler's troops marched into the Czech Sudetenland;
it was largely populated by Germans, who welcomed the invaders
warmly. In most of the region, a carnival atmosphere prevailed. . . .
Women wept or cheered at the sight of German soldiers, and garlanded
them with flowers."[14]

Again, Zanuck objected to Lawson's approach: "The personal
story has been submerged to give prominence to the March of Events.
It must be the other way around. Now it is a historical step-by-step
account of what happened in a small village and the people seem to be
of secondary importance. Handling it like this causes us to lose 50% of
the story's value as entertainment."[15] *Four Sons* received mixed reviews, although Lawson was commended for keeping propaganda to a
minimum. What the critics did not know was that he was also forced to
economize on history; the village sports homes with washing machines; the occupation of the Sudetenland appears in a newspaper
headline; the invasion of Poland is a communiqué item; and the
Führer's existence is acknowledged by the occasional "Heil, Hitler".

Like other Stalinists, Lawson was profoundly disturbed by the

Nazi-Soviet nonaggression pact of 1939 and wasted more than a year agonizing over its implications. He was elated that Germany's invasion of the Soviet Union in June 1941 made Russia an American ally, but at a time when other writers were racking up screen credits because they knew how to convert World War II into a cliché, Lawson was supporting the Communist candidate for the California state senate, championing a Communist teacher convicted of perjury, assisting in the formation of the Citizens Committee for Harry Bridges, serving as secretary of the National Committee for the Defense of Political Prisoners and the National Committee for People's Rights, backing the Sleepy Lagoon Defense Committee, the American Peace Mobilization, and other groups that were later denounced as Communist fronts.

Thus, when he had a chance to work at Warner Brothers in 1943—where his fascination with gangsters and his sympathy for the underdog would have found him a niche in the 1930s, fashioning vehicles for James Cagney, Edward G. Robinson, and Humphrey Bogart—he seized the opportunity because of both the studio and the nature of the assignment. *Action in the North Atlantic* (1943) enabled Lawson to show—indirectly, of course—his support for the Party and at the same time to write a commercially successful movie. The film, a tribute to the Merchant Marine, whose union was Communist-dominated, dramatized the hazards of shipping war materiel to our Russian allies; it was thoroughly pro-labor, glorifying the merchant seamen as workers who brook no criticism of the maritime union. When Dane Clark wavers between a shore job and a crew assignment, Sam Levene sets him straight: "So you want a safe job? Go ask the Czechs and the Poles and the Greeks. They were figuring on safe jobs. They're lined up in front of guns, digging each other's graves. The trouble with you . . . is that you think America is just a place to eat and sleep. You don't know what side your future is buttered on." Naturally, Clark signs up.

As the working-class studio, Warner Brothers could make such a film without incurring the wrath of the right; apart from its having appeared at the height of World War II, it was also an undisguised tribute to the Allies—all of them, including the Soviet Union. To criticize *Action in the North Atlantic* was to criticize the Allied cause; to support both was to support President Franklin D. Roosevelt, Jack Warner's idol (so much so that Warner Brothers was often dubbed the Roosevelt studio: during the 1930s it was pro–New Deal;[16] during the 1940s, pro-lend-lease and even pro-Soviet, as films like *Background to Danger*, 1943, and especially *Mission to Moscow*, 1943, indicate). Knowing this bias, Lawson used a direct quote from Roosevelt as an opening title: "Today in the face of this newest and greatest challenge of them all, we of the United Nations have cleared our decks and taken our battle stations. It is the will of the people that America shall deliver the goods. It can never be doubted that the goods will be delivered by this nation, which believes in the tradition of 'Damn the torpedoes; full speed ahead!' " The epilogue, spoken in a Rooseveltian voice, was equally assertive: "We shall build a bridge of ships to our allies."

Lawson, who even in his plays aimed at heterogeneity of character, assembled a variegated crew for the film's Liberty ship: a Pole, a Jew, a buffoon, a lovable oaf, a patriarch, a loner. Such a mix of characters is standard in the combat film; a Soviet subtext is not. Structurally and imagistically, *Action in the North Atlantic* owes much to *Potemkin*, the most influential of all the silent Soviet films and to Lawson "the most perfect example of a work constructed on the principle that the rhythm and the clash of visual images is the unifying element in the whole design."[17] By fashioning a screenplay that could only be rendered in montage—fast cuts, varied rhythm, alternations of light and dark-ness—and not in long takes, Lawson made director Lloyd Bacon's task easier; the script is a blueprint for the actual film which, like *Potemkin*, has a five-part structure and opens with an image of turbulence: the torpedoing of the *Northern Star*. Part II, the homecoming, contrasts a captain's return to his wife with the first mate's courting of a nightclub singer. As the setting changes, so does the rhythm; a loving reunion is succeeded by a whirlwind courtship. A study in contrast, this section culminates in the replacement of the torpedoed *Northern Star* by another Liberty ship, the *Sea Witch*. Part III, the gathering of the ships, like the third part of *Potemkin*, opens poetically: the convoy sets out at early dawn under a sky that ranges from opaque to sunshot, from sulfurous to translucent, as the ship moves in and out of the mist like a primordial phantom.

Part IV, the U-boat attack, repeats the rhythm of Part I; the pace intensifies, and the cutting is rapid. Lawson put his theory of dramatic action as system into practice by adding a plot twist, the separation of the *Sea Witch* from the rest of the convoy and its encounter with the U-boat. At the end, order returns to a system that has been subjected to sudden shifts and fluctuations of rhythm. Part V is Lawson's resolution of the root-idea, the completion of the mission; it is also the Marxist synthesis, for in addition to following the action/complication/resolution model, the plot has presented thesis (American Liberty ship), antithesis (U-boat menace), and now synthesis: Soviet planes save the ship from Nazi dive bombers and allow it to proceed to Murmansk, where the merchant seamen are hailed as "comrades" and reply in kind to the Russians. The cleverest piece of pro-Soviet propaganda occurs when Dane Clark spots the Soviet planes and cries, "They're ours!"

The Soviet subtext of *Sahara* (1943) is less evident, even though Lawson based his screenplay (for which director Zoltan Korda received co-credit) on a Soviet film, Mikhail Romm's *The Thirteen* (1937), about Russian soldiers attacked by bandits in the Karakum desert. Still, Lawson was able to make the ending both a resolution of the action and a reconciliation of opposites. A British-American detachment in North Africa is forced to retreat south under the command of Sergeant Joe Gunn (Humphrey Bogart, who had played the first mate in *Action*). The characters are an international aggregate: Americans, Britons, a French leftist who fought in Spain, an Italian who once believed in Mussolini, an Australian, an Irishman, a British Sudanese, and a Nazi. As a playwright, Lawson knew the difference between complicating a plot and encumbering it; he let the root-idea branch out until he was able to construct a network of relationships within the dramatic system, aligning the characters in pairs of opposites.

In *Sahara*, Lawson loaded the system to capacity; behind the desert trek is the myth of the Exodus. To reinforce the similarities, Lawson added further parallels between Moses and Joe Gunn, the Israelites and the detachment, the manna in the desert and the water that gushes in abundance at the end. Since both sides are suffering from thirst, Gunn makes water a condition of surrender, knowing that if his men are to survive, they need a miracle. The miracle occurs in the flooding of the wells. It is caused by excessive shelling rather than divine intervention, but the Nazis see only the water; crying *"Wasser!"*, they lay down their arms and surrender. Again, *Potemkin* gave Lawson his ending. Eisenstein's film concludes with a reconciliation when the Czarist squadron refrains from firing on the mutinous sailors; at that moment the title "Brothers!" appears on the screen, and so, however briefly, the Czarists and the rebels become one—just as Americans and Russians do in *Action*, and Allies and surrendering Nazis do in *Sahara*.

Lawson's last World War II film was the most Russophilic of the lot; in *Counter-Attack* (1945) a Soviet paratrooper, with the aid of a female partisan, holds eight Nazis at bay in a cellar. Based on a Broadway failure that starred Morris Carnovsky, the film featured Paul Muni as the paratrooper; it was another Korda-Lawson collaboration, though this time Lawson received sole screenplay credit. The film was generally well received, and Lawson was commended for wringing drama from a static situation; however, *Counter-Attack* was released after V-E Day and therefore received little attention.

Lawson's final screen credit was prematurely feminist, as *Blockade* was prematurely antifascist. *Smash-Up* (1947)—subtitled *The Story of a Woman* because RKO had already registered the first title—originated as a story idea by Dorothy Parker, whom Walter Wanger had hired in August 1945 to develop a plot along the lines of *The Lost Weekend* (1945) but from a woman's perspective and with a woman as the victim of alcoholism.[18] Wanger assigned Frank Cavett to work with Parker on the story; together, they produced an incomplete screenplay titled "Angelica," the name of the heroine—a name Lawson retained when he was entrusted with the writing after the services of Parker and Cavett had been terminated. It was about all he retained; the screenplay was entirely Lawson's (except for some additional dialogue by Lionel Wiggam) and "entirely new," as Wanger's legal department acknowledged. *Smash-Up* will always be known as either a woman's film or the movie that won Susan Hayward an Oscar nomination and established her as one of Hollywood's foremost interpreters of alcoholics; more important, it is a film created by a male which is unusually sympathetic to women whose marriages rob them of independence and force them to rely on whatever assuages their feelings of inadequacy.

Lawson did not proceed from *Counter-Attack* to *Smash-Up* without a transition; the link is another Columbia film, *The Jolson Story* (1946), for which he was uncredited—at his own request: "I disliked the final film. I felt that the use of black face was racist—of course, Jolson could not be detached from his black-face characterization, but I had recommended a more 'modern' treatment."[19] Actually, Lawson may have written *a* script, but not *the* script. Credits have as many lacunae as production files: like oracles, they can be deceptive. *The Jolson Story* credits attribute the screenplay to Stephen Longstreet, implying that there was only one writer; they also designate Sidney Skolsky, the movie columnist, as producer.

It is true that the idea for a Jolson bio-pic originated with Skolsky, but Sidney Buchman was the one Harry Cohn put in charge of determining the direction the script would take. Buchman, Columbia's most gifted screenwriter and one of the finest in the industry, had fulfilled another ambition in 1945: he turned producer with *A Song to Remember*, which he also wrote. For all practical purposes, he was *The Jolson Story*'s executive producer, a fact that he himself acknowledged and that was known in Hollywood at the time. Several years later, when he was facing contempt charges for failing to appear before HUAC, the *Hollywood Citizen-News* (9 March 1953) called him *The Jolson Story*'s author and producer. That may have been an exaggeration, but it does suggest the important role he played in the making of the film.

Buchman was frustrated by his inability to find the key to Jolson's personality until he realized that the entertainer's marital problems arose because he put his audiences before his wives. Then Buchman had his hook: the story would be "a love affair [in which] the lover is applause. Jolson's wife could handle other women, but she was no match against the applause."[20] Once he had tapped the source of the tension between Jolson and Julie (a composite of Jolson's wives but with more similarities to Ruby Keeler than to the others), Buchman may have passed the script on to Lawson, and with it, his plot points. *The Jolson Story* was clearly a Buchman production, so much so that he "spent six months in the cutting room assembling the final product."[21]

Lawson's association with Buchman was the natural outgrowth of a sequence of events that began fifteen years earlier. The men had much in common: both were playwrights, although Buchman's stage works (*This One Man; Storm Song*) are far less impressive than Lawson's. They were also similar in educational background: Lawson was a Williams alumnus; Buchman, a Columbia graduate who had also attended Oxford. Politically, they were both radicals—Screen Writers Guild activists and Communists (Buchman joined the Party four years after Lawson, but he left it in 1945 when he realized that Communism was unworkable in America.) Both came to Hollywood for the first time in the late 1920s and found themselves at Columbia in 1935, although Lawson's first tenure at the studio was short-lived. Buchman had arrived at Columbia the previous year and remained there until the blacklist forced him to leave in 1951; his scripts for such films as *She Married Her Boss, Theodora Goes Wild,* and especially *Mr. Smith Goes to Washington* and *Here Comes Mr. Jordan,* were instrumental—along with Frank Capra's movies—in ridding Columbia of the Poverty Row stigma.

In late 1934 Lawson was hired to work on a Jean Arthur comedy, *Party Wire* (1935), for which he received coadaptation credit. Harry Cohn fired him when he refused to contribute the obligatory dollar to the Frank Merriam reelection campaign. Even Buchman acquiesced, but Lawson refused—not because he favored Upton Sinclair and his "End Poverty in California" platform; on the contrary, he found EPIC counterrevolutionary. He refused on principle.

Eight years later Lawson returned to Columbia to write *Sahara* for Humphrey Bogart. Buchman was by then the studio's reigning writer as well as Harry Cohn's alter ego. A reference in *Theory and Technique of Playwriting and Screenwriting* shows Lawson's respect for Buchman, whom he called a master of continuity.[22] Buchman's talent for effecting changes in mood and pace was apparently utilized in *Sahara*—although he is no more credited for his contribution to *Sahara* than Lawson is for *The Jolson Story.* As Sidney Skolsky used to say in his column, "That's Hollywood!" And after his stint as *The Jolson Story's* "producer," he certainly should know.

Given the relationship that existed between the two men, then, Lawson's involvement in *The Jolson Story* should not be surprising. He had been at Columbia since 1942; after finishing *Counter-Attack,* he was free to take on another assignment. But here the drama ends; there is no last act, only an epilogue in which Lawson fought Harry Cohn to get his name removed from the credits—the reverse of what most writers do. Lawson won, and Stephen Longstreet, who had also written a script, was given sole credit.[23]

For *The Jolson Story*, Lawson was dealing with a plot, fashioned by Buchman, in which a wife who discovers that the man she has married has become an institution terminates the relationship like Ibsen's Nora: by walking out while her husband is wowing the audience. Interestingly, *Smash-Up* also dramatizes the effect of a husband's success on both his wife and their marriage within a show business context. Angelica's alcoholism is due not merely to her having abandoned her singing career; it is that the void once filled by her career has become a vacuum through a marriage that has reduced her to a member of her husband's entourage.

Although *Smash-Up* is one of Lawson's least political films, it is blatantly critical of a society that allows the affluent to pursue a life of leisure devoid of meaningful activity. To reinforce the socioeconomic connection between prosperity, leisure, and neurosis, Lawson has Dr. Lorenz, the pediatrician, blame Ken and his kind: "Men like you make their wives idle, useless. You give them servants to clean their homes, nurses to take care of their children, and then say, 'sit there and enjoy it'. . . . In doing so, you have taken all responsibility away from her and left her a life with no value. In despair, feeling she has lost you to your career in exchange for nothing she desires, your wife has turned to [alcohol]."

Lawson's argument is more sociological than psychological. The extremes of prosperity and poverty create a vacuum in human life— idleness among the rich, unemployment among the poor—which will continue to be filled unproductively until there is equalization. In the meantime, the only difference between the idle rich and the unemployed poor is the quality of the liquor they consume and the drugs they take. The argument is also anti-male, though Lawson's attack on men for diminishing women's self-worth is somewhat different from Ibsen's criticism of husbands who make dolls of their wives. Lawson's is a general accusation ("men like you") which, however, fails to take Angelica's psychological makeup into consideration. But then, Angelica's psyche does not interest Lawson, who made it clear in *Theory and Techniques of Playwriting* that his kind of dramatic action emphasizes the external over the internal because stressing the psychological inhibits the exercise of the conscious will and minimizes the possibility of meaningful activity.

Smash-Up is a woman's film in the sense that it makes a woman and her problems the film's focus. Yet like so much of Lawson's work, it contains the seeds of ideas that never grew and themes that were never developed. Since he abandoned the stage just when it seemed that he had found a form worth pursuing, he never had the opportunity to develop such characters as the upper-class liberal, the Broadway loser, or the blue-collar black. Similarly, the year of *Smash-Up* was also the year Lawson's subpoena arrived, ending his film career and, with it, the possibility of creating more women like Angelica, who went the way of Gwyn Ballantine into the realm of the might-have-beens.

Unlike Dalton Trumbo, Lawson had little success with black market writing; Trumbo, in fact, had to revise a Lawson script for *Terror in a Texas Town* (1958), which eventually bore one of Trumbo's pseudonyms, Ben L. Perry. Through Edward Lewis, one of Kirk Douglas's partners in Bryna (a production company Douglas founded in 1955), Lawson was able to earn approximately $33,000 in 1958-59—a far cry from his Hollywood days—by writing screenplays, pilots for television series, and original stories for Bryna, none of which came to fruition. He used the pseudonym of James Howard, which, in the middle of working on "The Mound Builders" script in 1959 became, for tax-reporting purposes, James Christopher. The change did not escape the attention of Bryna's internal auditor, who observed that for the first half of the never-to-be filmed "Mound Builders," "James Howard" received $4,500; for the second, "James Christopher" received $5,000. What the auditor did not know at the time was that Bryna paid Lewis for the first half and Lewis, in turn, paid Lawson/Howard; for the second half, Bryna paid Lawson/Christopher directly.

Although Lawson was grateful to Lewis, he felt that Bryna owed him $2,500 more.[24] Bryna, however, wanted an explanation: "We do not intend to pay James Christopher the balance of $2,500.00 due under the March 18, 1959 contract until we have an explanation of the $2,500 paid to James Howard, who is the same person, by check No. 3023 on February 3, 1959."[25] One hopes Lawson received what was due him. At any rate, as he was the first to admit, Lewis had at least found him employment: in a letter of 8 June 1959, which Lawson signed in his own name, placing "James Howard" below it in a parenthesis, he wrote: "I cannot conclude this dry recital without mentioning that our work together has been conducted with a cooperation and friendship which I value most highly. . . It is a sad thing that embarrassments and difficulties are occasioned by the curious situation in which [we] are placed. It is good to observe multiplying signs that these days of confusion are coming to an end."[26]

The year of deliverance varies with the blacklistee: 1960 for Dalton Trumbo; 1964 for Ring Lardner, Jr.; 1970 for Albert Maltz; never for Lester Cole. For Lawson, it mattered less; even before he was blacklisted, he found himself moving from writing plays and films to writing about them. In 1949 Putnam brought out a new edition of his *Theory and Technique* with an added section on screenwriting; the result, *Theory and Technique of Playwriting and Screenwriting*, made it evident that the years Lawson had spent in Hollywood were not in vain. He had seen an extraordinary number of American films and used them to illustrate a theory of film not significantly different from his theory of drama. While it may seem odd that Lawson drew so heavily on the Hollywood product which a few years later, in *Film in the Battle of Ideas* (1953), he would criticize as antiprogressive, he was no doubt thinking of a general readership, including students, whose knowledge of cinema came mainly from American movies.

Lawson is selective in his example, drawing whenever possible on films written by comrades (Dashiell Hammett's *Watch on the Rhine;* Lester Cole's *The Romance of Rosy Ridge;* Abraham Polonsky's *Body and Soul*) and films that in some way poked fun at the rich (*It Happened One Night*), glorified the masses (*The Grapes of Wrath*), or dramatized inhumanity (*Fury*). While the relationship of film and literature is a topic endlessly debated, Lawson understood the differences: as a time-space art, he asserts, film must capitalize on its uniqueness to create temporal-spatial relationships that the novel and drama cannot. By comparing Lillian Hellman's 1941 play *Watch on the Rhine* with Hammett's 1943 adaptation, Lawson is able to show how the play's first act, although it brings hero and villain into the same household, is spatially limited—as is the entire play, which retains the same set for three acts. Hammett opens up the play so that the action begins not in Washington, D.C., as the play does, but in Mexico, with the hero and his family about to leave for Washington; by intercutting scenes of the villain at the German embassy and the hero as he draws nearer to Washington, Hammett parallels their activities, making their eventual meeting an inevitable rather than a mechanical rendezvous.

Although Lawson explains the vocabulary of film, he retains his earlier terms (root-idea, conscious will), believing them applicable to film as well. And so that the section on film will not seem merely an appendix, he repeats the elements of drama (continuity, exposition, progression, the obligatory scene, climax, characterization, dialogue), discussing each one in the context of film.

The basis of discussion is, again, the conscious will—one capable of purposive action and therefore of bringing, voluntarily, a conflict to a state of crisis as that action moves toward a known end. Just as there are plays that are too fatalistic to qualify as drama of the conscious will, so too there are films in which the characters are alienated from objective reality or unconscious of their motivations. These, he argues in *Film, the Creative Process,* may be admirable for their technical skill, but they are not art: "Art has always dealt with man's struggle with the real circumstances of his existence. The alienated man abandons the struggle. He is not a genuinely tragic figure, because he is not stirred by rage or inspired by hope. He is not comic and he is incapable of inspiring laughter—the comic spirit expresses man's stubborn will to survive in spite of obstacles" (*FCP*, 255-56).

Like all theories that are rigidly postulated, Lawson's tend to suffer a breakdown in the very logic he has been so careful to maintain. Unwilling to give up "root-action" (the expression of the root-idea in terms of an action or system of events), for which he seems to have a special fondness, Lawson is forced to state that in film the root-action, or reflection of the conscious will, is manifested through the closeup. While admitting that directors have abused it, Lawson has no other choice than to maintain that the closeup reveals the character's will, particularly since it is one of the chief ways by which the audience can discern that will. While Lawson was thinking of the revolutionary power of D.W. Griffith's closeups, he was also thinking of Eisenstein's. To Eisenstein, their function was qualitative rather than quantitative, "not so much to *show* or to *present*, as to *signify*, to give *meaning*, to *designate*."[27] Lawson would simply add a direct object: signify, give meaning to, designate the *root-action*: "A person makes a decision. We then follow the train of events that is set in motion, the ultimate implications of the decision, and we come back to the closeup, to the eyes of the man or woman who is forced to face the consequences of what has been willed" (*TTPS*, 395).

Lawson posits the closeup as the bridge between exposition and progression, using as an example the closeup of Ingrid Bergman's face in *Spellbound* (1945) when, as she kisses Gregory Peck, a series of doors opens, symbolically suggesting that she will be the means of curing his amnesia. Again, Lawson is thinking in terms of beginning-middle-end narrative, in which the root-action begins with exposition, which is then linked, through a meaningful closeup, to progression. In film, however, the distinction between exposition and progression is an artificial one. In film, exposition can be handled in a variety of ways: in credits sequences, prologues, forewords, and the like; or piecemeal, with background information embedded in the dialogue or compressed within an image. The background may be intentionally vague, as in films about the unknowability of reality (Michelangelo Antonioni's *Blow Up; The Passenger*), although these Lawson would dismiss for their rejection of objective reality, which to him is the only reality. Progression, which is nothing other than rising action, is not really applicable to film. Unlike a play, in which an act can reach a climax of its own in anticipation of a grand climax, a film is built of sequences and thus contains many peaks. If charted or depicted graphically, its configuration would be not merely triangular but a series of small triangles that merge as if by an optical dissolve, into one large triangle at the end; or, if the action is nonlinear, a series of circles that grow concentrically out of one another, their circumferences becoming one at the end.

One problem is Lawson's ambivalence toward film. While his knowledge of the medium was almost as vast as his knowledge of drama, he was more at home with the latter. Yet since film was a mass medium when he was writing about it, as theater was not, he felt an obligation to be more Marxist when discussing film, the people's art. In the hastily written *Film in the Battle of Ideas* he attacks Hollywood pictures like *Viva Zapata* for showing people's movements that do not succeed, *A Streetcar Named Desire* for demeaning Poles, and *All About Eve* for the same reason: the unscrupulous Eve Harrington was born Gertrude Slescynski, and her machinations are doubly offensive because she may be Jewish as well as Polish.

Being a Marxist meant more to Lawson than being a critic, and acknowledgment by fellow Marxists meant more than acknowledgment by literary colleagues. Just as he apologized to Mike Gold in 1934 for the ideological confusion of his plays, so in 1953 he apologized to V.J. Jerome, the Party's cultural affairs commissar, because in a moment of optimism he had written that "there can be no permanent interference with the development of the American motion picture as a people's art" (*TTPS*, 361), when he should have known that there was a source of interference: Hollywood.[28] That Lawson should feel the need to apologize for a dream is unsettling; that he should also apologize for ignoring the political significance of *Fury* (*TTPS*, 420-21) because he had discussed it structurally—as if a critic must recant because he succumbed to the lure of form—is equally sad.[29]

Actually, Lawson's appreciation of form is one of the best features of his criticism. When he came to write *Film, the Creative Process*, he had refined some of the notions put forth in the 1949 edition of *Theory and Technique*. He no longer expected film to have an obligatory scene; he now saw that the unity of a film, which he once attributed to the root-action, is more dependent on theme; he realized that exposition in film is more complex than it is in drama. Assuming the role of a teacher, which he would do literally in the 1960s—at Reed College in 1960, San Fernando State College in 1961, San Jose State College and California State College in Los Angeles in 1965, and Stanford University in 1966—he offered a definition of film that, while rudimentary, illustrates the Aristotelian genus, species, and differentia: (1) A film is an audiovisual conflict; (2) it embodies time-space relationships; (3) it proceeds from a premise, (4) through a progression, (5) to a climax of ultimate term of the action (*FCP*, 292). It may be basic but it is accurate; students could learn worse. It is only when Lawson speaks of film dialogue that one realizes his heart is in literature: "I feel intensely that poetry, verbal poetry, is an essential aspect of cinematic expression, and that the present lack of poetry in film impoverishes and depletes the art" (*FCP* 196); and "Perhaps the time will come when the screen will speak with tongues of fire, restoring the potency of the spoken word" (*FCP*, 204).

There is much of value in *Theory and Technique* and *Film, the Creative Process;* they are excellent introductions to the well-written play and the well-crafted film. The difficulty lies in Lawson's desire to go beyond the classically constructed plot and beyond closure itself; he would want the climax to be both the culmination of the action and a call to action of a different kind—social action, purposeful action. Pushed to its logical conclusion, Lawson's theory would lead to a drama and cinema linearly Aristotelian in structure but without verisimilitude and therefore lacking the lifelikeness that Aristotle demands of art. Instead of beginning-middle-end construction, it would be beginning-middle-end-plus-end result—as in *Action in the North Atlantic*, which ends not with the convoy's arrival at Murmansk but with a gesture of unity between Russians and Americans; and *Sahara*, which concludes not with the Nazis' surrender but with their laying-down of arms in an act that betokens brotherhood. (Lawson, of course, was not the first to fashion dual endings. He may well have been influenced by such non-Marxist sources as D. W. Griffith's *Birth of a Nation* and *Intolerance* (1916), whose conclusions generate epilogues: war metamorphoses into peace in the former and prisons into meadows in the latter.) For all his Marxism, Lawson was really applying the Hollywood formula of the happy ending. Whether that ending is politically or merely emotionally significant is immaterial; in either case the resolution supersedes itself, occurring so fast that what follows cannot be anticlimactic, just anti-realistic.

Lawson's was a strange career. Although he spent two decades as a screenwriter, he wrote more regularly as a playwright: he had eight New York productions in eleven years. His screen record is erratic; the gaps between films, especially between *Four Sons* (1940) and *Action in the North Atlantic* (1943), would seem to be attributable to his involvement in antifascist and radical causes. However, that is not the sole explanation. Another interest had claimed his attention: history.

In 1938 Lawson began a monumental study of the period from the waning of the Middle Ages to the settlement of North America. Twelve years later the fruit of his labor, *The Hidden Heritage*, appeared just as its author was about to serve a ten-month sentence at the Ashland Federal Reformatory in Kentucky. If a major publisher had brought it out, the book might have attracted the attention it deserves. Few books have lived up to their title as literally, and ironically, as *The Hidden Heritage*. It is the least known of Lawson's works, yet it has a humanistic range and a panoramic breadth that would surprise even those familiar with the range of his critical work.

Like *Theory and Technique, The Hidden Heritage* is applied Marxism: seven centuries analyzed in terms of the class struggle. The author is less interested in the medieval church's preservation of learning or in the tension between the sacred and the profane than he is in the capitalism of the Benedictines and the erection of cathedrals from stone that was not "transported by the hands of gentlefolk."[30] The conventions of courtly love are not poetic embellishments but veils drawn over the reality of loveless marriages and adulterous unions between lady and knight. Sometimes a discussion that has seemed serpentine culminates in a revelation. Just as one is about to give up on Lawson's leap from Shakespeare's *Coriolanus* to Beethoven's Coriolan Overture and *Fidelio*, the links appear like the synthesis of a dialectic. In *Fidelio* Beethoven did what Coriolanus, in his contempt for the common people, could never do: he composed a hymn to freedom to be sung by the masses, a chorus of prisoners, thereby making them collectively as heroic as the opera's heroine, Leonore.

At times the arguments are tedious, the comparisons forced, and the vision opaque. Lawson's contention that myths are economic allegories would give a Jungian pause; it would also end mythopoesis. Since myths are polyvalent, they can be variously interpreted; however, using ancient myths about gold (the golden apple, the golden touch, the golden fleece) to explain the rise of Greece is to make the economic reality the only reality. It is here too that Lawson allows himself to cite a source out of context. To reinforce the connection between capitalism and tyranny, he quotes a diatribe against money without giving the source; one would think from the text that its author was a premature anticapitalist. But the excerpt is from Sophocles' *Antigone;* the context is Creon's invective against those who succumb to bribery. Creon is not inveighing against money; he is criticizing its abuse.

Nevertheless, the total effect of *The Hidden Heritage* outweighs its flaws. If it had been written by a professional historian, it would have been called *haute vulgarisation* because it is both readable and enjoyable. One would expect a screenwriter with such an ability to flee Hollywood for Academe; Lawson did—but only when nothing else was available.

Of the Ten, Lawson had the greatest potential for intellectual achievement. *The Hidden Heritage* offers evidence of what he might have accomplished if the circumstances—those he created for himself and those imposed on him—had been different.

4 HERBERT BIBERMAN
The Salt That Lost Its Savor

While John Howard Lawson's plays are discussed in standard histories of the American drama, Herbert Biberman's contribution to the theater merits a mere paragraph in one of them.[1] Yet Biberman might have become an important stage figure if he had not allowed politics to rule his life and had not alienated the Theatre Guild with his Marxist rhetoric.

The stage was Biberman's first love. After graduating from the University of Pennsylvania with a degree in economics, he realized he was more interested in the theater than in the vice-presidency of Biberman Brothers, the family's clothing firm. And so, in 1925, Biberman enrolled in Yale's School of Drama, where he studied playwriting and direction under George Pierce Baker—who had established the legendary '47 workshop at Harvard, whose pupils included Philip Barry and Eugene O'Neill, and who had just moved to Yale.

As one might expect from an American graduate student in the 1920s, Biberman began writing plays that were, for the most part, expressionistic. It is clear even from a cursory reading why they went unproduced. In "When the Blind See" (1925)—suggested by the plight of Floyd Collins, the Kentuckian who was trapped in a cave for eighteen days in 1925—a gas pocket explodes, causing a chasm that attracts a scientist who wants to investigate it, children who want to explore it, and a businessman who wants to turn it into a tourist attraction complete with circus tent, hurdy gurdy music, and a carousel.[2] Although the Collins case inspired one of Billy Wilder's best films, *The Big Carnival* (1951; also known as *Ace in the Hole*), it inspired Biberman only to attack venality and, when that theme was exhausted, to plumb the depths of expressionism by making the literal descent into the chasm a descent to the underworld, where the spelunkers encounter the dead and discover little difference between life below the earth and above it.

"Servants or Masters, or Majesty Machine" (1927) was written specifically for Baker's playwriting class, although one does not know what the professor thought of it.[3] If Baker was critical of O'Neill's *Bound East for Cardiff,* which he felt was not a play, it is difficult to imagine his liking "Servants or Masters." Elmer Rice might have done better with machines that assume a life of their own and begin controlling their operators; he had written something similar in *The Adding Machine* (1923), which had left its mark on the young Biberman.

Despite a lack of both originality and success, Biberman continued to write plays, yet by the end of the 1920s it was evident that if he were to have a career in the theater, it would be as a director. After receiving his master's degree from Yale in 1927, he toured Europe with his brother, Edward, an artist who specialized in painting workers and migrants. Biberman was especially taken with what he saw on the Moscow stage. Having experienced Socialist realism on its native soil, he was bent on recreating it in America. Upon his return to the United States in 1928, he approached the Theatre Guild, not for a job but in the hope of persuading the organization to produce some plays he had seen abroad. Nevertheless, a job resulted; Biberman became stage manager for such Theatre Guild productions as *The Camel through the Needle's Eye* (1929) and *Karl and Anna* (1929), in which he played a bit role; the cast also included Gale Sondergaard, whom he married the following year.

When Biberman was not stage-managing, he was at the American Laboratory Theatre. It was not the presence of Richard Boleslavsky, a former member of the Moscow Art Theatre and the school's coordinator, that drew him there; Boleslavsky had succumbed to the lure of capitalism. Rather, it was the presence of novices like Julius Garfinkle, later Jules Garfield and finally John Garfield, whom he hoped to convert to Communism because—as Garfield's biographer put it—Biberman believed that "the theatre existed as an agent for social revolution [and] evangelized his convictions."[4]

Biberman was determined to recruit the young Garfield, who never joined but whose associations with Party members eventually brought him before HUAC—an experience that contributed to his early death. Biberman was responsible for Garfield's unofficial debut in *The Camel through the Needle's Eye*; when George Freedley (later to become an outstanding theater historian), who was doing a walk-on in the play, became ill, Biberman arranged for Garfield to go on for him. After Biberman became one of the founders of the Theatre Guild Studio, he managed to get Garfield a part in *Red Rust*, a Russian play presented on Sundays for Guild subscribers. Although *Red Rust* was the Studio's only undertaking, the Guild was sufficiently impressed with Biberman's direction to put him in charge of a major production, the anti-imperialist Soviet drama *Roar China*.

Roar China was one of the most elaborately staged productions Broadway had seen. By removing the first four rows of the orchestra, Biberman was able to get a battleship on stage and extend the dock into the auditorium. He received excellent reviews and was similarly praised for his staging of Lynn Riggs's *Green Grow the Lilacs* a few months later. Just as Biberman believed in the anticapitalism of *Red Rust* and the anticolonialism of *Roar China*, he believed in the populism of *Green Grow the Lilacs*—as did Rodgers and Hammerstein when they set it to music, fashioning from it the pathbreaking *Oklahoma!* (1943). Biberman's belief in the play, however, was political. Curly, Aunt Eller, Laurey, and Ado Annie were "the people," a recurring word in Biberman's work, meaning humanity as an abstract idea or concept. Biberman was always more interested in the idea of the people than in persons, because the idea was the ideal: a classless, raceless entity beating with one heart.

Although the critics dismissed *Miracle at Verdun* (1931) as minor Theatre Guild, they commended Biberman for his innovative staging. Despite his good notices, Biberman's abrasiveness and his habit of banging his fist on anything handy during conferences led to the termination of his contract with the Guild in 1931. Solely because of his flair for historical drama, he was recalled three years later to codirect Maxwell Anderson's *Valley Forge* (1934) with John Houseman. Biberman was unaffected by the play's failure; he was no longer interested in Broadway. When Columbia Pictures beckoned with a two-movie deal in 1934, Biberman, like so many other easterners, journeyed west.

The two pictures—*One Way Ticket* (1935) and *Meet Nero Wolfe* (1936)—were not the sort to enhance any director's reputation, much less a radical's. The *Variety* reviewer even failed to mention the director of *One Way Ticket*, a prison melodrama with a dash of sociology, in which a citizen, learning that a banker who has defrauded his own bank has gone free, turns robber himself. *Meet Nero Wolfe* was slightly better; at least it had sophistication, but it was the sophistication of the stage, not the screen. Fresh from the theater, Biberman blocked shots instead of composing them. William Wyler could reproduce the wholeness of action characteristic of theater through long takes and deep focus; Biberman merely staged scenes that were whole in themselves—and looked it—but did not seem to be part of any totality. Some of the blame can be attributed to the character of the hero; of all the series detectives, Rex Stout's Nero Wolfe had the shortest tenure on the screen: two films. Neither as aphoristic as Charlie Chan nor as fast-talking as Ellery Queen, Wolfe was grossly overweight, a beer guzzler, a gourmand, and an orchid grower; in addition, he was penny-pinching and supercilious, especially toward his harried assistant, Archie. The real reason for his brief celluloid hour, however, was his hermetic existence; he never left his West Side brownstone.

Biberman opened up the action a bit, but the plot, based on Stout's *Fer-de-Lance* (1934), defeated him. He simply did not understand the medium; the cast reacts as it would on stage, but in film a stage reaction is overacting. Apart from some filmic touches—swish pans, dissolves, wipes, and an eerie shot of a dead man's hand clutching a newspaper clipping that another hand reaches down to retrieve—*Meet Nero Wolfe* is like a West End melodrama aimed at the tourist trade—slick, but so ephemeral that two days later the plot has vanished from the memory. All anyone seems to remember about it is the unusual murder weapon: a needle, treated with snake venom, concealed in a golf club head.

Biberman's only other screen credit in the 1930s was for the original story of Paramount's *King of Chinatown* (1938), which starred Anna May Wong, one of the few Asians to have achieved some fame in Hollywood. Throughout his life Biberman was committed to the betterment of minorities, working them into films whenever he could, not merely because the Party expected him to (he had joined in 1934) but essentially because minorities fell under the sacred rubric of The People. Although Biberman was not involved in writing the *King of Chinatown* screenplay, he was responsible for a story that would require the casting of orientals. The plot was not about the Tong Wars or the opium trade but about a racketeer's regeneration by a Chinese woman who is no ordinary mortal but a screen goddess type: a surgeon to whom the racketeer is so indebted that he offers to build her a clinic.

Biberman did not receive another screen credit for six years. Yet he wrote incessantly and in a variety of forms—essays, speeches, stories, plays, scripts, poems, radio dramas—on everything from steno pads to hotel stationery. Most of what he wrote is unpublished and unproduced. He was a classic case of the dilettante, well educated and widely read, who can neither find nor choose an outlet for his gifts; he moved from promising theater director to mediocre film director, from unproduced playwright to occasionally produced screenwriter.

Radical politics permeated everything Biberman did. With the Theatre Guild he was involved only with plays of a political nature. His stories, all written at the outbreak of World War II, are also political; like the plays, they are also unpublished.[5] If some were meant for the screen, it is small wonder they never made it. In "Cinderella in Uniform," a title suitable for a 1940s marquee, everyone in a family is patriotic except the husband, who joins the army only after his wife unmasks a saboteur. In "Our Greatest Hour" a woman with an aversion to foreigners opens her home to them when war comes. "Freedom's Children: A Story of a Can of Milk" proves that children who are given milk can rout Nazis.

To Biberman, a short story was an essay with a plot; a play, a dramatized message. Since his notions of fiction and drama were rooted in politics, his concept of film could only be political. Biberman was taken with film's collaborative nature, which he saw as the end of the individual artist and the beginning of collective art; he was not a champion of auteurism. Even the language in which he describes film is Marxist: its subject matter is "the quirk in the bowels of dialectical nature." Film is the ancilla of dialectical materialism because it enables the viewer "to understand the material world materially . . . the only way it can be understood."[6]

As the newest art form, film was free of tradition—to Biberman, an enviable condition. Freedom was Biberman's signature word; if he had had any fresh insights, his overuse of it might be overlooked. Sartre explored the connection between personal and political freedom; Biberman cannot even define freedom except to say that it is not a "sissy word" and that it is "endless and boundless."[7] Campaigning for Henry Wallace in 1948, he dubbed freedom one of the fruits of revolution and the goal of such "radicals" and "subversives" as Thomas Jefferson and Abraham Lincoln, who wanted freedom for all, not merely for the elect. Biberman's idol was Thomas Jefferson, who believed in The People—but not to the uncritical degree Biberman did; he might have reflected on Jefferson's acceptance of a natural hierarchy based on talent and virtue. Regardless, Jefferson could do no wrong, as Biberman attempted to show in an unproduced radio series, "Jefferson and Hamilton"; it portrayed Washington as a slave owner (as if Jefferson were not); Jefferson, as the great equalizer, proclaiming that "we are all Republicans; we are all Federalists."

Biberman was more successful with an earlier four-part radio series; The Legend of America, which aired on CBS in the fall of 1933, was a mammoth attempt to narrate the history of America in verse, from the Norsemen to the New Deal. Since even the films of the 1930s were critical of a society in which veterans were forgotten men and children of the unemployed rode the rails, Biberman was able to indulge in his favorite practice: inveighing against the evils of capitalist imperialism. The Spanish were a scourge; the British were murderers. America, "a gambler's paradise / Where every hazard nature flings / Is taken in stride for gold," awaited a messiah—who, naturally, turned out to be the Master of Monticello.

For a man who could not separate art from politics because his concept of art was political, Hollywood in the 1930s was the perfect place. In New York, Biberman might not have been able to consort with Lillian Hellman, John Steinbeck, Melvyn Douglas, and Dorothy Parker; as one of the founders of the Hollywood Anti-Nazi League and a member of the Committee for Loyalist Spain and the Los Angeles Chapter for Russian War Relief, he could. It is significant that the Hollywood Anti-Nazi League came into existence in 1936, the year that marked the end of Biberman's two-picture contract with Columbia. His involvement in the League and the Popular Front explains the gaps in his filmography. As the world girded for war, so did Biberman, who rapidly became one of Hollywood's leading progressives. When he was not deploring the exploitation of migrants, mobilizing support for Loyalist Spain, or attempting to convince disillusioned leftists that the 1939 Nazi-Soviet Pact was a fascist fabrication, he was writing—not scripts so much as stories and propaganda pieces. "Dangerous People," a one-acter written for the Southern California Union for Concerted Peace Efforts, almost makes obviousness a virtue. A veteran with one leg and another with one lung join forces with a young idealist—to what end one is not exactly certain, except to "wage war on war: the old and the new—together—in a fight against war."[8]

Just when it seemed that Biberman would never see another soundstage, RKO beckoned in September 1943, offering him a paltry $250 a week not to direct but to adapt a spy novel for a picture to be called "International Zone." The novel was abandoned; instead, Biberman and another writer, Philip McDonald, came up with an original story suggested by Nazi efforts to woo the Middle East away from the Allies in the early days of World War II. *Action in Arabia* (1944) did nothing to enhance the reputations of RKO or Biberman; nor did it advance the cause of truth. Even the title is a misnomer, since the setting is Syria, which was far more pro-Axis than the writers cared to admit. The film does, however, contain some interesting desert footage that RKO had intended to use in a movie (never made) about Lawrence of Arabia.

In *The Master Race* (1944), his next and last film for RKO, Biberman had a chance both to write and to direct. It began as an original 63-page treatment that Biberman had written on the assumption that though Germany's defeat was imminent, the spirit of Nazism would persist. In preparation for the Fourth Reich, what was left of the Third would go underground, its members assuming new identities and dispersing themselves throughout Europe.

The Master Race was produced by Edward and Robert Golden, the team that made the lurid but commercially successful *Hitler's Children* (1943), but does not depict love camps, sterilization, flagellation, and euthanasia—the ingredients of *Hitler's Children* that made RKO $3,335,000 richer. *The Master Race* is essentially about a Nazi colonel who, after assuming the identity of a dead Belgian patriot, perpetuates the scapegoat mentality on which the Third Reich thrived by turning the Belgians against their liberators. The notion that the liberated can reject their liberators, that the victims of Nazism could make victors of the Nazis, is compelling; the treatment, however, is so labored, the extremes of good and evil so pronounced, and the brotherhood theme so forced (an ecumenical service is held in a bombed-out Catholic church with a Protestant as celebrant and a menorah on the altar) that it is difficult to take the film seriously. RKO did not; although the studio had a seven-year option on Biberman, it chose not to exercise it even before *The Master Race* went into release. By 12 September 1944, Biberman's brief hour at RKO was over.

Having been a director and a writer, Biberman next became associate producer of *Abilene Town* (1946), which Jules Levey released through United Artists. Although Biberman had no official connection with the script, a copy of it among his papers bears the inscription of the director, Edwin L. Marin: "For Herbert—with sincere appreciation." Exactly what Biberman contributed is unknown. Superficially, *Abilene Town* is an oater about the familiar clash between cattlemen and homesteaders. The homesteaders, however, behave like populists, arguing that "the land's free," forming a protective association, and fencing in their property; to ensure justice, they march down the street on election day singing "The Battle Hymn of the Republic." Lines such as "A better time's comin' if people have the nerve to do their part," and "It's not this town you're fighting for, it's the right to live," may well have been written by the screenwriter, Harold Shumate; if so, they met with the associate producer's approval.

Jules Levey used an original story by Biberman and Elliot Paul, "Conspiracy in Jazz," as the basis of *New Orleans* (1947), Biberman's last screen credit until 1954. Although Paul coauthored the screenplay with Dick Hyland, Biberman exerted a considerable influence on it, as seen by the notes written on the final script.[9] *New Orleans* is often shown not for its plot—the old high culture/pop culture conflict—but for the presence of such jazz artists as Louis Armstrong, Billie Holiday, and Woody Herman. The story—can an aspiring concert artist (Dorothy Patrick) find happiness with the king of Basin Street (Arturo de Cordova)?—is pure Biberman; his answer is yes, if she broadens her repertoire to include the people's music.

New Orleans was released the year the HUAC hearings began. The blacklist that followed, though it curtailed and destroyed many promising careers, was responsible for the one film that assures Biberman a place in film history. Had it not been for the blacklist, it is doubtful that *Salt of the Earth* (1954) would ever have been made.

For a film that occasioned an eight-year antitrust suit, the picture is no more controversial than the Bill of Rights—which would be controversial only in an age when social injustice is the norm; similarly, *Salt of the Earth* could be inflammatory only in a time when racial and sexual equality is considered a noble goal because it has not been reached. In the long run, what may be significant is not the film itself but its history. The movie villains pale beside the real-life house-burners, FBI informants, and right-wing fanatics that people Biberman's *Salt of the Earth: The Story of a Film* (1965).[10]

Like much of the prose written by the Ten, Biberman's account of the filming attests to its author's years in the industry; told in short narrative segments framed by prologue and epilogue, it could easily have 'been converted into a screenplay. The cuts are marked; the transitions (especially the dissolves) are indicated. The beginning seems to iris out into a federal courthouse as Biberman awaits the jury's verdict in a suit brought by Independent Productions Corporation (IPC) and IPC Distributors, Inc., against sixty-eight defendants who conspired, first, to prevent *Salt of the Earth* from being made and then to keep it from being distributed. Between prologue and epilogue is a lengthy flashback on the film's production history, told without rancor, self-pity, or self-congratulation.

The flashback begins at the end of World War II when movies like *The Best Years of Our Lives* and *Crossfire* led the Hollywood left to believe that it had become possible to make films of greater maturity and social significance than in the past. Even after the HUAC investigation and a five-month prison sentence, Biberman still believed such films could be made—not within the studio system from which he was excluded but through independent production. The formation of a production company by Biberman, Paul Jarrico, and Simon Lazarus was followed by the formulation of its policy: to make films about "real people and real situations." The real situation turned out to be a strike; the real people, those involved in it. In 1951, Local 890 of the Mine, Mill and Smelter Works Union in Bayard, New Mexico, which had been expelled from the CIO for being Commnist-dominated, called a strike against New Jersey Zinc. What was unusual was the role women played: when a Taft-Hartley injunction prevented the miners from picketing, their wives went out on the line.

Any dramatization of the strike would have to reflect its uniqueness: a strike of Mexican-Americans seeking job equality with whites grew into a bid for sexual equality once the women joined it. A classic Hollywood screenplay would make the one concomitant with the other so that with the settlement of the strike the men would regard the women as equals. Such a resolution would also be in the best tradition of left-wing optimism, illustrating the penultimate leveling of distinctions—that between races and sexes. If classes had been included, the millenium would have been reached.

To call *Salt of the Earth* a semidocumentary merely because it is based on fact is to place it in the same category as *The House on 92nd Street* (1945), *Boomerang* (1947), and *Call Northside 777* (1948), with which it actually has only one feature in common: narrative structure. It boasts few professional actors, the best known being Will Geer; the cast is largely made up of amateurs, whereas Hollywood semidocumentaries cast the likes of James Stewart and Lee J. Cobb. Moreover, the conventional voice-over narration of the semidocumentary is an off-camera voice belonging to none of the characters, whereas *Salt of the Earth* is narrated by the heroine.

If *Salt* may be compared with any genre, perhaps it is Italian neorealism (*Open City*, 1946; *Paisan*, 1947), yet even that comparison needs qualification. Italian neorealism was a vital but short-lived movement whose themes, a world war and its aftermath, were far more historically significant than a little-remembered strike. In both the semidocumentary and neorealism, art and life meet halfway; in *Salt of the Earth*, life has an edge on art. To be oxymoronic, *Salt* is a fiction documentary; it is a fiction film based on an actual event, like the headlines-fresh Warner Brothers movies of the 1930s.

It was the film's narrative structure that warranted its being distributed like any other theatrical film, which is precisely what IPC wanted. While McCarthyism spawned some ludicrous incidents, the boycotts against *Salt of the Earth* went beyond ludicrous to incongruous: to reject this film is to repudiate classical Hollywood narrative, the time-honored situation-complication-resolution model. Had the opposition (which included Howard Hughes, who drafted a letter to a congressman outlining steps to prevent the film's release) detected Marxist elements in Michael Wilson's script, at least there would have been a philosophical basis for the boycott. But the backlash was the result not of philosophical differences but of prejudice, prejudice against a film made by Reds—in this instance, one must add, by Reds who knew how to write a script and how to film it.

The screenplay by Michael Wilson—a product of the studio system and an Oscar winner for *A Place in the Sun* (1952)—is a textbook illustration of the reduction of an action to a single theme: "the indivisibility of equality," which Biberman extended to include cast (black, white, Mexican-American, amateur, professional) and crew (union, nonunion, named, anonymous). Having found the spine of his narrative, Wilson proceeded to give it flesh; he began with a limited view of equality, which he then expanded until it became all-embracing. At the outset of the strike, equality is monolithic; it applies to the Anglos but not to the Mexican-Americans, who are willing to settle for even the most elementary form of equality: job safety—as if that should be a bargaining issue. When the wives argue that sanitation is more important than safety precautions (which ought to be axiomatic), they also find themselves caught up in the struggle—in their case, for sexual equality. Ironically, the same men who sought equality with the Anglos deny it to their wives. It is not until the women voice their demands and replace their husbands on the picket line that they are considered sisters in the same union in which the men are brothers. When the men who called each other brother begin to address their wives as sister, the film's point becomes clear: equality is upward-reaching; it begins simply and, as it progresses, makes whatever it encounters one with itself.

For the most part, Biberman's direction complemented Wilson's script; simplicity of plot was matched by simplicity of style. As Wilson reduced the plot to a single concept, Biberman defined that concept in terms of a central vision, that of Esperanza, the strike leader's wife, played by Rosaura Revueltas. Biberman's wife, Gale Sondergaard, was planning to play Esperanza until both she and her husband realized that only a Hispanic actress could do justice to the role (even though Sondergaard had successfully played a Eurasian in *The Letter* and a Thai in *Anna and the King of Siam*). Yet there is an uncanny similarity between Sondergaard and Revueltas; nature sculpted their faces so perfectly that when nobility of expression was required, the slightest glossing of the cheekbones would do it. Biberman was struck by the integrity radiating from Revueltas's face with a translucence no amount of front lighting can duplicate.

Initially, Esperanza is a reticent wife, but once she joins the pickets while her husband, Ramon, inherits the domestic chores, the film links them visually: when the deputies pummel Ramon, Biberman cuts abruptly to Esperanza crying out in labor; with the birth of their child, Ramon's face is superimposed on hers. Man is absorbed into woman as identities merge and differences disappear. Biberman had been moving toward such a synthesis from the very beginning when the men picket in a circle on a dirt road while the women watch atop a hill; when the women take over the picketing, the locations are reversed, as are the roles of superior and inferior, participant and spectator. As the strike moves toward a settlement, men and women, brothers and sisters, become one; the indivisibility of equality has been achieved.

Biberman's handling of the miners and their wives is much subtler than his depiction of the heavies: the sheriff and his deputies. The only embarrassing shot in the film occurs when the sheriff is photographed from the rear, a revolver in his holster assaulting the eye by its prominence. When Biberman wants a "hiss the villain" response from the audience, he has only to have a car drive into a striker, a woman scream, or a baby cry. Yet for all its faults—which include some dreadful acting by the locals and a sitcom quaintness when the men become domesticated—*Salt of the Earth* is an honorable achievement; it is impossible to watch it without feeling some gratitude to those who saw in an obscure strike humanity's perennial quest for dignity.

Salt of the Earth was IPC's only production. Its organizers had lofty aims when they decided to make films about "real people and real situations," but 1951 was not the time; the United States was not the place; and IPC's notion of reality was not the right one. At one point the company managed to get a script from Dalton Trumbo. When Trumbo

was annotating material for his collection at the State Historical Society
of Wisconsin, he came upon the script "An American Story," on which
he wrote, "This is not by me," then added, "Oh yes it is. For $2000 I
dramatized a local child custody case for a group composed of Paul
Jarrico, Adrian Scott, Herbert Biberman, et al. It was naturally never
made. A prime example of the dreamy propaganda piece that can
never succeed—even if you get the money to shoot it. All this, of
course, in depths of black market blacklist."[11] In fact, the propaganda
is far from "dreamy." The heroine of "An American Story," who is
battling for custody of her children, supports the Hollywood Ten, the
First Amendment, and North Korea, which decided to put an end to
the border warfare instigated by South Korea by embarking upon a war
of independence in June 1950. While the Korean War has been called a
police action, it is rarely if ever (at least in the West) termed a war of
independence. Naturally, "An American Story" was never filmed.

Biberman, however, did not give up. After a 1952 visit to New York
he was convinced that a black liberation movement was starting in the
United States and that the time was ripe for a film about it. Since IPC
was entirely white, Biberman proposed a People's Film Company with
himself, Scott, and Jarrico as vice-presidents and two blacks, Frances
Williams and Carlton Moss, as "co-owners"; the first production would
be the life of Frederick Douglass, starring Paul Robeson. That project
never materialized either. Biberman's motives were laudable, but his
attitude toward blacks was—however unconsciously—condescending.
By attempting to "win their confidence" and "give them the reality of
their own struggle to further inspire them," he implied that blacks
cannot inspire each other and must depend on whites to portray their
struggle as real, as if somehow it were not.[12] What blacks needed in the
early 1950s was civil rights; that, no movie could accomplish.

The only blacks Biberman had come close to in his career were the
jazz artists in New Orleans. Yet he wanted to go further; his goal was to
film Uncle Tom's Cabin. By December 1962 he had written a screenplay
called "Slaves," which, while relatively faithful to the abolitionist
novel, verged on the operatic: Tom's death would be accompanied by a
cleansing rain, and in the fade-out his grave would appear in silhouette, with Mozart on the soundtrack. Biberman elicited the support
of John Oliver Killens, who did an adaptation titled "The Slaves" (9
September 1963) that was inferior to Biberman's; next, the two collaborated on a screenplay, which also lacked the power of Biberman's first
script.

When Slaves (1969), Biberman's last film, was finally made, it bore
hardly any resemblance to Uncle Tom's Cabin. That it was a Theatre
Guild Films producion is doubly ironic: it was with the Theatre Guild
that Biberman began his career; it was with Theatre Guild Films that he

ended it. *Slaves* is theatrical in another sense, also; it is overripe melodrama, at times laughably so. It is hard not to smirk when the black mistress of a white plantation owner spits in her master's face while daring him to take her—which he does. Like Biberman's other films, *Slaves* seems staged rather than directed. Some directors can conceal their limitations when they are working with scripts that generate their own momentum; sheer kinesis can often hide an infertile imagination. But when the script lies somewhere between agitprop and shocker, the only substitutes for kinesis are sex and violence. Although Biberman felt as strongly about exploited blacks as he did about exploited workers, *Slaves* is no *Salt of the Earth*. Unrestrained by an indulgent script that was partly his own creation, Biberman made a film about slave owners as sexual tyrants and their chattels as sexual pawns. He would probably have replied that *Slaves* is about freedom—which is clear from the dialogue: the word is used so often (the soil of Ohio offers "the first smell of freedom"; to escape from bondage is to "haul ass to freedom") that one yearns for a synonym.

Subtlety was never Biberman's forte; he cuts from manacled feet to hooves of galloping horses, from a slave about to sleep with his wife for the last time to the irons that will encircle his feet the next morning. Interspersed between closeups of dejected faces and long shots so proscenium-bound that the characters are barely distinguishable are the homilies: black is a condition, not a color; missionaries convert black Africans, who are then sold as slaves to Christians, who require more missionaries to convert more blacks for more Christians to buy. *Slaves* is really an exploitation film; especially exploited are some good black performers who are forced to be not black stereotypes but white stereotypes in blackface. Dionne Warwick swigs rum and looks as if she belongs atop a piano in a waterfront dive, with a feather boa draped around her shoulders; Ossie Davis has the worst part as the Uncle Tom figure who is beaten to death when he refuses to divulge the whereabouts of the runaway mistress. In addition to the parallels between slave breeding and Nazism, slavery and totalitarianism, there is the self-referential analogy between the good slave who keeps his silence under the lash and the unfriendly witnesses of 1947 who kept theirs under the threat of imprisonment and unemployment.

When Herbert Biberman died of cancer in 1971, he left behind a slight filmography and a myriad of dreams: unfilmed scripts, unproduced plays, unpublished stories. As a fatalist, he would have appreciated the irony of having made the film by which he is remembered, *Salt of the Earth*, at a time when he was unemployable in Hollywood and when his chances for recognition were virtually nonexistent.

5 ALBERT MALTZ
Asking of Writers

When Albert Maltz graduated from Columbia University in 1930 with a B.A. in philosophy, he had no intention of pursuing the intellectual life. His sights were set on the stage; accordingly, he enrolled in Yale's School of Drama and, like Herbert Biberman, who preceded him by six years, studied under George Pierce Baker. There he formed a close friendship with another student, George Sklar, who became his collaborator on two plays.

As a Depression playwright, Maltz has suffered the fate of most dramatists who come under that heading. While some plays of the 1930s are revived and studied as drama, his are not, even though they reflect the era's preoccupation with political corruption, social injustice, capitalism, union-busting, the munitions industry, and profiteering. The problem with Maltz's plays is endemic to the radical theater: if a work is unsophisticated when it is first performed, once divorced from its era it seems even more so and in time becomes puerile. Clifford Odets is far from subtle, but *Awake and Sing* (1935) has had major revivals, as have *Golden Boy* (1937), *Paradise Lost* (1935), and *Rocket to the Moon* (1938). Even Sidney Kingsley's *Men in White* (1933) is occasionally staged. But Maltz's plays are lesser examples of an already limited genre; there is no reason to revive Maltz when one can revive Odets, who wrote less urgently and flamboyantly but whose characters are more realistic. What Odets would have considered revolutionary slogans ("The world is supposed to be for all of us" in *Waiting for Lefty*; "Go out and fight so life shouldn't be printed on dollar bills" in *Awake and Sing*), Maltz would have considered epigrams.

Although Maltz's *Private Hicks* (1935) and Odets's *Waiting for Lefty* are both represented in *The Best Short Plays of the Social Theatre*,[1] *Lefty* has had a life outside anthologies; *Hicks* has had virtually no life at all. While Maltz had a deeper knowledge of unionism than Odets, *Waiting for Lefty* remains the quintessential union play—not for its plot, which is negligible, but for its bold theatricality. *Lefty* is a succession of tabloid sketches combining the rhetoric of agitprop with the immediacy of the living newspaper play. The language is the vernacular revved up and embellished, a re-creation, not a replication, of working-class idiom.

Maltz would not insult the working class by elevating its speech; he writes the genuine article, with the "ain't," "tell'm," "oughta," and "yuh" intact.

Since Odets was more interested in evoking a strike atmosphere than in writing a tightly structured play, his medium was radical vaudeville, with blackouts instead of conventional scenes. Maltz, who understood drama but not theater, was more interested in making a point than in writing a play. In *Private Hicks* he raises a problem (a national guardsman's refusal to fire on strikers) and solves it (the guardsman's court-martial). Since the outcome is inevitable, there is no suspense; *Private Hicks* is a disguised short story that might have fared better had it been written as one.

Even after he had largely given up drama for fiction, Maltz was still determined to write the definitive union play. In *Rehearsal* (1938), which fell into oblivion after a Detroit production in May 1938, he tried to duplicate the qualities that made *Waiting for Lefty* and Marc Blitzstein's *The Cradle Will Rock* such galvanic theater pieces: chant, parody, and a climactic call for action. *Lefty* may not be a play nor *Cradle* an opera, yet each is unmistakably theater. *Rehearsal*, as the title implies, is a run-through for a play which, if performed, would be ritual agitprop, a requiem for a dead worker beginning where *Waiting for Lefty* leaves off. However, all is not clenched-fist rhetoric. Maltz adds a touch of the Freudian by attributing the heroine's neurosis to a past trauma: Vera, an actress in a labor play, cannot perform the final scene because it recalls a private agony. Yet once she admits that the fate of the dead unionist in the play parallels that of her brother in real life, she can speak the lines with the passion they require. The therapeutic value of theater is not the point here, nor is the Pirandellian interplay of illusion and reality. Maltz is arguing for the merging of life and theater in a symbiotic union, each feeding the other to produce not art but action.

Maltz thought he could surpass *Waiting for Lefty*: thus *Lefty*'s "Hello America" is repeated so often that Vera cries, "I won't say that God damn line again." By the end of *Rehearsal*, however, Maltz is not mocking Odets; he is echoing him. Agate's "This is your life and mine" speech in *Lefty* is the basis of Vera's exhortation: "There is no forgetting! Forgetting is a lie! There is no escape! Escape is a cheat! You are *here*! This is your home. This is your life. There is no hope except in struggle. There is no future that will come by itself. The future is here—the closed fist! Ours! The future is ours!"[2]

In Odets, a plot evolves into a thesis; in Maltz, the thesis precedes the plot. Maltz presents the action so that it appears to culminate naturally, although it is really moving with mock inexorability toward a preordained conclusion. Character does not determine outcome; Maltz does. In *Merry-Go-Round* (1932) a witness to a murder is convicted of that murder. The innocent bellboy who is framed and killed so that his death appears a suicide may be a victim of municipal corruption, but in terms of plot he is just a ploy. In *Peace on Earth* (1933) a college professor's support of a strike results in his death. Since the bellboy and the professor were scapegoats from the outset, they had no other choice but to die scapegoat deaths.

Of the two plays, both coauthored with George Sklar, *Peace on Earth* was the more successful. It ran sixteen weeks as the initial offering of the Theatre Union, whose policy was to present drama about the "economic, emotional, and cultural problems that confront the majority of people," offered at popular prices through subscriptions and theater parties.[3]

Although the published text of *Peace on Earth* carried the endorsement of Louis Untermeyer, Sherwood Anderson (who composed the hastily written introduction), and Sidney Howard,[4] it is best left to the seasoned play-reader, who can envision the work in its staged form and thus be more tolerant of its failings than would an academic who views drama chiefly in terms of language and structure. The play lies somewhere between the early expressionism of O'Neill, Lawson, and Rice and the social dramas of Sidney Kingsley and Sidney Howard. While the thrust of the action is forward and linear, the form is expressionistic; montages of short scenes alternate with choruslike interludes and culminate in a Walpurgisnacht in which fantasy becomes reality as quickly as scene merges with scene.

The tension between linearity and expressionism is the play's chief defect. While O'Neill in *The Hairy Ape* and Rice in *The Adding Machine* could make an expressionistic plot the basis of social commentary, the plots in both are nonrealistic. The plot of *Peace on Earth* is quite realistic: a psychology professor's radicalization, mock trial, and execution. At first Peter Owens remains aloof from the striking longshoremen who refuse to ship munitions intended for an imminent war. It is only when a friend is killed and his university votes to confer an honorary degree on a warmonger who has converted his mill from textiles to arms production that Owens becomes a radical, paying for it with his life. Owens recalls Jim Mahoney in Bertolt Brecht's *Rise and Fall of the City of Mahogonny*, who is put to death at the end because he has committed the mortal sin of capitalism: he has no money. Brecht's ending works for the same reason the endings of *The Hairy Ape* and *The Adding Machine* work: they are nonrealistic resolutions of nonrealistic plays. But there is no moon of Alabama shining on Peter Owens, no strangling ape, no reincarnation. Nor is there the eleventh-hour reprieve of Brecht's *The Threepenny Opera*, in which a messenger announces that Macheath, in addition to being pardoned, has also received a pension for life. The Messenger in *Peace on Earth* arrives with an envelope marked "Pardon," which actually contains Owens's death sentence.

Peace on Earth, with an economic theory of war partly Shavian and partly Marxist, was dated even in 1933; the assumption that the sinking of a ship would precipitate World War II suggests that Maltz was back in 1915 with the *Lusitania*. The play also explains why Maltz's hour on the stage was brief. Trained in drama as an academic discipline, he tended to see it in terms of movements and influences, falling under the spell of each. The play that most clearly reveals his failings as a dramatist is *The Black Pit* (1934), his last play for the Theatre Union. While one can admire his compassion for the miners of West Virginia, and even for the company informant (who is by no means a villain, although he would have been had he come from the middle class; being from the working class makes him a victim), *The Black Pit* is almost unreadable; the working-class dialogue is rendered phonetically, so that one must pause continually to figure out whether "heem" is "hem" or "him."

When Maltz turned to fiction in the mid-1930s, he encountered the same problem he had had with drama: a creative imagination at war with a social conscience. The latter usually won. Maltz was capable of devising plots which, if allowed to run their course, might have resulted in literature—maybe not of distinction but at least of merit. Instead, narrative became a means to an end: the awakening of the reader to a particular social problem. The characters of the short stories—dwellers in the lower depths, miners with black lung, blacks who jump from moving cars to their deaths to avoid a lynch mob, prematurely deaf factory workers, black women who give birth in the street because they are denied admission to a white hospital, unionists forced to run a gauntlet that leaves them hospitalized—are all such obvious victims of oppression, exploitation, and discrimination that their plight needs the starkness of a charcoal sketch, not the naturalism of a WPA mural.

Mike Gold's introduction to Maltz's first collection of short stories, *The Way Things Are* (1938), did not serve the author well. Insisting that Maltz was an artist despite his proletarian subject matter (which, to Gold, would make him an even greater one), he went on to equate Maltz's view of environmental determinism with the Greek sense of fate, making a bizarre comparison between Maltz's "Man on the Road" (1935) and *Oedipus the King*. Fate may be character, as the Greeks believed, but a driver who encounters a dying hitchhiker in West Virginia is not a son who encounters his father at the crossroads. In the story, there is no coinciding of destinies, only an awareness of human suffering. While Maltz felt deeply for the doomed miner, he did not allow the reader to feel differently; he determined that the reader's response would be the same as the narrator's mix of pity and anger: "In me, there was only mute emotion—pity and love for him, and a cold, deep hatred for what killed him."[5]

Maltz does this repeatedly, lessening the impact of otherwise effective stories. "The Game" (1936), in which a father works out a scenario with his son for stealing milk, could have been a powerful vignette except for the summary line: "You poor little monkey, they're not giving you the chance to grow up" (122). Even in one of his last stories, "The Cop" (1970), Maltz could not resist drawing a moral: "Take insects now . . . they know how to live their lives. But we who are human beings . . . we have such awful mixed up hearts . . . and what things they make us do, eh?"[6] Only in the title story of his second collection does Maltz allow the narrative to speak for itself. "Afternoon in the Jungle" (1941) is an ugly confrontation between a boy and a derelict as they contend for a half-dollar that has fallen into a subway grill. Neither comes off well, but the boy is beyond redemption.

As a short story writer, Maltz was a social, or Socialist, realist; as a novelist he was a radical. The novels illustrate his Marxism and antifascism better than his stories or screenplays. *The Underground Stream* (1940), his first, is solemnly subtitled *An Historical Novel of a Moment in the American Winter*—the moment being the CIO's attempt to unionize the automobile workers in 1936. Although the novel is dated, it is still an authentic account of the American Communist Party's infiltration of closed-shop companies to unionize the workers and recruit more minorities. The hero is, as one might expect, the Communist; the clue is his ungrammatical speech which, to Maltz, is a badge of honor.

For a Columbia Phi Beta Kappa, Maltz had a strange view of education. His radio play *Red-Head Baker*, which aired on CBS in 1937, was a plea for progressive education as a means of solving student indifference and delinquency. The arguments are naive and come down to allowing disaffected youths to study what they believe will be useful to them: "If [one's] going to use Latin in life, all right. But if he isn't, why waste time on it?" In *The Underground Stream* education is limited to Marxism which, like the synonymity of truth and beauty, is all one knows or needs to know. Since the book is politically monolinear, it cannot be criticized for its pervasive Marxism but can be for its excessive length.

The novel is really about the clash between fascism, as represented by Jeffrey Grebb, the personnel director of Jefferson Motors, who joins the Klan-like Black Legion because he believes America will go fascist; and Communism, as typified by Princey, who is committed to unionizing Jefferson Motors. Grebb has Princey kidnapped and, in an episode that makes undue demands on credibility, explains that he joined the Legion to subvert it in the belief that if fascism comes, it will be destroyed by an alliance between labor and management, with Socialism the next stage. Princey, who finds Grebb's reasoning preposterous, ends up a corpse. If Grebb is sincere, and one suspects he is, the form of Socialism he is advocating is totalitarian and scarcely different from fascism. Maltz hardly intended Grebb to be a Soviet prototype; yet Grebb's theory of destroying fascism by using right-wing coercion and left-wing ideology would lead to a totalitarian state complete with the internal exile of dissidents, gulags, religious and racial persecution. Thus, the book has become the opposite of what Maltz intended in 1940. To a modern reader, Grebb would be a Soviet type; Princey, a left-of-center trade unionist.

The Underground Stream enlarged upon the mock unity of time with which Maltz had experimented in "A Season of Celebration" (1937). The novel begins on a Saturday evening at 10:50 and ends at 6:00 the following morning. His second novel, The Cross and the Arrow (1944), has an even more unusual unity of time. It consists of three books, the first and third covering twenty-four hours (from 11:00 P.M. to 6:00 A.M., and from 6:00 A.M. to 11:00 P.M.). The middle book is a flashback to the period from December 1941 to August 1942. The three books could easily have been sequences in a film. Even within the main action of the twenty-four hours there are flashbacks. Still, the action seems continuous, with the present slipping in and out of the past without disturbing the narrative. The effect, then, is one of watching a film where a sense of the present is maintained despite spatial dislocations and temporal leaps.

Although the plot device Maltz chose—a seemingly inexplicable act that becomes intelligible at the end—is often used in thrillers (the first-page murder) and plays (the onstage corpse), it is also found in an unusually large number of films. Citizen Kane would never be the classic it is without the utterance of "Rosebud!" over which the audience puzzles for the next two hours. In The Cross and the Arrow, Willi Wegler, supposedly an exemplary Nazi and recipient of the War·Service Cross, fashions a cross out of hay and ignites it to direct British bombers to the site of the factory where he works as a drop-forge man.

The raid leaves Wegler seriously wounded but his ebbing consciousness becomes the medium through which much of the past is revealed. Filmmakers have always had a facility for entering the thoughts of the dying; a slow dissolve or blurred focus can take an audience from death to life so quickly that speed and logic are never questioned. To Faulkner and Tolstoy the consciousness of the dying was a source of insight. In The Cross and the Arrow there is no insight, only narrative. However, since the novel is so intensely cinematic, it is not so much a matter of Maltz's manipulating a character for the sake of a plot as of knowing why an apolitical man has made a political decision. The movies of the 1940s were filled with such types; in *Lucky Jordan* (1942), *This Land Is Mine* (1943), and *Edge of Darkness* (1943), the apathetic and cowardly have only to witness a single act of inhumanity to wax existential and join the ranks of the committed. It takes a series of acts to break Wegler's lifelong habit of silence. When a nurse boasted of quieting a screaming child by putting its head inside a gas oven, Wegler never reported her; he suppressed his rage at the death of his wife and son. But when he hears the son of the woman he plans to marry admit that the gifts he brought his mother came from a French woman he raped, Wegler cannot remain passive; he is now willing to betray a regime that even dishonors the spoils of its victims. When he learns that Germany is using slave labor from Poland, he discards his War Service Cross for an avenging arrow.

The Cross and the Arrow would have been less cinematic if Maltz had not been writing screenplays for two years. Actually, his Hollywood career might have begun a decade earlier than it did; in 1932 Universal invited him and George Sklar to write the screen version of *Merry-Go-Round*. When their treatment proved unsatisfactory (perhaps because they would not modify the conclusion), Tom Reed took over and gave the studio what it wanted—a crime melodrama with a happy ending. The result, *Afraid to Talk* (1932), would not have enhanced Maltz's reputation as a screenwriter.

In the late 1930s, although Maltz had not achieved any great success in the theater, he had learned enough about drama—both as a graduate student at Yale and as a practicing dramatist—to qualify for a position in the School of Adult Education at New York University's Writing Center, where he taught playwriting from 1937 to 1941. When the Selective Service Act resulted in declining enrollments, Maltz had little choice but to accept an offer from Paramount, to whom his literary credentials were more than acceptable. He was assigned the screen version of Graham Greene's *A Gun for Sale: An Entertainment* (1936), better known under its American title, *This Gun for Hire*, which was also the title of the 1942 film.

Maltz took screenwriting seriously, quickly learning format and terminology. He wrote the first draft of *This Gun for Hire* in pencil, beginning with the obligatory "fade in," breaking the action down into sequences, and designating scenes in terms of time and place.[7] He was sympathetic to Raven, Greene's professional killer; had he been able to develop the script in his own way, it would have been a dark romance on the order of *High Sierra* (1941), with Raven as a displaced romantic acting out his death wish in an alien world that believes death is the greatest evil.

Maltz's intentions could not be realized, because Greene's "entertainment" could not be filmed as written. For one thing, the time of the action had to be changed. Like Greene's *Confidential Agent* (1939), *A Gun for Sale* belongs to a body of pre-World War II works (Robert E. Sherwood's *Idiot's Delight*, Phyllis Bottome's *Mortal Storm*, Irwin Shaw's *Bury the Dead*, Sidney Kingsley's *Ten Million Ghosts*) that foreshadow the coming of war. A steel manufacturer, anxious to keep Britain on a war economy, instructs his henchman to hire a professional assassin, James Raven, to kill a pacifist war minister; war is averted because Raven kills the industrialist and his lackey instead. Still, the atmosphere is one of mobilization; the headlines are ominous; air raid drills are scheduled and gas masks issued. Another difficulty in adapting Greene is the aura of Christianity, specifically Catholicism, in his fiction, which is ample proof of G.K. Chesterton's thesis that the major symbols of twentieth-century literature are Christian symbols that have been inverted. Raven is both anti-Christ and Christ, predator and prey, Satan and savior. Anyone adapting *A Gun for Sale* in 1941 would have to dismantle the Catholic framework.

Between the book's publication in 1936 and the time the screenplay was written, the anticipated war had begun. The plot could remain the same—the unmasking of a traitor—but the setting would have to be Americanized, and the villain could not be a British warmonger but an agent in the employ of one of the two nations with which the United States was soon to be at war. This would pose no problem to Maltz, who had maintained in *Peace on Earth* that war was a capitalist conspiracy; the villain could still be a capitalist.

Because Maltz was a novice screenwriter (although one who learned the rudiments amazingly fast), he was expected to write the screenplay "under the supervision of Frank Tuttle," as the title page of one draft states. This meant working under a director, a Party member at the time, who would ten years later recant and name thirty-six names, including the writer he had supervised.[8] In 1941, however, Maltz was delighted at the prospect of writing a script that a comrade would direct. Both he and Tuttle knew that further changes were needed, especially in Raven, whom Greene had made a symbol of scarred humanity—doubly so, since Raven has a harelip as well as a scar on his wrist from a hot iron with which his mother had struck him. They need not have worried; the casting of Alan Ladd as Raven precluded a harelip, just as the casting of Joel McCrea in *Dead End* (1937) precluded his being the cripple of Sidney Kingsley's play.

Once Greene's setting was changed to San Francisco, Maltz scoured the city for authentic sites; his 114-page treatment (21 July 1941) is unusual in including snapshots of the sort of dilapidated boardinghouse in which Raven might live, a deserted Pullman car, railroad yards, footbridges, and gas works, all of which appear in the film.

While *This Gun for Hire* was a respectable movie melodrama, it lacked the novel's apocalyptic mood. As the summer of 1941 moved into autumn, the script acquired more World War II aspects. The villain is made an executive in a chemical cartel, planning to sell a poison gas formula to an unnamed foreign country—which after 7 December was no longer anonymous; whatever is sold to that country is, as Ellen Graham (the Anne Chowder of the novel) puts it, "Japanese breakfast food for Americans." Ellen is a World War II Mata Hari, like the heroines of *Paris Calling* (1941), *Tonight We Raid Calais* (1943), *First Comes Courage* (1943), and—the most famous—*Notorious* (1946), who are recruited because of their looks. Ellen even becomes so *engagée* that she gives Raven a pep talk: "This war is everybody's business, yours too."

Raven was a problem for Maltz. Greene saw nothing inconsistent in his being a killer and a Christ figure who, like his prototype, undergoes betrayal, passion, and death. The Catholic left, however, is not the Marxist left; and Maltz, even if he could have retained the Christ parallels, simply did not think in such terms. He saw Raven rather as a victim of society and thus found the context for Raven's criminality in his family background: a father who was hanged and a mother who cut her own throat. Although Greene makes little of the parents, Maltz believed they were the key to Raven's character. He planned to open the film with an expressionistic dream in which Raven, gripping a bloody icepick, runs through a forest of gibbets over which his mother's spirit hovers. He would have ended the film with a similar dream—of the terrible mother's face dissolving into Ellen's, a transformation allowing Raven to die in peace.

Since studios customarily assigned more than one writer to a film, each being unaware of the other's involvement, Paramount gave Maltz's 21 July 1941 treatment to veteran screenwriter W.R. Burnett, who was so influenced by it that his script concluded, like Maltz's, with the mother's face dissolving into Ellen's. In the actual film, for which Maltz and Burnett shared screenplay credit, there is neither an opening nor a closing dream and thus no final dissolve. Ellen betrays Raven, though not intentionally: her trail of face powder brings the police to him. Still, when Raven asks, "Did I do all right for you?" she nods. The Raven of the film dies with a smile on his face, whereas in the novel, his death is far from sentimental: "Death came to him in the form of unbearable pain. It was as if he had to deliver this pain as a woman delivers a child, and he sobbed and moaned in the effort. At last it came out of him and he followed his only child into a vast desolation."[9]

After *This Gun for Hire*, Maltz moved from Paramount to Warner Brothers where he was assigned to *Destination, Tokyo* (1943), for which Delmer Daves, the screenwriter-director, had done the first script; Maltz made changes in his own handwriting, as was his custom.[10]

Daves's basic plot included a scene in which a submarine pharmacist's mate removes a sailor's appendix by following instructions in a medical text. This dramatic incident was based on fact: a similar operation, performed aboard a submarine in 1942, was reported in the *Chicago Daily News* and other papers, reprinted in the *Reader's Digest*, and made the basis of a 1943 radio drama by Ranald MacDougall. The radio version disturbed Warner's legal department, but the incident had been too well publicized for a plagiarism charge. In any case, it was the one memorable sequence in the movie; the rest was wartime pietism. Christmas caroling makes it seem that everyone in the service was Christian; with a pretentious speech on the immortality of the soul, the pharmacist's mate, formerly a skeptic, is converted after the success of the appendectomy.

Maltz's contribution to *Destination, Tokyo* consisted mainly of blue-penciling some dialogue in the appendectomy sequence; humanizing the skipper (indifferently played by Cary Grant) by giving him a touching speech in which he recalls taking his four-year-old son for his first haircut; and inserting a salute to Mother Russia for comrades expecting it: a sailor whose uncle, a professor of philosophy in Greece, had been killed by the Nazis, remarks, "I read where a Russian guerrilla gets hanged and I think of my uncle." One wonders what paper he was reading.

Maltz's next film for Warner Brothers was both his best screenplay and a World War II movie still capable of moving an audience. *Pride of the Marines* (1945) was not any easy film to write; the plot appealed to all of Maltz's social instincts and to none of his aesthetic ones. As was often the case in Hollywood, Maltz was not the studio's first choice.[11] In March 1943 producer Jerry Wald had sent Al Besserides and Alvah Bessie a *Life* magazine article on Al Schmid, a Marine who had been blinded at Guadalcanal in 1942. Bessie and Besserides wrote a 26-page treatment, "The Al Schmid Story," that included a few scenes which eventually appeared in the film—the meeting of Ruth and Al, for example, and the Sunday dinner interrupted by the news of Pearl Harbor.

Exactly how Maltz became involved in *Pride of the Marines* is uncertain; perhaps because Bessie was needed for *The Very Thought of You*. Whatever the reason, by September 1943, Maltz was the screenwriter. At first he wanted to write the great proletarian film; it would start with Schmid as a street-smart kid tackling the local toughs and forcing them to recite "all men are created equal" while "bumping their foreheads on a democratic pavement."[12] Eventually, Maltz decided that giving bullies a lesson in equal rights was more characteristic of a scrapper from New York's Lower East Side than a Philadelphian of German-Irish extraction. Even so, he had not given up on using Al Schmid's story to illustrate the virtues of democracy. When the grenade that blinds Schmid is thrown into the machine gun nest, Maltz specified, an American Indian and a Jew should be in the same emplacement: "This is the meaning of America in the best sense, and an answer to the wolfish malice by which some people scorn others on a racist basis."[13] Exactly how their presence would minimize racism, especially since Schmid is the one who gets blinded, is uncertain; Maltz did not get an American Indian, only a Jew, Lee Diamond.

Diamond (Dane Clark) is an excellent foil for Schmid (John Garfield); it is Diamond who jolts his friend out of self-pity. It was also through Diamond that Maltz was able to introduce a theme that would recur in *Crossfire*, *The Best Years of Our Lives*, and *Till the End of Time*: the impossibility of recapturing the camaraderie of military life in postwar America. In a veterans' hospital, when Al, Lee, and other wounded marines wonder if their former jobs—however menial—will still be available for them, the racism that had been dormant in battle emerges: one marine assumes that his job has probably gone to a Mexican. When he realizes that one of his fellow patients is Mexican, he hurriedly adds, "But you're not like the other Mexicans." "I'm just a Mexican" is the disspirited reply. To Lee, returning to civilian life means facing anti-Semitism again; he is not sanguine about being back in an America where "there's guys who won't hire me because my name is Diamond instead of Jones, because I celebrate Passover instead of Easter."

Jerry Wald was deeply impressed by Maltz's script, as was John Gassner, who wrote Maltz to apologize for not including it in *The Best Film Plays of 1945-46*.[14] Frank Sinatra was also taken with the film: "You're the best goddam writer around," he exclaimed, referring to both *Pride of the Marines* and *The House I Live In* (1945), a promotional short that Maltz had written around Sinatra's song by that name.[15] In the short, Sinatra slips off into the alley for a smoke during a break in a recording session at the very moment some grade school Wasps are beating up a "dirty ———"; the noun is never uttered because Sinatra cuts the loudmouth off before he can say it and Sinatra gives the group a lecture on anti-Semitism before singing the title song.

Maltz did one last film for Warner Brothers, with Ring Lardner, Jr., as co-writer. The significance of *Cloak and Dagger* (1946) is not its having been written by two of the Ten but Warner's inability to release, intact, a movie that was simultaneously an attack on fascism, a tribute to the Italian Communist resistance, an exaggerated account of Germany's attempt to manufacture an atomic bomb, and a plea that the atomic age would not get off to as bad a start as Hiroshima seemed to indicate.

It is not always possible to distinguish Lardner's contribution from Maltz's, especially since they did not work together. Knowing Maltz's interest in resistance movements as revealed in *The Cross and the Arrow*, one might conclude that the Italian partisans' subplot was his and the main plot was Lardner's: an American physicist loosely modeled on J. Robert Oppenheimer is persuaded to defer work on the Manhattan Project (as if it were that simple) and embark for Europe to learn how the Nazis are progressing with their A-bomb. When the physicist arrives in Italy, the plot, never probable to begin with, revives at least momentarily when he makes contact with the partisans. One of them, forcefully played by Lilli Palmer, declares: "In this work we're comrades; we share." If this is Marxism, it has been diluted to such a watery base that it flows into the democratic mainstream.

Cloak and Dagger is a film of subplots, all of which are more interesting than the physicist's story. The third subplot would have shown the existence of Nazi atomic bomb factories, thereby vindicating Albert Einstein's 1939 letter to President Roosevelt, urging him to produce an atomic bomb before the Nazis could do so. Despite having as technical adviser a former OSS operative, Michael Burke (the same Burke who was president of the New York Yankees, 1966-73, and later of the New York Knickerbockers), Cloak and Dagger would have proved an embarrassment, if it had been released as written.[16] The screenplay had the Nazis conducting atomic research in four underground caves on the order of the rocket factories at Peenemünde. When the Nazis realize they have lost the war, they destroy three of the factories and dismantle the fourth for shipment to either Argentina or Spain—no one seems certain; perhaps Lardner and Maltz could not decide whether Peron or Franco would host the Fourth Reich.

Burke must have told the writers that Manhattan Project chief Leslie Groves had formed an investigative team late in 1943 to make contact with physicists in Naples in order to determine the extent of Germany's nuclear progress. The team learned nothing, however, because the Nazis had not confided in the Italians. What Burke could not tell Maltz and Lardner, because he did not know it, was that Nazi Germany had no atomic bomb. "The furthest German progress," historians tell us, "was a small experimental atomic pile that [Werner] Heisenberg had built in a brewery in the Swabian Alps. Because of a lack of enriched uranium, he had not even been able to start it up."[17] Ironically, in 1943, the year in which Cloak and Dagger is set, it was the Soviet Union that had just infiltrated the Manhattan Project.

Maltz and Lardner, who were premature antinuclear activists in addition to being early antifascists, intended to end Cloak and Dagger with a prayer. The physicist, realizing that we now live in the penumbra of the mushroom cloud, cries: "God have mercy on us if we ever thought we could really keep science a secret—or even wanted to. God have mercy on us if we think we can wage other wars without destroying ourselves, and God have mercy on us if we haven't the sense to keep the world at peace." This is how the film concluded when it was shown at a special critics' screening in August 1946. However, the version seen by the general public ends with the physicist's return to the United States and his promise to come back to the partisan in whose bed he slept because he was too tall for her couch (the physicist is played by Gary Cooper). Warner Brothers apparently realized the implications of the final speech: America might not have the sense to bottle up the genie it had liberated on 6 August 1945. Once the physicist's prayer was excised, the atomic subplot on which it depended had to go with it—and that is exactly what happened. Consequently, *Cloak and Dagger* became what its title implies: an espionage melodrama.

The Naked City (1948), Maltz's most famous screenplay, does not happen to be his best. The fame of the film is due to three factors: the authentic New York setting, the semidocumentary style, and the television series spinoff. Maltz worked from an original story by Malvin Wald, with whom he shared screen credit. What was basically an investigation of a homicide (by 1948 standards, a sensational one: a blonde found dead in a bathtub) became an occasionally pretentious and ambivalent portrait of a New York where life goes on amid death and violence—and because it does go on, and naked babies are born every minute into a naked city, there is always hope. Maltz determined the dispassionate tone whose visual equivalent would be an objective camera recording the "rich and infinite detail of the daily life of New York."[18] As usual, Maltz wanted more detail than most moviegoers would care to see, such as "an alley cat digging for its food in an open garbage pail."[19] The scavenging cat did not make it to the final cut, but much of Maltz's contributions did, particularly the off-screen narration by a disembodied voice—a combined alter ego, confidant, and conscience commenting on the action and even speaking to the characters in a language that vacillates between the urban vernacular and the urban poetic. The former does not wear well; even in 1948, when a voice from nowhere asked, "How are your feet holding out?" there were more than a few titters from the audience.

The Naked City was Maltz's last screen credit for twenty-two years; coincidentally, Universal gave him his last pre-blacklist credit as well as his first post-blacklist one, *Two Mules for Sister Sara* (1970). The blacklist cost him his credit for *The Robe* (1953); Maltz's collection at the State Historical Society of Wisconsin contains a script with the following note: "I wrote the original screenplay of *The Robe* in 1945-46. For reasons over which the producer had no control, the film was not able to be produced until 1952. In the interval the blacklist came into effect and my name was removed from the script."[20]

For the most part, Maltz is correct. In the early spring of 1945, though Jerry Wald was loath to see him go, Maltz left Warner Brothers for RKO—not because he felt more comfortable in the company of Adrian Scott and Edward Dmytryk but because he was writing the script of The Robe for independent producer Frank Ross (who had produced the Academy Award–winning short, The House I Live In, also an RKO release). Ross had purchased Lloyd C. Douglas's novel in 1945 and planned to release it through RKO.

It seems that Adrian Scott, who was to have been The Robe's associate producer, was quite critical of Maltz's 272-page script (21 August 1945), noting that it emphasized Christianity not as a way of life but as a religion of miracles. Maltz toiled over the script, writing three versions within a year, the last of which (11 December 1946) was shortened by 70 pages.

At this point Maltz's involvement ended; the following year his screenwriting career as well would virtually end, except for a brief comeback in the early 1970s. Philip Dunne recalls in his autobiography that Ross, unable to obtain financing for The Robe from RKO, approached Fox in the early 1950s. Zanuck agreed to a Fox release if Dunne rewrote the script, which Dunne assumed had been written by Ross. Not until the early 1970s did he learn that it was the work of a blacklisted writer, but even then he did not know which one. In 1953, when Dunne informed Ross that his revision of the script merited only co-credit, Ross insisted that his own name should appear only once—as producer—and Dunne had no choice but to accept sole credit for a script he had only revised.

Dunne is quite explicit about the changes he made: "I improved some of the characterizations, eliminated some of the religious hokum, interpolated some authentic Roman history, and sharpened the drama."[21] Unlike many filmmakers who suffer from selective memory, Dunne offers an honest assessment of his contribution to Maltz's script, as an examination of the production file in UCLA's Fox collection reveals. Zanuck considered Dunne's first-draft continuity (18 July 1952) an improvement on the original but wanted less talk: "I think we should examine every word of dialogue with a view to making cuts. I don't mean just taking out whole speeches; I mean taking out words, even two or three words in speeches. I think if we can tell this story with a minimum of talk it will be all to the good."[22] Dunne certainly rendered Maltz's script more succinct. He also clarified the time period, limiting the action to the last five years of Tiberius's reign so that the film could end with the accession of Caligula in 37 A.D. He deleted Maltz's scholarly explanation of Messianism and deemphasized Christ's miracles, believing they would detract from the main theme: the effect of Christ's robe on the tribune Marcellus.

But Dunne kept Maltz's narrative structure, his preliminary off-screen narration, and his handling of Marcellus's outbidding Caligula

for the slave Demetrius; Christ's triumphal entry into Jerusalem on
Palm Sunday; Demetrius's conversion to Christianity; Demetrius's encounter with Judas on the eve of Christ's death; the powerful crucifix-
ion scene with Christ's voice echoing through the thunder, "Father
forgive them; they know not what they do"; Marcellus's winning the
robe in a dice game at the foot of the cross and its transforming effect on
him; Marcellus's meeting with the Christians at Cana, an event that
brings about his own conversion; and Diana's embracing Christianity
and her decision to share Marcellus's fate.

Access to Maltz's adaptation would have simplified any screenwriter's task; Maltz incorporated the novel's major episodes, even
reproducing the conclusion in which Caligula scoffs at Diana and
Marcellus for choosing death: "They are going into a better kingdom!
They are going now to meet their king!" As the couple walk past the
raving emperor, Diana stops and hands the robe to the slave Mancipor,
speaking the novel's last line: "For the Big Fisherman."

When *The Robe* opened in the fall of 1953, Maltz's fortunes were at
their lowest ebb: "I am robbed of my ability to practice the art of
screenwriting where my work had previously been sought."[23]

Although fiction writing seemed open to him, he began to wonder
whether the blacklist had not also imperiled his future as a novelist.
In March 1949 Fox purchased his 1949 novel, *The Journey of Simon
McKeever*, for $35,000. At the beginning of April the trade papers
announced that Daniel Fuchs and John Collier would write the screenplay with Jules Dassin directing, Sol Siegel producing, and probably
Walter Brennan starring. On April 10 Zanuck suddenly did an about-
face, citing "heavy clamor from the public," although the clamor came
mainly from the right-wing Motion Picture Alliance for the Preservation of American Ideals. Yet Fox could never have acquired the novel,
nor could production details have been announced, without Zanuck's
permission. One can only conclude that despite the Waldorf Statement, which Fox had endorsed, Zanuck originally assumed that it applied to a blacklisted writer's screenplay but not a blacklisted writer's
novel. Still, even Zanuck knew the futility of kicking against the goad.
Maltz tried to enlist the aid of the Screen Writers Guild, arguing that it
was bad enough his screenplays could not be filmed without having his
novels suffer the same fate. The Guild did nothing. As for Zanuck, it
was sufficient that Fox was releasing *Forbidden Street* in 1949 with Ring
Lardner, Jr., listed as screenwriter; one act of daring a year was enough.

Maltz was partially correct about being a blacklisted novelist. Although *The Cross and the Arrow* had been distributed to 140,000 servicemen in a special Armed Forces edition during World War II, he soon
discovered that 1954 was not 1944. In 1954 he submitted *A Long Day in a
Short Life* to Little, Brown, which had published his first three novels;

not only did Little, Brown reject it, but so did other houses as well. Three years later it came out under the imprint of International Publishers, which had brought out his first collection of short stories.

In 1960 Maltz had reason to hope that his blacklisting was over: three months after the *New York Times* announced that Trumbo had been hired for *Exodus*, Frank Sinatra took out a full-page ad in *Variety* (28 March 1960), stating that Maltz would write the screenplay of *The Execution of Private Slovik*. Two weeks later Sinatra took out another full-page ad, conceding that "the American public had indicated it feels the morality of hiring Albert Maltz is the more crucial matter, and I will accept the majority decision." It did not seem to matter that there was no majority decision; most Americans would have had no idea who Albert Maltz and Eddie Slovik were. Maltz had been twice betrayed, first by Zanuck and then by Sinatra—the same Sinatra who, after seeing *Pride of the Marines*, had written to Maltz: "I have never been so emotionally moved by anything. . . . I know you *do* understand that my anxiety and interest in our social and discrimination (or what have you) problems have been hungrily awaiting such valuable assistance. . . . You've got to hit 'em right in the kisser with it and, baby, you really did."[24] Maltz did; Sinatra could not.

By the mid-1960s when there was less paranoia about hiring blacklisted writers, some studios began making overtures to Maltz. MGM asked him to revise a Robert Presnell, Jr., screenplay about Simon Bolivar, but it was never filmed either in Presnell's or in Maltz's version. Universal contemplated a film version of Ethel Waters's autobiography, *His Eye Is on the Sparrow*. Maltz spent three weeks trying to adapt it and then gave up. He admired Waters but felt that her religious views would inhibit him, especially since she would be scrutinizing the drafts. Maltz's Universal connection was producer Julian Blaustein, who asked Maltz to update his own *A Long Day in a Short Life* so that the main character would be a Vietnam veteran. Maltz wrote an overlong treatment and then an elaborate book-length draft in which he virtually retold his novel; nothing ever came of the project. It seems that whatever Maltz attempted was doomed to failure. Part of the problem was his inability to do hack work. When he was offered the script of *The Great Bank Robbery*, he noted in pencil that it was wrong for him: "I must get some philosophical depth here."[25] But what depth could there be in a western spoof starring Zero Mostel?

Maltz's relationship with Blaustein finally bore fruit, however, for it was Universal that gave him his first screen credit in over two decades. For Don Siegel's *Two Mules for Sister Sara* (1970) Maltz resurrected one of his favorite character types: the apathetic hero who acquires a political conscience—in this instance, an American mercenary (Clint Eastwood) who turns activist when he teams up with a whore masquerading as a nun (Shirley MacLaine), whose objective is to drive the French out of Mexico. When she persuades the mercenary to blow up a French garrison, the plan swells into a group endeavor with the Juaristas concealing dynamite sticks inside piñatas, which traditionally contain candy.

Maltz was next signed to write another film for Eastwood that would also be directed by Siegel and produced by Universal; in *The Beguiled* (1971) a Union soldier takes refuge in a southern girls' school, where his presence becomes a sexual threat as well as a sexual release. Maltz's screenplay (3 September 1969) was as elaborate as the one he had put together for *This Gun for Hire*, with photos and illustrations; the *Beguiled* script contained a floor plan of the school and a diagram of the grounds.[26] Even so, Siegel disliked it; writing to Eastwood a few weeks later, he complained that Maltz "is not with the story. He sees it as a kind of pale *Forever Amber* or *Raintree County*. He wrote it in a mid-Victorian style, the dialogue at times quite stilted. There's not near enough excitement, suspense, terror. It must be macabre, horrific in its intensity."[27]

"Mid-Victorian" is the wrong designation for Maltz's style, which mixed the language of Southern gentility ("I'm a Quaker, ma'am. . . . I carry bandages into battle, not a weapon") with the vernacular ("You don't want a man to have balls"). More important, Maltz had envisaged a drama of political (Union/Confederacy) and sexual (uninhibited male/repressed female) confrontations, with strong antiwar overtones and parallels with the French Resistance as the women hide the soldier from the authorities for reasons ranging from lust to compassion. Since at least two other writers revised Maltz's script (not to mention Siegel), Maltz had his name removed from the credits.

Had the blacklist not occurred, Maltz might well have enjoyed a dual career in fiction and screenwriting. Although he wrote only five novels, it is evident in his third, *The Journey of Simon McKeever*, that he had learned to make the length of the narrative commensurate with the theme. *Simon McKeever* is Maltz's most satisfying work; it is really a novella, a form that suited him. The screenplay had taught him the art of compression, which enabled him to distill the essence of an action—too fragile for expansion and too limited for a full-scale treatment—into a narrative whose length was determined by its significance. In *Simon McKeever* Maltz returned to an earlier character type, the hitchhiker; but unlike the dying miner of "The Man on the Road," Simon encounters more than one driver. He has access to a cross section of America, so that his odyssey results in knowledge of self, other, and society.

The novella was inspired by Maltz's encounter with an Irishman from the county poorhouse in Sacramento, who was hitchhiking to Los Angeles in the hope of locating a doctor who would cure him of crippling arthritis. Maltz understood that to be an odyssey in the mythic sense, the man's journey would require the same diversity that characterizes other odysseys, from Homer's to John Cheever's "The Swimmer" and Horton Foote's *The Trip to Bountiful*. If the road is a microcosm, those who travel it should represent humanity in all its variety and extremes. Simon accordingly encounters the self-absorbed, the malevolent, the mad, the uneducated humanized by nature, and the educated humanized by knowledge. Simon, an erratic reader familiar with Upton Sinclair, Walt Whitman, Mark Twain, and Jack London, comes upon Havelock Ellis's *The Dance of Life*, whose thesis of life as art spurs Simon to consider a reply, to be called *The Path of Life*, which would be the blue-collar application of white-collar theory. While life may be an art, some lives, like Simon's, are an applied art—a science.

Such a book would require a far greater command of language than Simon possesses, yet in his dreams he can be eloquent. Whether *The Path of Life* will be a dream fulfilled or an unachieved goal is irrelevant; Simon has succeeded in at least one undertaking: hitchhiking four hundred miles. Although he learns that his condition is untreatable and will in fact worsen, he is not defeated. At the close of the novella he returns to the poorhouse (or "rest home" as it is called) on his own terms, which include access to a library where he can research his book.

Maltz's achievement in *Simon McKeever* can best be appreciated by a comparison with an early short story, "The Happiest Man on Earth" (1938), with which it shares certain characteristics.[28] While the story was an O. Henry Memorial Award winner, it is really a vignette about economic injustice, and not for one of its five pages is the reader allowed to forget it. Like *Simon McKeever*, "The Happiest Man on Earth" also concerns an odyssey, but because of the story's brevity, Jesse's journey on foot from Kansas City to Tulsa is over when the story begins. Thus there is no narrative variety, only a dialogue between Jesse and his brother-in-law, whom he begs for a job. To regain his self-respect, Jesse is even willing to risk his life transporting nitroglycerine. Maltz intimates that Jesse's eagerness to do such work is the effect of economic fatalism, the death wish that the Great Depression provoked in the unemployed, but the suggestion is never pursued because Maltz ignores whatever would deflect the narrative from the paths of pathos. While Simon and Jesse are both grating in their stubbornness, Simon never descends to self-pity; Jesse does, with a whine that Maltz could not turn into a lament. Nor could he cease imposing collective guilt: a life-threatening job makes Jesse the happiest man on earth; his brother-in-law—and, by extension, the reader—the most wretched.

In *Simon McKeever*, Maltz has raised proletarian fiction to an art, an accomplishment most writers of working-class fiction would envy: had he done so a decade earlier and continued in that vein, Jack Salzman could have ended his monograph by calling Maltz not "one of the finest writers of social protest literature"[29]—a limited form with a limited number of worthwhile exponents—but one of the finest practitioners of the social novel. In *Simon McKeever* Maltz is not protesting; he is portraying, and portraying artistically. Except for a few words like "arthureetis," he abandoned the phonetic vernacular, emphasizing instead the rhythmic speech of the common man which, when heightened and cadenced, makes him a natural poet. The most poetic language in the novel occurs in one of Simon's dreams. In the waking state, Simon could never have been so articulate about the universe; in his dream—or what Nietzsche would call his Apollonian—state, Simon is at his most eloquent, maintaining that we may never be able to know others, but we can know the principle of continuity by which life proceeds and the evolutionary chain by which it is maintained: "Not for you to know of me or me of you. But to know the big thing only— the turning earth and the generations up from the apes, walking the path, striving and standing up, shouting and singing. I believe it . . . it aches in my heart. And all by the doing of people like us, it's the fine wonder of it."[30]

Maltz was forced to defer any further refinement of his writing until he had served his sentence. Unfortunately, the novel that came out of his prison experience, *A Long Day in a Short Life*, was a return to the narrative bloat of *The Underground Stream*; his ten months in the federal prison camp in Mill Point, West Virginia, made him so conscious of injustice that he resumed his 1930s role of social protester. In fact, *A Long Day* is a 1930s-style novel, passé in the mid-1950s when it was published; later generations, if they read it, will regard it as an extreme account of a miscarriage of justice and therefore the exception, not the rule. By contrast, though the days of the Okies are also past, *The Grapes of Wrath* is still read and will continue to be read because the myth, the journey to the promised land, is strong enough to support a narrative whose historical inspiration is barely a page in the history texts.

Unlike *Simon McKeever, Long Day* is mythless. Its most distinctive feature is its cinematic structure—montage conversations, flashbacks, and the intercutting of two stories: of Floyd Varney, who went to bed with the wrong woman and accidentally killed her husband when he discovered them together; and of Huey Wilson, a black youth who defended himself with a "deadly weapon"—his feet—when attacked by white toughs. The road was a metaphor for America's diversity in *Simon McKeever*; the prison is a metaphor for America's labyrinthine underside in *Long Day*.

The opening is promising. Facing the title page is a breakdown of the cell blocks showing prisoner, cell number, charge, sentence, and status. The reader enters the prison as if guided by the camera eye, which slowly pans the first tier of cells until it stops at Varney, half asleep in his bunk: "From where he lay he could see a small section of the cell block, as through a camera lens, and the scene was not without a certain cold, sombre beauty. The blend of night shadow and dim electric light, playing over austere lines and polished steel surfaces, over the expanse of immaculate floor and outer wall, had the quality and mood of fine chiaroscuro in a painting."[31]

Nothing else matches the opening description. Had Maltz limited himself to the stories of Varney and Wilson—who never meet, because the prison is segregated—*Long Day* would have been as tautly constructed as *Simon McKeever*, and as effective. Instead, he provided parallel subplots to a main action that itself is parallel; even if the result were narrative symmetry, which it is not, it would have been achieved at too great a price: the reader's lack of interest in any characters other than Varney and Wilson. While Maltz's dialect no longer stuns the eye and his reproduction of black English is uncannily accurate, he is again putting the thesis before the story, as evidenced early in the novel by italics that leave one no choice but to connect cause and effect: "His [Wilson's] father never had had schooling beyond four grades *because* he was a Negro; and his uncle had died on a Louisiana chain gang *because* he was a Negro; and his own namesake, his great grandfather, had been shot down on the streets of New Orleans *because* he was a Negro asking for equal rights for his people" (99).

Coming to *Long Day* after *Simon McKeever*, one is naturally disappointed. Perhaps in a career in which so much time was expended on ideology and antifascism, one perfect novel and a near perfect one are all a reader should ask for. The near perfect novel was his last, *A Tale of One January* (1966). Maltz needed a combination of financial security, a sense of self-worth, and recognition to do his best work. It is hardly coincidental that he produced a gem of a novella before he was blacklisted and a gemlike one when the blacklist was about to end for him (at least to the extent that his name was no longer anathema to the studios).

A Tale of One January is just that, a telling of an event: namely, the escape of six inmates—two women, four men—from Auschwitz in mid-January 1945. While the setting might have given *Tale* greater significance than any of his other works, Maltz took his title literally, writing an even shorter (by almost a hundred pages) novella than *Simon McKeever*. Having reduced the narrative to the length of a tale, Maltz chose to emphasize character over place, the group over the individual, and sexual tension over camaraderie: each of the women responds to the male presence in a different way, Lini by giving herself to one of the men, Claire by refraining not out of propriety but because Auschwitz has unsexed her.

Like *Simon McKeever, Tale* sustains interest to the end—which Maltz's other novels do not: in *Long Day,* Varney's suicide is as inevitable as Princey's death in *The Underground Stream;* in *The Cross and the Arrow,* the reason finally given for Wegler's betrayal of the Reich is not worth the wait. In *Tale,* on the other hand, though the six hope they will be rescued by the Russians, the denouement cannot be anticipated. The men are captured by the Nazis; the women, assumed to be Polish civilians, are left undisturbed. The tale, then, comes full circle: it began with the women, and it ends with them; the women, the first to escape, are the only ones to be rescued—by the Russians, as it happens.

Maltz lived for almost two decades after completing *A Tale of One January,* yet he never published another novel (a sixth, "Bel Canto" about the French Resistance, was supposedly finished at the time of his death in 1985, but whether it will see print is another matter). Maltz's screenwriting career also ended relatively early with *Scalawag* (1973), a Western reworking of *Treasure Island* which may be significant for Kirk Douglas's directorial debut but little else. The blacklist reduced Maltz to a writer of occasional fiction, and the frustration of being a nonperson took such a toll that even when he was no longer blacklisted, he could not regain his former drive. One would have thought that in 1968 when the *Saturday Evening Post* published two of his stories, "The Prisoner's Dog" and "The Spoils of War," under his own name, he would start writing prolifically again.[32] That never happened, however, even though the stories, written in the lapidary style of *A Tale of One January,* are his best; the language moves freely, and events occur uncontrivedly.

Both stories have a World War II background, and their outcome can no more be anticipated than that of *Tale.* In "The Prisoner's Dog," a Great Dane and his master are both conscripted by the Nazis, who train the dog to kill but cannot turn it against its master; the dog dies helping him escape. In "The Spoils of War," Maltz returned to one of the themes of *The Cross and the Arrow*: the Nazis' despoliation of the homes in which they had been quartered. The story is a postwar encounter between a Nazi who had occupied the apartment of a French family and a member of that family who finds himself a dinner guest in the Nazi's home. The chance encounter of former oppressor and oppressed is a difficult plot to execute; it works because Maltz wrote not a revenge tale but a cat-and-mouse game. The guest gradually reveals his identity and regains the paintings the Nazi had taken from his family. The character's satisfaction is only momentary, however, and a younger Maltz would have had him agonize over his action, berating himself for not taking revenge. Instead, the guest leaves without so much as an antifascist outburst. It took Maltz a lifetime to learn the art of restraint, yet once he had mastered it, he was no longer able to use it.

Toward the end of his life, he began to wonder whether the Party had not consumed valuable time that could have been spent more profitably in writing. Naturally, the Party had, yet Maltz's works have not gone unnoticed. His drama and fiction may not be discussed in general histories of the American stage or the American novel, but they are treated in studies of the theater of the Great Depression (Malcolm Goldstein's *The Political Stage*, Gerald Rabkin's *Drama and Commitment*) and the radical novel (Walter Rideout's *The Radical Novel in the United States, 1900-1954*). Could he have done more? In the *New Masses* for 12 February 1946 Maltz posed the question, "What Shall We Ask of Writers?" His answer, in brief, was that they should be judged on their merits, not on their politics; in other words, he was challenging the Party's axiom that art is a class weapon. Art is art, something the radical left, in its eagerness to enlist writers in the class struggle, failed to realize. But when Maltz's essay drew cries of protest from his comrades, he recanted in the same journal (9 April 1946), behaving, in a sense, no differently from Darryl F. Zanuck or Frank Sinatra.

There is no assurance that subordinating ideology to art would have made Maltz a better writer, but perhaps had he done so, posterity would not have had to wonder whether Albert Maltz was a case of unfulfilled promise.

6 ALVAH BESSIE
The Eternal Brigadier

Even the most militant supporters of the Ten would have to admit that Alvah Bessie's contribution to the American film—one original screen story and four scripts, all written from 1943 to 1947—is minor. Thus he cannot be accused of parlaying notoriety into celebrity; moreover, his screenwriting career had virtually ended in 1945—two years before the HUAC investigation—when Jack Warner fired him, allegedly for supporting the Conference of Studio Unions (CSU) strike. Any subsequent offers came not from major studios but from independent producers; that his last screen credit, *Smart Woman* (1948), was such an assignment reveals the extent of his options.

Bessie's forte was literature, not film; there was no reason for his coming to Hollywood except the usual one: money. After graduating from Columbia in 1924 with a B.A. in English and French, he drifted into the arts, first into the theater. For four years (1924-28) he acted and stage-managed; among other productions, he appeared in O'Neill's *Lazarus Laughed* (1928). During that period he realized that his talent lay not in acting but in writing. Like others of his generation he went to Paris, where he did rewrite work on the *Paris-Times;* it was in Paris that Bessie wrote his first short story, "Redbird" (1929).

If Bessie had worked seriously instead of intermittently at short fiction, he might have been able to turn a skill into an art; he had a gift that cannot be acquired but only cultivated: a love of storytelling. Occasionally, love became infatuation, not with self but with style, sometimes resulting in language that reads like a bad translation from the Latin: "There was still the final ritual to complete before he could let go, for since he had sketched in certain unattractive aspects of his married life in justification of his treachery, there still remained to erect the sophistry by whose aid he sought to expiate the mute desertion of his responsibilities, the cruelty of this silent ruthless criticism that his wife . . . was powerless to answer."[1] So many words, and the wrong ones, to delineate a doctor in midlife crisis.

Such neo-Jamesian puffery, fortunately, is sporadic; Bessie generally finds the right rhythms, the proper inflections, and the appropriate images to make stock themes—youthful disillusionment, the dis-

solution of a marriage, the transition from boyhood to manhood—
seem less familiar. A boy yearning to be a man is a would-be her-
petologist who writes so poetically of water snakes ("sliding volup-
tuously . . . like a stream of heavy lubricating oil") that his foray into
nature is merely a stopover on the road to being a writer ("The Serpent
Was More Subtil," 1982). An errant husband tries to interest a woman
in sharing a bottle with him, only to learn that she thinks he is someone
else ("Call It Love," 1941); an adolescent abandons his idol when the
idol dims his aura by revealing his weakness for women ("The Snake
Friend," 1982). In "Profession of Pain" (1935) Bessie brings to a comic
routine (a comedian could easily do the story as a monologue) the
spontaneity and art of a tall tale: an addict desperate for drugs feigns
nephrolithiasis so convincingly that a doctor removes one of his kid-
neys, not realizing that the addict will do anything in order to be
admitted to a hospital.

Despite his affinity for and mastery of the form, Bessie published
short stories sporadically: twelve between 1929 and 1935, seven between 1936 and 1941. In 1935 he turned to the novel but never achieved
the same degree of artistry. His first, *Dwell in the Wilderness* (1935),
traces the fortunes of a midwestern family over half a century, from the
1870s to the 1920s. Neither art novel nor pulp, it straddles social realism
and romanticism without really being in the same league as *The Magnificent Ambersons* and *Winesburg, Ohio*.

It was a respectable debut, revealing a writer who was well read
and not afraid to show it; quotations and allusions are interspersed
with letters, journal entries, and interior monologues. Yet for all his
knowledge of literature, Bessie was baffled by the novel form; long
fiction was too diffuse and its techniques too exacting for one who
could not sustain a lengthy narrative. Events that should have been
dramatized are related; the incidental frequently overshadows the
essential; cause and effect are separated, not in the nineteenth-century
way of withholding information and providing it piecemeal but by
allowing a situation to occur and offering an explanation later, almost as
an afterthought. The style ranges from the flat and colloquial to the
quaint and archaic; thoughts are often joined by a chain of hyphens,
and images cascade like a fall whose waters tumble noisily but without
grace: "the night came back with its idyllic background of early fireflies
in the shaded woods and flower-scents, heightened and intensified to
almost unbearable proportions by the mounting excitement of abandon and then ruptured and heightened and increased by the pain and
undercurrent of small, recognizable and torturing delight with its
foretaste of unallowed ecstasy."[2]

Although Bessie had difficulty curbing his muse, he could write
unaffectedly, even poignantly, when the occasion demanded. While

there is no real protagonist in *Dwell in the Wilderness*, Bessie's sympathies are clearly with Eben, a failure who, to get work, leaves his family and moves to Detroit where his prospects are no brighter. Unemployed and living in a rooming house, Eben writes to his wife (who is as sexually repressed as their daughter is sexually liberated), explaining that he cannot send the usual check and instead requesting money from her. The language is that of a man not yet broken but hardly proud, using his best English to make his petition less pathetic: *"I would like to know, my dear, if I might apply to you for some temporary assistance—two hundred dollars would tide me over the next few months, until I could find work again. I have held a few odd jobs, nothing to boast about, so if you could see your way clear to help me, I would be very grateful to you"* (212-13).

Six years elapsed before Bessie published another novel. The year after *Dwell in the Wilderness* appeared, the single most important event in his life occurred: the outbreak of the Spanish Civil War, in which he served as a member of the Abraham Lincoln Battalion of the Fourteenth International Brigade. Bessie saw himself as the war's chronicler, first with *Men in Battle* (1939), then with an anthology of poems and essays called *The Heart of Spain* (1952), and finally with *Spain Again* (1975).

Had Bessie sustained the level of excellence he reached in *Men in Battle*, he could have been a major writer. Even so, *Men in Battle* will keep Bessie's name alive; it is one of the few books on the Spanish Civil War (writing about which has become an industry in itself) that explains why this conflict was different from others. The title is a partial explanation; the book is about men—males—who are so conscious of their manhood that they speak of a less virile comrade as "more of a woman than a man." Bessie does this, too, yet he is never contemptuous of those less masculine than himself; rather, their fragility enhances his manhood. Manhood, its expression and apotheosis, was one of the reasons Bessie and so many others went to Spain: "There were two major reasons for my being there; to achieve self-integration, and to lend my individual strength (such as it was) to the fight against our eternal enemy—oppression; and the validity of the second reason was not impaired by the fact that it was a shade weaker than the first, for they were both a part of the same thing. It was necessary for me, at that stage of my development as a man, to work (for the first time) in a large body of men; to submerge myself in that mass, seeking neither distinction nor preferment . . . and in this way to achieve self-discipline, patience and unselfishness—the opposite of a long middle-class training—and the construction of a life that would be geared to other men and the world-events that circumscribed them. There is much truth in the old saws—for a desperate disease, a desperate cure."[3]

Spain unpurpled the prose that often turned gaudy when Bessie was holding communion with nature. In *Men in Battle* he writes with a painterly sense of place that conveys the tension in the Spanish landscape with its harshness and quiet beauty, its gargoyle mountains and lemon-laden trees. Unlike Ernest Hemingway, Bessie does not romanticize death by reveling in its odors and tastes, yet he explains better than any novelist why more than three thousand men came to fight for a country most of them had never even seen: "These men behind these fragile rocks, these men whose tender flesh is torn to pieces by the hot and ragged steel; they could not accept their death with such good grace if they did not love so deeply and so well—were not determined that love must come alive into the world" (291-92).

Naturally, Bessie is poeticizing the brigadiers' commitment, transmuting a motive into an idea and a goal into a dream. Whether it is called love of humanity or, as Bessie terms it, love of love (a desire to keep the force of love alive in the universe) is irrelevant. Love brought them to Spain; love—a different kind, not cosmic love but love of woman—sustained them there: "You think of love . . . the love you never had and could not give; the love that does not need words to create itself, but exists between the man and the woman who can look at each other and say inside their minds, I love and am loved" (291).

Unlike Hemingway and André Malraux, Bessie never wrote a novel about Spain; the closest he ever came to Spanish Civil War fiction is in the short story "My Brother, My Son" (1940). It was inspired by the death of Aaron Lopoff, his company commander, who was felled by a fascist's bullet that first cost him an eye and then his life. The exactness of the short story form drew from Bessie an explanation more concise than the one he gave in *Men in Battle* for 3,300 Americans' volunteering to fight for the Spanish Republic: "a strong and generalized love of people and a tortured lack of confidence." A generalized love also suited Bessie, who had encountered too many unlovable individuals, like the Jew-baiting boys who once cut his hair into shag and painted his scalp with iodine. Strangely, this childhood experience did not make Bessie vindictive, only introspective. Similarly, he bore no animus against Lopoff, ten years his junior, who had called him an old man and a mediocre soldier. Bessie knew that Lopoff's bravado was a facade concealing a fear rebels know better than anyone: the fear of being afraid, as Lillian Hellman termed it in *Julia*.

"My Brother, My Son," however, is not a paean to a man who was living out the myth of a Promethean rebel; it is a study in entangled emotions—grief, anger, incomprehension—which encoil around the unconscious, where they remain dormant until the slightest provocation releases their collective venom. When the narrator, clearly Bessie, visits the dead man's home, the amenities are displayed more effusively than ordinary hospitality requires. But when the narrator politely refuses to stay on as a boarder and, by implication, a surrogate son, the mother, who had been so gracious, says, "I'm sorry I can't say 'pleased to meet you' " (163). That line, the story's conclusion, is the culmination of a technique that never went further because too many detours, distractions, diversions, and finally soul-searching prevented the author from admitting that he had created a touchstone. It was a quarter of a century before Bessie returned to the short story, and then only briefly; yet of all the forms with which he experimented, it was the one at which he excelled.

In 1941 Bessie published his second novel, *Bread and a Stone*, which indirectly resulted in the second of the "two activities of which [he was] particularly proud": the first was fighting for Spain; the second, his refusal to answer HUAC's questions about his membership in the Screen Writers Guild and the Communist party.[4] It was *Bread and a Stone* that brought him to Warner Brothers as a screenwriter, at a salary that Jack Warner doubled (to $300 a week) when Bessie's agent reminded the mogul that although his client was a Red, the Reds were making it possible for Warner Brothers to gross its millions by keeping Germany occupied on the Russian front.[5]

It is understandable that of all the studios, Warner Brothers would be the one interested in Bessie. *Bread and a Stone* resembled the socially progressive sort of movie for which the studio was famous. If Warner's had ever decided to film it, casting would have posed no problem; any number of contract players—including Bette Davis, who was interested in the part of the heroine—could have done the roles. The novel was even written cinematically, in a series of flashbacks culminating in a revelation—which is, however, sadly anticlimactic: after 300 pages it comes as no surprise that the protagonist, an illiterate New Englander sentenced to death for first-degree murder, realizes that he has been "dead all [his] life." Bessie's empathy with the misbegotten did not result in a work of art like Flannery O'Connor's *Wise Blood* or Carson McCullers's *The Heart Is a Lonely Hunter*. His compassionate treatment reveals more about himself than his character; Bessie seems almost afraid to write poetically of misfits and grotesques for fear that art would demean them. Hence he chooses proletarian artlessness, allowing his hero to speak in dialect but think in the vernacular, perhaps to prevent monotony. Bessie dredges up every sociological cliché to make Ed Sloan a victim of his environment; in fact, the title of the Warner Brothers film, *They Made Me a Criminal* (1939), might well sum up the novel, "they" being Sloan's sadistic stepfather and an indifferent society. *Hard Travelling* was the title of the film version made in 1986; although sensitively directed and written by the author's son, Dan Bessie, it was neither a critical nor a popular success. The novel's time had passed.

Bessie did not write another novel for fifteen years. After having been a stage manager, translator, journalist, drama critic, short story writer, and novelist, he was now a screenwriter at a major studio. His first assignment was the Errol Flynn film *Northern Pursuit* (1943), which director Raoul Walsh dismissed as a "quickie" (it must have been, since Walsh had directed two others, *Background to Danger* and *Uncertain Glory,* the same year).[6] Except for the Canadian setting, which enabled the Mounties to pursue Nazis on skis and dogsleds, *Northern Pursuit* seems no different from other wartime melodramas, yet there are flashes of intelligence that at least point to a mind behind its creation. The mind, according to the credits, was dual: Frank Gruber and Alvah Bessie. Interestingly, Bessie's last screenplay for Warner's, *Hotel Berlin* (1945), contains a similar plot device: a woman is thought to be a Nazi sympathizer because she fraternizes with the Gestapo; in *Northern Pursuit* a similar assumption is made about the Errol Flynn character because he is German. (Originally, the character's surname was Patterson; it is clear from the revised script of 26 May 1943 that it was Bessie who changed the last name to Wagner and made him German-Canadian).[7]

Both *Northern Pursuit* and *Hotel Berlin* avoid the 1940s monolithic view of the Germans, who, unless painstakingly designated as "good," were presumed to be Nazis. Steve Wagner, the Mountie, is initially a political waif; as a German, he does not take the Nazi threat seriously until he discovers that a Canadian Luftwaffe (a historical improbability but a good plot peg) is ready to bomb waterways and canals. Nevertheless, he does not denigrate all Germans: "Just because he is an enemy, it doesn't mean he isn't human."

A similar sentiment occurs in Bessie's original screen story for *Objective, Burma!* (1945), which won him an Academy Award nomination. The film, also starring Errol Flynn, contains the most strident denunciation of the Japanese heard on the screen. When an American journalist sees a paratrooper's mutilated body, he calls for the extinction of the entire Japanese population in a speech ending "wipe them off the face of the earth." The scene in Bessie's story avoids the cry for vengeance: when a sergeant, after seeing the body, says, "Japs aren't human; they're animals," Nelson (the Flynn character) replies: "There's nothing especially Japanese about this. . . . You'll find it wherever you find fascists. There are even people who call themselves Americans who'd do it, too. But there are lots of people who haven't been turned into beasts—and you'll find them in Japan and Germany as well."[8]

Such level-headedness is totally absent from the film, written by Lester Cole and Ranald MacDougall. It would seem that MacDougall was responsible for the genocidal tirade, perhaps acting on the suggestion of producer Jerry Wald. There is no such outburst in the revised final script (1 May 1944), and the "wipe them off the face of the earth" speech was not Cole's idea, as is clear in a memo of 2 December 1944 from Bessie to Wald: "I've discussed this [speech] with Lester Cole, and he feels precisely the way I do about it—that the statement, as used, can be a very dangerous one and, in a film that so sedulously avoids political statements of any kind, this one highly political statement sticks out like a sore thumb."[9] Wald, however, thought otherwise: the speech stayed, much to the shock of the post–World War II generation, which sees *Objective, Burma!* on television and is embarrassed by its blatant racism.

The film displeased Bessie because of the liberties taken with the plot. He was proud of his screen story—a 53-page treatment (12 January 1944), part narrative and part dramatization—about American paratroopers who are dropped behind Japanese lines to destroy a Burmese communications center and munitions dump and, after completing their mission, are stranded in the jungle. What bothered Jerry Wald was not the gaffe about American paratroopers in Burma (which infuriated the British, who rightly insisted that the Burmese campaign was theirs) but Bessie's padding of the narrative: "It's hazy," the producer wrote on the treatment.[10]

Bessie's resolution was straight out of a jungle melodrama in which explorers are saved at the eleventh hour: the paratroopers are rescued by headhunters, who refuse to accept payment for their services because that would make them white man's slaves. It would also have made the film a racial, ethnic, and religious impasto, ending with a quotation from the left's beloved Jefferson: "The tree of liberty must be refreshed from time to time with the blood of patriots and tyrants." In the more plausible film version, the stranded men rendezvous with their plane. Except for its denunciation of the Japanese, the film of *Objective, Burma!* is superior to the original screen story.

Jefferson—specifically, a Jeffersonian epigraph—was also to have figured in Bessie's next film for Warner Brothers, *The Very Thought of You* (1944). Exactly what Jefferson's belief that human beings are their own masters had to do with a wartime romance is uncertain; perhaps Bessie intended to emphasize the characters' struggle to assert their independence, particularly that of the heroine from her family. In any case, Delmer Daves did not see the connection; consequently, the epigraph was scrapped, the New York setting was transferred to California, and Bessie ended up sharing credit with Daves, who also directed.[11] Their contributions were quite dissimilar. Daves was not the sort to meld romance and moral censure; he knew how to engineer a happy ending so the nasties could repent in time for the fade-out. Bessie preferred to explore the nether side of the home front; as a result, *The Very Thought of You* depicted the most disagreeable family to appear on the screen during the war. While American World War II films occasionally featured mercenary and self-satisfied citizens (one of the most infamous being the *grande dame* in *Since You Went Away* who frowned on girls' doing volunteer hospital work because it was "morbid"), the Americans who hoarded and complained about shortages were far more numerous in real life than in the movies, where only rarely would someone shrug off the war and go his or her own way. In *The Very Thought of You*, however, virtually the entire family does: the heroine's brother insists that "if we'd stop fooling around in Europe and take care of those Japs, we'd be better off"; her mother is quick to admit she is "in no hurry for the war to be over [because] this is the first prosperity we've had in this home for a long time"; her sister, who dates other men while her husband is overseas, discourages wartime marriage because "there's no promise of anything—home, security, or future"; her father is a decent sort, except for his racist comparisons: "You treated that nice boy with all the courtesy you'd show a Jap."

Hotel Berlin (1945), Bessie's last film for Warner Brothers, was an unpleasant experience for both him and his co-writer, Jo Pagano. First, they were constantly updating the plot to satisfy Jack Warner, who wanted the movie released before the Russians reached Berlin. Their main problem, however, was neither placating Jack Warner nor keeping up with the war in Europe; it was dealing with producer Louis Edelman, who exceeded his authority by rewriting key scenes—much to the annoyance of the unit manager: "This picture is being changed all the time, but no blue pages are being put through."[12] Edelman, whom Bessie considered monumentally vulgar, was also dissatisfied with the relationship in the script between Martin Richter, the resistance leader, and Lisa Dorn, the actress Richter kills when he discovers she is a traitor. On more than one occasion, Bessie and Pagano had to defend their characterization to Edelman, who wanted Richter and Lisa to be romantically involved. After several tedious conferences, Bessie finally agreed that Richter would pretend to be in love with Lisa as part of his job. The producer beamed: "All I wanted . . . was the bedroom scene."[13] He never got it; by conceding at the conference level, Bessie was able to do what he intended: have Richter shoot Lisa in the *film noir* tradition, à la *Double Indemnity* (1944), while she is vainly protesting her love for him.

The interference that Bessie and Pagano encountered resulted in a disjointed film. *Hotel Berlin* is an uneasy yoking of the ludicrous and the perceptive; it seems not so much coauthored as constructed from several perspectives, some more accurate than others. Certain details are improbable; one is tragically ludicrous: Jews roaming Berlin in

1945, wearing the Star of David and being told to return to their "district." Since *Hotel Berlin* is a World War II *Grand Hotel* (based on a novel by *Grand Hotel*'s author, Vicki Baum), the plot is no more uniform than a registry. Disunity, however, is minor compared to disharmony: plot clichés clash with ideology; *film noir* competes with espionage melodrama; slickness overshadows depth.

Yet it is precisely this disharmony that makes the film worth viewing. Bessie constantly tried to invest the material with a semblance of intelligence, making distinctions between informing and treachery, between repentant informants and unregenerate traitors. Tillie (Faye Emerson) is essentially decent despite her collaborationist ways. At least she was brave enough to defy the racial laws, even though it meant being paraded down a street with an "I Love a Jew" sign around her neck. As Hotel Berlin's hostess, she feels guilty about her intimacy with Nazis which, despite her euphemistic title, is sexual. When guilt gets the better of her, she joins the resistance, whose members accept her only after they are convinced of her sincerity. Conversely, Lisa, although attracted to the resistance leader, is willing to betray both him and his cause for a plane ticket to America. As in *Northern Pursuit*, Bessie avoids a wholesale condemnation of Germany; it is Nazism and collaborationism that the film condemns, not Germans and reconstructed collaborationists.

Even after he was fired by Warner, Bessie continued writing screenplays; since he had temporarily abandoned fiction, screenwriting was his livelihood. In March 1945, A&S Lyons, a talent agency, decided to enter film production as Producing Artists, Inc.; its sole property at the time was Dayton Stoddart's novel *Prelude to Night*, which Robert Rossen was to adapt and probably direct. Because Rossen, after more than a decade of screenwriting, was about to direct his first film (*Johnny O'Clock*, 1947) for Columbia, he arranged with Lyons for Bessie to do the adaptation. As Bessie recalled in his autobiography, it proved too radical for the fledgling company. When the film was made, his name was absent from the credits: "They had hired other writers and a new director, and the writers promptly wrote me out of the screenplay. This is a simple thing to do: you merely write enough new dialogue and create enough new scenes to guarantee that the original writer does not have a third of the final screenplay to his credit."[14]

Edgar G. Ulmer, the director of *Ruthless* (1948), as the film version was called, told a different story. He attributed the absence of Bessie's name to "McCarthyism," an expression he employed anachronistically as well as erroneously. In an interview with Peter Bogdanovich, the director labeled *Ruthless* "a dangerous script that had to be cut because McCarthy came in. It was written by Alvah Bessie." When Bogdanovich asked about the credited screenwriters, S.K. Lauren and G. Kahn, Ulmer replied: "They were names that were made up. It was in the panic time."[15] But Gordon Kahn is hardly an invented name; in addition to being a prolific screenwriter (*I Stand Accused; Buy Me That Town; A Yank on the Burma Road; Northwest Rangers; Her Kind of Man*) and one of the Hollywood Nineteen, he also wrote the first book about the blacklist, *Hollywood on Trial*, which was published in the same year *Ruthless* was released.

The truth is that by 4 April 1946, Bessie had written a treatment of *Prelude to Night* called "The Golden Calf" and structured along the lines of *Citizen Kane*: a flashback narrative explains the circumstances that have led to a millionaire's death by drowning.[16] Two weeks later, he had a screenplay ready under the novel's original title, though the concept remained the same: flashbacks recount the rise of an unprincipled financier from Boston slum to Wall Street. Like Kane, who fancied himself a champion of the people only to become their exploiter, Horace Vendig has been so corrupted by wealth that his plan for a peace foundation is an empty gesture.

The actual film adheres to Bessie's basic plot but not to the details. Bessie's script was more political; the action terminated in 1941 so that fascism could come under attack and Vendig's boyhood friend (and complete opposite) could go off to World War II. Nothing of the sort happens in *Ruthless*. The film also uses a frame narrative: one of the guests at a dinner party attended by people from Vendig's past is Buck Mansfield, whom Vendig has ruined. Buck and Vendig quarrel on the pier, falling into the water in a stranglehold; in Bessie's screenplay Vendig dies accidentally, and Buck is alive at the end. Also absent from Bessie's screenplay is the expressionistic scene in which Christa Mansfield mocks her husband by showing him his elephantine image in a mirror. Finally, Bessie's script lacks the fade-out line, which has had its share of admirers: "He wasn't a man; he was a way of life." Had it not been for the blacklist, Bessie would have been entitled to credit as adapter. But the final script of *Ruthless* was not Bessie's, as he admitted, however persistent the notion that it is.

Smart Woman (1948) was Bessie's last Hollywood screen credit. Like all his films, it was coauthored, this time by three writers: he was hired to revise a screenplay by Louis Morheim and Herbert Margolis, based on an original story by Adela Rogers St. John. As Bessie recalled the experience in *Inquisition in Eden*, Constance Bennett, who both produced and starred in the film, praised him for his revisions on those rare occasions when they met but at other times complained about his work, calling one scene unalloyed Communist propaganda because it discredited a district attorney. In his third-draft screenplay (8 September 1947), in an attempt to make the heroine a person instead of a

clotheshorse, Bessie introduced her playing shortstop on a kids' baseball team.[17] Bennett vetoed the idea; instead, she first appears in a
tailored suit. Bennett expected a star vehicle, though her star was not as
high in the firmament as it had been a decade earlier.

Smart Woman was a return to the lady lawyer film of the 1930s (such
as *Scarlet Pages* and *The Law in Her Hands*); here, however, the lawyer is
forced to defend criminals to conceal the fact that she was once married
to one. Her values are reshaped when she meets her opposite, an
idealistic prosecutor whose convictions—making a better world, refusing to compromise, fighting injustice—are Bessie's. When the pros-
ecuting attorney is questioned about his plans to clean up other people's yards, he delivers a typical Bessie reply: "We all live in the same
yard."

One of the yards in need of a cleanup is the defense lawyer's. In the
climax, she is defending her ex-husband against a murder charge of
which he is innocent. After all the witnesses have been called, she
dramatically asks the judge if she may summon one more: herself. It is
a real *coup de théâtre* and all Bessie's. So is her speech: the lawyer
explains that her former husband is a thief but not a murderer and that
he turned to crime because he was underprivileged. Later, she tells her
son that "sometimes, when people don't have anything, and they see
that other people do, they can't understand and it warps them"—
Bessie's sentiments, exactly.

Throughout the blacklist period Bessie continued writing screenplays but without success. Yet screenwriting had had its effect; when
he wrote the autobiographical *Inquisition in Eden*, he structured it as a
film script with camera instructions (Medium Two Shot) and transitions (Dissolve to . . .) carefully marked. His life had become a screenplay he could never sell to the movies, so he committed it to print, the
one medium open to him, even though he had deserted it when he
came to Hollywood.

Bessie's later fiction was never far from his life, whose axial ex-
tremities were the Spanish Civil War and HUAC; the two are chronologically juxtaposed in *The un-Americans* (1957), his first novel in more
than fifteen years. Although overly long and dated even by 1957
standards, the book is a technically ambitious work; time is not so
much layered, as it often is in literature, but intercut, as it is in film. The
interweaving has a synchronic effect—not that of the New Novel with
its metaphysical sameness of past and present but of biography, in
which past impinges on present; what was believed in 1938 is discarded, modified, or deepened in 1948. In the novel the past edges into
the present, 1938 gradually merges into 1948, so that by the end ten
years have dwindled to two.

There cannot be a perfect coinciding because the story is incomplete; the blood of Spain has not completely dried. In 1938 Ben Blau, a Communist journalist, and Francis Xavier Lang, a Catholic man of letters, are in Spain—Blau to fight, Lang to report. Like many progressives, Lang has become sufficiently radicalized in Spain to join the Party, if only for a year; he resigns when the Nazi-Soviet pact shatters his illusions about Communism. Nine years later, when the subpoenas started arriving, Lang is secure enough to scoff at HUAC until his short-lived membership in the Party is revealed; then he becomes increasingly cooperative until, while not exactly naming names (although the implication is that he will), he has no qualms about identifying the politics of anyone mentioned. Blau, emulating the stand of the Ten, refuses to cooperate, responding to the eternal question "Are you now or have you ever been . . . ," with "Are *you* kidding?" and being forcibly removed from the stand—not unlike John Howard Lawson et al. While Lang's reputation is intact at the end of the novel and supposedly will thrive in a Cold War climate, Blau's career is over, along with any chance of a normal life. A Russophobic prison inmate bashes his head in, with not one but two baseball bats. But although he will sport a steel plate in his head for the rest of his life, he is more determined than ever to fight for a just society, even changing his name from Blau (Blue) to Red, the color of his Party and the color of life.

The un-Americans also demonstrates Dalton Trumbo's thesis that, in "the time of the toad" there were only victims, whether victims of guilt like Lang or of innocence like Blau. Guilt and innocence are moral opposites: thus the guilty and the innocent are, in literary terms, villain and hero; in inquisitional terms, persecutor and martyr; in hagiographical terms, sinner and saint. Since these categories allow for only the slightest shades of difference, the novel becomes repetitive; what saves it from utter tedium are the mock synchronism and the passages of pure dialogue (for example, at the hearing), where Bessie's ability to capture tone and inflection makes one lament the infrequency with which that ability was exercised.

Bessie cannot meet the demands of the *roman à clef,* however. After a few pages it is evident that some of the characters are speaking through personae that are too large for them. Bessie admitted that while the relationship was fictional, Blau and Lang were suggested by real persons, but it is more accurate to say that each is a composite of several persons. Lang suggests Vincent Sheean, the correspondent and author who, like Lang, had been to Spain, flirted with Marxism (but never legitimized the romance), found love with a Spanish Communist as Lang does in the novel, mesmerized the Writers Congress in 1938 by his eloquence, and excoriated the Nazi-Soviet pact the following year; unlike Sheean, Lang is also a playwright on the order of

Emmet Lavery, a Catholic liberal whose views were often misin-
terpreted as Communistic; Lang's verse dramas recall those of Maxwell
Anderson, a liberal but not a radical. Blau is an amalgam of the author
(Jewish, Communist, former brigadier, ex-journalist, unfriendly witness), Jim Lardner, and Joe Hecht (to whom, with Aaron Lopoff, the
book is dedicated), but the differences are more striking than the
similarities. Unlike Blau, Bessie did not have his head bashed in; Jim
Lardner died in Spain; Joe Hecht survived Spain to die in World War II.

The characters are such exaggerated versions of real people that
they become their antitheses. They are also transparent in the manner
of minor allegory where, once the equivalents have been established,
the text admits of no further possibilities. The connections might have
been more challenging if Bessie had explored the deeper meaning of a
poem that affected him enough to quote from it but apparently not
enough to make it anything more than an analogue. Lang's all-suffer-
ing wife leaves him a copy of *Mainstream* containing Dalton Trumbo's
poem "Confessional" (1947), in which a former Party member explains
to a Stalinist friend why he has resigned and becomes increasingly
frustrated by his friend's stony silence. The speaker of the poem is at
first self-righteous, citing his impoverished youth, immigrant background, and courage in the face of controversy as proof of his integrity.
Then, to vindicate himself, he invokes the classic distinction between
liberal and radical, claiming that his friend's methods of improving
society are too revolutionary. The speaker protests too much: while he
has renounced Communism, he still claims to be a Socialist; while he
no longer believes in a classless society, he envisions a universal
brotherhood. Having timed his resignation with the descending of the
Iron Curtain, he encapsulates in an apothegm the reason for his defec-
tion: "I wish to be both rich and holy too."

The poem infuriates Lang, who takes it personally, seeing himself
as the speaker who is by turns sanctimonious, apologetic, whining,
and finally sacerdotal in his vision of a New Jerusalem where he and his
comrades can dwell without membership cards. However, if Lang is
the defector, Blau is the stalwart; since the voluble loathe the silent,
Lang grows angry with Blau, whose indifference to the props of poetry
makes him immune to the therapy of talk. If Bessie had made Trumbo's
poem the fulcrum, *The un-Americans* might have had a similar blend of
anguish and ambivalence; instead, for all its artful intercalation, the
novel is a study in monochrome with all shades of gray banished from
the moral spectrum.

In *The Symbol* (1966) Bessie fictionalized the life of another real
person, Marilyn Monroe. He sympathized with her as one of the
world's exploited, but the fact that he had never met her and that she
belonged to another era prevented the book from having an autobio-

graphical aspect; thus, while Bessie's last three novels were all *romans à clef, The Symbol* is the least personal and, perhaps for that reason, the best.

Like *The un-Americans, The Symbol* is cinematically structured. Instead of chapters there are sequencelike Monologues, Dialogues, and Scenes. The monologues and dialogues, set in March 1957, consist of diary entries and psychiatric sessions representing the present; the scenes, often intercalated with the monologues and dialogues, are dramatizations of a past that began in 1943. As the past approaches the present, the intercalation ceases, and time flows into a single channel, narrowing progressively until it contracts and disappears. The stream of life is no different for a movie star than for anyone else; it only overflows its banks more often, or so it seems in the case of Wanda Oliver, formerly Emmaline Smith, who proceeds from an orphanage to the soundstages of Hollywood and whose career ends in suicide.

While the book could easily have become gaudily packaged glitz, Bessie is too serious for class trash. *The Symbol*, which made more money than Bessie's other novels (although it never became a best seller), won him some thoughtful reviews lauding his ability to enter the soul of a woman who, in death, became the patron saint of the fame-destroyed. That Bessie, who was so critical of womanish males in *Men in Battle*, could identify with a woman, writing monologues of such candor that one seems to be inside Wanda's consciousness, is a tribute to his empathetic sense.

Wanda is a woman whose screen image is the inverse of her real self; unable to experience orgasm, she allows her public to enjoy it vicariously; the public, however, does not know what Wanda's husbands and lovers know: the sex goddess is a snow queen. Since Bessie is more interested in the symbolic Marilyn (hence the title) than in specific correspondences, he forges only the most basic links and makes the most obvious substitutions: Wanda is a redhead instead of a blonde; she marries a football player rather than baseball star Joe DiMaggio and an artist in place of dramatist Arthur Miller.

At times the book intentionally discourages parallels by making Wanda seem more like Jayne Mansfield or Mamie Van Doren. The studios where she works (Dialogue Pictures, Spectacular Studios) evoke, if not Poverty Row, then Gower Gulch; her films have B-movie titles: *Madness at Midnight, Juke Box, Deep Purple, Passion Flower.* Wanda, then, is not really Marilyn, who was primarily associated with Fox and made films of which no actress need be ashamed. Wanda is Marilyn as she might have been had she never advanced beyond movies like Columbia's *Ladies of the Chorus* (1949). The transparent parallels and wild deviations are Bessie's way of saying that the historical basis of the novel is, like any foundation, a support for the edifice; the banal movie titles are his way of manifesting contempt for Hollywood and of distancing readers from the character they assume is la Monroe but who is only the personification of her death wish, which the moguls exploited to convert a girl-woman into an icon.

In an odd way, *The Symbol* is the proletarian novel that Bessie tried to write in the 1930s when he kept confusing proletarian with protest. If anything symbolizes exploitation, it is the studio system that requires a sex symbol to live out a myth completely alien to her nature, causing such tension between person and persona that the hapless star grows to hate her private self as much as her public image. The industry engenders self-hate which, if it becomes all-consuming as in Wanda's case, leads to self-destruction.

The Symbol was a natural film property; Bessie started working on the screen version in 1973, but nothing came of it. Then he turned it into a teleplay, which was so radically altered that when *The Sex Symbol*, as it was called, was aired on ABC in 1974, it seemed as if the heroine— renamed Kelly Williams for the tube—had wandered into the valley of the dolls.

Bessie wrote screen adaptations of his last three novels but got no further than the television disemboweling of *The Symbol* and a BBC radio dramatization of *The un-Americans*, with Lionel Stander as Lang, in 1964. Still, he did not give up writing film and television scripts, even though in 1972 an agent told him bluntly that his work was not marketable. His last novel, *One for My Baby* (1980), took eight years to find a publisher. *Spain Again* (1975), a collagelike memoir about the filming of *España otra vez* (1968), was rejected by eighteen publishers before a northern California press, Chandler & Sharp, brought it out.

It is not so much that *Spain Again* is uninteresting, merely that it is inconsequential. Only a fan of Bessie's would even care that in 1967 he returned to a Spain whose government he abominated to write a screenplay about a neurosurgeon's return to a country he had not seen since he fought there. The premise called for a film of spiraling irony: the producer was a Francoist; the director was born the year the Spanish Civil War began; the star was Mark Stevens, who had made his movie debut in *Objective, Burma!* but had no idea who Alvah Bessie was; and Bessie himself was acting for the first time since the 1920s, playing a Texas doctor. Irony compounded deepens a shallow narrative, but Bessie could not ford the stream of time. Instead, he juggled past and present, intending the present to be inferior to and unworthy of the past. His interest was not in Franco's Spain of the 1960s—a land of tourism, condos, luxury hotels, tortured dissidents, and emigrating workers—but in the Spain of the 1930s, his Spain. Bessie's Spain, part real, part dream, made every other subject pale by comparison; nothing else he wrote measured up to *Men in Battle*. Spain made Bessie a writer, but what Spain wrought, antifascism undid.

España otra vez was a success in Spain, but the film failed to find a distributor in the United States. Bessie's last novel, *One for My Baby* (1980), did not fare much better; it neither sold well nor garnered good reviews. The book is, to use the subtitle of Gore Vidal's *Two Sisters*, a memoir in the form of a novel—a reminiscence sometimes humorous, sometimes rueful, of the types he encountered at San Francisco's hungry i, the nightclub where for seven years (1956-63) he worked as combination light man, stage manager, and announcer. Bessie should have been in his element, but he had descended only into the limbo of the lost, not into their hell. He could only limn the denizens of North Beach, as if they were material for an etching; they needed brush strokes.

Bessie planned *One for My Baby* as a crossroads novel with the Night Box, clearly the hungry i, as the site of intersecting destinies. In the book, lives do intersect, but they fail to collide, forming instead a static grid. Thus little happens dramatically; it is like watching a play with only one set, although the action calls for more, and with psychological types instead of individuals. The novel, then, becomes a study in self-loathing, failure, and strength—the last quality being the rarest; it belongs only to Monica Butler, the antithesis of Wanda Oliver. Monica, a promising starlet, loses her legs in one accident and is facially disfigured by another. Still, she has the ability to reject pity, even when it comes in the form of a marriage proposal from Bessie's persona, Dan Noble. Noble works the lights at the Night Box; previously he had been a journalist who, predictably, supported Loyalist Spain during the Civil War.

Unfortunately, Monica is not the main character, though her story is the most compelling. Besides portraying the misbegotten, Bessie also wanted to evoke their milieu, in which sleaze is softened by baby spots and curtained by cigarette smoke. Although he was successful in his recreation of the club's ambience, he could not people his microcosm with genuinely sympathetic characters; Monica is the exception. The dominant figure is Dr. Sour, a Lennie Bruce type (with traces of Mort Sahl and Irwin Corey) who makes his life his act and whose self-love is disguised self-hatred, which spills over to the audience he strokes and insults and to the women he deifies and abuses. It is a fascinating portrait but not enough to constitute a novel. Monica and Dr. Sour are short-story figures imprisoned in a novel in which too many uninteresting and unworthy characters compete for the reader's attention. At least *One for My Baby* is too short to be tedious; it is only exasperating in its revelation of misdirected art.

Bessie's final book was a 1982 collection of short stories that he had hoped to publish fifteen years earlier. The exhilaration of being back in print in the 1950s, first with his anthology *Heart of Spain* (1952) and then with *The un-Americans*, had encouraged him to press for a collection, even though the most recent story had been written in 1941. He petitioned his friend Angus Cameron, who for political reasons had been forced to resign from Little, Brown in 1951; when he later formed his own company, Bessie thought it would be a logical publisher for his stories. Cameron was not encouraging; he advised Bessie to write a novel about something he knew, such as American progressivism. Cameron also did more than twist the knife in an already wounded ego when he inquired; "Aren't you working on anything new? I know the difficulties but you are a writer, aren't you? And writers write, don't they?"[18]

Since Cameron was such a close friend (*The Symbol* is dedicated to him), Bessie took the criticism well: "Let's say I am an occasional writer, once in 11 years when I have something to say."[19] Actually, his problem was that he had too much to say and said it in too many different ways. The Alvah C. Bessie Collection in Wisconsin contains some twenty-five unproduced scripts, written between the mid-1940s and 1973. But perhaps the most surprising feature of the collection is his personal correspondence, which comprises two boxes. Bessie may not have been a model epistolographer, but he faithfully answered his mail, addressing the correspondent by first name because, no doubt, he wanted (and generally received) a first-name salutation in return. Journalism teachers invited him to address their classes; Spanish Civil War buffs deluged him with questions; undergraduates hearing him lecture yearned to learn more about the left; and graduate students in search of information discovered a willing correspondent who gave them far more time than they probably received from their mentors.

Bessie suffered from prodigality; a natural writer, he simply wrote, letting his ideas take whatever form circumstances or inclination dictated. There were many forces acting on him during his lifetime, any one of which (the Great Depression, the Spanish Civil War, Communism, Hollywood, the witch-hunt) might have made him a writer of substance. Collectively, however, they restricted a vision that may already have been limited. One force diminished the energy another had generated, so that at the end of a life that spanned four decades there was a vast body of writing—translations, criticism, novels, short stories, poetry, screenplays, autobiography—but no genuine corpus. Individually, there is some excellent work, but it is the failures like *One for My Baby* that magnify the nerve ends of Bessie's talent—a talent that could never direct itself because it could never be confined.

Some of the Hollywood Ten gather with families and supporters to protest their sentencing. Left to right: Edward Dmytryk (holding sign), Lester Cole, Alvah Bessie (with cap), Dalton Trumbo, Albert Maltz (face partially obscured), Ring Lardner, Jr., beside lawyer Ben Marolis (lighting cigarette), and Herbert Biberman. Southern California Library for Social Studies and Research.

Above, Samuel Ornitz, patriarch of the Ten, who charged the others to be "as brave as the people we write about." Right, Alvah Bessie after refusing to answer HUAC's $64 question on 28 October 1947. AP/Wide World Photos.

Unless otherwise noted, photos are courtesy of the Academy of Motion Picture Arts and Sciences.

Above left, Lester Cole in 1981, practicing his politics. Courtesy of Michael Cole. Below, Van Johnson and Janet Leigh in *The Romance of Rosy Ridge* (1947), Cole's favorite screenplay. Above right, John Howard Lawson, the "Hollywood Commissar," who preferred the approval of the Party to that of the critics.

Above, Madeleine Carroll in *Blockade* (1937), Lawson's tribute to Loyalist Spain. Wisconsin Center for Film and Theater Research. Below, Edward Dmytryk directing Dick Powell and Claire Trevor in *Murder, My Sweet* (1944).

Above, Franchot Tone (left) in the Theatre Guild's production of *Green Grow the Lilacs* (1930), directed by Herbert Biberman. Below, Biberman on location during filming of *Salt of the Earth* (1954). Top photo, Wisconsin Center for Film and Theater Research.

Above, Albert Maltz just before being ordered from the witness chair on 28 October 1947. Copyright *Washington Post;* reprinted by permission of the D.C. Public Library. Just two years before, Maltz had been praised for his screenplay for *Pride of the Marines* (below), starring John Garfield as Al Schmid.

Right, Adrian Scott in the critical fall of 1947, four years after his coauthored screenplay for *Mr. Lucky* (below), starring Cary Grant and Laraine Day, made him a producer at RKO. Top photo courtesy Joan Scott.

Above, Ginger Rogers and Robert Ryan in Dalton Trumbo's *Tender Comrade* (1943), which Ginger's mother denounced as Red propaganda. RKO. Right, Walter Mirisch presents Trumbo with his belated *Brave One* Oscar in 1975, the year before Trumbo's death.

Left, Ring Lardner, Jr.,
at the Ring Lardner
Centennary Observance in
1985. Below, the Last Supper
parody in *M*A*S*H* (1970),
Lardner's second Oscar-
winning script.

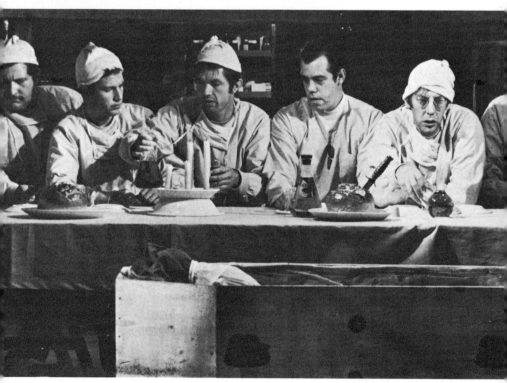

7 ADRIAN SCOTT
A Decent Man

Stage, the chic precursor of *Theatre Arts,* was "The Magazine of After-Dark Entertainment," as its cover proclaimed. Notables from the literary and performing arts such as Clifton Fadiman, Deems Taylor, Burgess Meredith, and Marcia Davenport graced its pages with their essays and reviews. It was something of a surprise, then, that the December 1936 issue included a satire on Dish Night (the practice of including a piece of dinnerware in the price of a movie ticket) written in gamy prose that was as much at variance with the magazine's urbane image as the topic. The author was John Paxton, a recent journalism graduate of the University of Missouri. Readers apparently welcomed the diversion, and *Stage* published a few more of his pieces. When the editors realized that Paxton could offer the magazine more than jottings and ruminations, he was made an associate editor beginning with the August 1937 issue, which also announced another addition to the staff: Amherst-educated Adrian Scott. By November, both had become assistant editors—Scott for film, Paxton for theater.

Since *Stage* already had a film editor, Katharine Best, Scott had little opportunity to write about the medium that fascinated him. In the seven months he spent at *Stage,* not one review or article carried his name, although he may have written some of the unsigned briefs in the "Pictures Now Showing" column. Paxton stayed on until the magazine's demise in 1939. But within five years the two men were working together in Hollywood, where Paxton would write scripts of five of the six films Scott produced at RKO.

Eventually, RKO became Scott's home studio, but his first screen credits came from minor films at other major studios: MGM's *Keeping Company* (1940), a domestic comedy; and Fox's *We Go Fast* (1941), which at least one critic remembers for its wisecracking dialogue.[1] Earlier, however, RKO had given him his first taste of Hollywood. Adrian's brother Allan Scott, who was as comfortable writing for Broadway as he was for Hollywood, went to RKO in 1934 and soon found his metier in musicals, collaborating on the scripts of such successes as *Roberta* (1935), *Top Hat* (1935), *Follow the Fleet* (1936), *Swing Time* (1936), and *Shall We Dance* (1937); it was also Allan Scott who enabled Ginger

Rogers to reveal her comedic talent in *Fifth Avenue Girl* (1939). No doubt because of his brother's association with the studio, Adrian Scott was put on the RKO payroll in 1934, at the munificent salary of $25 a week, to work on the film that became *The Gridiron Flash* (1934). What he contributed is unknown, since his efforts are uncredited.[2]

Although four years elapsed before he tried screenwriting again, Scott's brief exposure to the medium, followed by his stint at *Stage* magazine, had left its mark. So had two other events which, in combination, defined an entire generation: the Great Depression and the rise of fascism. In 1938 Scott was interested in writing not fiction films, like his brother, but documentaries. After reading Paul de Kruif's *Fight for Life* (1938), he was convinced that the book could spawn any number of documentaries about diseases such as pellagra, tuberculosis, and polio, which had reached epidemic proportions during the 1930s. Scott endorsed de Kruif's premise that humankind has a right to life and that whatever endangers that right (such as poverty and disease) must be eradicated. He also agreed that the fight for life was a people's fight that could be won only through a national health program. De Kruif's conclusion became Adrian Scott's credo: "The relief of suffering and the prevention of dying cannot be best served, for all, as long as there remains any money consideration between the people and the fighters for their lives."[3]

Determined to make a series of shorts based on *The Fight for Life*, Scott approached RKO, which had acquired Pathé News and its parent organization in 1931. Pathé would have been a logical choice for the series; so would *The March of Time*, for which RKO had acquired distribution rights in 1935. Scott was not alone in wishing to make a film from de Kruif's book. While he went to work on the book's eleventh chapter, "Tuberculosis in Detroit," Pare Lorentz focused on the first, which described the harrowing conditions under which the poor gave birth in maternity wards. Lorentz succeeded in making his film, which bore the name of the book, *The Fight for Life* (1939). Scott was less fortunate; when he submitted his script, Frederick Ullman, Jr., of Pathé, though sympathetic to the subject matter, had to reject it on the basis of cost.[4]

Scott did not give up on RKO. As the threat of fascism increased, he moved further to the left which meant, in Hollywood and elsewhere, belonging to liberal or progressive groups, to the Communist Party, or to the all-embracing Popular Front. He began traveling in antifascist circles where he encountered those who shared his beliefs—if not always about Marxism as a panacea, then at least about the danger of fascism. One such circle was the Motion Picture Guild, a progressive organization that included both radicals and liberals. In 1939 the Guild purchased the rights to Erika Mann's *School for Barbarians*. Scott was so eager to become involved in the film version that he invited J.R. McDonough, former president of RKO, to attend a party in honor of Erika. McDonough declined, and the project never materialized.

In 1939, then, Scott did not yet have a single screen credit. By the time of Pearl Harbor, he had three. *Keeping Company* and *We Go Fast* are inconsequential; *The Parson of Panamint* (1941), a Paramount release, revealed Scott's vision of human nature for the first time. For all his idealism, he was not blind to the darkness of the heart; it is that darkness, in the form of venality and hypocrisy, that destroys the town of Panamint and leads to the persecution of its parson, whose gospel of brotherly love falls on deaf ears. Scott shared screenplay credit with Harold Shumate, whose screenplay he revised.[5] Whether it was Scott or Shumate who devised the frame narrative, a campfire story that makes the film a flashback, is unknown, but flashbacks do occur not only in films Scott wrote but in most of those he produced (*Murder, My Sweet; Cornered; Deadline at Dawn; Crossfire*).

The Parson of Panamint traces the rise and fall of a utopia, a once thriving mining community that degenerates into a ghost town. To gain respectability, Panamint hires a preacher who turns out to be a genuine Christ figure, able to win over prostitutes and gamblers but unable to remain silent about the danger that flooded mines pose to the town. Because of their integrity, the parson and the prostitute, who plays Magdalen to his Christ, are hounded out of Panamint on a trumped-up murder charge. What happens to them is uncertain, but as the narrator observes in closing, "Wherever they are, people will be a little better, a little finer, and a little closer to God."

Since it was Scott who added a spiritual dimension to *Mr. Lucky* (1943) by having the protagonist's regeneration take place inside a church, it was probably he who invested *Panamint* with a religious ambiance. If Scott did not write the parson's sermon about an impoverished man who becomes a thief, he certainly concurred with it: "He wasn't doing very well, and his wife and children were hungry, although there was plenty all around them. Well, so he broke into a store and stole a lot of canned goods and a warm coat for his wife. But the next day they caught him and the owner of the store filed a complaint against him. However, a strange thing happened. During the trial, the owner of the store was himself arrested for stealing a huge sum of money from his stockholders." For those unsure of the moral, the parson sums it up biblically: "He that is without sin among you, let him cast the first stone."

Art not only imitates life; sometimes it foreshadows and mocks it. Six years after the film's release, Scott, like the parson, became a pariah in his community. And like the store owner of the sermon, HUAC chairman J. Parnell Thomas was indicted on 8 November 1948 for defrauding the United States Treasury; on 2 January 1949, he was convicted and sentenced to serve eight months to two years in the Danbury Federal Correctional Institution, where Lester Cole and Ring Lardner, Jr. served their sentences. (Thomas's prison duties included cleaning the chicken coops, a task that merited him the title, Congressman Chickenshit.)

Throughout the 1930s Scott and RKO had constantly crossed paths. On 20 July 1942 Scott was hired at $300 a week—twelve times his 1934 salary—to write "Bundles for Freedom," which finally became the Cary Grant film, *Mr. Lucky*. In August, RKO producer David Hempstead wrote to the Los Angeles Induction Center, asking that Scott's entrance into the army be delayed for five weeks so that he could complete an important "war propaganda" film. Since it was customary during World War II for studios to request such deferments for their writers, the letter could have ended there, but it went on: "The movie is important to Mr. Scott personally. He has been what is known as a writer of 'B' pictures in the industry. It is a stage a writer goes through against that day he gets that opportunity. 'Bundles for Freedom' is his opportunity. If he is permitted to finish his script and receives the writing credit, his career is secure when he returns from the war."[6]

As it happened, Scott did not have to serve. But Hempstead's letter, which went beyond the routine, is typical of the feelings Scott evoked in people. Those who knew him speak of two qualities that made Adrian Scott unique in an industry not especially known for either: sincerity and integrity. On the basis of only one meeting, Dalton Trumbo's biographer, Bruce Cook, wrote: "He was one of the most decent men I have ever met."[7]

The evolution of *Mr. Lucky* sounds like Hollywood legend; in this instance, the legend is history.[8] Around the time of Pearl Harbor, Milton Holmes, the former manager of the Beverly Hills Tennis Club, happened to see Cary Grant in *Suspicion* (1941), which convinced him that the actor's range extended beyond romantic comedy and even beyond Hitchcockian melodrama. He decided to fashion a serious vehicle for Grant, writing it first as a short story; *Cosmopolitan* published "Bundles for Freedom" in June 1941. Spotting Grant in Beverly Hills, Holmes literally approached him on the street with the story and sold him on the film version.

The creation of a screenplay has always been a complex procedure, especially during the studio years when a writer assigned to a film might not be told that others were also at work on it. Details from one draft were often added to another, frequently by someone brought in at the very end, who then received screen credit for what publishers call creative editing. This method was expected to result in a filmable script, whatever the expense to the writers' pride. Even before Scott became involved with *Mr. Lucky*, Holmes and Charles Brackett had written two treatments (24 June and 1 July 1942) under the title "Joe the Greek." Since Holmes was a novice, RKO was taking no chances; the studio gave him a collaborator who had already proved himself (*Enter Madame*, 1935; *Bluebeard's Eighth Wife*, 1938; *Arise My Love*, 1940; *The Major and the Minor*, 1942).

When Scott arrived at RKO in July 1942, he had no idea that it was Brackett and Holmes who had already sketched out the plot, nor did he know that while he was trying to construct a script from their treatments, Dudley Nichols was doing likewise. Eventually, Scott obtained the Nichols script, from which he kept only a few details: among them the rhyming slang (Briney Marlin = My darlin'), and the heroine's liberal family dating back to an abolitionist ancestor who died at Harpers Ferry.

The original story's ending was too downbeat for either a Cary Grant vehicle or a World War II movie. Joe Boscopolous, a gambler who attempts to fleece a war relief organization run by wealthy socialites, blossoms into a patriot when he learns that the Nazis have killed his brothers in Greece; he turns his gambling boat into a relief ship which, it is implied, will never dock again in New York. Brackett and Holmes worked out a framing device in which Joe, now a merchant seaman, tells his story to a pilot on a raft that is really the top of a crap table—all that survives when the relief ship is torpedoed. Since Brackett excelled at scripts about assumed identity, it may have been he who thought up the idea of the gambler's having taken the name of Joe Boscopolous from a dead man whose 4-F draft status he acquired along with his new identity. Concerned only with avoiding induction, the gambler has no qualms about what he has done until he learns that the Greek village where the Boscopolous family lived has been destroyed by the Nazis. After the gambler is regenerated, Brackett returned to the two-men-on-the-raft ending. Because the ersatz raft can accommodate only one person, Joe tosses a coin; the pilot stays, and Joe slips into the mid-Atlantic.

The idea of a frame narrative appealed to Scott but he set it on a pier, where a ship's captain explains to a watchman that the beautiful woman keeping a nightly vigil is awaiting the gambler's return. Scott also liked the coin resolution but not what it portended. His coin, instead, is a trick one that always comes up heads and is tossed to determine whether or not the gambler rushes into the heroine's arms. Since the coin cannot come up tails, neither can the ending.

Some of Scott's changes illustrate his belief in a universal brotherhood. When the gambler receives a letter from the Greek mother of the man whose identity he has assumed, he takes it to a priest for translation. The priest assumes that the gambler really is the Joe Boscopolous whose brothers have been killed by Nazis and who is now expected to continue their fight against fascism. As the gambler and the priest kneel in prayer, the priest asks God to "direct Joseph, who in Thine eyes, is the brother of all men." Although Joe mends his con man's ways in the earlier versions, he is not regenerated in a church. Scott's Joe, moreover, is renewed not only spiritually but politically, becoming a nephew of Uncle Sam and a member of the merchant marine.

Scott's work on *Mr. Lucky* was more than editorial refurbishing; he deserved the screenplay credit he shared with Milton Holmes. On the basis of *Mr. Lucky's* success, RKO negotiated a new contract with Scott that virtually made him a producer, raising his salary to $500 a week and stipulating that he could be asked to write the script of any film he was assigned to produce.

Reconstructing a life from legal files, clippings, production notes, and marked-up scripts makes one appreciate the way events, sometimes only a day apart, can, by their proximity, bridge a gap without quite covering it. By 14 December 1943, the day after RKO made Scott a producer, a Paramount Pictures executive could have had access to the 96-page treatment of *Miss Susie Slagle's* (1946) by Ann Froelick and Adrian Scott which bears that date. Scott must have started working on it immediately after he finished *Mr. Lucky*. Although *Susie* was not released until 1946, and was by then so far from what Scott intended that he received only coadaptation credit, it was obviously a film with which he wanted to be associated.

Scott was not the first writer to work on the story.[9] As early as 1939, Paramount had wanted to film Augusta Tucker's novel about Johns Hopkins medical students who roomed at Miss Susie Slagle's boardinghouse. In that year, veteran screenwriter Frances Marion was the first to attempt an adaptation, completing a 126-page script by early 1940 which marked the end of her association with the film. She remained relatively close to the source, which had a surface proletarianism that a radical—which Marion was not—could deepen. In fact, some of the characters were a Marxist's dream, especially the working-class student who inveighs against privilege and condescension, and the self-effacing Jew whose confidence returns when he hears that Jews are natural doctors because of their history of persecution. The problem lay with the title character, whose death from cancer was so exemplary and uplifting as to make oncology obsolete.

Paramount, however, had not given up. It is not surprising that Adrian Scott would play a role in the studio's six-year attempt to bring the novel to the screen. The plot with its overtones of racial prejudice and class consciousness would have appealed to him; but something else attracted him even more: the possibility of writing as a feature film the documentary on poverty and disease he had yearned to make in the late 1930s. Medicine had remained one of Scott's interests; in "Some of My Worst Friends," his apologia for *Crossfire*, he drew on it for analogies with anti-Semitism: "Medicine would not put a highly infectious patient in a fine hospital and deny him the use of penicillin. Motion pictures cannot make two or five or even ten films and announce their responsibility has been discharged. If the industry believes, and not simply pays lip service to the notion that American life guarantees freedom from prejudice, as the pictures on anti-Semitism will say directly or indirectly, then clearly there is a responsibility facing the industry." Even films about the subject "are no permanent cure." Anti-Semitism is an infection that needs megadoses of antibiotics: "To destroy a mass prejudice a mass instrument is necessary." That instrument, Scott insisted, was a series of shorts on prejudice and intolerance. Even when he was trying to convince RKO to make *Crossfire*, he compared anti-Semitism to "a cancer [that] will grow unless heroic measures can be taken to stop [it]."[10] This is not liberal cant but a liberal's credo, as genuine as a profession of religious faith. While Scott believed in God, he also believed in Man. His approach to *Miss Susie Slagle's* expressed this joint belief.

The 14 December 1943 treatment of *Susie* is coauthored, and there must have been a consensus; otherwise, it would never have achieved such homogeneity. Anyone interested in medicine would want a movie about aspiring doctors to include scenes in clinics, classrooms, and laboratories, but since Scott—like Lester Cole—worked blacks into his plots whenever possible, it was probably he who inserted the scene in which one of the students delivers a black woman's child, as well as the one in which a black choir moves from ward to ward singing a spiritual so poignantly that the interns (one of whom is Chinese) join in. As a racially heterogeneous group of children responds to the choir, a Jewish intern remarks, "It's good to be reminded that prejudice isn't congenital. What a great world this would be if we could all grow up to be children!" If Scott did not write these lines, he easily could have. And the title character's envoi—"It is the passionate people who make the world progress. Use your brains, my dears, but never stop thinking with your hearts"—expresses Adrian Scott's sentiments precisely.

As the script passed from Scott and Froelick to others, however, its conscience dissipated and finally disappeared. What had been conceived as a film blending love and commitment became a medical school romance. There is no impassioned peroration by Miss Susie because she does not die of cancer but goes on renting rooms; the role of the Jewish intern is reduced to a walk-on; no black choir entertains the patients; the medical student delivers a white woman's baby.

By the time Paramount released *Miss Susie Slagle's* in 1946, Scott had already produced four films at RKO. The first was not *Murder, My Sweet*, as is usually thought, but *My Pal Wolf* (1944), written by his friend from *Stage* magazine days, John Paxton. Even before December 1943, Scott had arranged for Paxton to come to RKO as a writer, and with his elevation to producer, he was able to get Paxton his first screen credit.

When Scott became a producer, he was fresh from his work on *Miss Susie Slagle's*, and *My Pal Wolf* was the perfect illustration of the intern's wish that we might all grow up to be children. Paxton's unusually sensitive script concerns a girl who, because of parental neglect, forms a close attachment to a German Shepherd she calls Wolf. Even when she discovers that Wolf belongs to the army, she refuses to give him up, going so far as to petition the secretary of war to keep him. The secretary explains Wolf's importance to the war effort, arguing that making an exception for her would be like exempting a physically fit man from the draft because of a mother's plea. The child gets a substitute until Wolf is discharged, and her career-conscious parents are shamed into mending their ways; they do grow up to be children.

Despite *My Pal Wolf*'s moderate success, it was not a film to advance anyone's career. Scott, a producer in RKO's B unit, was interested in making an A product—a classic melodrama. He found his film in the studio's discard pile; there amid the literary jetsam was Raymond Chandler's *Farewell, My Lovely*, which RKO had purchased in 1940 and relegated to the Falcon series, where it had appeared in radically altered form as *The Falcon Takes Over* (1942). After convincing RKO that *Farewell, My Lovely* could be filmed pretty much as written, Scott gave Paxton a morning to read the novel; then the two set out to adapt it. Their collaboration is paradigmatic of what can result when producer and writer share the same outlook. While *Murder, My Sweet* (1944) is generally regarded as an Edward Dmytryk (director) and John Paxton film, Scott's contribution went beyond merely producing. It was Scott who was responsible for the flashback structure, which he preferred to sequential narrative.[11] He felt that having Philip Marlowe narrate would preserve the novel's first-person quality. Scott was also responsible for the transformation of Chandler's Anne Riordan into Ann Grayle; thus Dmytryk was able to make doubles of Ann and her stepmother, Mrs. Lewin Lockridge Grayle, the sought-after Velma.

Murder, My Sweet made Scott a producer to be reckoned with and Paxton one of RKO's most valuable writers. The film netted Paxton a $2,500 bonus, a far cry from the $150 a week he received in 1943 when the studio put him to work on two Great Gildersleeve movies for which he received no screen credit. In fact, RKO was so determined to keep Paxton that in order to justify a raise, the studio wrote the Treasury

Department's Salary Stabilization Unit that he was "one of the top writers in the motion picture industry."[12]

For Scott, *Murder, My Sweet* was a beginning and an end; of all his films, it is the only one without a political subtext and human values, both of which would have been out of place in a milieu where decency is an aberration. *Deadline at Dawn* (1946)—directed by Harold Clurman and written by Clifford Odets, who freely adapted Cornell Woolrich's novel—is a more typical Scott production; it brims with humanity. The characters speak Odetese, a poeticized version of the working-class vernacular. It is a crazy kind of dialogue, as unrealistic in its way as is Philip Barry's at the other extreme. Yet Odets and Barry were able to capture the rhythm and phrasing of their respective worlds, the street and the drawing room. By giving a lilt to the language, inverting conventional word order, and using stylized and nuanced speech, both were able to convince audiences that their characters were authentic, that Bronx families and Main Line Philadelphians sound as they do in *Awake and Sing* and *The Philadelphia Story*.

Deadline at Dawn is a unity-of-time film in which a sailor has from midnight to dawn to clear himself of a murder charge. With the aid of a prostitute who keeps calling him "son" and the cooperation of the most helpful New Yorkers this side of a liberal's imagination, the villain is revealed to be a benign taxi driver; in killing a blackmailer, he has only rid the world of a parasite, according to the Odetsian ethic. Paul Lukas, in fact, plays the cabbie so sympathetically that he seems to have committed only a misdemeanor—which is what Odets intended, obviously with the producer's approval.

Scott's fourth production, *Crossfire* (1947), was his most personal. Again Paxton wrote the screenplay and Dmytryk directed, but the film originated with Scott; the words and images, though created by others, reflect everything he represented. It started on 11 May 1945 when an RKO story analyst summarized Richard Brooks's novel *The Brick Foxhole* (1945), as follows: "A soldier fed up to the breaking point with being left behind at a desk job, hears a rumor that his wife has been unfaithful to him. He goes completely to pieces and on a wild binge in Washington becomes involved in murder. Through the efforts of a loyal friend he is finally extricated from all his difficulties."[13] The analyst neglected to add that the murder victim was a homosexual killed by a homophobic soldier; perhaps he realized that the Production Code forbade any reference to homosexuality and assumed that the plot would have to be altered—as indeed it was. On 19 February 1947 another story analyst summarized "Crossfire," John Paxton's 102-page adaptation of *The Brick Foxhole*: "Theme: A drunken soldier murders a Jewish civilian for no apparent reason unless it be his hatred of Jews.

He almost succeeds in pinning the guilt on one of his buddies, a corporal whose recent strange behavior, attributable to imaginary matrimonial difficulties, makes him a likely suspect. A second crime, committed to prevent the victim from giving information about the first, proves a pitfall for the murderer."

In the two-year interlude, *Crossfire* was born. It was not an easy birth; in fact, it gave Adrian Scott the ulcers that worsened his chronic colitis. Scott campaigned to make *Crossfire*; he believed Brooks's novel could be turned into an attack on anti-Semitism without a corresponding loss of power, simply by substituting one prejudice (anti-Semitism) for another (homophobia). Although World War II was over and the Axis defeated, Scott believed fascism was still alive in the form of social injustice and racism. The most virulent fascism was Nazism; inseparable from Nazism was anti-Semitism; hence Scott reasoned, wherever there is anti-Semitism, there is incipient Nazism. In an undated letter to two RKO executives Scott fervently argued his case, claiming that in addition to being topical, *Crossfire* would also show how some American anti-Semites could easily have become Hitlerites: "Anti-Semitism is not declining as a result of Hitler's defeat. The recent Negro race riots even in a high school (an unheard of event in this country) is symptomatic of the whole cancer. Anti-Semitism and Anti-Negroism will grow unless heroic measures can be undertaken to stop them. This picture is one such measure."

Whether Scott convinced Charlie Koerner and Bill Dozier, to whom the letter was addressed, is unknown; he certainly convinced RKO's new head of production, Dore Schary. Although Schary would help formulate the Waldorf Statement a few months after *Crossfire* was released, he had a reputation as a liberal (which he was, in addition to being a survivor). He became so enamored of the project that he even fancied himself *Crossfire*'s "executive producer" and was designated as such on the Bulletin of Screen Achievement Records sheet (10 April 1947). Actually, there was no executive producer; there was only a producer, Adrian Scott. Not until 29 January 1948 was a revised sheet filed indicating that *Crossfire* was "presented by Dore Schary." The change accomplished little except to set the record straight. In the meantime, the producer had been fired from the studio where he was building an impressive career.

As soon as *Crossfire* was released, a controversy arose as to whether it might encourage anti-Semitism by appealing to bigots who would enjoy seeing a Jew murdered. Schary, never one to abandon a film he had presented, stepped into the fray. In a letter to *Commentary* (October 1947), after admitting that he "made contributions to [*Crossfire*], stimulated its production, and presented it with pride as a contribution . . . to a better world," he went on to defend the film's plausibility, arguing that there are often motiveless murders and murders whose only motive is irrational hatred. The film, Schary insisted, was made to "insulate" people against anti-Semitism. One assumes he meant "innoculate," yet *Crossfire* does insulate against anti-Semitism in a way that neither Schary nor Scott would have understood: it portrays an extreme form of it, avoiding the more common manifestations such as job discrimination, ghettoization, ostracism, restricted communities, and swastikas on synagogues. Everything Scott said about *Crossfire* indicates that he considered anti-Semitism indistinguishable from Nazism: "We have failed to understand that with existing prejudices against the Jews and the Negroes and other minorities, it would be simple—so very simple—for an American Fuhrer to whip this country into a violent and ghastly hatred as a step toward the eventual destruction of our democratic institutions."

Conceptually, *Crossfire* is an antifascist film that uses anti-Semitism as a point of departure. It is less about prejudice than about the paranoia of prejudice; what it really depicts is not just anti-Semitism but the sickness behind it, much as *M* (1931) portrays the sickness behind child-killing but is not *about* the murdering of children. Why M kills is never satisfactorily explained; "I can't help it," he cries. *Crossfire* does better at pinpointing the source of the problem. Since it was a liberal and leftwing venture, it shows the source of the disease, not surprisingly, as an ultra-right mentality acquired from the military. Monty, the murderer, is devoted to military service because it demands unquestioning obedience and corrects laxity with discipline. He is contemptuous of those who shirk their military obligations, assuming that Jews fall into that category and that as draft dodgers they have forfeited their right to live.

The irony is that Samuels, the Jew Monty kills, is not a draft dodger; he has been discharged from the army after being wounded at Okinawa, one of the bloodiest battles of the war. Just as ironic is the common source of Monty's anti-Semitism and Samuels's loneliness (which prompts him to invite Monty to his apartment): postwar malaise. Monty no longer has the regimentation that gave his life meaning; Samuels is trying to cope with an America where there is no longer an identifiable enemy: "I think maybe it's suddenly not having a lot of enemies to hate anymore. . . . Now we start looking at each other again. A whole lot of fight and hate that doesn't know where to go." Unwittingly, Samuels has hit upon the motive for his own murder: hate, lacking an outlet, is vented upon another.

Because *Crossfire* equated anti-Semitism with right-wing extremism, which also gave rise to fascism and Nazism, it implied that America had become anomic because its wartime unity had been lost. Consequently, the film aroused the ire of anti-Communist witch-hunters who believed that any movie exposing prejudice in America was intended solely to stir up racial hatred: "The job of creating racial antagonisms and minorities' grievances was handed over to the Hollywood Reds! And they accomplished it to perfection with such films as 'Gentleman's Agreement,' 'Crossfire,' 'Home of the Brave,' 'All My Sons,' 'Pinky,' 'Lost Boundaries,' etc."[14]

So Well Remembered was the final collaboration of Paxton, Dmytryk, and Scott; it was also Scott's last screen credit. The film opened in the spring of 1948 when Scott and Dmytryk had become known as two of the Hollywood Ten; naturally, it was a failure. It was also considered subversive because the main character, a doctor, espoused decent housing and adequate health care—regarded as radical goals in certain quarters. Although the film had Paxton's flashback structure and one of Dmytryk's favorite character types, the irredeemable heroine (a supposedly dutiful daughter who allows her father to go to certain death), it also epitomized everything in which Scott believed: the improvement of humanity's lot. As the doctor explains simply, "I just want men to have it better than I had."

Scott and Dmytryk were both terminated at 2:30 P.M. on 26 November 1947, the day after the Waldorf Statement was delivered; the studio obviously did not believe in wasting time. N. Peter Rathvon, corporate president of RKO, personally handed each of them a letter that read like a dishonorable discharge: "By your actions, attitude, associations, public statements, and general conduct . . . you have brought yourself into disrepute with a large section of the public, have offended the community, have prejudiced this corporation as your employer and the motion picture industry in general, have lessened your capacity fully to comply with your employment agreement, and have otherwise violated the provisions of Article 16 of your employment agreement with us."[15]

Article 16 was a morals clause which, if invoked, meant that the individual had flouted morality in a way reflecting unfavorably on both the studio and the industry: "At all times commencing on the date hereof and continuing throughout the production and distribution of the Pictures, the Producer will conduct himself with due regard to the public conventions and morals and will not do anything which will tend to degrade him in society or bring him into public disrepute, contempt, scorn or ridicule, or that will tend to shock, insult or offend the community or public morals or decency or prejudice the corporation or the motion picture industry in general; and he will not willfully do any act which will tend to lessen his capacity fully to comply with this agreement, or which will injure him physically or mentally." Even the most apolitical of moviemakers would have difficulty living up to these conditions.

Both Scott and Dmytryk sued RKO for wrongful discharge and the compensation owed them on the remainder of their contracts. RKO considered settling out of court, but both men refused. Dmytryk dropped his suit when he recanted in 1951. Scott pressed on, but when a jury awarded him $84,000 in April 1952, RKO appealed the decision and was upheld; the case dragged on for five more years, coming to an end in 1957 when the Supreme Court refused to hear it.

While Scott never received another screen credit after *So Well Remembered*, Dmytryk went on to direct more than twenty-five films. Paxton, who was not a Communist, may have been tainted for a while by his association with Scott—he had no credits between 1947 and 1950—but continued in his profession, writing such successful films as *Fourteen Hours* (1951), *The Wild One* (1954), and *On the Beach* (1959).

Scott was the unfortunate one. His wife, Anne Shirley, divorced him when he refused to cooperate with HUAC. His colitis ulcerated so badly that he had to be hospitalized and was therefore the last of the Ten to be sentenced—on 27 September 1950; a brutal proctological examination prior to imprisonment did not help his condition. Psychoanalysis eventually cured his colitis, and his luck began to change when he met aspiring television writer Joan La Cour, who first fronted for him on television scripts, then collaborated with him, and eventually became his wife. Yet he was still a producer with no prospects of producing in his own country. Consequently, the Scotts went abroad, settling in London in 1961 where Adrian found a position as executive assistant to Larry Bachmann, head of MGM's British division. The job was supposed to lead to producing, but through a series of misfortunes often known to befall the undeserving, every production that Scott planned failed to materialize. One such film was to have starred Warren Beatty, with Paxton as screenwriter and Joseph Losey as director; it was never made, nor was Scott credited for the films (such as the 1964 remake of *Night Must Fall*) to which he did contribute.

He had one last production before he died—not on the big screen, but on the tube; the same production reunited him with John Paxton. In 1947 Scott had written a charming one-acter, *Mr. Lincoln's Whiskers*, which was produced by the Actors Lab in Hollywood the same year. The play's point of departure is eleven-year-old Grace Bedell's letter to Lincoln suggesting that if he grew whiskers, he would look less formidable and would also win the presidential election. Lincoln replied almost immediately, wondering whether it might not be a piece of "silly affectation" if a hitherto beardless man suddenly sported whiskers.[16] Scott imagines what might have happened if Lincoln, to demonstrate his faith in "the people's will," had paid the child a visit.

Paxton adapted the play as a television movie, which was filmed in 1969. In the fall of 1972, when Scott was terminally ill with lung cancer,

Dalton Trumbo pressured Universal to televise it in time for Scott to see his name on the screen, albeit the small screen, before he died. When Joan Scott told her husband that it would be aired sooner than scheduled, he replied, "It's too late." *The Great Man's Whiskers*, as the teleplay was called, was shown on 13 February 1973. Scott had died the previous Christmas at the age of sixty-one.

In the spring of 1947 Adrian Scott's expectations were boundless. He believed he would finally be able to make those documentaries about minorities and prejudice that he had long envisioned. It was an ambitious project whose aim was neither wealth nor fame but the education of the American public, and he was convinced that enough prominent people in the industry were interested in such films and even willing to donate their services to make them: "A number of gifted people said they were available for use in combating minority prejudice. This was enough encouragement to ask other people among our actors, directors, producers, and writers if they would be willing to give their services. . . . No one refused. They agreed to make time if they were busy."[17]

One suspects they agreed because the request came from Adrian Scott.

8 EDWARD DMYTRYK
To Work, Perchance to Dream

"My life has been one long roller-coaster ride. I've had more ups and downs than a two-bit whore in a lumber camp. And I've learned one thing. Every time fate beckons with her middle finger, it's a complete surprise. Misfortune doesn't take off her coat, put up her dukes, and say, 'Come on, let's fight.' She creeps up on you when you're not looking, clobbers you, then keeps hitting you while you're down."[1]

This quotation suggests a weary gumshoe in a dented fedora; one might be hearing the late afternoon ruminations of Philip Marlowe in his best screen incarnation, *Murder, My Sweet* (1944), Edward Dmytryk's first major film. Marlowe could turn a similarly tough phrase and flex language as if it were muscle.

Actually, the source is not a Dmytryk movie but Dmytryk's autobiography. If the director sounds like one of his characters, it is because nature and destiny conspired to give him a hide that was never in danger of reverting to skin. The son of Ukrainian immigrants, Dmytryk began peddling papers at six. Family squabbles turned him into an unsuccessful runaway, and the desire for decent clothes prompted his enlistment in the ROTC. Despite a childhood that most psychologists would consider deprived, Dmytryk looked upon the film industry not as a means of compensating for a lost youth but as a means of earning a living. Beginning as a messenger boy at Famous Players–Lasky, the precursor of Paramount, he graduated to assistant cutter, then to editor; after snipping celluloid for thirteen years, he got his first directing job at twenty-eight.

A survivor who came up from the ranks, Dmytryk learned early to adhere to a shooting schedule and stay within budget, sometimes surprising a studio by bringing a film in ahead of time and under budget. Given his unglamorous apprenticeship, he could hardly be expected to evidence much interest in languorous long takes, sequence shots, pictorialism, romance, or humor; the characters in his best films move within an oppressively closed universe, tightly framed by a camera that replicates the archway in which life has trapped them. But that apprenticeship gave him the technology to survive for more than fifty years in an industry where longevity is the exception to the rule. It was his pragmatism—bred of years of hustling, studying by the light of a projector, and handsplicing film—that influenced his decision to recant in 1951 and to name names, if that meant reinstatement in the only profession he knew.

Unlike most directors, whose hands had rarely touched the stuff of which their films were made, Dmytryk began by cutting strips of celluloid and piecing them together, using razor blades, spit, and cement; with the coming of the editing machine, he was able to improve the movies of such directors as Henry Hathaway and Leo McCarey by imparting rhythm and momentum to scenes in which they were either lacking or inchoate.

Dmytryk became a director in a way that was not exactly atypical; just as Alfred Hitchcock was corralled into completing a film that someone else had started, Dmytryk was asked to finish *Million Dollar Legs* (1939; not to be confused with the W.C. Fields film of the same name) when Nick Grinde became demoralized by Paramount's lack of confidence in him. Paramount was impressed with his work even though musical comedy was not his forte; the studio must have sensed that someone who had touched the raw material of film and thus knew how to energize it would be more suited to thrillers. Paramount's judgment was borne out by *Television Spy* (1939), which was followed by three others, all for Paramount: *Emergency Squad* (1939), *Golden Gloves* (1939), and *Mystery Sea Raider* (1940).

Although these films are not typical Dmytryk except for the speed with which they were made and the pace at which they moved, within a year (1939-40) he had demonstrated his capacity for melodrama, which is far less limited in movies than in fiction or drama. Movie melodrama can assume such forms as *film noir*, thriller, science fiction, horror, crime, and exploitation—the last being one to which Dmytryk returned periodically, mining it for whatever sensationalism the times would allow.

In 1941 the times were far from lenient; a film about prostitution required encoded dialogue and intentionally ambiguous situations that the knowledgeable would take one way, the Breen Office and the Legion of Decency the other. Thus, when Dmytryk made *Under Age* (1941) for Columbia, his direction allowed the naive to assume that the girls recruited to steer men to a motel chain known as "The House by the Side of the Road" were "hostesses," and that the "houses" were homes away from home; more seasoned moviegoers knew that "hostesses" are whores and that a "house" is not a home. *Under Age*, in fact, is a cheap imitation of *Marked Woman* (1937), right down to the "two sisters" plot. When the younger sister is brutally killed, the older seeks revenge; when the avenging sister is beaten, what is done to her is intentionally vague, inviting the unhealthiest sort of speculation.

Dmytryk reveled in sleazy plots and gave them the look of premium trash. *Under Age* includes a classy Depression montage with canted shots of grim faces dissolving into feet wearily pounding the pavement as the sisters look in vain for work. The film also introduced a favorite Dmytryk motif: the interrogation in which the victim—here, the older sister—is menaced by inquisitors whose faces are masked in shadow.

Made the same year as *Under Age* was *The Devil Commands* (1941), also a Columbia production, which embodies the most distinctive feature of Dmytryk's style: low-key or, as he would preferred to call it, high-contrast photography. Low-key photography is characteristic of *film noir*,[2] a genre (if it is one) that eludes definition because, for all its realism, it is a mannered portrayal of menace: faces are stark white or flecked with shadow; streets are tar-black and glistening; mirrors reflect anti-selves; light falls in circles. The roots of *noir* lie in expressionism pruned of its excesses and confined to the shadowy interplay of light and darkness in a world as askew as the chimneys in *The Cabinet of Dr. Caligari* (1919) but less exaggerated and therefore more recognizable. While *film noir* illustrates a calculated use of monochrome, it is incorrect to say that Dmytryk is consciously trying to be painterly or to imitate Rembrandt, whose blacks have always fascinated moviemakers. *Noir* became his specialty because it corresponded to his vision of the world as a place of dark theatrics.

Technically a "mad scientist" movie, *The Devil Commands* features a scientist who is neither deranged nor murderous, although his subjects do tend to die from his experiments in contacting the dead through the brain waves of their survivors. The plot is a combination of *Frankenstein* and *The Old Dark House* (1932), perhaps to capitalize on the persona of Boris Karloff, who appeared in both and starred in *The Devil Commands*. Thus there are the house on the cliff, rainswept and lit by lightning; the streets that look wet from perpetual rain; the combination of high-contrast and low-key photography (which, despite Dmytryk's insistence, are distinct); and such monochromatic juxtapositions as a jet-black cake in an ivory box and black-clad mourners beside a blindingly white tombstone.

The film's outstanding feature is Dmytryk's creative use of shadows, which fall across faces like masks or turn walls and balustrades into dark latticework. Equally imaginative is his incorporation of light sources into the action: headlights, flashlights, and electrodes. One sequence is particularly notable for its amalgamation of natural light and shadow: when a former spiritualist descends the staircase, brandishing a lamp, and her shadow intersects with that of the balustrade, the wall becomes a study in chiaroscuro.

The success of *The Devil Commands* led to six more films at Columbia made within a period of eighteen months, the most notable of these being *Confessions of Boston Blackie* (1941) and *Counter-Espionage* (1942), which enabled Dmytryk to demonstrate further his flair for stylized, low-budget melodrama. *Confessions of Boston Blackie* was part of a series of such varying quality—in directors, scripts, and casts—that any sort of consistency was impossible. *Confessions* had an interesting premise—forgery in the art world—buried in a script that, had it been better written, might have challenged the director instead of affording him an easy victory.

Dmytryk reduced the plot to real versus fake and proceeded accordingly. In the opening shot the camera pulls back from a statue of Augustus to reveal a studio where forgers are busy at work; thus he establishes the plot peg without recourse to dialogue, most of which turns out to be pedestrian. Dmytryk occasionally framed characters between the original and the forgery—the latter doing double duty as a storage place for a corpse. Such compositions were by no means merely ornamental; he was able to compress so much into sixty-eight minutes because, before "editing in camera" became a stock description for the method of John Ford and Raoul Walsh, Dmytryk was doing it automatically: editing while shooting, composing shots in such a way that little real editing was required. His days as a cutter had taught him economy; hence he used few closeups (like Hitchcock, he disdained talking heads and facial adoration), relying primarily on medium and long shots and favoring group shots—especially three-shots, with the trio arranged in such a way that others can enter the frame by an invisible cut or a pullback of the camera.

Dmytryk also practiced another form of economy: full use of the frame, as if it were a canvas to be filled with images of such diversity that the eye does not lose interest in them. Even when he leaves part of the frame empty—as he does in *Broken Lance* (1954), his first encounter with CinemaScope, in which a shot at one end of the frame is not balanced by a corresponding shot at the other—that spatial void is still functional; in *Broken Lance* it has less to do with the wide screen than with the dramatic effect of family disunity.

Once the frame is regarded as a canvas with borders and a center, it can be used more imaginatively than if it is perceived merely as a rectangular surface. Dmytryk introduces the main characters in *Confessions* not from the front but from the back. What fills the right of the frame is their hats, one of which is so outrageous that it is like a clever joke in a witless play: it keeps the audience laughing into the next few lines, which are then mercifully unheard. Another director might simply have faded in on the women. Dmytryk uses their hats as a fade-in; instead of the screen's brightening to reveal the character, the hat does it, gradually giving way to the wearer.

Confessions also reveals Dmytryk's ability to distinguish between melodrama and film noir. He must have sensed that the picture was melodramatic hokum and not sufficiently menacing for noirisme (which he would have considered expressionism, Hollywood-style). Half of Confessions takes place in daylight, the other half at night—but not the nighttime world of film noir: the streets look like urban thoroughfares, not infernal roads; the bars of shadow on the walls come from the French doors, not from the collective unconscious.

In Counter-Espionage, Dmytryk was able to use a style midway between urban melodrama and film noir because the setting, London during the blitz, called for it. Dmytryk belongs to the breed of director who finds his or her style in the subject matter; a city subjected to blackouts and air raids hardly lends itself to high-key lighting. Thus jet-black cars with silvery hoods careen down streets that look as if they had been inked rather than paved; fog swirls, and a pub mirror catches the reflections of the apprehensive patrons. The plot—the Lone Wolf's attempt to keep a beam detector out of Nazi hands—is not the thing here; atmosphere is. In one extraordinary scene the Lone Wolf disguises himself as a blind man in an attempt to find the Nazis' hiding place, where he had once been taken blindfolded. Hoping the sounds he heard on that occasion will recur and lead him there, he proceeds into a night whose silence is broken by the mewing of a cat, the crackling of roasting chestnuts, the tapping of a cane. Naturally, one thinks of Fritz Lang's M (1931) and the blind beggar, tapping his way along the streets of Düsseldorf. Although Dmytryk may be imitating Lang, he is not imitating Lang's expressionism, which is visually in an altogether different league. There is nothing in Counter-Espionage comparable to the shot of Peter Lorre looking into a cutlery shop window, his face and that of a potential victim framed in a rhomboid of knives. Dmytryk's style is an amalgam of expressionism without self-consciousness, and crime melodrama without stridency. It was ideally suited to movies like Counter-Espionage, almost all of which takes place at night—Dmytryk's time of day.

Dmytryk's career falls into four distinct but chronologically unequal phases: the 1939-42 melodramas at Paramount and Columbia; the RKO years (1942-47); the blacklist interim (1948-49); the post-recantation period (1951-75). Before moving to RKO in 1942—where he would make his two most famous films, Murder, My Sweet and Crossfire (1947)—he put in a few weeks at Universal, which was interested in adding to a gallery of monsters that already included Frankenstein, Dracula, the Mummy, and the Wolf Man. Its latest creation was an ape woman, who first appears in *Captive Wild Woman* (1943), again in *Jungle Woman* (1944), and finally in *Jungle Captive* (1945). Dmytryk was involved only in the first of the trilogy, which explains the creature's origin: she is the result of an experiment conducted by the prototypical mad scientist (John Carradine), who graduates from grafting the glands of a frog into a mouse to inserting a woman's brain into an ape. The victim's reversion to simian status when aroused prompted many reviewers to consider the film unhealthy. A post-Auschwitz audience would find it evocative of Nazism, not only in terms of the depraved experiments but also in the scientist's obsession with breeding the master race, a topic on which he discourses rapturously. In 1943, however, audiences would hardly have known that what John Carradine was doing in his soundstage laboratory paralleled what Nazi doctors were doing in death camps.

Moreover, like the vastly superior *Cat People* (1942), *Captive Wild Woman* takes an atavistic view of the female, reducing her to an animal id when she is aroused. In *Cat People*, sexual jealousy transforms the heroine into a black leopard, at least offering women a less insulting avatar; *Captive Wild Woman* gives them a Darwinian model that in the hierarchy of beasts is far from flattering.

Yet whatever one's reservations about the film's moral tone, it is still solid grade-B moviemaking. Within sixty-one minutes Dmytryk not only tells an incredibly lurid story; he also incorporates footage of Clyde Beatty from *The Big Cage* (1932) and edits it so cleverly into *Captive Wild Woman* that shots of Beatty holding lions at bay blend in naturally with those of Milburn Stone in the same pose and dress.

Dmytryk's ability to turn out movies that would nicely fill out a double bill or play singly in side-street theaters also enabled him to meet the demands of World War II, one of which was the propaganda film. Although RKO originally hired him at $500 a week to direct *Seven Miles from Alcatraz* (1942), it was his third film for the studio that established him as a master of the B movie. Here again, fate intervened, as it had with *Million Dollar Legs*: Dmytryk had not been slated to direct *Hitler's Children* (1943) but inherited the assignment from Irving Reis.

The result turned out to be a blockbuster. While *Captive Wild Woman* is grotesque, *Hitler's Children* is fascinatingly morbid. Because of the Production Code, whose limits had already been stretched to the breaking point in the interests of patriotism, screenwriter Emmet Lavery used transparently discreet euphemisms for such matters as fornication (young men and women "may meet and decide to share the experience that makes them worthy of the Führer"), sterilization ("special treatment at the Frauenklinick in Berlin"), and lobotomies (which eradicate "dangerous political thinking"). But while Lavery reduced Nazism to an oily euphemism, Dmytryk treated it as a sado-masochistic fantasy. Flagellation has never been staged in quite the same way; perhaps that is why the scene has left such a lasting impression. When Anna (Bonita Granville) proves to be a less than exemplary Nazi, she is sentenced to be whipped publicly. The lashing is done as ritual—coldly, formally. In contrast to the human circle the Hitler Youths formed on Midsummer Eve, the girls from the labor force form a rectangle as they march into the compound to a relentless drumbeat. In the middle of the compound is a totemic flagpole to which Anna is tied. A bullwhip is uncoiled, the back of Anna's blouse is ripped open—but the flagellation never goes beyond the second lash. Anna's Nazi lover suddenly sees the light and seizes the whip, using it on the flagellator.

Hitler's Children was such a success that Dmytryk and Lavery made the Japanese follow-up, *Behind the Rising Sun* (1943), into which they crammed more atrocities than would have been thought possible in a ninety-minute movie. A Japanese minister is assassinated in his bed; a female journalist is brutally slapped in the face for occupying the same sidewalk as a Japanese officer, and later, pieces of bamboo are driven under her fingernails. Chinese children plied with opium are the lucky ones; the other children are tossed into the air and bayoneted for sport. A newsman becomes a human ashtray as a lighted cigarette is put out on his chin; a boxer is strung up like a puppet, blood gushing down his arms. Eventually the Japanese memoirist narrating the film, as he prepares to disembowel himself, begs "whatever gods are left in the world" to "destroy us before it is too late."

Dmytryk's sadistic bent became increasingly obvious during the 1940s; it was the sadism of the pulps, recalling the workover scene in which the cop carefully puts on his brass knuckles or takes out his blackjack as the victim, interrogated into senselessness, slowly looks up—exhaustion changing to terror. When it came to torture and execution, Dmytryk seemed to share Augustus's philosophy: Make haste slowly. The hanging of the Filipino principal in *Back to Bataan* (1945), for example, proceeds at a deliberately slow pace. The rhythm is that of the flagellation scene in *Hitler's Children*, and even the setting is similar: a flagpole doubles as a gallows, and children are spectators.

Dmytryk's fascination with violence and its various forms—torture, beatings, murder, bizarre deaths by burial in cement or forced feeding with dirt—continued to manifest itself throughout his career; so did his ambivalence toward women, which was revealed as early as *The Blonde from Singapore* (1941), in which Leif Erickson's attraction to Florence Rice does not prevent his kicking her in the rear. In 1943 RKO assigned him to a film featuring Ginger Rogers, the biggest star he had yet directed. Although *Tender Comrade* (1943), a home-front drama in which four servicemen's wives rent a house while their husbands are at war, seemed light years away from *Hitler's Children* and *Behind the Rising Sun*, his direction of Rogers was a continuation of his overall approach to women, whom he transmogrified, humiliated, or ignored. Here he exaggerated.

Rogers had a combination of spunk and allure, girl and woman, that the right director could bring out, as Billy Wilder did in *The Major and the Minor* (1942) and Sam Wood in *Kitty Foyle* (1940), which won her an Oscar for Best Actress. In *Tender Comrade*, Rogers was overbearing; even as Kitty the working girl, she had more class. There is a vast difference between the scene in which Kitty Foyle speaks to the child that will never be born alive and the one in *Tender Comrade* in which Jo speaks to the child of the father who will never return. In the former, Rogers is warm and maternal; in the latter, she is grating and shrill, insisting that the tyke never forget what his father died for. Although Dalton Trumbo's screenplay, with its paeans to democracy, ruled out any subtlety, it was Dmytryk who had Rogers use the hard sell, promoting America as if it were a detergent that permanently banished all stains.

In 1944 Dmytryk made the film that is generally considered his best. *Murder, My Sweet*, based on Raymond Chandler's *Farewell, My Lovely*, called for the full *noir* treatment, which Dmytryk had no difficulty providing. Unfortunately, just as real *noir* (as opposed to crime melodrama and the gangster film) was emerging as a kind of subgenre and one whose conventions Dmytryk had helped establish, the blacklist intruded and prevented his joining the ranks of such postwar practitioners as Henry Hathaway and Samuel Fuller. However, even his few bona fide examples demonstrate that this was a form for which Dmytryk was suited. For one thing, it allowed him to dramatize his vision of life as an expressionist tabloid. *Noir* sanctioned the embellishment of sleaze, its elevation to the tawdry baroque. *Noir* also furnished a context for the Dmytryk woman. The *noir* lady—murderous housewife, bored matron, thrill-seeker, gun fetishist, hooker on a bar stool— is the dark side of woman, a shadow self whose own shadow extends the length of a sidewalk or a staircase. Everything about her is exaggerated: her manacle bracelet, her hair lacquered into metallic splendor and adorned with a white gardenia, her cashmere sweater with its look of calculated casualness, her white turban that mocks its symbolic color.

As William Luhr has noted, John Paxton's screenplay for *Murder, My Sweet*, with its intimations of homosexuality (Marriott's less than masculine cologne), incest (Ann Grayle's more than filial love for her father), and promiscuity (Mrs. Grayle's admission that she has not been "good"), challenged Dmytryk's ability to sustain an atmosphere of corruption and satisfy the requirements of the Production Code at the same time.[3] Like so much detective fiction, Chandler's story is a quest, certainly for Velma Valento, who turns out to be Mrs. Grayle. Chandler's Philip Marlowe is something of a quester himself, not merely because he is a private eye but because he is in quest of *his* grail—his ideal woman. Yet as Marlowe laments in Chandler's *The Long Goodbye*, he finds only "blondes and blondes"—some who play helpless; others who are soft, willing, but alcoholic; languid types made even more desirable by their aloofness; and showpieces that are well outside his price range. Moose Malloy, who hires Marlowe to find Velma, is yet another quester, seeking something as lifegiving as the grail: a dream.

In writing the screenplay, John Paxton understood that the dual quest of Marlowe and Malloy was at the heart of the novel, and that duality suggests doubling, something that Dmytryk grasped intuitively. The double is a literary device; in film, anti-selves and alter egos must be *shown* to be similar or bipolar. In *Psycho* (1960), for example, Hitchcock makes it clear by the way they are photographed in conversation that the murderer and his victim share the common bond of loneliness: each appears separately at the extremity of the frame. In expressionist film the double is often seen as a reflection in a mirror or a pane of glass.[4] In *Murder, My Sweet* Moose appears for the first time as a reflection in the window of Marlowe's office, becoming Marlowe's anti-self. Instead of looking up and seeing his own image, Marlowe sees Moose's—not unlike Henry Jekyll in Rouben Mamoulian's *Dr. Jekyll and Mr. Hyde* (1932), who, after drinking the potion, looks into the mirror and sees Hyde. When Mrs. Grayle comes to Marlowe's apartment, she is reflected in the mirror before which he is standing and thus joins the mirror images that dwell in Marlowe's mirror world. Mrs. Grayle is an extension of Marlowe in a double sense; as the unknown object of his quest and as the femme fatale of *noir* who objectifies the hero's love of danger.

Further doubling occurs between Ann Grayle, who should be the "good girl," and her stepmother. Twice, Dmytryk frames them in the same shot; in one, Ann sits in an armchair directly behind her stepmother—the latter's legs suggestively apart, the former's demurely crossed. Mrs. Grayle wears a two-piece white outfit with a bare midriff; Ann is dressed in a beige suit and a pillbox hat. As the women change, however, so does their attire. When Mrs. Grayle graduates to basic black, there is always a touch of white or silver. When she is killed at the end, black and white join in her shroudlike gown with its shimmering vertical stripes. Ann also has a penchant for silver. In a dimly lit nightclub, she wears a black dress with a silver clasp at the neck and silver bars on the shoulders. And although the finale implies a bright future for Marlowe and Ann, there is something unsettling about it, still something of Mrs. Grayle in Ann—who is sporting a pin-striped suit, set off by a coat draped around her shoulders.

Murder, My Sweet is a dark quest as well as one in which the quester is in the dark—often literally, moving through creeping fog or slipping into a black pool of unconsciousness from a blow on the head or an injection that sends him spinning through space. Dmytryk planned every detail of the film. The credits begin with a circle of light that expands into a rectangle by the time the last credit appears. The first shot reveals the source of the illumination: a light in a police station where Marlowe, wearing a white blindfold, is being interrogated. As in the credits, the light in the station falls in a rectangular block so that the table top seems made of lucite.

The film, then, is a study in monochrome, with black and white complementing and commenting on each other as light calls attention to the absence of darkness, darkness to the absence of light. The narration contributes to the periodic tension between black and white by creating a form of asynchronization; as Paxton himself explained it, the narration served "not so much for the purposes of direct storytelling . . . but what I choose to think of as syncopated narration, or narration that is not directly related to the images one is seeing on the screen at the time."[5] The plot is also at odds with itself; causal links always seem to be missing as the events unfold in time: the sudden appearances of Moose and Marriott, Marlowe's awakening to Ann Grayle's out-of-focus face. In detective fiction, what happens is often its own explanation; there is no real causality, or at least plausible causality, because one is in a world without an Efficient, much less a Final, Cause—only chance: chance meetings, chance deaths.

Despite the inevitable changes that had to be made in Chandler's novel, Paxton preserved its essence: the paradox of regulated unpredictability where random events form a pattern fashioned not by destiny but by fortune's symmetry. As fine as Paxton's screenplay is, however, *Murder, My Sweet* is Dmytryk's film: it corroborates his vision of life as a roller-coaster ride—a roller coaster whose rails are silver-edged, whose seats are onyx-black, and whose inclines are Art Deco sleek.

In 1945 Dmytryk made the film that irrevocably changed his life. It was his experience with *Cornered* (1945), his eighth film for RKO, that convinced him to break with the Communist Party, as he explained to HUAC on 25 April 1951 when he did what he had refused to do four years earlier: discuss his Communist past and identify Party members.[6] According to Dmytryk's autobiography, *Cornered* originated as a 20-page treatment by Ben Hecht which RKO executive William Dozier purchased, mainly on the strength of Hecht's reputation. Since the plot was weak, John Wexley—who had shown some expertise in writing thrillers and whose prison drama, *The Last Mile*, had been a Broadway success—was hired to develop the plot along the lines of a manhunt. Wexley arranged the events in such a way that the manhunt terminated in Argentina, thereby allowing for an attack on Argentina as pro-Nazi. When both Dmytryk and producer Adrian Scott objected to the script—presumably because of the ponderous writing but more likely because it violated the Good Neighbor Policy—John Paxton was commissioned to soften the polemics and restore the manhunt theme.

The RKO archives tell a slightly different story.[7] Ben Hecht may well have written a separate treatment at some point, but the project originated as a 54-page original screen story written by Hecht, Herman Mankiewicz, and Czenzi Ormonde in August 1944. The plot involved an American seaman who, after being liberated from a prison camp in Vichy France, sets out to find the man responsible for his brother's death. His search brings him to the Caribbean where, just as he is about to take his revenge, someone else kills the man he has been seeking. All Wexley retained was the vengeance motif and the serviceman hero.

RKO must have felt that the Hecht-Mankiewicz-Ormonde treatment still had possibilities; between December 1945 (two months after *Cornered*'s release) and August 1946, two screenwriters working independently did a series of step outlines and treatments for a film to be called "Revenge," which was never made. Saddled with the brother-avenging-brother theme, the writers expanded the plot to include a search for a buried treasure that belonged, depending on which script one was reading, either to the Aztecs or to American prisoners of war whose money had been expropriated by their Japanese captors. Whether by clerical error or by intent, the "Revenge" drafts ended up in the *Cornered* file at RKO so that the file consists of (1) a treatment that inspired a film to which it bears no resemblance; and (2) drafts for a film that was never made. Wexley's original script and Paxton's revision seem to have disappeared in the cloud of controversy that *Cornered* created.

Since Scott, Dmytryk, and Wexley were all Party members at the time, Wexley, who believed he deserved screen credit for *Cornered*, brought the matter to John Howard Lawson.

Lawson's behavior on this occasion was more like a Pooh-Bah's than a commissar's. It was not merely his siding with Wexley that soured Dmytryk on the Party; it was his authoritarianism. Since Paxton's screenplay allowed the fascist villain to express his point of view, the question arose as to whether fascists should be permitted to voice their opinions on the screen. Dmytryk argued that freedom of speech is everyone's right, fascists' and Communists' alike. Lawson ruled differently.[8]

After the *Cornered* imbroglio, Dmytryk knew he would be leaving the Party. Yet it is odd how minor incidents cause major decisions. *Cornered* is a poorly constructed thriller. Whether its faults should be attributed to Wexley (who made the brother of the treatment a husband tracking down the collaborationist who betrayed his wife to the Nazis) or to Paxton is problematical. One can respect the film's rejection of vigilantism and its insistence on evidence in the prosecution of war criminals: "There is no place for revenge or murderous hate," one of the characters states. But there is also no place for an anticlimactic ending in a thriller. If Wexley's original script favored ideology over action, Paxton's revision favors action over plausibility; Paxton, an excellent screenwriter, should have known that when a manhunt is a whodunit, the culprit should not be introduced at the very end. Throughout the film, the hero keeps encountering suspicious types, any one of whom could be the collaborationist he is seeking, yet the suspects are the opposite of what they seem: the lawyer who appears to be a fascist isn't one; his nephew is. Not until the very end of the movie does the villain pop up, assuring the hero that Nazism is far from passé: "Wherever you find the hungry, you find us. Remember you plastered us off the map once before. You held the fruit of victory in your hands, but you let it decay. You continue to attack wrong things in the wrong way. We accept the evil in man; we find it good and fertile."

These were quite possibly the Paxton lines to which Lawson and Wexley objected on the grounds that they allowed a collaborationist freedom of expression. Perhaps Lawson and Wexley were disturbed, too, by the reference to Nazism's appeal to the disaffected, which could be said of Communism as well. If so, they were correct; *Cornered* could easily be remade with a contemporary setting, given a little updating and the substitution of "Communist" for "Nazi" and "fascist." One line could remain intact: "Wherever you find the hungry you find us."

In any event, *Cornered* changed Dmytryk's politics; his next film, *Till the End of Time* (1946), changed his life. It was during the filming of the latter that he met his second wife, Jean Porter, who was playing the supporting role of a teenager who discovers that ex-servicemen are sexier than the neighborhood boys. It is Jean Porter to whom his autobiography is dedicated; it was Jean Porter who picked him up at Mill Point Prison Camp in West Virginia after he had finished serving his sentence, restoring him not only to society but also to the only life he knew—moviemaking. If she seems like the "but for whom" woman, she was.

Jean Porter came into Dmytryk's life at a critical time; his first marriage, always rocky, had ended in divorce, and what had been terminated by decree was later ratified by choice when his ex-wife committed suicide. In Jean Porter, Dmytryk found an entirely different sort of woman, the converse of the black widow of *noir*. It was Dmytryk's discovery, at forty-two, that purity and passion are not mutually exclusive which enabled him to present a complete woman on the screen for the first time: Pat (Dorothy McGuire) in *Till the End of Time*.

Till the End of Time has always been considered a poor relation of *The Best Years of Our Lives*, a Samuel Goldwyn production released through RKO the same year. Both deal with the adjustment of three veterans to civilian life; however, the difference between them is not so much that of an epyllion as opposed to an epic, but of a liberal as opposed to a democratic point of view. *Till the End of Time* was a liberal collaboration between Dmytryk, committed but no longer to the Party; Allen Rivkin, a liberal anti-Communist screenwriter; and producer Dore Schary, who was thought to be a liberal, and was so by his definition (one who stands up for the rights of others when it is prudent to do so). Since *Till the End of Time* lacked the *Best Years* team—a deep-focus cinematographer (Gregg Toland), a screenwriter from the Broadway stage (Robert E. Sherwood), and an Academy Award–winning director (William Wyler) known for his long takes—the film has been judged to have less art than its rival. It is neither as civilized nor as poignant as *Best Years*; *Time* is blunt in its assertion that as "good" a war as World War II was, it left in its wake demoralization and trauma. None of the vets can function as a civilian: one refuses to wear his prostheses until his mother shames him into doing so by invoking Franklin Roosevelt's polio; another cannot take orders; the third balks at seeing a doctor about the headaches he gets from the steel plate in his skull. Instead, the men dream of being buddies forever, owning a ranch, and hiring only ex-GIs.

While both films feature the woman whose morals have been loosened by the war, Pat is radically different from Marie (Virginia Mayo) of *Best Years*, who found that life without her husband was more remunerative than it was with him. If Dmytryk had not met Jean Porter, he might have turned Pat into a Marie. Dorothy McGuire had usually been cast in roles like the childlike wife in *Claudia* (1943)—wide-eyed, fluttery, but unalluring. Yet as Pat, she had to play a woman who, while not promiscuous, spent afternoons on a barstool, telegraphing her loneliness and availability. Pat has an affair with a much younger man (played by Guy Madison). Still, she never becomes a mother surrogate; rather, she plays woman to a boy. In a scene that anticipates the roll in the sand in *From Here to Eternity* (1953), McGuire, lying on the beach, raises her body toward Madison as he sinks down, fitting himself against her. Surprisingly, no one objected, not even the Legion of Decency, which gave *Best Years* a B rating (Morally Objectionable in Part for All) because it condoned divorce.

Best Years ends with a wedding; *Time*, with a brawl. Right-wingers approach the vets in a bar in an attempt to recruit them for an organization that excludes blacks, Catholics, and Jews. In a climax that looks forward to the end of *Giant* (1956)—in which Rock Hudson takes on a diner full of bigots as "The Yellow Rose of Texas" blares approval from the jukebox—the men reject the invitation with their fists, showing that liberalism in its most elementary form is a right cross to a racist's jaw.

Best Years is no longer a movie; it has become cinema, studied for its deep-focus photography and long takes. *Till the End of Time* is a movie, frequently reprised on afternoon television, where it can be enjoyed as a serious but undemanding flick. Dmytryk, who had to hitchhike to school and once ran away from home, at least has the satisfaction of knowing that he was better able to deal with raw reality, as opposed to cinematic realism, than an auteur like Wyler.

Circumstances interposed once more to prevent Dmytryk from pursuing that integrated vision of which he now seemed capable. *Crossfire* (1947) found him back in *noir* country, canting the camera, setting up low shots, and sending shadows up and down walls. *Crossfire*, like *Murder, My Sweet*, is textbook *noir*, the initial sequence being the first lesson. A table lamp juts into the frame, freeing the wall to act as a screen that reflects the shadows of two men, one of whom is pummeling the other to death. The victim falls to the floor, knocking over the lamp and thus producing a natural fade-out. The lamp also provides the corresponding fade-in as a hand switches it on in the next scene; it is not the hand of the murderer, who exited swiftly against an asymmetrical latticework of light, but that of a police detective. As the detective converses with the medical examiner, the camera reveals someone sitting on the sofa—the victim's flashily dressed girlfriend. Suddenly a soldier appears at the door; he will be revealed to be the murderer of a man whose only crime was that he was born a Jew. Lamps with cheap shades, darkness streaked with sickly light, and shadows on a wall provide a natural setting for an unnatural act.

Despite John Paxton's claim that this script gave him the greatest satisfaction of any he had written, *Crossfire* is a director's film. Paxton gave Dmytryk a plot, a whodunit with racial overtones, which Dmytryk broke down into its visual components. Again, one of these was doubling, but not merely of paired characters. The double can also be internal—the second self which, in expressionist film, is lit in low key to suggest duality. In *Crossfire*, however, the technique is more complex than the demarcation of light and darkness. Monty (Robert Ryan) does not behave like a typical murderer, yet beneath his good-natured exterior lies a killer's soul. Lighting can only imply duality, by blanching the face or inking the hair (or vice versa); it cannot suggest the nature of the duality. An actor can, and Ryan did. No one who mangles English as ingenuously as Monty can be evil—yet that is precisely the point: outwardly Monty is an ignoramus; inwardly he is a bigot. When the inner self overpowers the outer, ignorance joins with prejudice, erupting in an act of violence caused by both.

When Monty kills again, the second murder is visually the opposite of the first. The shabby room in the boardinghouse where Monty murders his buddy Floyd, who he thinks has betrayed him to the police, is the reverse of the apartment where he killed Samuels. Everything, in fact, has been reversed: rooming house/apartment; lamp left of frame in boardinghouse/right of frame in apartment; struggle in full view instead of in silhouette.

The scene in which Leroy, Monty's buddy, tricks Monty into returning to the boardinghouse occurs in a washroom where each man is shaving in front of a mirror. (Dmytryk was probably influenced by the scene in Wyler's Little Foxes (1941) in which Oscar Hubbard and his son Leo shave opposite each other, Wyler's way of indicating that one is the mirror image of the other.) It is an artful way of suggesting another dualism. Leroy is Monty's double in that he is poorly read, ignorant, and fearful of Jews because he has never encountered one; in fact, he thinks Finlay, the police inspector, may be a Jew because the officer has such strong feelings about prejudice. But Leroy does not cross over from ignorance to violence, because his inner self is not violent but merely as ignorant as his outer self.

Monty, on the other hand, is both an illiterate and a psychopath, given to analogies that only point up his sickness: anyone who does not respect the army does not respect his mother; "draft dodger" equates with a last name like "Samuels." Reflected in mirrors in washrooms and bars, Monty is not the classic dual personality; this is no mere cleavage of good and evil but the face of illogic and unreason, which finally leads to murder.

Following 1947—the year of Crossfire, So Well Remembered, and HUAC—the chronology of Dmytryk's career was an unusual one among the Ten. Although he did not recant until April 1951 (and had three films out the next year), and in spite of the time spent in litigation, personal appearances, and jail, his employment record in the interim is not a blank; he made two films abroad, The Hidden Room (1949) and Give Us This Day (1949). Of the Ten, Dmytryk was the least committed to the Party, as borne out not only by his recantation but also by his having joined much later—in 1944. (Although Trumbo did not join until 1943, for him it was more like legitimizing a long-standing relationship).

Perhaps being at RKO had something to do with Dmytryk's decision to join when he did. Unlike the major studios, RKO had no patriarchal head, monolithic structure, or central philosophy of movie-making. It attracted directors and writers eager to make a career for themselves and caught in that intermediate stage between obscurity and fame. Those who stayed on did so because it was lucrative; generally, though, the studio was a stopping-off place, especially for such stage liberals (and some radicals) as Orson Welles, John Houseman, Emmet Lavery, Clifford Odets, and Garson Kanin. Harold Clurman directed his only film at RKO: *Deadline at Dawn* (1946), produced by Adrian Scott and written by Clifford Odets. It is not coincidental that of the Ten, seven had passed through RKO. That Dmytryk socialized with Adrian Scott, who produced three of his films; that he worked with Dalton Trumbo on *Tender Comrade*; that he and Biberman were at the studio at the same time all suggest that the associations he made at RKO may well have influenced him to become a Communist. Significantly, it was also an experience at RKO that drove him to leave the Party.

The RKO years, however, do not tell the whole story, nor did Dmytryk in his HUAC testimony; for that, one must go to his autobiography. Like countless others in 1941, Dmytryk was an antifascist; he wanted to enlist in the Signal Corps but claimed he was rejected because he was considered a premature antifascist.[9] Dmytryk could have continued as an antifascist, premature or otherwise, without joining the Party; by 1944 the argument that Communists were the only ones who unilaterally opposed fascism carried no weight. In his autobiography, Dmytryk explains the Party's appeal: it was a tribe in which acceptance meant adhering to the rules; one thinks of the youth who suffers through an initiation not because he understands its meaning but because he wants to impress his peers and his elders by his endurance. That Dmytryk likens the Party to the Boy Scouts and its challenges suggests that even in middle age there was more than a bit of the boy-man in him.

Dmytryk's desire to prove himself to his peers, especially those at RKO, also explains some of the contradictions in his HUAC testimony, as Albert Maltz noted in his response to a *Saturday Evening Post* article about Dmytryk that appeared less than a month after his recantation.[10] Having left the Party in the fall of 1945 after being in it only a year, Dmytryk should have had no qualms about answering HUAC's questions in 1947, yet he refused. If he wanted to disassociate himself from Communism, he had more than enough reasons for doing so in 1947; Churchill had made his "Iron Curtain" speech the previous year, and it was impossible not to feel the chill in the air. Between 1947 and 1949 there were even better reasons—the Hiss trial, Judith Coplan's arrest for espionage, the Communist takeover of China; Dmytryk did not have to wait until the outbreak of the Korean War. Others might have recanted to avoid jail, but Dmytryk served his sentence, then recanted;

to have done otherwise would have made him less of a man. Having performed his ritual obligation once, however, he saw no reason to repeat it; manhood proved is manhood vindicated. Besides, as he explained to Ring Lardner, Jr., a director cannot be anonymous; screenwriters could use pseudonyms or peddle their scripts through a front, but "I have to work," he insisted.[11] So did Frank Tuttle, Robert Rossen, and Elia Kazan—other directors who also became informants.

Obviously, all Dmytryk learned from being in the Party was that instead of liberating artists, Communism enslaves them. In Hollywood, as he noted in his HUAC testimony, the Party was guilty of other wrongs: tithing salaries, attempting to influence film content, and vying for a place in the entertainment capital of the world. Dmytryk may have been right about the first allegation, but even Alvah Bessie and Lester Cole, Stalinists by any definition, had to admit that no screenwriter could insert Communist propaganda into a script without detection. The most one could do, and it would elude the average moviegoer, was to incorporate a casual reference to the Soviet Union on the order of James Cagney's toast (in *Blood on the Sun*, written by Lester Cole) to the "ten days that shook the world"; he was referring not to the Russian revolution but to ten days with Sylvia Sidney, though a comrade might have thought differently.

In fact, most of the films cited as examples of wartime Russophilia were not written by Communists. Howard Koch (*Mission to Moscow*, 1943), though one of the Unfriendly Nineteen, was never a Communist; Lillian Hellman (*The North Star*, 1943), though she lived with Dashiell Hammett for over thirty years, was (probably) not a Communist even though he was; Casey Robinson (*Days of Glory*, 1944) was apolitical and best known for his Bette Davis movies. *Song of Russia* (1943) was the exception; it was written by two Communists, Paul Jarrico and Richard Collins (the latter turned informant and named twenty-three names, however). Even so, the film's power of persuasion was overshadowed by its ability to evoke boos when Lenin's picture appeared on the screen, and laughter when Robert Taylor, looking totally guileless, confessed after a night in Moscow that he had never expected Russians to be happy.

The few Communist directors were equally powerless. Apart from the fact that Communism did not seem to dominate their lives, the subject matter of Soviet cinema (revolutions, strikes, harvests) and its techniques (dialectical montage, Socialist realism) would have been alien to American moviegoers; only under the protection of traditional narrative could social-consciousness films succeed. While radical directors made their share of hard-hitting movies exposing fight fixes (Robert Rossen's *Body and Soul*, 1946), anti-Semitism (Elia Kazan's *Gentlemen's Agreement*, 1947), wartime opportunism (Irving Pichel's *A

Medal for Benny, 1945), and the rackets (Frank Tuttle's *Suspense*, 1946), they were not the only ones. Liberal anti-Communists and apolitical directors did likewise: Mark Robson's *Champion* (1949) and Robert Wise's *The Set-Up* (1949) also dealt with the boxing world; Mark Robson's *Home of the Brave* (1949) and Joseph L. Mankiewicz's *No Way Out* (1950) both attacked racism.

Directors are pegged by the kinds of films they make, not by their political content (unless form and content are one, as they are in the work of Costa-Garvas and Marcel Ophuls). Dmytryk would have been a director of melodramas and *film noir* in any era, whether he had joined the Communist Party or the John Birch Society. It was on the basis of his success in such genres that he was able to continue working when he came off the blacklist. In the idiom of the workplace, Dmytryk's skills were marketable. He also worked fast: three of his films (*Mutiny; The Sniper; Eight Iron Men*) were in the theaters in 1952. The King Brothers, who hired him for his first post-recantation film— *Mutiny*, which was shot in eighteen days—knew his capabilities.

So did Stanley Kramer, who saw them in a different light, however. To Kramer, Dmytryk was the director of *Crossfire*, which was to anti-Semitism what Kramer's production, *Home of the Brave* (1949), was to racism: a powerful if overwrought indictment. Dmytryk's next four films would be for Stanley Kramer, each attacking some excess in the name of liberalism: oedipalism (*The Sniper*), Nazism (*Eight Iron Men*), self-withdrawal (*The Juggler*), authoritarianism (*The Caine Mutiny*). By 1951, Kramer, a genuine liberal if not a great filmmaker, had alerted audiences to the plight of paraplegics (*The Men*) and blacks in a white man's army (*Home of the Brave*). That Dmytryk made four films for Kramer indicates that he had become accepted as an anti-Communist liberal, not unlike Kramer himself.

Of the three 1952 releases, *The Sniper* is the most representative of Dmytryk's work. Had it been made at RKO in the late 1940s, it might have been a superior study in terror. However, like Dore Schary, who wore his social conscience on his sleeve, Kramer refused to settle just for a movie about a woman killer. The sniper picks off women because he hates his mother; once, when his mother's name is mentioned, he reacts like a prude hearing an obscenity.

Confronted with a plot in which a man kills because his dop-pelganger takes possession of him, driving him to murder women who are more like his mother than his feminine ideal, Dmytryk—master of the mirror as metaphor for the split self—has each woman shot through glass, as if the sniper is trying to kill both the woman and what she represents. Women are shot as they see their reflection or while they are standing by a window. The killer does not even have to see his victim in the flesh; an image on a television screen is sufficient.

The Juggler (1953), also a Kramer production, promises to be a film of power and punch, yet both are curiously absent. The main character (Kirk Douglas), a death-camp survivor haunted by the memory of his wife, who died in the gas chamber, is a misfit; he is unable to function even in Israel because the Israeli police remind him of the SS. Although his plight is moving, it is a plight without a plot other than the conventional man-on-the-run, which makes *The Juggler* another man-hunt film. That the man is a Jew is important to Michael Blankfort, who adapted his own novel, but not to the director; while Dmytryk may have empathized with the character, he did not identify with him, as Sidney Lumet did with the title character in *The Pawnbroker* (1965). Dmytryk had no feeling for Israel; the exteriors could easily have been shot in Griffith Park. Uprooted from the world of the soundstage and transplanted to Haifa, he had little opportunity to demonstrate the art of high contrast except in one scene: a hora danced around a bonfire illuminating the faces and clothes of the dancers, turning white shirts silver and washing complexions clean of imperfections; when Dmytryk moves to a high shot, the hora becomes a concentric study in black and white.

It is ironic that the Kirk Douglas character is a Dmytryk type whose dark and bright sides are in disharmony. The problem was the setting; Dmytryk could not portray a dual personality in kibbutzim and refugee camps. Only once did he succeed in depicting a psychic split; when the juggler entertains an audience of children, his shadow on the wall mimics his every movement. But when the juggler barricades himself and defies the police, one has the feeling that the film is an Israeli *Sniper*; both sniper and juggler admit that they want to be caught, the juggler going so far as to cry, "I'm sick; help me." And what might have been a film about Israel becomes a film about a neurotic rehabilitated by Stanley Kramer, who was wise enough to know that Israel alone is not the answer for disturbed Jews.

Equally ironic, but in a different sense, is a scene that looks back to Josef von Sternberg's *Blue Angel* (1930) and forward to Dmytryk's 1959 remake. When the juggler, in order to get a laugh, lets one of the eggs he is balancing land on his head, it is impossible not to think of a similar scene in *The Blue Angel* in which the magician breaks an egg on the head of Professor Unrath who, like Dmytryk's juggler, is in white face. While the circumstances are different (feigned embarrassment as distinct from debasement), the imagery is the same—and seven years later, Dmytryk would repeat the egg-breaking scene in its original context.

With the exception of Ginger Rogers in *Tender Comrade*, Dmytryk rarely directed screen icons until his reinstatement in the industry; then he worked not only with major stars but also at major studios such as MGM, Fox, and Warner's. Yet if Spencer Tracy had not made *The Mountain* (1956), Clark Gable *Soldier of Fortune* (1955), or Bette Davis *Where Love Has Gone* (1964), cinema would not have been the poorer. The problem was the scripts offered to Dmytryk, which, out of habit or preference, he accepted. When he had the opportunity to distinguish himself, as he did in MGM's *Raintree County* (1957), he was unable to provide the epic sweep a Civil War film required. Instead, he repeated himself, isolating characters at the extremity of the frame and using the mirror as an alter ego. Thus, Elizabeth Taylor sits right of frame as she bids farewell to her children; in anger, she lashes out at a mirror, though she stops short of smashing it, as George Peppard does in *The Carpetbaggers* (1964) when he discovers he has become the father he loathes.

Anzio (1968) might have been a blockbuster but is curiously small-scaled; the liberation of Rome, which should have been a spectacle, is just a parade. Although the star is Robert Mitchum, the best moments are Peter Falk's; he plays a soldier so badly wounded that surgical repairs have made him almost literally a man of steel—recalling the Mitchum character of *Till the End of Time*, whose head throbs from the steel plate. The only effective moment in *Anzio* has nothing to do with the war; it is Falk's frenetic rendition of "Bye, Bye Blackbird," which sends his steel-girded interior into trauma.

Dmytryk's inability to draw a stellar performance from a cast capable of it can be seen in *The Caine Mutiny* (1954), his last film for Stanley Kramer, which featured Humphrey Bogart, Fred MacMurray, Jose Ferrer, and Van Johnson. Dmytryk could not get the acting styles to mesh: Ferrer sounded like an elocutionist; Bogart's Queeg was more like the paranoid he played in *The Two Mrs. Carrolls* (1947) than the craven captain of Herman Wouk's novel; Van Johnson looked as if he missed June Allyson and the MGM backlot.

Perhaps the interrelated themes of informing, guilt, and betrayal were too much for the director. On 22 May 1951, less than a month after Dmytryk's recantation, Jose Ferrer had appeared before HUAC, cooperative to the point of obsequiousness. A year later, Dmytryk was directing Ferrer in *The Caine Mutiny*: an informant directing a friendly witness playing a hero. The film may have touched a nerve in Dmytryk, who seemed more interested in Keefer (MacMurray), in many ways the director's alter ego, than in Queeg, for whom he had no sympathy. Dmytryk's indifferent direction of Bogart left no doubt that Queeg was incompetent; in the stage version, *The Caine Mutiny Court Martial* (1953), the best Queegs (Lloyd Nolan in the original, Michael Moriarty in the 1983 revival) left room for uncertainty. Keefer should be the villain, yet Dmytryk downplayed Keefer's villainy, allowing MacMurray to substitute slickness for malevolence. Thus, in the penultimate scene, when Greenwald—realizing that wars are won by the Queegs who, whatever they are, at least keep Jews from ending up as bars of soap—throws a drink in Keefer's face, the gesture is a melo-dramatic cliché, like gauntlet-flinging or face-slapping. Keefer is no more responsible than Fred MacMurray.

Of the films Dmytryk made after his recantation, *Mirage* (1965) is closest to the kind on which he made his reputation. In addition to being in black and white, it allowed him to triumph over the improba-ble story of an amnesiac scientist's discovery of a way to neutralize nuclear energy, much to the alarm of a peace foundation with ties to a chemical combine that is interested in the atom only for wartime use. *Mirage* also evidences Dmytryk's talent for adapting to the newest form of flashback. In the 1940s the flashback was usually a fade-out/fade-in; influenced perhaps by the flashcutting in *Hiroshima Mon Amour* (1960), filmmakers started abandoning the fade-out for the quick cut. Since the flashbacks in *Mirage* are intended to prod the hero's memory, they seem more like epiphanies than episodes. The climax is staged in the *noir* manner: the room is elegantly appointed and the *noir* lady in black, yet just when it seems that the hero is doomed, a shot rings out; the villain falls to the floor; and the dark lady, now the avenging angel, stands behind a mahogany desk with a smoking revolver in her hand.

Although Dmytryk calls himself an agnostic, he has made four films on religious themes which reveal a good deal about himself. When the plot affects him, he displays the reverence of a believer; when the plot merely interests him, he simulates belief without conde-scending to the material. In either case, he is respectful.

In 1948, jobless and willing to direct anything, he accepted an offer from producer Lou Geiger to do the film version of Pietro DiDonato's novel, *Christ in Concrete*. Since Dmytryk and screenwriter Ben Barzman had been blacklisted, the film was shot in London and released by Eagle-Lion. The plot, in which a bricklayer is buried alive in concrete at the very moment he puts humanitarian concerns above self-interest, needed an Italian neorealist like Vittorio deSica or Roberto Rossellini or else an American pictorialist on the order of Ford or Wyler. It needed the look of the streets, even if shot on a soundstage, like Ford's *Informer* or Wyler's *Dead End*.

At the time, Dmytryk, though no longer a Communist, was still one of the Ten and thus should have been sufficiently committed to improving society to inject passion, if not rage, into *Give Us This Day*, as the film was titled. However, what attracted him to the project was not, it seems, the novel's virulent anticapitalism but the final scene. Yet when Geremio's head disappears beneath the concrete, the effect is less shattering than it should be, perhaps because the concrete looks like oatmeal.

The opening—Geremio stumbling along a Brooklyn street as smoke rises from a manhole and a lamppost imparts an eerie sheen to the cobblestones—leads one to expect more than Dmytryk proves capable of offering. The film is more effective technically than it is emotionally. When high contrast is required, Dmytryk supplies it; when the camera must mount scaffolds and pan construction sites, Dmytryk is there, supervising every moment. Yet in intimate moments like an Italian wedding or a family dinner, he resorts to clichés: a row of empty wine bottles spells inebriation; a pasta-eating contest passes for ethnicity. Give Us This Day demands iconography; the title calls for it. Yet when Geremio in despair brings his hand down on an iron picket, stigmatizing himself in the first of a series of Christ associations, Dmytryk does nothing with the stigmata.

Similar problems occurred twelve years later when Dmytryk read a script about the seventeenth-century saint Joseph of Cupertino (1603-63). That Dmytryk was able to persuade Columbia to finance a movie with dubious box-office prospects shows how dramatically his stock had risen after a string of undistinguished but commercially successful films. That he produced and directed The Reluctant Saint (1962) proves that, unlike Give Us This Day, The Reluctant Saint was not a job, but a choice.

But again, he was not the ideal director, although he may have sympathized with a man who, despite his lowly origins (not unlike Dmytryk's), became a miracle worker and saint. The film needed the earthborn simplicity that Franco Zeffirelli brought to Brother Sun, Sister Moon (1973), as well as Zeffirelli's unabashed love for his hero, St. Francis of Assisi. Dmytryk has Maximillian Schell play Joseph as more of a retardate than a simpleton. While Joseph may have been the village joke, he was not the village idiot.

Again, Dmytryk was involved with a film that cried out for iconography, at which he was never successful. When Joseph is robbed and stripped of his cassock while begging, his condition should evoke the traveler in the parable of the Good Samaritan or Christ on his way to Calvary. Instead, a woman covers Joseph's bare back with a cloak. The closest Dmytryk comes to iconography is a shot of Joseph, his hands clasped anxiously, standing next to a picture of the Virgin in a similar pose.

Even in a film about a saint, Dmytryk could not resist the temptation of low-key lighting; when Joseph and the Vicar General roast chestnuts in an open field, one almost expects Moose Malloy to step out of the darkness. But believing that the life of a saint needs bursts of light and shining corollas, Dmytryk switches to high-key for the climax; when the monk (Ricardo Montalban) who has always been skeptical of Joseph's miraculous powers sees him levitating, the skeptic is bombarded with such a blast of front lighting that he looks electrified.

As a film of faith, *The Reluctant Saint* lacks the purity of *The Song of Bernadette* (1943), even though it contains two of the same plot ingredients: the persecution of the saint and the conversion of the skeptic. Dmytryk may have envied Joseph's simple faith or related to his vindication, but there is not the identification with the material that Henry King brought to *Song of Bernadette*, Robert Bresson to *Diary of a Country Priest* (1951), and even Leo McCarey to *The Bells of St. Mary's* (1945).

Dmytryk's best films on religious themes are *The Left Hand of God* (1955) and *The End of the Affair* (1955), perhaps because they evoke his personal and cinematic past. Understandably, there is an intersubjective quality in Dmytryk's post-HUAC films: within two years he directed a friendly witness (Jose Ferrer) and an informant (Lee J. Cobb, who recanted a year later than Dmytryk); trials, investigations, and admissions are recurrent themes in his films; Dore Schary produced *Raintree County* when it was Schary who, by supporting the Waldorf Statement, was partly responsible for the blacklist that caused Dmytryk to be fired from RKO. Such incidents may not turn saints into agnostics, but they at least make them sensitive to life's incongruities.

The Left Hand of God could easily have been maudlin had it not been for Dmytryk's apprenticeship in B melodramas; thus the plot—a flier, masquerading as a priest in postwar China, saves a village from a savage warlord (read Communist)—becomes less a noble deception and more a conversion story in which the change is from tough to tender, but never from sinewy to simple-minded. Humphrey Bogart's "priest," Father O'Shea, recalls a character Bogart had played in Warner's *It All Came True* (1940): a gangster who eventually softens without melting into buttery wholesomeness.

Although little is made of the time of the action, it is clear from references to China's being "in a state of civil war," that its fall to the Communists in 1949 is just a few years away. Thus Yang the warlord (Lee J. Cobb), whose minions kill priests, can only be a Communist; he recalls another Chinese warlord, also named Yang, in *The General Died at Dawn* (1936), written by Clifford Odets, who modeled the character after Chiang Kai-shek—much to the delight of the left, which despised the Generalissimo. Two decades later, Yang is the name of a Communist despot in a film whose director and second lead had also undergone a 180-degree turn.

Although *The Left Hand of God* has overtones of *Going My Way* (1944) and *Guys and Dolls* (1955), with sing-along songs for children and a crap game whose outcome determines the fate of the village, it never becomes as treacly as the former or as brash as the latter. Dmytryk is in control of both the material and the CinemaScope screen, which he fills with some impressive vistas, favoring the colors of which he is fondest: blue and red, the blues making the night look almost sacred.

Dmytryk's most spiritual, as distinct from religious, film is the screen version of *The End of the Affair*; although it was not a commercial success, it was certainly a triumph of taste. *The End of the Affair* is Graham Greene's most complex Catholic novel; its theme is not so much belief in God, although that is part of it, as belief in belief. The paradox of having faith in faith and of aligning the human will with the divine will without any diminution of free choice is difficult to express on the screen in any era, let alone the mid-1950s. Dmytryk was fortunate in his producer and screenwriter, David Lewis and Lenore Coffee. Lewis, known primarily as a producer of women's films, learned from his involvement with *Camille* (1936), *Dark Victory* (1939), and *The Other Love* (1947) that popular tragedy is not middle-brow romanticism and that what is serious need not be solemn. For the production to remain on the same theological plane as the novel, in which adultery becomes the occasion for dramatizing the interrelationship between guilt, belief, and salvation, a screenwriter must be attuned to Greene's civilized and at times jesuitical Catholicism. Lenore Coffee was; while she omitted the novel's final miracle (the disappearance of a birthmark from the face of an atheist whose hatred of God had been caused by his disfiguration), she was remarkably faithful to the plot and to Greene's carefully sustained atmosphere of drawing room infidelity.

Greene's novels and plays generally revolve around a moral dilemma: in *The End of the Affair* it is a married woman's decision to give up a lover. Although this is a common literary theme (and it may have been the *Camille*-like premise that attracted Lewis to the project), Greene's Sarah is not a courtesan relinquishing her lover for his family's honor; she is a woman who, when she thinks her lover has been killed in a bombing raid, makes a bargain with God that she will give him up if he lives. When Maurice survives, Sarah must, like Camille, make the sacrifice without disclosing the reason; it is only through her diary that he learns the nature of her sacrifice. It was a sacrifice that enabled her to find God, beginning—as such quests do—with finding God's opposite: an atheist whose faith is even stronger than Sarah's because it is really bitterness at being born with a facially disfiguring birthmark. Sarah then falls into belief as she had fallen into love.

Coffee even includes the novel's most shattering revelation: Sarah, who seeks solace in Catholic churches, does not know why she is drawn to Catholicism. The reason, one discovers at the end, is that she had been baptized a Catholic but had never been told. Thus her pact with God stems from an unconscious awareness that adultery is more than the breaking of a marriage vow; it is the breaking of a commandment. Sarah, who fancied herself an agnostic, really behaves like a

Catholic raised on the sixth commandment, which always seemed to take precedence over the other nine.

As Sarah, Deborah Kerr had one of the most difficult roles of her career; in a sense, playing the adulterous Karen in *From Here to Eternity* (1953) prepared her for it. Yet Sarah does not engage in extramarital affairs out of self-pity or boredom; she has so internalized her passion that by a spiritual alchemy it has been refined into yearning and then into selflessness. Kerr caught every nuance of the character: her casual approach to infidelity, revealed by the matter-of-fact way she puts on her earrings after she and Maurice have made love for the first time; her insensitivity to Maurice's embarrassment when he is mistaken for her husband; her gradual realization that her husband, a dull civil servant, needs her; her own knowledge that she could have broken her covenant with God and remained a happy sinner instead of a tortured saint. *The End of the Affair* is Deborah Kerr's and Edward Dmytryk's film.

By coincidence or destiny, which is controlled coincidence, Dmytryk found himself repeating a theme and a setting from two earlier films that are light years removed from *The End of the Affair*. *Murder, My Sweet* employs the same plot device: the hiring of a private investigator to learn something about a woman. In *Affair* the investigation leads to the knowledge of the real Sarah, acquired through her diary, just as Philip Marlowe's investigation led to the discovery of the real Velma. Dmytryk also went back to the London of *Counter-Espionage*—a London of blackouts and air raids—but not to high-contrast photography. A romance in the shadows, evening visits to churches, a lover pursuing his beloved down a dark street in a rain that does not blacken because the rain is regenerative—these require chiaroscuro, which Dmytryk achieved by making light and shadow as real as they are symbolic. Mirrors, the expressionistic symbols of the other and Dmytryk's favorite props, are reflectors of the characters' private selves, which must be concealed from the public eye. The inner selves of Maurice and Sarah are mirror images, viewed, appropriately, through glass. Maurice sees Sarah for the first time in a mirror as she kisses one of her lovers. When she and Maurice are about to become lovers, the mirror behind the bar in a pub catches their reflections. When the rocket hits, a shattering of glass portends the end of the affair and the end of their mirror selves as the real Sarah and Maurice emerge from the rubble.

The one flashback in *The End of the Affair*,[12] which explains Sarah's refusal to see Maurice after the bombing raid, is characteristic of Dmytryk; he treats the diary as a clue and dramatizes its revelations, as he so often did in his melodramas. Dmytryk survived by recycling the old and adapting to the new, particularly to new technology. With the advent of CinemaScope in 1953 and the wide-screen revolution that followed, filmmakers had to adapt to a process that George Stevens claimed was better suited to a python than a person: the creative deployment of space is difficult when the image is more than twice as wide as it is high. When Dmytryk made *Broken Lance* (1954) at Fox, CinemaScope was in its second year (Fox had introduced it in *The Robe* in 1953).

He was fortunate in making his CinemaScope debut with a western, a genre which, like the adventure film and the biblical spectacular, was ideal for the new screen. Like many CinemaScope productions, *Broken Lance* is a better example of cinematography than of direction. The movie itself is a remake of Fox's earlier *House of Strangers* (1949); had it been remade as the melodrama it was, it would have shown Dmytryk in his element. Instead, the saga of an Italian immigrant who rises from barber to banker, carving an empire out of embezzlement and usury and leaving his sons a legacy of greed and divisiveness, was transformed into a western dynasty film on the order of *Duel in the Sun* (1947) and *The Furies* (1950); the banker was transformed into a cattle baron (Spencer Tracy) whose only decent son is the offspring of his father's second marriage, to an Indian woman.

In 1947, a movie with an interracial theme would have been ideal for Dmytryk; having attacked anti-Semitism, he could have gone on to make the first antiracist western. As it happened, Fox's *Broken Arrow* (1950), which obviously inspired the title of *Broken Lance*, has that distinction. Fox envisioned *Broken Lance* as *Broken Arrow*'s successor but with a happy ending in which the mixed-breed son and his white bride would live happily ever after. *Broken Lance* does not allow for much sermonizing on race; still, when Tracy denounces the governor for opposing the marriage between his daughter and Tracy's son, Dmytryk does not waffle. Some of the old anger is still there; it does not cut through like acid, but at least it has a chance to surface.

Although Dmytryk made many other films that are nominally westerns (*Alvarez Kelly*, 1966; *Warlock*, 1959; *Shalako*, 1968), he could never emulate John Ford, who once said in a self-effacing moment, "My name is John Ford and I make westerns" Dmytryk made a few films that happened to be set in the West but starred actors (Richard Widmark, Spencer Tracy, William Holden) who were not identified with the genre. However, when revisionism caught up with the western, as it did with other types of films, Dmytryk, who was never at home on the range, was able to spread his own brand of cynicism over the sagebrush.

By the mid-1960s, the Civil War was ripe for revisionism to the extent that in *Alvarez Kelly* (1966) it was possible to have a war profiteer (William Holden) working both sides of the Mason-Dixon line until he encounters a one-eyed Confederate colonel (Richard Widmark), who has more integrity than his Union counterparts with twenty-twenty vision. Kelly is an apolitical Mexican national who first sells his cattle to the Union; when he and his herd are kidnapped by Confederates, Kelly agrees, after losing his money and a finger, to teach the rebels the art of the cattle drive; the drive itself becomes the film's climax.

The bipolar characterization appealed to Dmytryk. Even without the customary mirrors and windows, which were precluded by the setting, he was able to make a movie about doubles. Kelly loses a finger, the colonel an eye; Kelly is apathetic, the colonel committed; Kelly knows how to herd cattle, the colonel how to steal it. Finally, Kelly saves the colonel's life by an act of heroism that makes sense only for one who is saving an alter ego—or himself.

Dmytryk, always aware of the actor's persona, often capitalized on it, using it as a cross-reference in the evolution of the actor's screen image by repeating gestures, mannerisms, or attitudes from previous films. In *Alvarez Kelly* he provided William Holden with a role that combined in one character the two types for which Holden was known: the double-crosser and the double-crossed. In the final scene, when Kelly raises his hand in a farewell salute, he is Sefton in *Stalag 17* (1953), making the same parting gesture to the men in the prison camp who made his life miserable but against whom he bears no grudge.

For *Walk on the Wild Side* (1961) Dmytryk had Barbara Stanwyck wear the kind of suits that had become her trademark. Most movie-goers remember the film for Saul Bass's credits: a black cat prowls around construction pipes, slipping into one of them and emerging to attack (not accidentally) a white cat, while all the time Elmer Bernstein's honky-tonk score provides a low-life mood of its own. Much of the action is set in a New Orleans brothel whose madam stalks the girls like the cat in the credits. With Barbara Stanwyck playing the lesbianic madam, the mannish suit fit the character. However, on the Jane Fonda character, a homeless girl from Texas who drifts into prostitution, Dmytryk imposed a set of exaggerated mannerisms and a perverse postural geometry; she is constantly bending over in such a way that her rump looks perpendicular to her waist, and sitting with her legs apart at an ungainly angle.

For twenty years Dmytryk had been exploring the dark side of woman, usually within the parameters of *film noir*, where women had the frozen allure of an exotic drink, overly garnished and congealed in a mound of shaved ice. Like Art Deco, which streamlines, exaggerates, and blends the new with the primitive, the women were themselves blends—amalgamations of conventions, some derived from feminine psychology but most from a male consciousness.

The *noir* woman is only anatomically female; her essence is exaggeration. As a creature of the shadows, she has a shadowy look which is an extreme form of her daylight visage. Reduced to a set of mannerisms, the *noir* woman does not breathe but purr; she neither walks nor strides, but sways; her hair is lacquered; her lips are painted beyond their natural borders. Even when the *noir* woman wears something feminine, like a white cashmere sweater with a single strand of pearls, her movements belie her appearance; her breasts, unaccustomed to softness, project defiantly, turning the sweater into a sheath.

Although Dmytryk's marriage to Jean Porter offered him an alternative to the *noir* woman, he was rarely able to avail himself of it; Pat in *Till the End of Time* was an exception. Jean, "my only love," as the dedication to Dmytryk's autobiography reads, may have been the spiritual force behind the man but not always behind the director. While Dmytryk tried to make the Capucine character in *Walk on the Wild Side* a woman of flesh and blood, he staged her death in the *noir* manner, with her body jutting into the frame as it falls.

As the 1960s progressed, so did Dmytryk, from the tabloid sensationalism of *The Carpetbaggers* and *Where Love Has Gone* to *Shalako* (1968), in the course of which a dog's throat is cut, a flaming arrow is shot through a man's chest, and a woman is killed by having dirt forced down her throat. *Shalako* was followed by the film that reduced the Dmytryk signature to an obscene scrawl. Whatever else *Bluebeard* (1972) may be, it is opulently mounted trash refracted through a rainbow prism that leaves only two colors, the red and blue of Dmytryk's *mise-en scène*. Having advanced from melodrama to *noir* and from *noir* to pulp, he moves from pulp to perversion. Dmytryk's talent for sensationalism was manifested early in his career, but though he had the distinction of making Universal's most tasteless horror film, *Captive Wild Woman*, the Production Code had prevented degradation from turning into depravity. With a system that would assign an R rating to two such diverse films as *Carnal Knowledge* (1971) and *The Godfather* (1972), however, Dmytryk could go well beyond the understated lesbianic tension between Barbara Stanwyck and Capucine in *Walk on the Wild Side*. *Bluebeard* contains as graphic a scene of lesbian lovemaking as one will find in an R-rated theatrical film.

"If sex were all, then every trembling hand / Could make us squeal like dolls, the wished-for words," the speaker of Wallace Stevens's *Le monocle de mon oncle* muses. In a movie that runs more than two hours, sex should not be all yet it constitutes a good deal of it. When Dmytryk is not indulging his sexual fantasies, he is hauling out the old baggage: the revelatory flashbacks, one of which is incomplete until the end; the high contrast of *noir* rendered as variations of red and blue; tight framing and cuts so quick that at times they are virtually subliminal. The theme is also 1940s Dmytryk: Bluebeard is a World War I hero in search of the ideal woman; Germany is in search of a scapegoat to take the blame for economic depression. The two quests merge as Bluebeard becomes a brownshirt whose sexual aberrations keep pace with his Nazism. The connection between depravity and fascism is not new; Dmytryk had explored it metaphorically in Captive Wild Woman and literally in his RKO atrocity films.

Because Bluebeard is sexually bizarre to the point of generating laughter, it has become something of a camp classic. Its ludicrousness is compounded by the atrocious acting of Joey Heatherton as the American bride who escapes death and refrigeration (the fate of Bluebeard's wives) and by the appearance of Raquel Welch as a nun who fingers her beads while reminiscing en déshabillé about her former lovers. What is particularly depressing is that the film shows Dmytryk in a state of cinematic bankruptcy as his career comes to an end; it resonates with echoes from the films of others as well as his own. Bluebeard's oedipus complex, which leaves no room for any other woman than his mother, makes him kin to Norman Bates, who preserved his mother's rotting corpse in the basement—as does Bluebeard. That Dmytryk intended moviegoers to notice his hommage to Hitchcock is evident from the appearance of the mother's face; like Mrs. Bates's, it has the look of a striated pumpkin ready to cave in from decay. And like Norman Bates watching from behind a painting as his victims undressed, Bluebeard peers through slits in a portrait to observe a prostitute instructing his wife in the art of love.

Dmytryk's most advanced form of self-quotation is an autobiographical subtext. Bluebeard is an anti-Communist; when his friends show fear of an owl, he is appalled that men who have endured "bombs, even Communists" would be afraid of a bird. He kills his penultimate bride because her lover was both a Russian and a Communist, a death-deserving combination that merits suffocation in a casket. If Dmytryk is trying to bury his Communist past in Bluebeard, he succeeds only in burying his antifascist past. It is strange that the two should have converged at the end of his career, as they had at the beginning, when Communism and fascism were political antonyms whose antagonism often made Communists out of antifascists. The one bride who escapes death is saved by a Jew who, it is intimated, is also a Communist. In the finale, she and her rescuer whisk past Bluebeard's body, which lies in state in a swastika-draped chapel. Fascism may be embalmed, but Communism refuses to stay interred. That the conclusion should be an American's rescue from fascism by a Communist is the perfect commentary on a career that thrived on the portrayal of the evils of fascism and sustained itself by an admission of the evils of Communism.

In his autobiography as well as in the film textbooks he has written, Dmytryk would have one believe that the film that followed Bluebeard was his last, *The Human Factor* (1975); he omits *He Is My Brother* (1974) from his filmography.[13] One can understand his reluctance to discuss it, but to dismiss it when the credits identify him as director and his son Michael as assistant director is to invite speculation. A film with such a righteous title must have a message; here, it is that one's brother may be both racially and physically different. In this instance the brother is a dark-skinned leper confined to a Hawaiian island where two ship-wrecked boys rethink their views on leprosy and race, and, as the epilogue hopes, so will the audience. Dmytryk's previous attacks on fascism and racism had bordered on the pugilistic, but there is nothing hard-hitting about *He Is My Brother*, which is merely a cheaply made travelogue. Although filmed on location, there is no poetry in the landscape, no awe in the rituals; it has the look of a B western promising panoramic vistas but at such a distance that their majesty must be taken on faith.

Since careers rarely end the way they should, a director's last film often turns out to be unmemorable or even unworthy. For D.W. Griffith it was *The Struggle* (1930); for Raoul Walsh, *A Distant Trumpet* (1964). *The Human Factor*, far from bringing Edward Dmytryk's career full circle, veered off in the opposite direction, circumscribing an anti-world. It is a former antifascist's nightmare, incorporating the themes and situations associated with the antifascist film into a fascist setting that mocks the notion of a political conscience as well as those who have—or had—one.

A continental *Death Wish*, *The Human Factor* derives from the same premise as the Charles Bronson film: a husband's revenge on the killers of his family. *Death Wish* is set in New York but directed by a Briton (Michael Winner); *The Human Factor* is set in Itay but directed by an American who has no more feeling for Naples than Winner did for Manhattan's Upper West Side. *Death Wish* was at least apolitical, merely a revenge odyssey. The avenger in *The Human Factor* is a Naples-based American whose entire family is killed by terrorists.

And *The Human Factor* goes a step further than the neofascist films of the period (*Straw Dogs*; the "Dirty Harry" movies) in which individuals, despairing of justice, take the law into their hands and wreak R-rated vengeance; it makes the international terrorists not religious fanatics or members of the lunatic fringe but Berkeley dropouts. The film's position is unequivocal: if Berkeley political science majors are in the vanguard of world revolution, it is because they were radicalized on the campus where the Free Speech movement began. Filled with hatred of what in the 1960s was alternately called the System and the Establishment, they have become so desensitized that the babysitter thinks nothing of killing a child and taking the child's doll for herself. When the avenging father tracks her down, she spits in his face; he retaliates by firing a revolver into hers and then lassoing her accomplice with an iron chain.

When *The Human Factor* is dismantled, Dmytryk's contempt is laid bare: contempt for the material, the characters, even for himself. That he made it at all illustrates a career that was an odd amalgam of chance and choice. As America moved to the right, so did Dmytryk; politically it was easy after his recantation; professionally it was easier because there was no alternative. *The Human Factor* is the reverse of an earlier revenge film, *Cornered*, with right-wing vengeance instead of a left-wing manhunt and a fascist mentality supplanting an antifascist one. In *Cornered*, the Nazi was at least given his day in court; in the tradition of the fascist film, the terrorists of *The Human Factor* are unworthy of trial. Besides, all one needs to know about them has been gleaned from a computer, which adds a high-tech touch to the film and makes the father's revenge an impersonal act. Somehow one feels that even if Dick Powell had had access to a computer in *Cornered*, he would still have found the collaborationist on his own. But George Kennedy is not Dick Powell, any more than 1975 is 1945.

That Dmytryk's last film should end in a PX where a voice dispassionately announces the day's specials amid a barrage of bullets and a cascade of cans is a perfect metaphor for a career that endured wreckage of a different sort. Survival comes down to gathering up the scattered goods and reshelving them or, if that does not work, rearranging them in interesting configurations to catch the consumer's eye.

9 RING LARDNER, JR.
Radical Wit

The supreme moment in *A Star Is Born* (1937) occurs at the end of the film when Vicki Lester (Janet Gaynor) steps before a microphone and introduces herself by her married name: "Hello, everybody. This is Mrs. Norman Maine." Budd Schulberg, Jr., and Ring Lardner, Jr., the creators of that scene, were never credited for it, although their fade-out line is now legendary.[1] The same year, Lardner, with the help of George Oppenheimer, devised the memorable finale of *Nothing Sacred* (1937), in which Hazel Flagg (Carole Lombard) becomes a celebrity when she is erroneously believed to be dying of radium poisoning. To preserve the myth and prevent disillusionment, Hazel feigns death but, in reality, goes off on a honeymoon cruise with the newspaperman who made her a national figure. When a passenger recognizes her, Hazel insists that she is not the "phony" media creation, only to be berated for speaking disrespectfully of an idol.[2] Also on board is the alcoholic doctor, in league with Hazel, who wakes up in his cabin and, not realizing he is at sea, cries, "Run, Hazel, the hotel is flooded."

If Ring Lardner, Jr., seems the wittiest of the Ten, it is not only because he had the best sense of humor, as befits the son of one of America's great humorists, but also because aphorism comes naturally to him. At the HUAC hearings, his response to the formulaic "Are you now or have you ever been . . ." would, if it had appeared in a movie, have merited a place in the thesaurus of one-liners that includes "Play it, Sam" and "Fasten your seat belts; it's going to be a bumpy night." Quipped Lardner: "I could answer it, but if I did, I would hate myself in the morning."[3]

While the rejoinder was not atypical of a Lardner, the circumstances were. Because the respondent was the son of a uniquely American writer, the conservative press felt justified in asking "What's a nice boy like you doing in a place like this?" or, more precisely, "What's old Ring's son doing at the Federal Correctional Institution in Danbury, Connecticut, for contempt of Congress?" Lardner was portrayed as an ingrate who turned on the country that had given his father fame and himself a charmed life: "Here is an American citizen who enjoyed advantages far beyond those which are the lot of the average young man; he came from a talented family and showed unusual talents himself; he received the best possible education and used it to acquire profitable jobs; he had every reason for following the political philosophy shared by the vast majority of American citizens. But like a few others of his generation, young Ring decided that this philosophy was not for him."[4]

Actually, the road to Danbury was a direct route from a father who despised privilege and hypocrisy all his life, and finally showed it by voting Socialist the year before he died, to a son who took up where his father had left off: joining the Socialist Club at Princeton; campaigning for Socialist candidate Norman Thomas in the 1932 presidential election; traveling to the Soviet Union in the summer of 1934; and joining the Party two years later.[5]

Nor was Lardner's Hollywood period a deviation from that journey. It was no surprise that he became a writer, as his father was, and as his three brothers were: John Lardner became a sports columnist; David Lardner died in Germany as a war correspondent; and Jim Lardner intended to cover the civil war in Spain but lost his life there— the last American volunteer in the Abraham Lincoln Battalion and one of the last to be killed.

Like his father, young Ring started out as a reporter, covering bridge tournaments for the New York *Daily Mirror*. It was at the *Mirror* in 1935 that he met Ian McLellan Hunter, who became his closest friend. Hunter too became a screenwriter, and although he was never subpoenaed to appear before HUAC, he was nonetheless blacklisted.

Dissatisfied with the kind of writing he was doing at the *Mirror* yet uncertain about the direction his career should take, Lardner had no objection when the eminent publisher and family friend Herbert Bayard Swope recommended him to David O. Selznick, who was about to form Selznick International. In Hollywood, where life and art are mutually reflective, mistaken identity is a stock theme; it was also the way Lardner got into film. Selznick's secretary, Silvia Schulman—later the first Mrs. Ring Lardner, Jr.—confused Ring with his brother John and so introduced him to the producer, who apparently did not care which member of the family he was speaking to; since he had been told that Lardner could also act, a screen test was arranged. The result was so dreadful that Ian McLellan Hunter still laughs when he speaks of it. Once Selznick discovered that Lardner was not meant to be seen on the screen, he hired the young man to promote it, first as publicity director and then as one of the studio's uncredited writers. At the *Mirror* Lardner had at least occasionally received a byline, but not at Selznick International—even though Dorothy Parker and her husband Alan Campbell, the main writers of *A Star Is Born*, petitioned Selznick to add Lardner's name to the screenplay credits.

Nor did he fare much better during his brief tenure in Bryan Foy's B unit at Warner Brothers; none of the four scripts he wrote between 1937 and 1939 was ever filmed.[6] Moreover, he infuriated Jack Warner by soliciting contributions to buy ambulances for the Spanish Loyalists and by organizing a boycott against the Hollywood visit of Mussolini's son, Vittorio.

Still, Hollywood in the 1930s was the right place for Lardner. The Hollywood Communists were a mix of militants, solitaries, and idealists; being a bit of all three, Lardner fit in easily. His new radicalism, which manifested itself in defending Stalin's purge trials and preaching isolationism until Hitler's invasion of Mother Russia made World War II a people's war, began to appear when his scripts finally reached the screen. Not surprisingly, Lardner's first credits were at RKO, which was always looking for new writers and had hired Dalton Trumbo in 1938—the year before Lardner came to the studio.

Lardner's first RKO script, *Meet Dr. Christian* (1939), on which he collaborated with Harvey Gates (author of the original story) and his good friend Ian McLellan Hunter, was the first in a series based on the beloved radio character whose popularity RKO hoped to duplicate on the screen. While the film is not unusual in its portrayal of the poor, it does reflect a more than casual awareness of the health problems that existed during the Great Depression, particularly the epidemics that were often traced to squatters and their unhygienic living conditions.

The Courageous Dr. Christian (1940), next in the series, was coauthored by Lardner and Hunter and directed by Bernard Vorhaus. The three had met a year earlier at Republic, where they had worked on the screen version of Irving Stone's *False Witness*, an attack on small-town maliciousness. When Vorhaus discovered that Republic planned the film—finally known as *Arkansas Judge* (1941)—as a vehicle for the Weavers and Elviry, a well-known vaudeville act that had appeared in some hillbilly musicals, he would have nothing more to do with the project. Lardner and Hunter at least received adaptation credit for their efforts, although the final screenplay was not theirs.

Vorhaus's attitude was understandable. Although even film buffs might not be familiar with his work, he had achieved considerable success in Britain where, between 1933 and 1936, he directed several melodramas (*Crime on the Hill; The Ghost Camera; The Last Journey; Dusty Ermine*) that are still highly regarded, especially by David Lean, who called Vorhaus the one British (even though he was New York–born) filmmaker of the 1930s that he admired. In America, Vorhaus had less success. Since his political leanings were similar to Lardner's and Hunter's, he was also blacklisted; he returned to London in the 1950s and remained in obscurity until he was rediscovered in 1986 and given a retrospective by the National Film Archive in London; the following year, the Museum of Modern Art in New York included some of his work in its British Film Traditions series.

With writers and director sharing the same views, it was only natural that the second Dr. Christian film would reveal an even deeper commitment to humanitarian ideals. In the debut film Dr. Christian defends the squatters but is not blind to the health hazards they pose; in the second film (which, unlike the first, had an original screenplay) he improves the squatters' lot despite opposition from a conservative minority that maintains, "These people are not like us." The doctor does not court a minority view, especially when it is the wrong minority: "I'm not counting on everybody, just the majority." He also believes that since most people are intrinsically good, they will rally around the persecuted: "There isn't a community in this country that won't meet a responsibility if it's pointed out to them clearly." When spinal meningitis breaks out among the squatters, the citizenry shows its true colors; the town council approves low-income housing; and the local dowager finds she enjoys being the champion of the poor. Although the "goodness will out" resolution was mandated by the nature of the series, the film insists that the poor are not responsible for their poverty and that what seems to be an extreme attempt to alleviate it (the erection of a shantytown) is an expression of frustration, not lawlessness.

The year 1940 was memorable not because of *The Courageous Dr. Christian* but because of Katharine Hepburn's triumph as Tracy Lord in the screen version of Philip Barry's *The Philadelphia Story*, which lifted the miasma that had for a time hung so thick over her career that she had been called box office poison. Subsequently, Hepburn was looking for a similar script about a single, strong-willed woman who, while she is any man's equal, is willing to change her status and modify her independent ways for the right partner. Lardner, together with Michael Kanin (Garson's brother), wrote a story for Hepburn called "Woman of the Year," for which she paid $40,000 on the condition set forth in a contract (1 August 1941) that they "transfer . . . to the purchaser all of [their] rights, title and interest in and to said title."[7] Then she brought the story to Louis B. Mayer's attention, and after it was approved as her next MGM film, she put together a $211,000 package that included $100,000 for her salary, $10,000 for the agent (who was none other than Hepburn), $1,000 for travel expenses, and $100,000 for the screenwriters: she wanted the same team of unknowns who had written the story to write the script.

By 23 August 1941, Lardner and Kanin had a script ready with the same title as their story. The heroine embodied everything associated with the Hepburn persona: flair, style, and a mind that a genius would envy. Tess Harding was a politically conscious Tracy Lord, awesomely well-informed and so polylingual that she would break into Russian when greeting Soviet visitors. Since Russia had become an ally on 21 June 1941, the scene might have been Lardner's way of acknowledging the fighters in the People's War, and perhaps the allusion lit up the eyes of the comrades—but the audience's eyes were on Katharine Hepburn and Spencer Tracy.

In its original form, *Woman of the Year* (1942) handled the emancipated woman theme more intelligently than did *Philadelphia Story*. In a battle of the sexes between a news commentator and a sportscaster, Lardner and Kanin reversed the familiar sexual stereotypes, making the woman the man's intellectual superior. Tess Harding is not only more politically astute than Sam Craig (Tracy); she is also better informed. When Tess remarks that her network has only one man at Vichy, Sam asks, "Vichy? Are they still in the League? Who's pitching?"

Lardner and Kanin knew that Tess and Sam would finally do what audiences wanted and resolve their differences in time for a happy ending. But the writers had no intention of having Tess relinquish her career or compromise her principles. Their script, which bore the approval of producer Joseph L. Mankiewicz, ended with Tess and Sam at a boxing match in which a seemingly washed-up fighter reclaims his title, as Tess has predicted he would. Sam, forced to consider Tess an equal, proposes a mean between career and conformity: his wife will be known neither as Tess Harding nor as Mrs. Sam Craig but as Tess Harding Craig. Had *Woman of the Year* ended as Lardner and Kanin planned, it would have lived up to its title, becoming the prototype of film feminism.

A few months later, Mankiewicz decided that moviegoers would be loath to see a man yield to a woman, especially Tracy to Hepburn; rather, males would feel vindicated and females would be delighted if a woman like Hepburn had to do for her husband what more ordinary wives do for theirs: cook breakfast. And so, instead of settling their differences ringside, Tess plays the dutiful wife and makes Sam's breakfast, although she has not the slightest idea even of how to toast bread. The new ending—written by John Lee Mahin, whom Mankiewicz brought in at the end of November 1941—so disgusted Hepburn that she termed it "a bunch of shit."[8] In addition, it is excruciatingly long. As batter oozes out of the waffle iron, coffee boils over, and toast flies into the air, Tess's effeminate secretary, Gerald, enters to tell her she is due to launch a battleship. After escorting him out of the kitchen, Sam returns for the closing line: "I've just launched Gerald." And the vessel that might have launched film feminism on its maiden voyage was scuttled by a producer who thought, in 1942, that the ship was not seaworthy.

Despite the revised ending, *Woman of the Year* made Lardner and

Kanin $140,000 richer and won them an Oscar for Best Original Screenplay. While Hepburn went on to *Keeper of the Flame* (1943) and *Dragon Seed* (1944), Lardner found himself working on *The Cross of Lorraine* (1943) with three other writers, including Michael Kanin. For MGM, whose forte was the film of bourgeois gentility, *The Cross of Lorraine* was a significant departure. The setting is a Nazi prison camp after the fall of France in 1940; brutality abounds, and the dialogue is mildly left-wing. If Lardner's voice is audible (and it is difficult to detect it among so many), it is in the character of a Chilean "who fought wherever the people's armies were on the march," the International Brigades being one such army. It is not improbable that Lardner, who has had a lifelong interest in the Spanish conflict in which his brother died, was responsible for the character and his dialogue. As a Party member in 1943, he might also have had a hand in the ending, which is a tribute to Stalin's scorched-earth policy: the villagers burn their homes and head for the mountains to become guerrillas, making the setting seem more like Russia than France.

At MGM Lardner also had a chance to work on a Lana Turner movie, *Marriage Is a Private Affair* (1944). His contribution is uncredited, but he was in distinguished company, since Tennessee Williams and Christopher Isherwood worked on the film, also without credit.

The 1940s, while they ended as abruptly for him as they did for the others, revealed an ability in Lardner that under different circumstances could have resulted in his becoming a major screenwriter—a view shared by Richard Corliss.[9] While antifascism stalled the careers of Biberman and Ornitz, Lardner could distinguish between politics and subject matter: an antifascist plot requires an antifascist treatment; an apolitical plot requires an apolitical approach. In 1944, he showed he could write either kind.

In adapting the Broadway play, *Tomorrow the World*, for which he shared credit with Leopold Atlas, Lardner stayed relatively close to the original, which dramatized the impact of Nazism on a German boy living in the United States but still bearing the marks of Nazi indoctrination; introduced to an oriental student whom he assumes to be Japanese, the boy recoils in horror to learn that he is Chinese and not from a member country of the Triple Axis. Lardner wrote a speech for the boy which is not in the play, implying that South America was not unreceptive to National Socialism. He did not go so far as to suggest that Brazil might be a Nazi microcosm (as Ben Hecht would do two years later in *Notorious*), but he did have the boy contradict one of his peers during a geography class: "If I may say so, he has left out some of the most important facts. . . . Politically, Brazil is the key to the western hemisphere. It is the closest to Europe because there is the smallest crossing of the ocean and because there are two-and-a-half million

Germans and three million Italians, almost one-fifth of the population." The speech is wonderfully ambiguous; it can mean that Brazil is
central to Germany's plan for world conquest ("tomorrow the world"),
that the fascist nations are well represented there, or that because of
such representation Brazil is ripe for fascism. Since the speech is
delivered by a child programmed to spout Naxi propaganda, the
implications went unnoticed; besides, Brazil had joined the Allies in
1942.

   Tomorrow the World (United Artists) and *Laura* (Twentieth Century–Fox) were both released in 1944. Lardner had screen credit for the
former, but not the latter. It is commonly thought that he was hired to
provide witty lines for Clifton Webb as Waldo Lydecker, *Laura's* epi-
cene art critic. Actually, he did much more: he wrote a script (19
November 1943) that was a revision of Jay Dratler's first-draft continuity
of 30 October 1943.[10] Dratler's first draft had left Darryl F. Zanuck
unimpressed: "As a dialogue job I find it very ordinary. Waldo is the
only well drawn character throughout, and even his lines can be
punched up with more sarcastic humor and ironic, sadistic wise-
cracks."[11] The latter was Lardner's specialty. He was also able to provide something else that Zanuck wanted, tougher dialogue for police
detective Mark McPherson; Lardner added a bit of vernacular ("rubbed
out," "two-timing dame") and made Mark more the cop and less the
romantic lead. To render the characters less synthetic, Lardner had
Mark, Waldo, and the sybaritic Shelby go to a baseball game, which
might have worked with a different cast. However, the thought of Dana
Andrews (Mark), flanked on either side by Clifton Webb (Waldo) and
Vincent Price (Shelby) at Ebbets Field requires a suspension of disbelief
of which only a saint is capable.

   Neither the bulk of Lardner's script nor the so-called "final" that he
wrote with Dratler (29 November 1943) reached the screen. It is not that
his work was inferior; its texture was not glossy enough for a murder
mystery set at the glittering intersection of art and fashion where no
one would know the difference between a homer and a bunt. Nevertheless, some of Lardner's dialogue was used. Waldo's unsurpassa-
ble response when Laura asks him to endorse a pen for an ad she has
designed was retained: "I don't use a pen. I write with a goose quill
dipped in venom." Also Lardner's is Waldo's verbal assault on the artist
who paints Laura's portrait. The judicious choice of words implies
latent homosexuality; in Clifton Webb's delivery it is no longer latent:
"He [the artist] was so obviously conscious of looking more like an
athlete than an artist. I sat up the rest of the night writing a column
about him. I demolished his affectations, exposed his camouflaged
imitation of better painters. . . . It was a masterpiece because it was a
labor of love."

Lardner's contribution to *Laura* may have been slight, but Otto Preminger, who directed the film, thought enough of it to request his services for *Forever Amber* (1947), which Preminger was never supposed to direct (any more than he was supposed to direct *Laura*),[12] Lardner to write, or Linda Darnell to star in. Jerry Cady, *Amber*'s first writer, worked on the script for about six months, from the end of 1944 to May 1945.[13] Then Philip Dunne took it over and labored even longer, completing the shooting final in February 1946. This was the script that Zanuck had planned to film with Peggy Cummins as Amber and John Stahl directing. Shooting terminated abruptly on 1 May 1946 when it became evident that Cummins was wrong for the part. Zanuck did not abandon the film, however; Dunne was retained, but Cummins was replaced by Darnell and Stahl by Preminger, who insisted on Lardner's being assigned to the script. Dunne did not object; the men worked well together and had much in common. Both were well educated: Dunne had a Harvard B.A., and Lardner was a former Princetonian without a degree but clearly anyone's intellectual peer. When Dunne went off the film on 30 September 1946 to start writing *The Ghost and Mrs. Muir* (1947), Lardner put together the revised shooting final (10 October 1946), which reflected his joint work with Dunne, Zanuck's suggestions, and Lardner's revisions.

Lardner's credit for *Forever Amber* was more than deserved. The original opening sequence was a lengthy title summarizing the events between 1644 and 1660, the rise of Cromwell and the Restoration. Lardner broke up the title, making it a true film prologue that incorporated text and image. After the 1644 title a child, wrapped in a shawl on which is embroidered "Amber," is abandoned at the door of an English cottage; after the 1660 title the child is a mature sixteen-year-old, being forced by her adoptive father to marry a farmer she does not love. Since Amber will abandon the provinces for London, Lardner explains why: Amber fancies herself a lady. In her room she studies the picture of a woman of breeding at the moment that Bruce Carlton is outside her window, asking directions to the nearest inn, to which Amber immediately heads. That one incident sets the rest of the film in motion; Amber becomes Bruce's inamorata and, like Moll Flanders, proceeds from one adventure to another, including imprisonment at Newgate, a fling on the stage, and a fling of another sort with Charles II, whose mistress she becomes.

Dunne did most of the work on the scenes at the Theatre Royal, implying parallels between Amber and Nell Gwynn. Lardner shortened the scenes but stressed Amber's comedic talent—something she shared with Gwynn—by showing her in a Restoration comedy.

Lardner was responsible for the film's ending, although he was carrying out Zanuck's instructions. The 31 July 1946 script ended with

Amber's marriage to the Earl of Radclyffe after Bruce and their son go off to America. In Lardner's revision, which is reflected in the film, Amber marries the earl much earlier in the plot, then leaves him in order to nurse Bruce, who has fallen victim to the plague. The earl's violent death is also Lardner's work: when the great fire reaches Radclyffe House, a servant whom the earl had abused hurls his master into the flames.

Knowing he would have to placate the Legion of Decency (which he did in several ways, including a "wages of sin is death" voice-over introduction and an off-screen *mea culpa* from Bruce at the end), Zanuck had to insist on an unhappy ending, which Lardner supplied. Thus Amber foolishly allows her son the choice of staying in London with her or going to the New World with his father; the boy chooses America, and a moist-eyed Amber stands at the window, watching her husband and son recede from view.

Once Dunne had completed *The Ghost and Mrs. Muir*, he and Lardner made a few more revisions for *Amber* between 20 March and 8 April 1947. Theirs was a genuine collaboration, one in which two writers—working sometimes together, sometimes separately—created a script signed by two hands so alike they could have been one.

It was evident after *Forever Amber* that Lardner had a firm place at Fox—or would have had, without the blacklist—for Zanuck found that he could be counted on when a script was in trouble. Fox had bought Margery Sharp's novel *Brittania Mews*, dealing with a well-bred Englishwoman who succeeds, through various twists of plot and fate, in transforming a Dickensian slum into a middle-class enclave. The book proved difficult to adapt. Zanuck first commissioned David Hertz to do the screenplay in 1946; by the end of the year, he knew he needed someone else.[14] Since Lardner had finished *Amber*, he was assigned to *Mews*, making the screenplay so much his own that he received sole credit for it. Neither knew it at the time, but Zanuck had given Lardner his last screen credit for sixteen years.

Lardner incorporated all of Zanuck's suggestions, thus winning a commendation from the producer for his "flair and humor" because he had made the heroine's first husband, a puppeteer, more of a bounder than a scoundrel.[15] The puppets, as Lardner discovered, were the means of unifying a plot that Zanuck had found too diffuse. Just as in the Dr. Christian films, group endeavors restore the poor's self-esteem, so in *Forbidden Street* (1949), as the adaptation was called, do puppet shows; "the Mews began to wash its face and scrub behind its ears," as did the squatters in *The Courageous Dr. Christian* once they got soap and water.

Of the writers among the Ten, Lardner received the last screen credit for the duration. When *Forbidden Street* came out in 1949, it bore

Lardner's name. Although that may seem to have been courageous of Fox, it should be remembered, first, that Lardner had not yet been sentenced (Lawson and Trumbo had been, in May 1948); and second, that discrimination is notoriously indiscriminate. Lardner was actually the first to be targeted for dismissal—not directly, of course, since Fox prided itself on being ethical. After Lardner received his subpoena, Zanuck informed him that he would honor his contract unless the board decreed otherwise—which it did. Anticipating a blacklist, Spyros Skouras, president of Fox, formally announced the board's decision on 20 November 1947 (five days before the Waldorf Statement): "Resolved that the officers of this corporation be, and they are hereby directed, to the extent that the same is lawful, to dispense with the services of any acknowledged Communist, or of any employee who refuses to answer a question with respect thereto by any committee of the Congress of the United States and is cited for contempt by reason thereof."[16] The only Fox employee cited for contempt was Lardner, who was formally discharged on 28 November.

During the nine and a half months that Lardner spent at the Danbury Federal Correctional Institution, he contemplated the circumstances that put him there—circumstances under which ten men who considered themselves Americans and, in their naiveté, believed they enjoyed First Amendment rights had found themselves jobless. What was so alarming was the swiftness with which the public's indifference changed not to passion—for that would portend a cause—but to revenge. In part, it was the usual reaction of the righteous to those who they believe have betrayed them. Yet it was also anger at being roused from postwar slumber to discover that there was a new enemy—the Communist, a word that would soon replace Nazi and Jap in the lexicon of fear. The 1950s were an era not of the gentle transition but of the sudden switch: from Russophilia to Russophobia, from friendship to enmity, from a popular front to a monolithic position—from employment to anonymity. There was no middle ground, as the title character lamented in Lardner's first novel, *The Ecstasy of Owen Muir* (1954).

The story, conceived in prison, was Lardner's parable—neither dark not crepuscular but slightly bilious—about the ease with which neutrality can change to involvement, involvement to obsession. If Catholicism, with its scapegoat founder and history of persecution, could encourage the anti-Communist hysteria of the 1950s with redundant sermons on "godless atheistic Communism," it showed how poorly Catholics recall their own radical past; if the United States, itself the product of a revolution, could allow an embezzler's gavel and a senator's whiskey breath to silence dissenting voices, it showed how short a memory Americans have.

The situation, however, is tragic only to those with a tragic sense of life, which Ring Lardner, Jr., does not have. Since comedy and tragedy are different expressions on the same countenance, the prospect of an awakening apathy moving first to the left, then to the right, and finally to the extreme right can be wonderfully funny if it is reduced to the absurd. In *Owen Muir* the title character goes from teenage bookworm to draft resister to Purple Heart patriot, from anticapitalist to failed entrepreneur, Episcopalian to Roman Catholic, married man to Trappist monk. What fascinates Owen about Catholicism is what fascinated Lardner: its ability to offer explanations of misfortune that are either coldly coherent (unbaptized babies go to Limbo because they never had any desire to see God and would never miss what they never had) or eerily logical (America entered World War II on 8 December, the Feast of the Immaculate Conception; the war ended in Tokyo on 15 August, the Feast of Mary's Assumption). Instructed by Monsignor Frasso (modeled far from loosely on Fulton J. Sheen, who competed with Milton Berle in television popularity in the 1950s), Owen absorbs the fine points of Catholic theory without being able to put them into practice.

Owen Muir is Lardner's *reductio ad absurdum* of noninvolvement; while Owen goes from one position to another, he is surrounded by people who have not done even that but remain in the same amoral mode, topping one action with another more outrageous. A supposed Communist is really an FBI informant; he is also such a convincing Marxist that he recruits his own mother into the Party, where she becomes so militant that she lands in jail.

Since Lardner is too genial to be Juvenalian (as Victor Navasky has observed, his wife refuses to speak to informants, while Lardner speaks to anyone),[17] he approaches Owen like a bemused observer who is able to see the canker in the rose and marvel at the irony of beauty going to rot. Thus the novel never becomes a diatribe, because Lardner keeps undercutting himself; the narrative remains an exercise in pushing a thesis to the limit. Only once does he lower the satirist's voice: in his re-creation of Paul Robeson's 1949 concert in Peekskill, New York, which culminated in a vicious right-wing attack on the departing audience whose members, in addition to being verbally abused, drove home with smashed windshields. Owen is disturbed by the violence of the attack yet does nothing about it. Soon he is so steeped in Catholic dogma that nothing can satisfy him short of the contemplative life. There he discovers his own canker in the rose: boils consign him to a bath, where his sole pleasure derives from watching the pus drain.

The Ecstasy of Owen Muir is Lardner's portrait of the good who pursue The Good without knowing what it is; once it is identified for them, they strive to make themselves good but are incapable of doing good for others. What makes the novel a touchstone of the 1950s is the author's evocation of the morality of an era when merely taking an anti-Communist stand, something even the affectless can do, results in an onrush of righteousness. The Allies/Axis mentality of World War II had yielded to Communist/anti-Communist with antinomic subdivisions (evil/good, Soviet Union/America, Khruschev/Eisenhower) among which one could not pick and choose. It was block booking: one bought the package.

Eventually, *Owen Muir* found an audience, particularly among academics.[18] In the meantime, Lardner had to survive. He tried writing for the black market but with little success. While Dalton Trumbo could turn out scripts under a variety of pseudonyms, Lardner found it difficult. As a result, his uncredited film work between 1950 and 1960 amounts to little. It is impossible to know exactly what he contributed to *The Big Night* (1951), a psychological melodrama about a son victimized by his father's past; the movie owes more to Hugo Butler, who seems to have done most of the work on the script, and to director Joseph Losey, than to Lardner. Under the pseudonym Philip Rush, Lardner and Ian McLellan Hunter adapted Robb White's novel *Virgin Island* (1959), which director Pat Jackson revised without their knowledge, sharing screenplay credit with "Philip Rush."

It was not film but television that made it possible for Lardner to pay the rent during the plague years. Hannah Weinstein, an acquaintance from his *Daily Mirror* days, a genuine liberal, and one of Lillian Hellman's closest friends, had become a television producer. It was she who made it possible for Lardner and Hunter to write for British television in the mid-1950s; in 1955 they created the *Robin Hood* series, which proved so successful that they went on to develop two others, *Sir Lancelot* and *The Pirates.*

The Adventures of Robin Hood, with Richard Greene in the title role, was one of the first British series to appear on American television; it was so popular that it ran on CBS for three seasons (1955-58). Lardner and Hunter wrote their scripts under a series of pseudonyms, the most common being Samuel B. West and Oliver Skene. The latter, the name of a deceased sportswriter friend, proved to be an apt choice. In familiarizing themselves with the source material, Lardner and Hunter returned to *Ivanhoe*, in whose dedicatory epistle Scott acknowledges sketches made by his friend James Skene of some of the sites described in the novel. The plot of one episode, "Secret Mission" (1955), draws on *Ivanhoe* for the incident in which Richard the Lion-Heart joins Robin Hood's band of outlaws.

Lardner and Hunter admit there is no way of distinguishing their individual contributions to the *Robin Hood* series, for which they wrote approximately forty scripts. After they talked out the stories, says Hunter, "Ring would write one half of the teleplay while I did the other. Then we'd put the pieces together, polish them up a bit, and ship them off."[19] While others, including the blacklisted Gordon Kahn and Waldo Salt, also wrote for the series, the first two episodes (written under the transparent pseudonyms Lawrence McLellan and Ian Larkin) set the stage for the subsequent ones. Robin Hood has been variously called Norman and Saxon, yeoman and disinherited earl. Lardner and Hunter do not equivocate: their hero is Robin of Locksley, a Saxon who returns from the Crusades to find himself dispossessed and the family castle occupied by Normans. The sides are as clearly defined as they are in *Ivanhoe*: Saxon versus Norman.

The pilot, "The Coming of Robin Hood" (which Hunter recalls as the only one written solely by Lardner; Hunter was completing another project at the time) opens, as all the episodes do, with a short ballad suggestive of the popular medieval forms in which the story of Robin Hood was told. The villain is the Norman Roger de Lisle, whose name recalls Brian de Lisle, a historical figure in league with Robin's traditional foe, the Sheriff of Nottingham. Lardner follows the version of the legend in which Robin joins an already existing band of outlaws, reasoning that since Robin had returned from the Crusades to find signs of Norman oppression everywhere, it was natural that the despoiled and proscribed would already have banded together. It is their leader, Howard FitzWilliam, who supplies Robin's traditional surname, dubbing him Robin of the Hood from the hooded cape he wears over his coat of mail. Before he dies, FitzWilliam names Robin his successor, and Robin immediately institutes a new policy: instead of robbing indiscriminately as in the past, the bandits of Sherwood Forest will waylay only the rich or their lackeys—like the usurer in the second episode, whose money is returned to those from whom it was expropriated.

It is unfortunate that the flair Lardner exhibited for the teleplay could not have been utilized during America's Golden Age of Television; instead of working under pseudonyms for Sapphire Films in Britain, he might have written for Studio One or Playhouse 90 in his own name. Until his reinstatement as a screenwriter in 1964, the only media open to Lardner in which he could use his own name were fiction and the theater; he tried both with mixed results. *The Ecstasy of Owen Muir* was rejected by all the American publishers to whom it was submitted; it was finally accepted by Jonathan Cape, a small British house, and eventually went from obscurity to the status of cult classic. The same fortune will probably not befall *Foxy* (1964), a musical version of *Volpone* starring Bert Lahr, with music by Robert Emmett Dolan, lyrics by Johnny Mercer, and book by Lardner and Hunter.

Foxy may have had a brief run, but Gerald Boardman, one of the American musical theater's foremost historians, regards it highly.[20] The Lardner-Hunter libretto is a clever reworking of the Elizabethan play that preserves the transparent names of the original: Volpone becomes Foxy; Mosca, Doc Mosk; Corbaccio, Buzzard; Bonario, Ben. Celia's name is unchanged, and while she and Bonario are not romantically paired in the original, Celia and Ben are in *Foxy*.

Taking their cue from Volpone's apostrophe to gold at the beginning of Ben Jonson's play (which ties in nicely with the comic gold lust in Chaplin's *Gold Rush*, 1925, another source of inspiration), Lardner and Hunter moved the time of the action to 1896 and changed the setting from Venice to the Yukon. Foxy is not the embodiment of avarice that Volpone is but merely a prospector who wants satisfaction when his three partners make off with his gold. With Lahr in the lead and the musical comedy format, there is no room for misanthropy; Foxy's revenge is more of a practical joke than retaliation. The librettists devised some wonderfully comic material for Lahr in what turned out to be his last stage appearance; he enters with his leg in a bear trap; later he arrives on a sled. But the most hilarious scene is Celia's attempt to seduce him. When she cries, "Play me, like a harp," Foxy replies with the kind of one-liner that Lardner writes best and that Lahr could deliver with deadpan brilliance: "I got a sore pinky."

Lardner's next stage venture was a radical departure from musical comedy. At Avery Fisher Hall in Lincoln Center on 7 April 1986, the fortieth anniversary of the beginning of the Spanish Civil War was commemorated in a program in which such performers as Jack Gilford, Frances Cheyney (Mrs. Lardner), and three members of the Weavers— Ronnie Gilbert, Fred Hellerman, and Pete Seeger—recalled the war in the words of Ernest Hemingway, Lillian Hellman, Dorothy Parker, Alvah Bessie, and others. Lardner wrote the script, interweaving commentary with text and song. Among the most moving moments of the evening was his reading of his brother Jim's letter to their mother explaining why he was quitting his job with the *Herald-Tribune* in Paris and joining the Abraham Lincoln Battalion. The letter is typical of a Lardner; some of it is tongue-in-cheek ("because I am tired of working for the Herald Tribune in particular and newspapers in general . . . because there may be a chance to do some reading and I won't have to wear a necktie"), but Jim Lardner's real motive was never in doubt: "Because I believe that fascism is wrong and must be exterminated."[21]

The year of *Foxy*, 1964, was also the year the blacklist ended for Lardner when MGM hired him for *The Cincinnati Kid* (1965), an adaptation of Richard Jessup's novel. Although he and Terry Southern shared screenplay credit, Lardner's ability to be both droll and compassionate comes through in his delineation of characters that could easily have been charmless riffraff; instead, although they are the flotsam of society, they are genuinely picaresque. One suspects that Ring Lardner, Sr., would have commended the terse writing in the poker sequences as well as the film's moral: you can play every card right and still lose— as his son had learned in 1947.

After sixteen years, the cards were right; after a quarter of a century, it was a royal flush. Lardner's real comeback film was *M*A*S*H* (1970), which won him his second Oscar. Over the years, however, *M*A*S*H* has acquired such legendary status—both as the spinoff television series and as Robert Altman's first commercial success—that its fame has eclipsed Lardner's script. Altman made it a director's film by imposing his distinctive style (zooms, overlapping sound, offscreen conversations that cut into and often engulf on-screen dialogue) on a literary script, which became less literate in the process.

Lardner took Richard Hooker's novel about a madcap medical unit in Korea and, instead of blackening the humor further, repeated what he had done in *Owen Muir*: he reduced the situation to the absurd, working on the premise that the acronym of the Mobile Army Surgical Hospital was the key to the plot. While the medics mend, they also mash, hacking away at bodies like butchers, trading quips while blood spurts onto their gowns and gloves, humiliating women, and behaving like the zanies of the commedia dell'arte or characters in an absurdist farce. Since the absurd is the far side of the existential, absurdist farce is existentialism transmogrified. The characters in *M*A*S*H* mock existential commitment by treating their work as a job, which, although they do it well, is done—like everything else—for the sake of doing. Action, doing, is all; what one does, how one acts, is irrelevant. When they are not operating, they are debasing women, seducing but not loving them. The key is to resist stasis, for with stasis comes immobility; with immobility, death.

The context of their actions is the Korean War, itself absurd: a "police action" that dragged on for three years in a country which before 25 June 1950 had no more meaning to most Americans than Vietnam before 1966. Since the absurd can be countered only by the absurd, the world of *M*A*S*H* is an inverted one in which not values but antivalues predominate. Sex is not love but a release from tension or a form of therapy. Immature behavior becomes the highest form of maturity because it is a means of warding off the presence of death. In this type of comedy there is no question of laughing with the characters; you laugh *at* them because they would laugh at you.

On paper, *M*A*S*H* is a typical Lardner script, a cross between a novel and a play. Meticulously written passages of narration and description alternate with dialogue; complex scenes (incidents in surgery; the climactic football game) requiring little dialogue are described in detail. The football game is more interesting to read than to watch. In the script it runs to ten pages; every play is described, every move indicated. When the action must be dramatized, Lardner uses dialogue alone. Since much of the plot takes the form of gags, Lardner writes gag scenes rather like burlesque blackout sketches—short, pointed, and culminating in a punch line. The first mention of Painless's ample organ occurs when Hawkeye explains to Trapper why all the men are watching Painless shower. As a black man takes his turn at the peephole, he remarks, "Ah'd surely love to see it angry"; the line is a perfect cue for a quick cut or, in burlesque, a blackout.

Since life in M*A*S*H approximates what it is in the musical Zorba, something that is done while one is waiting to die, there is remarkably little tenderness. The only sequence that even aspires to anything human is the Last Supper parody—and not all of that. When Painless plans to commit suicide because a temporary bout of impotence has convinced him he is gay, Hawkeye finds a cure in the form of a nurse, Lieutenant Dish, whose name is of course frequently punned upon. Hawkeye brings the nurse to the bed on which Painless lies and lifts the sheet, which rises like a tent as the "Suicide Is Painless" theme rises to a crescendo. Just as the nurse begins to show some compassion for Painless, one realizes it is the size of his organ, not himself, that attracts her.

Despite a second Oscar, Lardner did little screenwriting after M*A*S*H. Early in 1971 Variety announced he would be writing the screenplay for René Clement's The House under the Trees; the following year, when the film—retitled The Deadly Trap—was released, the screenwriters were Sidney Buchman and Eleanor Perry. Lardner's last script was The Greatest (1977), based on the career of Muhammed Ali. Inevitably, The Greatest was compared with Rocky (1976), which to critics and public alike was the real contender. Traditionally, the sports figure movie is either a bio-pic (Pride of the Yankees; The Stratton Story), allowing for a leisurely unfolding of the character's life, or it depicts a social microcosm, appropriately small-scaled and physically confining (Body and Soul; The Set-Up). The Greatest lay in between; it emphasized the fifteen-year period from the 1960 Olympics to Ali's winning the heavyweight crown in 1975. The director, Tom Gries, died of a heart attack before he completed the editing, but the film's problems could not have been solved in the cutting room. Too many wrong choices had been made at the script level; while Lardner respected Ali's pacifism and Muslim beliefs, he did little but extol them.

After the failure of The Greatest, Lardner returned to fiction but encountered critical indifference there, too. While All for Love (1985) has similarities to Owen Muir, it is not as good. Lardner's second novel represents the kind of satire which, like Juvenal's, works from a rhetorical rather than a narrative premise; the narrative is an act of rhetoric. *All for Love* pushes the scientific method to the extreme. A molecular biologist reaches such a state of detachment and moral indifference that he becomes a cross between Dr. Kinsey and Dr. Frankenstein. Sexually unsuccessful himself, he decides to regulate the sexual behavior of others through a drug called eroticin, thereby attracting women whom he would ordinarily have repelled. Ultimately, eroticin prevents World War III when it is dropped into a punch bowl at a nuclear arms conference; the Soviets are so affected that they agree to disarm. The biologist, however, winds up as a mental patient. Lardner chose the most difficult form of satire, one that requires the illogical to seem at least possible if not probable. In *All for Love* only the conceit is believable, not the fiction built on it; what results is a comic fable but not a novel.

While some might confuse his wit with frivolousness and his drollness with insouciance, Ring Lardner, Jr., is a serious writer who has puzzled and even disturbed those who expected him to produce a greater body of work. Philip Dunne, an anti-Communist liberal (who for a time was mistaken for a fellow traveler) and not one to pay undeserved compliments, has said, "If there is one thing about the blacklist that angers me more than any other, it is that we were all deprived of the movies Ring Lardner . . . [was] not allowed to write."[22] There are also scripts that he wrote, before and after the blacklist, which for various reasons were never filmed: the Warner Brothers scripts of the late 1930s; an anti-Nazi screenplay for Fox in 1943 based on William Dodd's *Ambassador Dodd's Diary, 1933-38* and his daughter Martha Dodd's *My Years in Germany* (1939); a General Custer screenplay for William Cagney Productions. Even after he won the Oscar for *M*A*S*H*, none of his projected work except *The Greatest* came to fruition: a *Pal Joey* script (for which Lardner would have been ideal) for Ray Stark; an adaptation of Tom McHale's *Farragan's Retreat*; a Spanish Civil War movie commissioned by a Columbia Pictures executive whose successor vetoed the idea.

Some of the frustration of Lardner's career was endemic to a business in which more scripts go unproduced than produced. But a major source of that frustration has to do not with the profession of screenwriting but with a political climate that prevented Lardner from practicing that profession for fifteen years.

10 DALTON TRUMBO
The Bull That Broke the Blacklist

Although none of the Ten has ever become a household name, "Dalton Trumbo" at least comes close. When I was researching this book in Los Angeles in the summer of 1985, a waiter in a Westwood Hamburger Hamlet, sensing that I was not an Angeleno, asked what brought me to the environs of UCLA. When I mentioned the Hollywood Ten, he reacted automatically, as if he were on a quiz show: "Dalton Trumbo." Trumbo has come to epitomize the Ten for two reasons: the wide readership of his novel *Johnny Got His Gun* (1939), and the prevalence of undergraduate film history courses where students discover that Trumbo's name is often worth a few points on an exam if they can match it up with "broke the blacklist."

Although the blacklist could not have been broken without the help of someone high up in the industry, it was Trumbo who set the machinery in action, Trumbo who made it possible for Otto Preminger to become a matching-test item himself: "hired Dalton Trumbo to adapt Leon Uris's *Exodus* in 1960."[1] If Trumbo had not persisted in writing under pseudonyms, peddling stories and scripts on the black market, and finding people who would front for him, he would never have succeeded in embarrassing the Academy of Motion Picture Arts and Sciences when it awarded an Oscar for Best Screen Story to Robert Rich for *The Brave One* (1956), not knowing that Robert Rich was Dalton Trumbo. Trumbo turned the blacklist to gray so that Preminger could lighten it to off-white, accomplishing what only a writer could appreciate: the restoring of his name. Trumbo had learned the importance of signing his work when the editor of Colorado's *Grand Junction Sentinel*, for which the adolescent Trumbo was a cub reporter, congratulated him on a story but reminded him to use a byline.[2] Trumbo's name in the opening credits of *Exodus* was in the same size lettering as Uris's (although not so large as Preminger's).

Writing came naturally to Trumbo, as one can see even in his high school essays. Unlike the work of most young oratorical contestants of the period—whose style might have delighted the Asianists of antiquity but not the Atticists who favored plain speech—Trumbo's oration on the unknown soldier is without affectation, though idealistic: "The

United States is composed of individuals, the vast majority of whom would make the same sacrifice made by the unknown soldier."[3] In another contest speech he preached that "the golden text of the twentieth century is service to God, service to country, service to our fellow man"—a conviction expressed in his screenplays, especially those of the 1938-45 period.

Trumbo's short stories are quite different. For the most part they are not didactic; ranging from mood pieces to vignettes, they became more traditional as Trumbo began tailoring them for the magazine market.[4] His very first, "The Return," written in the early 1920s when he was still a student at Grand Junction High School, was never published but reveals his ability to describe the underside of Main Street America, where mental breakdowns, murder, suicide, and madness are all the more disquieting because they are unexpected—or at least, a Colorado teenager from a family of Christian Scientists is not supposed to be aware of them.

Trumbo continued writing stories—most of them unpublished—during the eight years (1925-33) he worked at the Davis Perfection Bakery in Los Angeles, where he graduated from wrapper to estimator. In these, he celebrates the world's losers: orphans who grow up to be poet killers ("Johnny, My Johnny"); drifters who spend Christmas Eve listening to Handel's Messiah ("A Young Guy Meets Christmas"); a blind man and a tubercular woman who ignore their afflictions and become street singers ("Chanson de Paris"); a husband in financial disgrace who commits suicide ("Idyll—1933").

Trumbo began to experiment with the novel form; as early as 1927 he sketched out "The Quest of David Bonham," supposedly about the perennial quest for happiness. In 1930, he completed a 463-page typescript dedicated to his father, to be entitled either "Bleak Street" or "American Sonata."[5] The story grew out of his experiences in the bakery, "a principality in itself with its overlords, its serfs and its rebels," where there is "an endless certainty about getting out the bread twenty-four hours a day, so that time does not leap ahead by the week or month, but slips past like a swift calm river." It is a flashback novel, anticipating the structure of Johnny Got His Gun and many of the screenplays; it also emphasizes what would be a major theme in his novels and scripts: Christmas Eve. To Trumbo, Christmas Eve was more significant than Christmas; one of the characters in "Bleak Street" wistfully reflects on the "deliciously dreamy anticipation of the thing we shall never attain" because, with the dawn, the dream fades. Christmas Eve is a time of hopes that may never be realized; Christmas Day is one of responsibilities that must be shouldered. As the Nativity story in Johnny Got His Gun makes clear, Christ's birth is an occasion for meditating on His death. For a twenty-five-year-old writer, "Bleak

Street" was an impressive accomplishment despite its moralizing and length. Although it never saw print, Trumbo was the kind of writer who never discards what might be transferable. The funeral train in "Bleak Street," for example, became the death train in *Johnny Got His Gun,* where the engineer is Christ. Also transferred almost verbatim to *Johnny* is a swimming sequence from his early story "The Green Young Things," in which some Mexicans dive into a river and emerge covered with thistles. Moreover, "The Green Young Things" is set in "Shale City," which is really Grand Junction. Shale City, so called because of the shale oil developments in the vicinity of Grand Junction, became a familiar setting in Trumbo's fiction and screenplays: his first novel, *Eclipse* (1935); his only play, *The Biggest Thief in Town* (1949); and his original screenplays *The Remarkable Andrew* (1942) and *Tender Comrade* (1943).

After a decade as an unpublished fiction writer Trumbo was finally able to place a story in *Topics of the Town* in the fall of 1931; it was a mock Depression piece, "The Governor Enters Heaven," in which a governor commits suicide and is doomed to fall through space for eternity. His first appearance in print, though, was in January 1931 when the *Film Spectator* published his rebuttal of George Jean Nathan's attack on movies, which had appeared in *Vanity Fair.* Trumbo's defense of film, says his biographer, was "no more a serious defense of the movies than Nathan's attack was to be taken seriously."[6] Still, it brought him to the attention of *Vanity Fair,* which published his satire "Bootlegging for Junior" in 1932.

Gradually Trumbo was being drawn into the world of film. When the opportunity arose to become associate editor of the *Hollywood Spectator* (*Film Spectator's* new name), he quit his job at the bakery to accept. But the journal's financial condition was so precarious that Trumbo never received his full salary. Money was always important to Trumbo; he worked at the bakery to support his mother and sisters; he wrote black market scripts to provide his wife and children with some semblance of the life they enjoyed when he was the highest paid writer in Hollywood. For whatever he did, Trumbo expected compensation; when the *Spectator* could not pay him, he left in 1934 to become a story analyst at Warner Brothers.

The following year his first novel, *Eclipse,* was published. It did not take the citizens of Grand Junction long to realize that "Shale City" was their town and that the characters were thinly disguised Grand Junction types. But although the editor of the *Sentinel* issued a mild reprimand to the author, hoping he would use his talent for something better than caricature, *Eclipse* received good reviews; the *Times Literary Supplement* went so far as to compare Trumbo with Sinclair Lewis.

His second novel, *Washington Jitters,* appeared a year later, reveal-

ing Trumbo at his most obvious: the satire is broad, the politics un-
apologetically liberal, and the message clarion-clear. When a sign
painter is mistaken for the head of a New Deal agency and grilled about
his politics, he replies with Trumbo's credo: "I just feel that everyone
should have jobs, and that the money should be divided up more
equally so that everybody can go to school and have enough to eat and
all that, and so that the poor man won't always be going to war to fight
for the rich man's investments."[7] The book is Capraesque in its elevation of common sense over partisanship; indeed, Frank Capra might
have turned Trumbo's novel into the companion piece of *Mr. Deeds Goes
to Town* (1936), which it resembles in its political ingenuousness.

Still, Trumbo's career as a novelist and short story writer (he had by
this time appeared in the *Saturday Evening Post* and *Liberty*) was bur-
geoning in 1936 when he accepted a screenwriting offer from Warner
Brothers, the studio apparently realizing that he was more valuable as a
writer than a reader. Trumbo took the job because he expected to
intersperse screenplays with fiction; instead, he discovered that a full-
time screenwriter must be a part-time novelist. The gaps between his
fourth novel, *The Remarkable Andrew* (1940), and the posthumously
published and incomplete *Night of the Aurochs* (1979) is revealing. In
between were a play and some poetry, essays, and pamphlets, but the
bulk of his writing was for the screen. Even *Johnny Got His Gun* (1939) is
a disguised script; Trumbo makes liberal use of flashbacks introduced
by quick cuts or slow dissolves, and fragments the plot into discrete
narrative units that are more like film sequences than chapters. In fact,
he had to use flashbacks; when the main character is a double amputee, fed intravenously, deaf and speechless with a gaping hole for a
face, and confined to a hospital bed where he is an object alternately of
pity and disgust, there is not the remotest possibility of a plot without
them. The only suspense possible is the character's gradual realization
that he is a living stump. First Joe Bonham discovers that he is deaf,
then that he is armless and legless and, finally, faceless. Once he makes
the discovery, Trumbo must try another tactic: Joe attempts to communicate his thoughts, requiring more flashbacks.

In the screenwriters' vernacular, Joe Bonham is Dalton Trumbo's
hook. If this seems blasphemous to those who revere *Johnny Got His
Gun* as one of the world's great pacifist novels, the only reply is that
Trumbo has used one of the Great War's mutilated to inveigh against
war; his manipulation of Joe's consciousness leaves the reader no other
choice but to react as Joe does. Trumbo achieves this dual manipulation
by drawing on a full range of film techniques, demonstrating that
within a scant three years in the industry, he had mastered the art of
screenwriting.

Trumbo excelled at the motivated flashback, the best example of which is in *Kitty Foyle* (1940), where a paperweight serves as a visual link with the heroine's past. The flashbacks in *Johnny Got His Gun* are, for the most part, occasioned by an image or a sound; in fact, the novel begins with a ringing sensation that Joe mistakes for a phone, not knowing it is the sound of silence—the hollow reverberations of deafness. The ringing cues the first flashback: a phone call that summoned Joe home from work when his father died. Then the action dissolves back to the hospital, where Joe's next sensation, the feeling of swimming in space, conjures up the days of the old swimming hole.

Sometimes Joe resurfaces from the pools of memory with a shuddering inference: he cannot be wearing Kareen's ring because he has no arms: "There was a ring on my hand, what have you done with it?" Kareen provides a scene prior to Joe's sendoff to the war: Joe spends his last night with her, and she is down at the station the next morning with the other flag-wavers. The departure is pure cinema, the farewells intercut with World War I songs:

> His [Joe's] mother and his sisters were there and Kareen was there and Mike was there muttering goddam fools and glaring at everybody and watching Kareen sharply.
> "And their lives if necessary that democracy may not perish from the face of the earth."
> It's a long way to Tipperary it's a long way to go
> "Don't get scared Kareen. It's all right.". . .
> And we won't be back till it's over over there
> "Step lively boy you're in the army now."
> Pack up your troubles in your old kit bag and smile smile smile.[8]

Like Charles Ives's dissonant arrangements of traditional melodies which seem to question their sincerity, Trumbo's jarring juxtapositions of sentiment and jingoism confirm that without song, war would lose its appeal.

Joe's awareness of sensation leads him to certain conclusions as he starts using all the war has left him: his mind. He knows he is awake when he feels the nurse's hand. He senses that evening is coming from the warmth of the setting sun; soon he learns to tell time from the nurses' shift changes. Finally, he begins to communicate in code by moving his head against a pillow. His first attempt is with a nurse whose massaging fingers revive the memory of his first sexual experience. Since the motivation for the flashback is sexual, so is the message, at least from the nurse's point of view (although in 1939 Trumbo had to be circumspect about the nurse's erotic side).

A few of the flashbacks (a Puerto Rican who works at getting fired because he cannot bring himself to quit; Joe's last fishing trip with his father) are true vignettes that offer further proof of Trumbo's talent for short fiction. Although they are essentially filler, they are at least artistic filler; as character sketches, they reveal Trumbo's ability to find drama in people as well as situations.

The novel's climaxes (there are two) have a pulp sensationalism about them. After Joe taps out his wish to be a one-man freak show illustrating the horrors of war, he receives by way of a reply: "What You Want Is Against Regulations. Who Are You?" Had the novel ended there, it might have had a certain shock effect, with the realization that what Joe lacks is even worse than missing organs and limbs: his dog tag having been destroyed with his other parts, he lacks an identity. That point, however, is lost because Trumbo indulges his passion for sermonizing and launches into a diatribe against warmongers, thereby undermining what might have been a chilling conclusion. While some moralists provoke fear, Trumbo provokes guilt, as if not to take a stand on war is equivalent to waging one.

Trumbo could not have written *Johnny Got His Gun* if he had not written several screenplays first, starting with *Love Begins at Twenty* (1936), the film version of the 1929 play *Broken Dishes*, which brought Bette Davis to the attention of Hollywood. It was a "revolt of the meek" comedy about a uxorious husband who regains his manhood after tangling with bank robbers. Trumbo coauthored the script with Tom Reed, but his next film for Warner's, *Road Gang* (1936), won him sole credit.

Murder, suicide, blackmail, and kidnapping are recurring themes in Trumbo's early stories, both published and unpublished, but his screenplays rarely gave him a chance to exhibit his fascination with violence. *Road Gang*, set in a Southern prison camp, is an exception.[9] Perhaps because he believed *I Am a Fugitive from a Chain Gang* (1932) and *Hell's Highway* (1932) did not go far enough, Trumbo sensationalized the material: inmates are electrocuted on a high-voltage fence, or lashed and sent to coal mines. The Breen Office wanted the crack of the whips muted and the number of lashes limited to six; in Britain, the electrocution scene had to be cut; in Australia a foreword stated that "the story has no reference to Australia where the conditions depicted in this film do not exist." In the United States, they did, and since Warner's prided itself on hard-hitting movies, Trumbo hit as hard as he could.

At RKO, Trumbo's next studio, the B unit to which he was assigned in 1938 was under the supervision of corporate president Leo Spitz, who was primarily interested in "crime subject, 'exploitation' films and homespun, sentimental diversions."[10] Trumbo had a chance to experiment with all but the exploitation film. *Fugitives for a Night* (1938), Trumbo's first film for RKO, took a dim view of the movie business, which by the late 1930s was accustomed to being portrayed as either maganimous or corrupt, the gamut running from "hooray for Hollywood" to "what price Hollywood." In between were films like *Fugitives*, which used the movies as a backdrop for a "man on the run" plot; here the man is a studio publicist involved in the murder of a producer, who was really killed by a fading star. The picture is forgettable, but its history shows that Trumbo knew the ability to write was not enough; just as important to a screenwriter's survival was the ability to revise. Between 7 May and 4 June 1938, *Fugitives* went through three drafts and various revisions; on 11 June a final script was ready.[11] Trumbo learned early in life that the product is all, whether it is cellophane-wrapped bread or a minor script reworked to a studio's satisfaction.

In 1939 RKO released five films for which Trumbo received screen credit: for two sole credit (*Career; Sorority House*) and co-credit for three (*Five Came Back; Heaven with a Barbed Wire Fence; The Flying Irishman*). His 1940 RKO films were all sole credit ones: *Never to Love, Curtain Call*, and *Kitty Foyle*. Except for *The Flying Irishman* (based on the career of an American pilot) and *Heaven with a Barbed Wire Fence* (for which Trumbo had written the original story), none of his 1938-40 RKO scripts was original: two were remakes (*A Man to Remember; Never to Love*); four were derived from other sources; and the most famous was an adaptation of a novel, Christopher Morley's *Kitty Foyle*. Yet through a combination of chance and temperament, the incalculable and the innate, Trumbo was able to make the right creative choices even when he had not chosen the themes; something in him responded to the material he was expected to turn into scripts; stories about small town playwrights, rural doctors, barnstormers, and general store owners tapped a source within him considerably deeper than the rivulets that circulated in studio hacks.

That source, however, might never have been tapped if Trumbo had not been at RKO. It was his luck to be there when the studio was in its Americana phase, typified by *Anne of Green Gables* (1934), which capitalized on the myth of pastoralism and the superiority of rural values. Such films appealed to audiences who prided themselves on practicing the virtues of yore and expected those virtues to be glorified on the screen. *Anne* showed that nature is a better teacher than the university; wisdom of the heart can be learned only from those who live off the land. Dawn O'Day, the actress who played the heroine, Anne Shirley, took the character's name as her professional name, and three of her next four movies came from Trumbo: the edifying *A Man to Remember* (1938); *Sorority House* (1939), in which Anne played another spunky maiden who would not compromise her integrity, even rejecting an invitation to join the sorority that had initially rejected her; and *Career* (1939), in which Anne played the daughter of a banker whom a noble country doctor saves from ruin.

Career, set in the mythical Pittsville, revolves around three major holidays: the Fourth of July, Thanksgiving, and Christmas. The climax occurs when an Iowa storekeeper, accused of precipitating a financial crisis by refusing to deposit money in a mismanaged bank, lectures an angry mob on the nature of liberty. The speech reveals that Trumbo had not changed since his days as a high school orator: "If the liberty of one man in this country is illegally threatened, then the liberty of all of us is threatened. The thing that is happening to me now, once started, can happen to any one of you tomorrow. Liberty and justice aren't things to be tampered with. They aren't things to be qualified. They're absolute. Either they exist or they don't. There is no compromise."

Five Came Back (1939) gave Trumbo a sabbatical from the cracker barrel and the general store. The plot, derived from Richard Carroll's original story, was a variation of the old ethics class puzzler about the lifeboat with six people that can hold only five; in the film, it is a plane able to fly only five people out of a South American jungle, leaving others to face certain death at the hands of headhunters.

Five Came Back is important not so much because of Trumbo, who shared credit with two other writers, but because one of those writers was Nathanael West.[12] By 11 June 1938, West had completed an unusually literary outline, which left no doubt that he was a better writer of fiction than of screenplays. It was a short short story without dialogue; its only concession to screenplay form was its division into sequences, which read like fragmentary chapters in a projected novel. The survivors (one of whom is described by her "prehistoric undergarments") organize themselves into a commune; West, though not a Communist, was sympathetic to the radical left.

West next enlarged the outline into a screenplay, burdening it with 1930s agrarianism in the form of a paean to the soil; one of the passengers extols agriculture for freeing humankind from the shackles of superstition and wresting nature's secrets from her. The script was unfilmable for various reasons, chiefly the unambiguous ending in which the three who are left behind have a gun with exactly three bullets.

When Jerry Cady, a better than average writer, became involved early in 1939, he built up the character of the anarchist Vasquez, who finds the communal life spiritually invigorating. Since Vasquez has nothing to look forward to except hanging, he agrees to act as impartial judge, determining who will stay and who will go. In one version Vasquez decides to risk a return but is shot; in another he stays behind, uses two of the three bullets on an elderly couple who prefer quick death to decapitation, but refuses to use the third, resigning himself to his fate.

The last writer on *Five Came Back* was Trumbo, who knew that anyone who could be ecstatic about living in a classless society was no more a villain than Christ or Marx. Trumbo even added a coda to Vasquez's speech in which the jungle commune is compared to Eden: "By all theories ours is an ideal community. And yet everyone here except myself is living for the day when all this will come to an end. That is how tightly modern living has become wrapped up in non-essentials." Trumbo has Vasquez remain incorruptible to the end, resisting bribes and even killing the briber. Trumbo also knew that the Legion of Decency and the Breen Office, which frowned on suicide, would raise objections to the killing of the couple; thus Vasquez stays with them as they await whatever fate is lurking in the shadows.

In 1939 Trumbo's first child, Nikola, was born; he planned to commemorate the event by naming the heroine of *Heaven with a Barbed Wire Fence* after his daughter, but as the script evolved into a Depression fable, the Russian Nikola became the Hispanic Anita. Mother Russia, however, was not completely discarded; the characters, typical Depression figures (runaways, freight-hoppers, dreamers, professors gone to seed), find their utopia in a southwestern mining town settled by Russian immigrants. Strangely, the film was as unknown to HUAC in 1947 as it is to film historians today.

The influence of Nikola's birth can also be felt in Trumbo's script of *Never to Love*, the 1940 remake of *Bill of Divorcement* (1932) and the first of several Trumbo films about father-daughter relationships. In both the original and the remake, a daughter sacrifices personal happiness to remain with her mentally ill composer-father. The 1932 version ended with a fiery-eyed John Barrymore flailing the ivories as he attempts to finish his sonata; in the remake, the daughter joins her father, and they complete the composition together.

Trumbo's most complex treatment of the father-daughter relationship appears in *The Last Sunset* (1961), which he adapted from Howard Rigsby's novel. Trumbo's radical revision of the original resulted in an *Oedipus* in reverse: a young girl falls in love with a man who happens to be her father. Rather than merely settle for irony, Trumbo tried to poeticize the infatuation so that it would not lose its innocence. He went back to the May Day episode in *Johnny Got His Gun*, in which children left baskets of primroses on doorsteps. In the book, the primrose was a vestige of a bygone era; in the film it has much the same meaning: it is the flower that a man once gave to his wife and that he also planned to give to his daughter before he died. As the film's final image, a primrose bouquet restores the family to its original purity. The image did not save *The Last Sunset* from the indifference of critics and ference of critics and audiences, however, despite Trumbo's discreet handling of a subject that could easily have been sensationalized.

When 1940 began, Trumbo had been writing scripts for four years, none of them destined to become even minor classics. Finally, in the summer of 1940, he wrote a screenplay that would prove an exception to the rule that an adaptation is generally inferior to the original. His screenplay for *Kitty Foyle*, which won him an Academy Award nomination, was a vast improvement over Christopher Morley's novel. In *Kitty Foyle*, Trumbo was able to reveal his feelings about the working class, subjecting it to gentle criticism but respecting its integrity.

Trumbo, however, was not RKO's first choice to adapt Morley's novel. Donald Ogden Stewart, who ended up with a credit for additional dialogue,[13] had already written a complete screenplay, to which Trumbo referred, although he was not bound by it. Influenced by the novel's first-person narration, Stewart determined that the film would be a flashback: the title character reviews the past in order to decide whether she should marry a struggling doctor or a Main Line plutocrat. Stewart worked out an elaborate flashback; as Kitty thumbs through a scrapbook, her inner self speaks to her from a mirror on which the pages of the scrapbook appear; transitions within the flashback were initiated by an object integral to the plot: a glass paperweight containing the figure of a girl on a sled. When the paperweight is shaken, the artificial snow inside dissolves into actual snow.

Trumbo kept the framing device of Kitty's reminiscence but combined the mirror dialogue and the snow dissolves into a single transition. The first flashback called for a shot of the paperweight at such an angle that "we are staring through the ornament to Kitty's face." The glass ball and the mirror are joint reflectors of the two Kittys, whom Stewart had called Mocking Kitty and Calm Kitty—the inner and outer selves in a state of disharmony. Once duality has been established visually, Kitty can then speak to her mirror image, appropriately enough, in a mirror. Trumbo made the dissolves functional rather than ornamental by having the mirror image compare Kitty to the girl on the sleigh in the paperweight. In the various drafts, Trumbo termed the transitions the "sleigh-ride ornament dissolves": the entire film seems to occur within the glass ball as a kind of surrogate memory.

As the script of *Kitty Foyle* evolved at RKO during the summer of 1940, Orson Welles was also at the studio, filming *Citizen Kane*. Of the many memorable images in Welles's film, two have special relevance to *Kitty Foyle*: the glass paperweight with the snow-covered house and snowman inside it that falls from Kane's hand at the moment of his death, and the snow that falls gracefully to the music of the "Rosebud" theme in the first flashback when the young Kane is seen sleigh-riding.

Welles and/or his screenwriter Herman J. Mankiewicz were clearly impressed by the snow dissolves in *Kitty Foyle* and even more by Kitty's paperweight.[14] In both films the paperweight with its winter setting is a symbol of youthful innocence, as it was in the novel: the Foyles have a glass ball with the figure of "a little girl [inside] on a sled coasting down a hillside with a red scarf flying around her neck and a castle in the background. When you shook the ball she was surrounded by a whirling blizzard, then gradually it would settle down and was clear and peaceful."[15] Here was an image that cried for visualization, as Stewart realized, but it was Trumbo who knew the conjuring power of such an object. The glass bibelots we shook to see the swirling snow and the sea shells through which we heard the ocean's roar are the stuff of childhood. But the snow in a paperweight is not autonomous; like Kitty's inner and outer selves, it is part of a nexus of associations that cooperate in evoking the past.

Trumbo's next scripts were not of the same quality as *Kitty Foyle*. As he became increasingly antifascist, he grew more didactic, taking it upon himself to be the spokesman of the democratic way of life. *The Remarkable Andrew* (1942), which he adapted from his own novel, originated as a short story that he sold to Paramount; the story was a democracy lesson presented as a fantasy, a genre of which Trumbo was fond, perhaps because it is through fantasy (especially the dead speaking to the living, as they do in *Tender Comrade* and *A Guy Named Joe*) that aspirations which in real life would seem fantastic (such as a world at peace) appear possible.

There are two Andrews in the film: the seventh president of the United States, and a Shale City bookkeeper accused of embezzlement. To the latter's rescue comes the former, along with Washington, Jefferson, Franklin, and (for variety) Jesse James; together, they provide Andrew with enough evidence to convict the corrupt officials who framed him. Trumbo's inclusion of Jefferson among the gods from the machine is not surprising. Trumbo saw himself in Jefferson's position: a humanitarian with the mind of an aristocrat. The left wing of the intellectual elite has never been able to limit its elitism to matters of the mind; there is always a conflict between privilege, which enables intellectuals to advocate change, and the lack of privilege that exists in the lives they want to change and which, if changed, might mean the end of privilege. That conflict manifests the dichotomy between what is and what should be and creates tension in those who experience the dichotomy most deeply. Although that tension may result in acts that appear inconsistent (such as living the good life while accusing others of the same), ultimately the wisdom of those acts will be revealed, as was the case with Jefferson, whom Trumbo portrayed as one who resolved the seeming contradictions within himself: "Here a valiant fight for the rights of the community and a sincere desire for the absolute minimum of federal power; there a staggering assumption of executive authority for the purchase of Louisiana. It matched up. It made sense. There was no getting around it."[16] It made sense because Trumbo's Jefferson was, like Augustus, *primus inter pares;* he could consider himself one of the people as well as *the* one who, by representing and serving them, is therefore superior to them.

Although *The Remarkable Andrew* is an unremarkable movie, it reveals much about Trumbo. What Andrew Jackson tells his namesake, "one man with courage makes a majority," is for Trumbo the motto from which all else follows. Thus, one man with courage cannot stand by and allow those without it to subvert the common good. When Jefferson asks Andrew why he remained silent about the corruption in Shale City, Andrew replies that he was hired to keep books. Jefferson's reply reinforces the motto: "It isn't enough to do your job. There's no particular virtue in that. Democracy isn't a gift; it's a responsibility." Although this is Popular Frontism with a dash of collective security propaganda, it is nonetheless a logical consequence of Trumbo's belief in the inseparability of freedom and democracy. If they are identical (at least in theory), any challenge to democracy must be met with whatever weapons one has; Trumbo's weapon was language.

Throughout his life, Trumbo wanted a better world for himself and others. This interlinking of the individual and the community goes back to something even more basic: the interlinking of the living and the dead. Trumbo believed that the dead work through the living (a point made in several of his films) in the form of values and traditions, and even at times by their presence. As the war progressed, Trumbo found himself expressing that belief with increasing conviction, to the extent of having a dead pilot act as guardian angel for rookie fliers (*A Guy Named Joe*).

A similar situation exists in his home-front drama *Tender Comrade* (1943). Although Trumbo's contract with RKO had expired with *Kitty Foyle,* he sold the studio on a vehicle for Ginger Rogers on the strength of the former film's success. *Tender Comrade* was only a financial success whose claim to fame is that Ginger's mother cited it as an example of Red propaganda in 1947. The film was propaganda, all right, but its colors were red, white, and blue, with panegyrics to the democratic process delivered by Ginger Rogers as if she were addressing members of the ILGWU. The film's most offensive feature, however, is its sanctimoniousness. The plot centers on four women, working in a munitions plant, who learn to share responsibilities when they rent a house together. When Jo (Rogers) announces that once the expenses have been paid, everything will be shared equally, boasting that "we'll run this joint like a democracy," the housekeeper replies that she once lived in a democracy (meaning, mistakenly, the Weimar Republic) that was "murdered, like a little child." When the housekeeper declares that she will no longer patronize a butcher who gives her not less but more than she asks for, thereby depriving others, she argues that just as for want of a nail a shoe is lost, so too could the war be lost for an extra pound of bacon. Anyone presuming to disagree with such thinking, with the way the Allies are conducting the war, or with the way Jo is running the household is called a fifth columnist.

Since the movie was planned for Ginger Rogers, Trumbo simply repeated the *Kitty Foyle* format, right down to the image-triggered flashbacks, the image here being a picture of Jo's husband, Chris, who dies in the war. Just as each flashback in *Kitty Foyle* made some reference to the political scene in America, those in *Tender Comrade* offer some news about the war's progress. The greatest similarity between the two films is the relationship between mother and child: a child that dies in childbirth (*Kitty Foyle*); a child that lived while his father died (*Tender Comrade*).

By the end of the film, democracy is reduced to the basic act of caring for another as a mother cares for her child. Trumbo planned an elaborate coda in which conversations would parallel and balance each other: as Jo talked to her child, Chris would talk to Jo. It might have worked had Trumbo not turned the scene into a catechism lesson. Jo asks Chris why he is fighting; Chris answers, "You." Confused, Jo replies that most people would have said, "your way of life." Chris has an answer for everything: "You're my way of life." The indefatigable Jo persists, citing democracy as a reason for fighting. When Chris asks Jo to define democracy, he receives a typical Trumbo definition: "Letting everybody be free; letting them love, with enough to eat, and a home." Jo had apparently seen *The Remarkable Andrew*.

Trumbo must have known that the scene went on too long; he shortened it but kept the idea of parallel dialogue, dropping the question-and-answer approach and minimizing Chris's role—though Chris is allowed to explain, as only the dead can, why he fought and died: "To be free, to live with you—enough food, and our own home. That's what the war's about, I guess." Not really; that's what the film was about.

Having gone from waving the flag to draping himself in it, Trumbo chose to end the film with Jo's address to her child who, if he had not fallen asleep in the middle of it, would have been traumatized by the lecture: "He [Chris] dies for a good thing, little guy. And if you ever let it slip away from you, if you ever let anyone talk you out of it, then you might as well be dead too."[17]

Tender Comrade was an embarrassment but won a place in the history of film when Ginger's mother, Lela Rogers, found the movie subversive and said so to HUAC. What particularly rankled Lela

Rogers was Ginger's line, "Share and share alike; that's democracy."
Yet no one objected when, also in 1947, RKO released *Sinbad the Sailor*,
in which Douglas Fairbanks, Jr., said "share and share alike" to George
Tobias. Mrs. Rogers ignored the context: Jo was explaining that the
women could save money if they sold one of their two cars and shared
the use of the other. Mrs. Rogers apparently did not come from a one-
car family, but then, she was a movie star's mother.

In 1943 Trumbo had the opportunity to return to MGM, which had
fired him in 1938 after he failed to come up with a single screenplay in
two years. By 1943, however, his credentials were sufficiently impressive for Hollywood's biggest studio to take him back. His politics
notwithstanding, Trumbo was the kind of writer MGM wanted in the
1940s: someone who would uphold the sanctity of home and hearth,
and compose paeans to democracy that were slightly more sophisticated than those he had written for RKO. MGM offered him
Spencer Tracy, Lionel Barrymore, Irene Dunne, and Van Johnson for *A
Guy Named Joe* (1943), and Trumbo went back to his vision of life as a
cosmic concatenation in which the dead are interlinked with the living:
a pilot, who had balked at being a flying instructor when he was alive,
fulfills his destiny by returning to become mentor to a new generation
of fliers and communicate with the woman he loved.

A Guy Named Joe occasioned requests from editors seeking permission to reprint Tracy's monologue on the thrill of flying ("the underdrift
comes straight off the morning star, and beautiful white clouds drift
toward you, and they're like old friends") and from ministers asking
for copies of Lionel Barrymore's speech on cosmic unity for use in their
sermons. The speech is a semipoetic blend of mysticism and optimism
about the music of the spirit (as opposed to that of the spheres) that
fliers hear; its purity brings them back to their childhood and temporarily restores their innocence. Those who have heard that music
(which, in less metaphysical terms, is simply keeping the child alive in
the adult or, in New Testament terms, of maintaining a child's purity of
heart in order to enter the kingdom of heaven) have an obligation to see
that it continues; if war persists and there are no children to hear the
heavenly music, the chain of unity binding young and old, living and
dead, will be broken. The speech elaborates the paradox that "no man
is really dead unless he breaks faith with the future, and no man is
really alive unless he accepts his responsibility to it."

The ideas in Trumbo's 1942-45 scripts take precedence over plot
and structure because Trumbo was more interested in expounding
than in narrating. That Trumbo could wring 102 minutes out of *Tender
Comrade*, and that Edward Dmytryk allowed it, must be attributed to a
war effort that sanctioned self-indulgence. How Trumbo managed to
stretch Doolittle's raid on Tokyo, a morale-booster that did little dam-

age, into a 142-minute movie is less mysterious. When he was writing *Thirty Seconds over Tokyo* (1944), he was in an epic mood; consequently, he wrote an epic-length screenplay with a tripartite plot, each segment of which could have been expanded into a film of its own. Instead, the three parts—the raid, the crash in China, and the aftermath—were interconnected like the links in Trumbo's great chain of being.

There is something Saroyanesque about Trumbo's MGM films; Saroyan's *The Human Comedy* (1943), an MGM success, was also Louis B. Mayer's favorite film because it confirmed the indestructability of the family—not just in the sense of child replacing parent but of stranger replacing, and therefore becoming, kin; in the human family, there are no strangers. In *Thirty Seconds*, the characters were even pure in their racism; the most charitable remark made about the Japanese in a World War II movie occurs when Robert Mitchum states with stolid ingenuousness, "I don't like Japs—yet. Funny, isn't it. I don't hate 'em. But I don't like 'em."

During World War II Trumbo's patriotism, which had been heading down the old freedom road of western populism, exited onto the ramp of repetition, where it remained for the duration. Much of the tediousness of his films, especially *Thirty Seconds*, can be traced to his self-appointed role of priest-screenwriter. When Van Johnson cannot bring himself to tell his wife that his leg was amputated in China, Spencer Tracy bluntly informs him that the loss of a limb will make the future better. But even the uncritical patriotism is less disturbing than the film's cavalier attitude toward everything a writer should hold dear: characterization, motivation, and structure seem to have been rationed.

Never did Trumbo pontificate more grandly than in *Our Vines Have Tender Grapes* (1945), and rarely have audiences been so willing to be patronized (of course, to be patronized by Trumbo is to be flattered for being human). Although the war had ended, Trumbo was not giving up; there was still a lesson to be taught to postwar America, a lesson as old as the story of the Nativity. Again, MGM was innundated with requests, this time for copies of Margaret O'Brien's account of the birth of Christ. Actually, Trumbo took it from *Johnny Got His Gun*, making only minor variations. In the novel, the Christmas story begins: "All the people were going to Bethlehem because it was tax time and they had to appear at the court house and register and pay up" (208); in the film: "It was tax time in Palestine, and all the people had to go to the county seat to pay what they owed." Both versions end with Mary's fear for the child as she "hugged her baby closer."

At the end of *Vines*, a newsman, whose father believed in collectivism and advocated pooling crops and supplies, takes up a collection for a needy farmer, arguing—as did Andrew Jackson, the General in *A*

Guy Named Joe, and Jimmy Doolittle in *Thirty Seconds*—that "we are all children by adoption of the land in which we live. . . . If we have within ourselves the nobility to share in times of stress with those who are destitute, then we can raise our heads with dignity among the princes of the earth."

Our Vines Have Tender Grapes had moviegoers scrambling for handkerchiefs so often during the film that everyone was relieved to walk out into a world where there might be more suffering but less misery. Still, the Christmas story sequence registers an impact far greater than it does in the novel, where it seems to be a set piece rather than a natural outgrowth of the action. It would probably have been less effective, however, without Margaret O'Brien, whose elfin face alone made eyes well up. Nevertheless, it is thoroughly representative of Trumbo's proto-Christian philosophy of life—which is no different from his philosophy of death, since both derive from the Christian paradox that to live is to die, and to live forever requires death within time. Whether because of his Christian Science background or his ability to view life and death as synonymous, the Nativity according to Trumbo was still as much the story of Jesus' death as it is of His birth.

On 3 October 1947, J. Robert Rubin of Loew's Incorporated wrote to Irwin Margulies at MGM, inquiring whether the critics had found "communistic propaganda" in *Our Vines Have Tender Grapes*.[18] On 28 October, Trumbo appeared before HUAC; six months later he was convicted of contempt of Congress. *Vines* was his last screen credit for fifteen years. On 30 March 1949, however, Trumbo's only produced play, *The Biggest Thief in Town*, opened in New York—and closed after thirteen performances, although it had a lengthy London run in 1951-52. The New York reviews, while negative, were not damning. The play's premise calls for a dark comedy: an undertaker concocts a scheme to embalm a plutocrat's corpse before a competitor is called, only to discover that the plutocrat is both alive and penniless. Trumbo treated the material as if it were a folktale about a couple of small-town oddballs, but for this kind of comedy to succeed, the oddballs needed a touch of the grotesque that Trumbo was unable to provide. What is lacking is a sense of the macabre; thus one is left with a yarn about a widower who turns body snatcher in order to send his daughter to New York and (through Trumbo's magnanimity) profits financially from the scam because, as he confesses in the curtain line, "I only steal what I absolutely have to have—and then I work for the rest."

The Biggest Thief in Town was another indication of Trumbo's need to write, as distinct from a need to write in a particular medium. In 1948 he may have thought that the time was right for a play, since the witchhunt had not yet reached Broadway; perhaps he believed that playwriting would not be an entirely new experience because, like screenwriting, it required the reduction of character to dialogue—a technique he had mastered. Yet he had also mastered the short story, although he did little with it. *Thief* is essentially a dramatized short story that can no more conceal its true nature than *The Remarkable Andrew* could. With some care and the elimination of the romantic subplot, it could have been converted into the kind of short story that gets anthologized; as a play its appeal is limited to community theatre groups performing in converted barns.

About the same time that *The Biggest Thief in Town* opened and closed on Broadway, Trumbo made a critical decision about his future in the movie industry. Since he knew the blacklist would not last forever (but also that it would not end immediately), he had only one alternative if he wished to survive as a screenwriter in the interim: the black market. Thus, working through fronts (Ian McLellan Hunter, Robert Presnell, Jr.) and pseudonyms (Sam Jackson, Robert Rich, Ben L. Perry, Marcel Klauber), he chose this alternative, beginning in 1949. It is impossible to determine exactly how many such scripts Trumbo wrote; the figure usually cited is thirty, and the Trumbo collection at Wisconsin contains about that number; however, six of those never reached the screen, and the collection lacks two of the most famous: *Gun Crazy* and *The Prowler*.

Two factors complicate any discussion of the black market scripts: Trumbo's habit of taking credit for films he had not written, merely to expose the capriciousness of the blacklist; and the confusion between scripts he actually wrote (*Carnival Story; The Boss; The Brave One*), those on which he was consulted (*No Down Payment*), those that he polished (*Heaven Knows, Mr. Allison*), and those for which he provided the original story (*Roman Holiday.*). Often it comes down to the difference between the definite and the indefinite article: did Trumbo write *a* script or *the* script? Though not every fallacy can be disproved, some can be refuted.

Fallacy. "When jobs were not immediately forthcoming he managed . . . to get work on some original screenplay or screen story. This is how he came to write *Furia*, which was made as *Wild Is the Wind* in 1957."[19]

Fact. The second sentence requires so much qualification that it is meaningless. In 1955, Anna Magnani pressed Hal Wallis to do an English remake of *Furia* (1947), a pseudo-Lawrentian melodrama about a horsebreeder, his daughter, and his second wife, who takes up with the groom. In the course of the steamy proceedings, the husband, assuming it is his daughter who is sleeping with the groom, forces marriage upon them. Eventually, the husband dies; a spurned suitor murders the wife; and the daughter and the groom realize they love each other. Eugene Daniell and Stella Linden (Anna Sten) wrote the screenplay for the remake of the Italian film, changing the setting to nineteenth-century Texas. Philip Yordan was hired to adapt the screenplay, and later Trumbo was brought in to rewrite Yordan's adaptation.[20] The film that became *Wild Is the Wind*, however, bears absolutely no resemblance to the 1947 *Furia*. In 1957 Arnold Schulman took over the script, making the action contemporary and the plot a hybrid of *They Knew What They Wanted* and *Desire under the Elms*. To perpetuate a belief in Trumbo's authorship is to deny Arnold Schulman his rightful role in the creation of the script and, worse, make "Arnold Schulman" seem a pseudonym of Dalton Trumbo. When Schulman was writing *Wild Is the Wind*, his comedy, *A Hole in the Head*, was playing on Broadway.

Fallacy. Sally Stubblefield was a pseudonym Trumbo used for *The Green-Eyed Blonde*.

Fact. Sally Stubblefield was as real as Dalton Trumbo. In 1954, as recreation director of a girl's correctional school in Los Angeles, she decided that an effective film could be made about life in such an institution. According to the production notes, "she came to Warner Bros. with the completed script and several months later the story went before the camera."[21] The completed script was written by Trumbo, to whom Stubblefield was introduced by Adrian Scott. Stubblefield had the idea for a film; Trumbo the talent to dramatize the idea. In short, Sally Stubblefield was Trumbo's front. Since he could not promote the movie, she gave the interviews, impressing journalists with her charm, her brown eyes, and her prematurely gray hair.

The Green-Eyed Blonde was not badly reviewed; some critics, in fact, commented on the sympathetic script. Essentially, the movie was a mild exploitation film with the usual mix of delinquents and their elders. While not vintage Trumbo, it does bear his imprint: during a riot one of the girls is impaled on a barbed wire fence (compare *Road Gang*); the news of Green Eyes's death in a car crash comes over the radio, interrupting a program of Christmas carols (music for which Trumbo had a special fondness).

Fallacy. Dalton Trumbo was responsible for *The Beautiful Blonde from Bashful Bend* (1949).

Fact. He did write the original screen story, "The Lady from Laredo," which was sold to Twentieth Century–Fox under the name of his screenwriter friend Earl Felton. Preston Sturges used the story as the basis of *Beautiful Blonde*, an ill-fated Betty Grable movie. He adhered to the story line (a female cardsharp mistaken for a schoolteacher), but his changes resulted in a Preston Sturges film. By contrast, the 40-page story—which can be found in the Fox collections at USC and UCLA—is unalloyed Trumbo. It is written in the style of Trumbo's best letters; incongruities multiply until they subside into deadpan humor, as the opening illustrates: "The year 1885 is not particularly auspicious for honest, law-abiding men—or women—in the old west. The settlers are swindling the Indians, the progress-makers are swindling the settlers, the speculators are swindling the progress-makers, the bankers are swindling the speculators, the outlaws are swindling the bankers and the climate is swindling them all. . . . The Santa Fe is unwisely changing from a trail to a railroad, and now it is running clean across the state of Arizona, thus making easier the hop from one saloon to the next: steel rails fanning out to bind America together, the fanning out frequently accompanied by a catastrophic splitting asunder, with horrifying results to cars and passengers, and nobody left at all to sue the railroad. Those who survive are frequently scalped by their passing brothers, the Red men."

Fallacy. Trumbo wrote an "original script," *From the Earth to the Moon* (1958), for Benedict Bogeaus.

Fact. It could hardly have been an original, since it was based on a Jules Verne story. Trumbo may have written *a* script for Bogeaus, but the film by that name, which Bogeaus produced and Warner Brothers distributed in the United States, was written almost entirely by Robert Blees, a highly respected screenwriter (*Paid in Full; Magnificent Obsession; All I Desire; Slightly Scarlet*).

Fallacy. Screenwriter James Poe was responsible for *Last Train from Gun Hill* (1959).

Fact. The opening credits would lead one to assume so, but story credit is given to "Les Crutchfield," who is none other than Dalton Trumbo. James Poe and Edmund North wrote a script in March 1958, known as "Last Train from Laredo," as a costarring vehicle for Anthony Quinn as a cattle baron and Kirk Douglas as the marshal who kills him. After reading Poe's later version of the script, Kirk Douglas fired off a detailed letter to Hal Wallis, who was producing the film for Paramount, expressing his dissatisfaction with it.[22] Douglas's objections were valid; the script was riddled with inconsistencies, the most glaring of which was the relationship between the cattleman and his mistress, whose brutalization at his hands has not altered her devotion to him. As Douglas pointed out, the cattleman is not the sadist in the movie; his son is. If anyone should be roughing up women, it should be the son who raped and killed the marshal's wife.

Through Edward Lewis (whom Alvah Bessie hailed as one of the few progressive producers in Hollywood and who at the time was executive vice-president of Douglas's production company, Bryna), Douglas was able to secure the rewriting services of "Sam Jackson" of 6231 Annan Trail, Los Angeles—Trumbo's address—for $10,000. Jackson/Trumbo made the changes Douglas requested, but they do not appear in the film; thus, Poe is the writer of *Last Train from Gun Hill*.

Since "Les Crutchfield" received story credit, one assumes that Trumbo's story was the basis of the screenplay; one might also assume that "Sam Jackson" tried to carry out "Les Crutchfield's" intentions but could not.

Fallacy. Robert Presnell, Jr., was the screenwriter of *Conspiracy of Hearts* (1960), which was based on a teleplay by Dale Pitt, a Trumbo alias.

Fact. In 1956, the year in which she met Trumbo, Sally Stubblefield was about to become a partner in an independent production company, one of whose projects was the film version of an hour-long teleplay, *Conspiracy of Hearts* by Dale Pitt, who was not an alias but a front—for Adrian Scott.[23] The film version is another matter; since Stubblefield was about to front for Trumbo on *The Green-Eyed Blonde,* she could not do so on *Conspiracy of Hearts.* Accordingly, the trades carried a story in August 1956 that Robert Presnell, Jr., had been hired to write the screenplay for $20,000. Presumably, Presnell was Trumbo's front; whether he contributed at all to the script is unknown. Whatever the case, a screenplay was ready by April 1957. The teleplay was set in 1946 and dealt with nuns helping Jewish refugee children find their way to Palestine; the screenwriter(s) moved the time back to 1943, with the nuns helping Jewish children escape deportation to the death camps. Unfortunately, the suspense is undermined by some incredible plotting. While it is true that with nuns all things are possible—as moviegoers know from *The Bells of St. Mary's* and *Come to the Stable*—finding a rabbi in a German-led region to conduct Yom Kippur services for the children does strain the suspension of disbelief. Adrian Scott's teleplay was vastly superior to the screenplay.

In 1958 *Variety* (13 August) reported that Albert C. Gannaway, known principally as a director of Republic westerns, had optioned Presnell's script, planning to direct and coproduce it with Stubblefield. But *Conspiracy of Hearts* was finally filmed not in Hollywood, but in Italy; it was produced not by Gannaway and Stubblefield but by Betty Box for the Rank Organization; and it was directed not by an American but by a Briton, Ralph Thomas. The history of the script between 1957 and 1959 is impossible to determine.

Fallacy. Trumbo was denied screen credit for *The Cavern* (1966), Edgar G. Ulmer's last film.

Fact. Trumbo wrote *The Cavern* while he was blacklisted; when the movie was made, he was no longer blacklisted. But he believed that a film should bear the author's name; if pseudonymously written, it should carry the pseudonym. In any case, *The Cavern* is a director's film, revealing Ulmer's talent for inducing claustrophobia by confining the action to one setting: an underground cave in which seven people are trapped during World War II. The quintessential Trumbo touch remains, however: a Christmas Eve celebration in which the group sings carols, framed by stalactites and glistening rock.

Fallacy. Trumbo had a role in fashioning the script of *The Abominable Snowman* (1957).

Fact. A 1956 newspaper account about the reappearance of the Abominable Snowman in the Himalayas prompted Trumbo to try his hand at a genre he had never attempted: science fiction. He was also motivated by the possibility of becoming "stinking rich," as he explained in a 12-page letter to Frank King (16 July 1956) in which he outlined his ideas.[24] Having done a great deal of research on the Yeti, he wanted to portray the Snowman as "a human being . . . such as we once were." He would explain the creatures' physical appearance as the result of natural catastrophes in the Vale of Kashmir which caused them to develop furry bodies and grow to an enormous size.

As it happened, Regal Films in Britain had similar plans; it was that studio's film that Fox released in the fall of 1957. The screenplay was by Nigel Kneale, known for his science fiction serials on British television, who based his script on his own play *The Creature.* Trumbo's script bears an April 1957 date; the British film would have been finished by then, and it is quite different from anything Trumbo envisioned. He included a romance between the British explorer's wife and a British-educated Indian anthropologist; the explorer's death so the two could be together and remain to teach the Yeti the use of fire; and the Snowman's plunge, King Kong–style, from the mountain peak to which he had taken the heroine.

Fallacy. Trumbo wrote *Roman Holiday* (1953) with Ian McLellan Hunter as his front.

Fact. Trumbo wrote the story on which it was based; it was sold to Frank Capra, who, sensing that it was by a blacklisted writer, sold it to William Wyler.[25] One can understand the story's initial appeal to Capra: it was in the tradition of *It Happened One Night* but princess/reporter instead of heiress/reporter. One can also see it as not atypical Trumbo: the plot, in which a princess takes a sabbatical from the rigors of royalty until the chimes tell her she must leave the real world and return to her throne, is the reverse of *Kitty Foyle,* in which Kitty ascended from the working class to the upper class before returning to her roots.

Trumbo did not write the screenplay of *Roman Holiday;* Hunter wrote *a* screenplay, but not the only one. There were at least four others: two by Ben Hecht (one of which had a happy ending); one by Preston Sturges;[26] and one by John Dighton, Suso Cecchi d'Amico, and Ennio Flaiano. A member of Paramount's story department compared the scripts and concluded that "although there is a good deal of new material in the final screenplay of Dighton-d'Amico-Flaiano, dated June 5, 1952, the authors have also borrowed some dialogue and action from the screenplays of Ian McLellan Hunter, Ben Hecht, and Preston Sturges."[27] Hunter's script was the basis of the others because it derived from the original and included the main plot points: the princess's disappearance, the American newsman's discovery of her asleep on a ledge, her tour of the people's Rome, her romance with the newsman, and his decision not to publish an account of their escapade. Hecht added the character of the photographer who generously returns the photographs of her Roman Holiday to the princess instead of printing them; Hunter had the newsman return them himself and still feels it would have been more in character.

The credits for *Roman Holiday* read: "Screenplay, Ian McLellan Hunter and John Dighton, story by Ian McLellan Hunter." It has always bothered Hunter that when *Roman Holiday* won the Oscar for best story, the award went to him rather than to Trumbo.

Many of Trumbo's black market scripts were for crime films, giving him an opportunity to indulge his penchant for climactic violence: western villains are gunned down in vengeance (*Last Train from Gun Hill*); characters expire operatically in ghost towns (*The Prowler*), swamps (*Gun Crazy*), atop a ferris wheel (*Carnival Story*), on a barbed wire fence (*The Green-Eyed Blonde*), and in a stalactitic cave (*The Cavern*). Three films on which Trumbo worked prior to entering Ashland State Penitentiary in June 1950 all depict criminal types—sympathetically for the most part; all three climax in settings that would have delighted Verdi and Puccini. In *Gun Crazy* (1950) a young man, whose fascination with weapons lands him in reform school, meets a carnival sharpshooter and ends up playing Clyde Barrow to her Bonnie Parker, eventually shooting her in a fogbound marsh. In *The Prowler* (1951) a policeman seduces the wife of a disc jockey whose radio voice is recognizably Trumbo's cross between a drawl and a twang, enumerating vegetable prices with mock-folksy dispassion and signing off with "The cost of living is going up." When the policeman learns that the wife will inherit a modest estate from her husband, he murders the husband, making the death seem accidental. Pregnant with the policeman's child, the wife delivers in a desert ghost town, where the policeman meets his fate. In *He Ran All the Way* (1951), John Garfield's last film, a killer who takes a family hostage is eventually shot by the daughter, even though she and the killer are attracted to each other. To Trumbo, love between father and daughter is sacred; when her father's life is threatened, the daughter pulls the trigger, and in typical *noir* fashion the killer dies on a rain-slick street.

These three films also include variations on the love death, the lover either killing or betraying the beloved. Although *Gun Crazy* was based on a *Saturday Evening Post* story by MacKinlay Kantor—who received screenplay credit with Millard Kaufman, Trumbo's front—the opening is pure Trumbo: the Clyde figure is shown as a boy whose attraction to guns is mistaken for criminal behavior. The policeman in *The Prowler* is a victim of his own avarice; even so, he cannot let his wife die in childbirth in the middle of a desert, and by summoning a doctor, he seals his own doom. In *He Ran All the Way* a killer's lack of a family drives him to seek out a surrogate one.

One of Trumbo's best black market scripts is *The Boss* (1956), a rarely shown political melodrama written under the name Ben L. Perry, which Trumbo also used for *Terror in a Texas Town* (1958).[28] Both were Walter Seltzer productions; whenever Seltzer wrote to Trumbo, he used "Sam" in the salutation (that is, Sam Jackson, a favorite Trumbo pseudonym) and signed the letter "Bromo." *The Boss* roughly parallels the career of Kansas City political boss Tom Pendergast, who backed Harry Truman when he ran for presiding judge of Jackson County in 1926 and whose conviction for over a million dollars in income tax evasion saddened Truman. Trumbo treats the Pendergast figure, Matt Brady, sympathetically; he is by no means evil, just a little corrupt. At the end, when Matt is facing imprisonment, he says to his friend Ernie Jackson, unequivocally modeled on Harry Truman (whom Trumbo portrays as politically incorruptible), "You're an important man, Ernie. You're a senator in the Congress of the United States of America. That's big; it is something to be proud of. And you may grow even bigger."

Trumbo's most celebrated black market film was *The Brave One* (1956), which netted him an Oscar for best story; however, he did not receive it until 1975, the year before he died. When the awards were presented, Trumbo was still blacklisted; besides, the winner was not Dalton Trumbo, but "Robert Rich." Jesse Lasky, Jr., vice-president of the Screen Writers Guild, accepted the award for his "friend," explaining that Robert Rich was about to become a father and was at his wife's bedside.[29] Lasky was only repeating what he had been told; the next day, he learned that there was no Robert Rich on the Guild's membership list. Soon he was besieged with calls from the lunatic fringe; next, eleven Robert Riches tried to claim the Oscar. As climax to the farce, there had indeed been a Robert Rich in the audience on Oscar night: the nephew of Frank King, of King Brothers, who had produced *The Brave One.*

That a film which few American moviegoers saw in 1956-57 and virtually no one sees today should have become a media event is another illustration of the excesses to which the blacklist led. By April 1957 it was fairly obvious that Dalton Trumbo was Robert Rich; deciding to embarrass the industry further and thus point out the ludicrousness of the situation, Trumbo would neither deny nor affirm that he had written *The Brave One* (soon, he was admitting to the authorship of scripts he had not written, thus creating even greater confusion among the curious). Frank King further complicated matters by telling the press that in Europe in 1952 he had met a struggling goateed writer by the name of Robert Rich, who sold him the script of *The Brave One* for a modest sum.

The necessity of such subterfuge is a bizarre commentary on a film of uncommon simplicity, a story about a Mexican boy and a bull that he comes to regard as a brother; when the bull is sent to the *corrida*, the spectators insist on the *indulto*, the sparing of the animal's life. Trumbo wrote *The Brave One* while he was living in self-imposed exile in Mexico City. When he was writing a script based on fact, he frequently kept a file of pertinent newspaper clippings and magazine articles, in addition to taking copious notes from a variety of sources. His research notes in this case consist of seven handwritten legal-size pages on the bull fight, which he considered an unfair contest: in it man reverts to his lower nature, thereby becoming morally inferior to the bull, which transcends its nature and becomes a noble victim.[30] Although Trumbo could not incorporate all his theories into the film—especially his belief that bullfighting is a confrontation between the forces of homosexuality (the matador) and heterosexuality (the bull), and a variation on the sacrifice of the Year King—his notes are fascinating to read and reveal a depth never attained in the film.

The Brave One's merits, which may have been modest, were eclipsed by lawsuits and charges of unoriginality. Plagiarism suits are not uncommon in a medium where plots are often so similar that one need not be telepathic to duplicate someone else's story line. While Trumbo's story was fiction, the *indulto* was not. The studio production notes stated that "the story of *The Brave One* is based on an actual incident which occurred at the Plaza del Toros in Barcelona on April 12th 1936"; there had been another instance in Madrid in 1912. History provided a point of departure; all a writer had to do was provide a plot, and apparently other writers besides Trumbo had done so. Orson Welles maintained that Robert Flaherty had an idea for such a film; Fred Zinnemann agreed. Welles further claimed that he had bought the story from Flaherty and shot "thousands of feet of film." In a letter to *Variety* (10 October 1956) Kenneth McGowan corroborated Welles's claim, alleging that Welles had tried to make such a film for RKO but was stopped in midproduction.

Zinnemann, Welles, and McGowan were correct. Flaherty contemplated such a film in the late 1920s; by the mid-1930s he had almost persuaded Alexander Korda to make it, but Korda was more interested in elephants than bulls and hired Flaherty to direct *Elephant Boy* (1937). Four years later, Welles, who had been interested in Flaherty's boy-and-bull story since 1936, finally bought it. The "thousands of feet of film" make up *My Friend Bonito*, an episode that was to have been part of *It's All True*, a Latin American semidocumentary that John Hay Whitney and Nelson Rockefeller (then Coordinator of Inter-American Affairs and a major stockholder in RKO) persuaded Welles to make as part of President Roosevelt's Good Neighbor Policy. However, in June 1942 reports of Welles's extravagance in Rio de Janeiro filtered back to RKO, along with rumors of a possible Brazilian boycott when a national figure accidentally drowned during the shooting of one of the segments. Moreover, when the unedited footage was screened, it appeared unintelligible. RKO canceled the project.

In *The Films of Orson Welles*, Charles Higham described what he had seen of *It's All True* in a chapter that whets the appetite for more.[31] The appetite may now be satisfied; in 1984 some eighteen to twenty hours of footage running to about 100,000 feet were discovered, including what Norman Foster had directed of *My Friend Bonito* (slightly more than half) before RKO recalled him for *Journey into Fear* (1942).[32]

Even with the discovery of the footage, the riddle of *The Brave One* has not been solved. In April 1957, Paul Rader, the production director of an educational television station in Boston, admitted that he had sold a similar story to Nassour Brothers for $5,000, claiming that the inspiration came from special-effects genius Willis O'Brien.[33] RKO was interested enough in Rader's story to have Jesse L. Lasky develop it but, for some reason, lost enthusiasm. Rader then wrote his own script and submitted it to several studios, including RKO. The Nassours asserted that the boy-and-bull script they purchased was "Emilio and the Bull," but that was in 1944! Still, they claimed that *The Brave One* was identical to "Emilio" and sued King Brothers for $750,000 but settled out of court.

The story does not end here. In 1975 a Nassour production appeared titled *Emilio and His Magical Bull*—an animated feature of less than an hour, filmed in a process called Compu-Vision, which gave the figures added depth. After almost two decades, Paul Rader finally received screen credit for his work, sharing it with three other writers. In this production, too, the bull's life is spared in the arena.

Juan Duval was not so fortunate as Paul Rader. In 1958 one Carmen Duval claimed $300,000 in damages from King Brothers, alleging that her late husband, Juan, had submitted a script to them in 1954, two years before his death, entitled "Corrida de Toros" and that *The Brave One* duplicated scenes and characters in her husband's script. Again, the case was settled out of court—this time for only $12,500.

Trumbo was sympathetic to Carmen Duval, whom he regarded as a "sincere woman with an honest conviction supported by an amazing sequence of events which coincided with her contention."[34] Nevertheless, he wanted a quick settlement, and with good reason. The

Trumbo and Duval scripts were very similar; both reached King Brothers at about the same time. Maurice King had corresponded with Trumbo in Mexico City, suggesting revisions that included a blessing-of-the-animals sequence. Such an episode did not exist in Trumbo's original script though it appears in a "corrected" one (16 December 1954); it did, however, exist in the Duval script—and, oddly enough, in *My Friend Bonito*. Evidently, some of Duval's material had ended up in Trumbo's script, as Trumbo realized. Hence, he wrote a 15-page letter to Frank King, urging him to settle the Duval claim for reasons ranging from Maurey King's excitable nature (which, in a courtroom, could be construed as belligerence) to the Kings' unorthodox practice of circulating scripts they received to writers working on similar projects: "You not only accept scripts at random; you also distribute your own with equal abandon."

The real irony is that RKO distributed *The Brave One*; had it not canceled the filming of *It's All True*, there would probably never have been the litigation, duplication, and confusion that ensued.

By 1958 the end of the blacklist was imminent; the Robert Rich Oscar had made the Academy look foolish, and the Nedrick Young affair made it look absurd: when *The Defiant Ones* received an Oscar for Best Original Screenplay of 1958, the winners were Harold Jacob Smith and "Nathan E. Douglas," the pseudonym of blacklisted writer Nedrick Young.

In 1958, too, Trumbo was hired to rewrite Howard Fast's screenplay of *Spartacus* (1960) for Kirk Douglas's Bryna Productions; the liaison was again Edward Lewis. Trumbo was elated even though he had to use the name of Sam Jackson (with which the Bryna accountants had become familiar); it was the biggest movie he had yet worked on. He researched the background of the famous Roman slave revolt of 73 B.C., typing up detailed notes on Roman life and institutions.[35] He had his own theory of the revolt. According to most historians, it failed because dissension among the slaves was intensified by their greed and depravity. Trumbo, still the left-winger, would have none of this; in fact, he wanted a mass marriage scene that would show the slaves at their noblest. To Trumbo, the rebellion was a confrontation between freedom and enslavement, led by an ex-gladiator who shook Roman society to its foundations by organizing a band not of outlaws and cutthroats but of "uncorrupt" and "undemoralized" slaves who went to "valorous deaths."

Douglas detested the mass marriage scene, as did Stanley Kubrick, who took over the direction from Anthony Mann. Kubrick was the most difficult director Trumbo had ever encountered; he was furious when Kubrick rejected the scene in which Spartacus asks Varinia, the slave who later becomes his wife, to teach him to read. Trumbo had intended the scene to illustrate the connection between education and advancement and at the same time make Spartacus a seeker of wisdom rather than a beef-witted hulk.

After a year of trying to please Douglas, who objected to the righteousness of Trumbo's Spartacus; Laurence Olivier, who wanted changes in wording; and Peter Ustinov, who did not wait for revisions but made them himself, Trumbo complained that the script was being written by a committee. He had never known such disregard for his work. At first he was civil, almost deferential; he called Kubrick's attention to his mode of screenwriting, which he compared to a crossword puzzle, implying that any change would require a new configuration of his script. What really bothered him was not the need for revisions but the way they were being made—without him. To have some assurance that he was not being written out of his own film, Trumbo asked to see the rushes—an extraordinary request, especially from one who was still blacklisted.

The request was denied, and Trumbo grew increasingly testy; complaints about the quality of typing paper he was using were the last thrust of the knife. He reserved most of his wrath for Kubrick (though never in public); since Trumbo had rarely worked with auteurs, he found it difficult to deal with someone who was more interested in the script's visualization than in its language. Spewing out his anger in diarist fashion, Trumbo railed at directors who "hate dialogue because it presents ideas (which directors abominate), causes a thought reaction (which directors fear) and diverts attention from the visual composition of the scene (which, to a director, is the only valid reason for making the film in the first place)."[36] He even parodied Kubrick's name, calling him Young Doctor Kubrick, Stanley Kupper, Stanley Kupprock, P. Saratoga Kubric, Stanley Pepper, Stanwick Kubrick.

Trumbo's infantilism is regrettable, but more regrettable is his misconception of Kubrick, whose films are often based on unusually literate scripts (*Lolita; Barry Lyndon*). He even speculated on why Kubrick would marry a German: "Did he marry her because he loved her or did he marry her because he wanted to marry a German girl in order to punish the Germans through her for what they had done to the Jews?"[37] What Kubrick's religion and marriage had to do with *Spartacus* is difficult to say, except that to Trumbo they might explain why Kubrick refused to go along with his conception of the title character, who was turning into a proto-Christ. When Kubrick decided to emphasize the love between Spartacus and Antoninus, Trumbo accused him of introducing homosexuality into the plot.[38] The scene in which Spartacus (Kirk Douglas) embraces the dying Antoninus (Tony Curtis) did raise a few eyebrows in 1960, yet Trumbo had written it as a love scene: "I love you, Antoninus, like the son I will never see."

Trumbo became so frustrated that he concluded notes for the pregnancy scene with the plea "Give me back this film." On 31 May 1959 he sent two telegrams to Edward Lewis within twenty minutes. "I have rewritten as much as I intend to," declared the first; the second was more decisive: "I quit this picture absolutely." He didn't, however. Within three months he managed to see a rough cut of *Spartacus*, which so appalled him that he typed up five pages of notes as to how it could be improved with recutting, reshooting, and looping. By cajoling, complaining, and conniving—in short, by being Dalton Trumbo—he managed to convince Douglas and even Kubrick of the worth of some of his suggestions.

Although *Spartacus* was his trial by fire, Trumbo received sole screen credit for the script which, while not pure Trumbo (Howard Fast apparently did some revisions, along with the "committee"), certainly reflects his view of the slave revolt. It may not have been presented as ideologically as he would have liked, and the slaves may not have been the noble band he envisioned, but neither are they dregs of Roman society; ranging in age from toddlers to octogenarians, they behave like a family and live like commune dwellers. And there are enough speeches that use Trumbo's favorite word, freedom, to leave no doubt that Spartacus's war on Rome was a war of liberation. Universal had planned to release the film without a screenwriter's name, but when the *New York Times* (19 January 1960) announced that Trumbo had been hired for *Exodus*, the studio could follow Otto Preminger's lead and acknowledge his existence.

Trumbo was not Preminger's first choice for *Exodus*; as in the case of *Spartacus*, the book's author had done the first adaptation. When Leon Uris's script was deemed unfilmable, Trumbo was pressed into service, playing the role that had become second nature to him: *deus ex machina* for despairing producers. *Exodus* was a difficult novel to adapt, consisting as it does of several interwoven stories told out of chronology and interspersed with summaries of Jewish and World War II history. Paul Newman and Eva Marie Saint were cast in the leading roles, yet theirs was the least important story. Still, Trumbo managed to retain the multi-narrative structure without making any story the central one. His main difficulty was not juggling plots but creating suspense, since the saga of the real *Exodus* that sailed out of Cyprus for Palestine in 1947 was already well known. But where there can be no suspense, there can at least be surprise, and Trumbo found it in the most undeveloped subplot in the novel: the story of Dov Landau, the Auschwitz survivor. As the rewrites progressed, Dov became a more prominent character; consequently, the most impressive performance in the film is by Sal Mineo as Dov, and the most dramatic moment is Dov's confession of his past to the Irgun.

In the novel, Dov, an expert forger, is shipped to Auschwitz and immediately marked for extermination but is spared when he convinces a guard of his talent for counterfeiting. Later, he is forced to work as a *Sonderkommando*, a point that Uris downplays, emphasizing instead the boy's "indomitable spirit." For that spirit to remain indomitable, Dov had to perform one of the most loathsome jobs in the camp: *Sonderkommandos* did not just wash down the gas chambers and haul away the corpses but also extracted gold fillings from the corpses' teeth. Dov, then, had been little more than a collaborationist. Now Trumbo had the link between Dov's Auschwitz experience and his overriding desire to join the terrorists: to atone for his collaborationism. Yet forgery did not seem a sufficient explanation for Dov's ability to survive after having been marked for death. Then Trumbo noticed something about Uris's description of the way the Jews were classified when they arrived at the camp: some went immediately to the gas chambers; others, to forced labor; the rest, both males and females, to the brothels. Trumbo had his explanation: Dov survived by prostituting himself.

Trumbo built up to Dov's agonized admission during the interrogation. Unlike Uris, Trumbo chose not to show Dov at Auschwitz; all that is known is that he is eager to join the radical Irgun so he can blow up British installations. When he is cross-examined by the Irgun, he boasts of his dynamiting prowess, claiming he acquired it in the Warsaw ghetto. His examiner, an Auschwitz survivor himself, notes that there was no dynamite in the ghetto. Gradually, Dov reveals that he learned about dynamiting at Auschwitz where, until the crematoria were built, explosives were detonated to create mass graves. Finally, he admits the worst: "They used me. They used me like you use a woman."

The sequence that builds to the revelation ends in the administering of the Irgun oath. If this is the most artfully constructed part of the film, it is mainly because it embodies Trumbo's personal belief that guilt, if atoned for, is forgivable. Like the HUAC informants, the *Sonderkommandos* were only victims. The will to survive manifests itself in different ways; often survival is a matter of quantity: how long can one last? how many names can one name? how many black market scripts can one write? how many corpses can one dispose of? Trumbo felt no contempt for Dov; rather, he wanted to portray someone who was his exact opposite: the survivor as collaborator. Everyone is victimized by an extreme stand; extremes produce doubles, reverse images, as the films of Edward Dmytryk have shown.

When Dov swears never to divulge the name of an Irgun member, that oath, taken from the novel, is Trumbo's way not so much of evening the score—for the scales of justice can never be balanced perfectly—but of vindicating history through fiction. In *Exodus*, Trumbo's comeback film, self-interest produces collaboration, which results in guilt that is expiated and an oath that precludes the possibility of informing. In the case of the Ten, it happened in reverse: a united stand led to betrayal, imprisonment, recantation, guilt, and in some cases self-knowledge.

A film about the partitioning of Palestine gave Trumbo another opportunity to express his hope, which he never abandoned, of reconciling orders and classes—here, Arab and Jew. Uris's novel, however, was both anti-Arab and anti-British. Trumbo retained the anti-British sentiments and even added to them, but he could not follow Uris in the dissolution of the friendship between Ari (Newman) and his boyhood friend, the Arab Taja, the *Muktar* of the village of Abu Yesha. Their friendship, which becomes strained because of Taja's love for Ari's sister, deteriorates with the partitioning and Ari's call for the destruction of Abu Yesha. In the novel, the relationship between Ari and Taja was the reverse of the one between their fathers, David and Kammal. Trumbo could not mitigate the effect of the state of Israel on the Arabs, nor could he allow Taja to live. Instead, he transfers Kammal's mode of death to his son; he is killed for being a Jewish sympathizer. Thus the film cannot end with a Seder, as the novel does; it concludes with Karen and Taja buried in a common grave as Ari prays for the day when Arabs and Jews will share in a "peaceful life." History has not yet answered Ari's prayer, but then, as Trumbo knew, history often inverts the order of fiction.

Exodus forced Trumbo to reflect on the Holocaust. The sailing of a refugee ship to Palestine is only one incident in a sprawling narrative about the struggle to extract the promise from the promised land. The Holocaust altered the need for a Jewish state from a legitimate claim to an immediate priority; reading the novel was also an enlightening experience for those who did not know the difference between concentration camps and death camps, between mass murder and genocide. Using the most innocent character to convey information about the camps, Uris has the teenage Karen recall atrocity stories she has heard, one more horrifying than the other. Realizing that immunity follows surfeit, Uris knew when to stop cataloguing horrors. Yet those pages, the most graphic in the book, are vital to an explanation of the birth of Israel from the ashes of the Holocaust.

Uris's novel affected Trumbo for better—his screenplay—and for worse: Trumbo's own Holocaust novel, which outdoes the atrocity accounts in *Exodus*. He began writing *Night of the Aurochs* in November 1960, a year almost to the day after he took over the *Exodus* screenplay. *Exodus* heightened his awareness and produced what knowledge of the Holocaust often does: guilt that can be personal or collective; in Trumbo's case, it was both. It is curious that for all his antifascism, Trumbo had never written a script about Nazism during World War II. While Bessie was working on *Hotel Berlin*, Biberman on *The Master Race*, and Lardner on *The Cross of Lorraine*, Trumbo was defending democracy.

After reading *Night of the Aurochs*, one is grateful that during the war he avoided Nazism, which he regarded as a sexual aberration. *Aurochs* was to have been a study in graduated depravity, the sort that culminates not in the sin of sins but in the degeneration of the protagonist into a fantasist whose object of reverie is one of the Holocaust's greatest martyrs, Anne Frank. Although Trumbo had finished barely a third of the novel when he died, the plot can be reconstructed from his synopsis and notes. The synopsis reads like a treatment, leading one to suspect either that Trumbo was thinking of it as a potential film or that he had become so accustomed to screenwriting that he structured the novel in the same way.

Ludwig Richard Johann Grieben's descent into fantasy is by no means atypical of Trumbo; only the nature of the fantasies is. Before Grieben reaches the fantasy stage, Trumbo laboriously traces his odyssey to Auschwitz, viewed as the crossroads of Eros and Thanatos—a hell that became a heaven, a place meant for death that became the setting of fertility rites. What fascinated Trumbo was not the degradation as much as the depravity that existed there: "strange cults for the celebration of sex, which is the origin of life, rather than death, which is its end. In the very shadow of the ovens by day, in the flow of their fires by night, men and women and sometimes even children came together in strange, unplanned saturnalias through which life and love are perceived purely as sex—pornographic sex, obscene sex, unnatural sex, wild, abandoned, and sometimes excremental sex."[39]

Whatever orgies existed at Auschwitz are a footnote to the Holocaust, not the text; yet to Trumbo they seemed to derive from the "mystical fuck up" (158) that led to Nazism, in which the cult of masculine superiority was counterbalanced by the glorification of motherhood—the one resulting in homoeroticism, the other in a mania for breeding, and both in a Dionysianism that deifies passions and drives as if they were autonomous forces within the cosmos rather than in the individual. Trumbo's choice of a sexual obscenity, "fuck up," to encapsulate his vision of the Third Reich reveals what was on his mind: *Aurochs* is a Freudian reading of the Holocaust, with the camps as the channels into which a nation's sexual energy was diverted.

Trumbo begins with Grieben's boyhood of erotically tinged violence. After crushing a rabbit to death when it cannot stretch to accommodate his penis, he focuses his attention on the local maidens, one of whom is blackmailed into urinating for him and then stripping for a friend. Grieben wishes both to possess and humiliate women.

When he learns that a ballerina with whom he is infatuated has a Jewish mother, he has the ballerina shipped to Auschwitz as his mistress. After she is killed in the liberation of Auschwitz, Grieben buries her in the forest as he did the rabbit "done to death by love on a summer lawn." At the end of the war Grieben is sentenced to six years in prison, where he reads Anne Frank's diary, wondering if he had met her at Auschwitz before she was transferred to Bergen-Belsen. He imagines her as still alive, visiting him periodically and then dying at the same age as the ballerina.

Having advanced from infantilism to genocide, with a detour into sadism, homosexuality, and finally fantasy, Grieben was supposed to emerge as a satanic hero, a Nazi Abraham profoundly affected by the atrocities. What Trumbo did not live to show was that "Grieben did his job and suffered his punishment for a cause he believed encompassed the salvation of mankind" (161).

For this, one must take the author's word; it will never be known whether Trumbo could have pulled off a coup worthy of Jean Genet or Norman Mailer and extracted some good out of an evil that transcends human forgiveness. What exists of the novel indicates that *Aurochs* would have embodied the worst feature of Holocaust fiction: an unrelenting emphasis on human depravity. Mailer might have rescued the plot from sinking into the mire of inhumanity along with Grieben, but Trumbo might not have thought a rescue was necessary. The novel was self-purgation; Trumbo, who so readily taught history to others, was teaching it to himself, but the lesson was too painful to learn without the sugary incentives that he provided himself.

The main incentive was an intentionally literary style alternating between the exactness of chronicle and the abandon of romance. Words are not so much chosen as weighed; adjectives are epithets, affixing themselves to nouns like parasites. When Grieben recalls a mass murder, the words pile on each other like bodies, and one phrase folds into another: males stand naked with scrotums like "doughy crepe bags," and their blood seeps into the "soft-sucking" earth.

The excessive language may seem new for Trumbo, but it reflects the prose in some of his letters. When he writes to his son Christopher about the joys of masturbation, he adopts a mock-heroic style that is effective for a page or two—but not for seven. In describing the after-effects, Trumbo writes: "I turned thin and pale; my odor changed from sour to stercoraceous; reflexes vanished altogether; palpitations of the heart set in, accompanied by giddy spells and sudden faints."[40] In *Aurochs*, Inge produces the same effect on Grieben: "My temples throbbed, my throat tightened, my vision blurred. . . . I gasped, I panted, I whimpered, I sobbed. I fawned" (51). The adolescent Trumbo spent summer nights fantasizing about sex, as he tells his son in the same letter: "On warm summer nights . . . I, dedicated fool, lay swooning in my bed with no companion in seminal darkness . . . I celebrated rites . . . with sullen resignation." The adolescent Grieben did the same: "It is not remarkable that I, a healthy, lynx-eared boy, throbbing to the promise of his thirteenth year, lying on a cot . . . should ultimately hear the dainty hiss of Inge's salute. . . . Once discovered I bècame a lad obsessed" (50).

Naturally, one wishes that Trumbo had finished the novel; still, it is unlikely that a complete *Night of the Aurochs* would have added to his reputation. It reveals a Trumbo quite different from the screenwriter on whose speeches ministers based their sermons: a Trumbo who abandoned himself to the erotic lure of the camps in an attempt to find a sexual metaphor for an event for which no metaphor exists.

He had one final opportunity to deal with the persecution of Jews when he did the adaptation of *The Fixer* (1968). Bernard Malamud's novel was inspired by the trial of Mendel Bellis, a Jew in Czarist Russia who was falsely accused of murdering a Christian boy in 1911 and spent two years languishing in prison before his case came to court. Trumbo was attracted to the Bellis figure, Yakov Bok, who is transformed from an apolitical Jew into one of literature's most tragically recognizable prototypes of humanity. Betrayed, reviled, and physically abused, Yakov undergoes a passion not unlike Christ's, which was Malamud's intention: just as Christ was a Jewish scapegoat, Yakov is a Jewish Christ. At the end of the novel, he has acquired a knowledge born of suffering: "There's no such thing as an unpolitical man, especially a Jew. You cannot be one without the other." Trumbo repeats these sentiments in his screenplay: "There's no such thing as an unpolitical man. Where there's no fight for it, there's no freedom. Spinoza said it best. . . . He said you can't stand still and let yourself be destroyed. He said if the state acts in ways that are abhorrent to human nature, then it's the lesser evil to destroy the state."

Spinoza's philosophy, which is central to the novel, is barely suggested in the film, but it could hardly have been otherwise. Spinoza's God is not determined by external causality, yet He is not free *not* to create the world, since the only way God can prove He is infinite is through finite creation. These are hardly ideas for an MGM movie, nor is Malamud's thesis that humankind must compensate for its lack of existential freedom by becoming politically free. Trumbo kept the novel's structure but had to abandon its texture; when this happens, it is generally an indication that the work has reached its level of excellence in its own medium and cannot be transplanted.

Except for *Lonely Are the Brave* (1962), Trumbo's post-*Exodus* scripts are disappointing; even his black market work was better than *Hawaii* (1966), *The Horsemen* (1971), and *Executive Action* (1973). *Papillion* (1973) might have been the exception if Trumbo could have completed the script; but even then, it would not have been his completely. Perhaps what makes *Lonely Are the Brave* special is that it originated in 1958 as a Kirk Douglas film, to be produced by Bryna. The *Spartacus* affair had not yet occurred, and Trumbo had a relatively free hand in the screenplay, an adaptation of Edward Abbey's novel *Brave Cowboy*. Since Trumbo was still blacklisted, he was hired by Bryna as Sam Jackson and paid an advance of $2,500; he was to deliver a first-draft screenplay by 15 May 1958 for an additional $1,250 and receive the same amount for the revisions, $10,000 on commencement of principal photography, and an additional 5 percent of the producer's share of the net profits. No date was specified for the revisions because a shooting schedule had not been determined—nor would one be for three more years.

In the interim, Douglas did *Last Train from Gun Hill*, *Spartacus*, and *The Last Sunset*, all of which involved Trumbo. *Lonely Are the Brave* did not reach the theaters until the spring of 1962. When it did, it was no longer a Bryna production but a Joel production released by Universal; the screenplay was not by Sam Jackson, who had ceased to exist, but by Dalton Trumbo. No longer blacklisted when the script was completed, he used his real name. The film was a commercial failure in 1962 but has since become a minor classic, thanks to Howard Thompson, the former *New York Times* film critic, who rescued it from oblivion first by promoting it on visits to college campuses during the 1960s and then by alerting viewers to its TV appearances when he began writing movie squibs for the *Times* television page.

After more than a quarter-century as a screenwriter, Trumbo had finally mastered the art of obliquity. Although the plot, a cowboy's inability to adjust to the mid-twentieth century, lent itself to homilies, Trumbo suppressed the urge to preach and let the action speak for itself. The presence of Kirk Douglas and Walter Matthau discouraged didacticism. When Burns, the Douglas character, disparages private ownership, Douglas flashes such an expansive grin that one knows he is sincere but also apolitical. Trumbo is not recreating the proletarian atmosphere of his 1930s films; he is writing a character study. Burns is an anachronism, a cowboy whose home is on the range, but the range has yielded to the expressway. More an epic than a tragic hero, Burns is such a survivor that he elicits a "Judas priest!"—Trumbo's favorite expletive (not to mention Kitty Foyle's and Jo's of *Tender Comrade*)— from a policeman who is awed by his indomitability.

In a moment of despair over *Spartacus*, Trumbo asserted that his scripts were so economically written that nothing could be excised without damage to the whole. A decade on the blacklist entitles anyone to moments of self-delusion, but the truth is that many of his screenplays could have profited from a blue pencil. His remark is correct, however, with respect to *Lonely Are the Brave*. Realizing that the plot was not linear, Trumbo took a circular approach, allowing the climax to curve rather than peak, so that it could connect with the rest of the action. The film begins with a truck proceeding along a four-lane highway onto which Burns drives his horse, causing chaos but no accidents. It ends with Burns and the truck on the same highway; this time, heavy rain causes a collision between horse and truck. Burns survives, as does the film, because Trumbo makes it possible. Until that moment, humanity has not been winning; even a one-armed veteran, whose condition should engender sympathy, is such a sadist that his disability suggests an amputated soul. Yet when the accident brings traffic to a standstill, the plight of Burns and his horse—which is so badly injured that it must be shot—deeply affects the other drivers: they look with compassion and admiration on a horseman who dared compete with the automobile.

The scripts that followed *Lonely Are the Brave* were, at best, perfunctory (*The Sandpiper*); at worst, indulgent (*Johnny Got His Gun*). *The Sandpiper* (1965) was one of Richard Burton and Elizabeth Taylor's biggest flops, but Trumbo must shoulder some of the blame (although he wrote the screenplay with Michael Wilson, most of it was his). If he thought that mid-1960s moviegoers were interested in being shriven when the Vietnam War was being escalated, he completely misjudged his audience. Burton's final speech was one of the great cinematic turnoffs: "I've learned that total adjustment to society is quite as bad as total maladjustment, that principled disobedience of unjust law is more Christian, more truly law-abiding than unprincipled respect, and that only freedom can tame the wild, rebellious palpitating heart of man. Encagement, never. . . . Life, unfettered, moves toward life, and love to love."

Amen.

Five years before his death, Trumbo finally managed to see the work by which he will be remembered, for both good and ill, brought to the screen. It would seem that a novel as cinematically conceived as *Johnny Got His Gun* would transfer well, yet the film version was a failure and a pretentious one at that. As both screenwriter and director, Trumbo must be held accountable. Trumbo the novelist exploited a situation that was static; Trumbo the screenwriter exploited an audience that was not. That *Johnny Got His Gun* (1971) received an R rating indicates that Trumbo and his producing company did not expect the movie version to get by on the novel's reputation. There was no reason for Kareen to be photographed in the buff unless Trumbo thought an R rating would improve chances at the box office. The nudity, however, is less objectionable than Trumbo's heavy-handedness, which even extends to the part he wrote for himself: in one dreadful fantasy sequence he plays a warmonger extolling the speed with which the maimed will be able to return to battle in future wars.

The flashbacks Trumbo devised fall below the level of their weakest counterparts in the novel. Joe's meditation on life as a card game is the cue for the Christ fantasy in which a hip Jesus kibitzes over the shoulders of doomed soldiers; in the novel it began more imaginatively with a sound of a woman crying for her son, who turns out to be Christ. Never one for waste, Trumbo saves the woman for another sequence—an expressionistic dance into which she wanders, searching for her boy. The fantasy sequences in the film are not even good surrealism; they resemble Maoist theater where a fable is acted out so literally that one is too appalled by the crudeness to feel insulted. At least in the novel there is the interesting suggestion that Christ is the escort of the dead, like Hermes in Greek mythology; in the film Christ continues in the carpenter's trade but makes only crosses.

The film's most depressing feature is not its physical production, which calls attention to the budgetary restrictions it tried to conceal and to the poorly handled flashbacks; nor is it the one-note theme without variations. It is the characterization of the fourth nurse, who taps out "Merry Christmas" on Joe's chest—a touching moment in the book but perverted in the film: her achieving orgasm implies that a legless, armless torso is the perfect Christmas gift for the sexually repressed.

Trumbo no more knew how to end the film than he did the novel. In the film, when Joe's request to be an antiwar symbol is denied, he signals his desire to die: "Kill me." The fourth nurse is about to cut his life support system when she is discovered by her superior. Joe will be kept alive. His final tirade is inserted into a carnival sequence in which his mother and father, a barker and a hooch dancer, enumerate the benefits of being a double amputee, especially the money saved on shoes and clothing. The last speech is shorter than the one in the novel but as repetitive in its own way: "SOS help, SOS help . . . "

The novel came out three days after Hitler invaded Poland; Trumbo thought the film would be equally timely, since the Vietnam protests were at their height, and the flower children were finding the road to peace tough going. He may not have realized that the flower children wanted the message leavened with satire and dark humor, and they already had it—in *M*A*S*H*.

Throughout his career, Trumbo pursued the same goal that he espoused repeatedly in his work: freedom. However, Trumbo the screenwriter who celebrates freedom with moist-eyed panegyrics to democracy is not Trumbo the pamphleteer who composed a reasoned defense of Harry Bridges, justified the Ten's First Amendment stand, and enumerated the abuses of the Smith Act. In his pamphlets the ideas are organized more logically than they could be in the scripts; it is also evident from the pamphlets that Trumbo's preoccupation with freedom was not the result of romantic idealism but derived from a study of the Constitution, the Bill of Rights, and specific cases of civil rights violations.

In his scripts Trumbo propagandized for freedom; in his pamphlets—*Harry Bridges* (1941), *The Time of the Toad* (1949), and *The Devil in the Book* (1956)—he argued for it by appealing to the minds and emotions of an audience through language. In the pamphlets he showed that he could treat freedom not as a theme but as a topic. Their style is a continuation of the classical exordium-narration-confirmation-division-refutation-peroration form of his high school orations. Although screenwriting left him little time for the art of persuasion, he enjoyed practicing it when he could, and even studying it; at the University of Southern California (1928-29) he took courses in advanced expository writing, advanced composition, and criticism. He played the essayist in his letters as well, recapitulating the background of World War II for FBI agents who were supposed to be investigating the anti-Semitic letters he received but who were really investigating him; or providing statistics to his lawyer to prove that an American Legion boycott of *Spartacus* would have no effect at the box office.

Trumbo's first pamphlet, *Harry Bridges*, is a defense of the West Coast labor leader and president of the International Longshoremen's and Warehousemen's Union (ILWU), who, in 1941, was facing the second of what would be four unsuccessful deportation attempts. Trumbo moves deductively from the general (the rights of all) to the particular (Harry Bridges's right). He draws analogies between the brutal treatment of strikers in 1934 and Vienna and 1934 America; cites jurists, the Bill of Rights, and the Constitution; catalogues Bridges's achievements in improving the standard of living for longshoremen; and quotes Dean Landis's 1939 decision—which was at odds with the government's view—that Bridges was not a Communist. After appealing to the reader's intellect with facts, figures, and quotations, Trumbo proceeds to the emotions—but not manipulatively, as he does in his films. Almost matter of factly he brings up Bridges's Catholicism, his family life, and the selfless nature that has made him the lowest-paid labor leader in America, his only possessions a mortgaged car and a vacant lot in his native Australia. Finally, Trumbo makes an ethical pitch: no one of sound sense would allow Bridges to be deported; to send him back to Australia would be to send freedom into exile. Trumbo almost, but not quite, resorts to John Donne's argument in *Meditation XVII* to the effect that the diminution of one person's liberty diminishes the liberty of all.

As a pamphleteer, Trumbo believed that the issue could be even more important than the individual. In defending Harry Bridges, the Hollywood Ten, and the California Fourteen, he saw more at stake than a labor leader's facing deportation, ten men cited for contempt, and fourteen Californians accused of advocating the violent overthrow of the United States government. What was at stake was freedom, not the quixotic dream of his screenplays but a constitutionally guaranteed right that was being violated—in Bridges's case, by union-busters; in the case of the Ten and the Fourteen, by Cold Warriors.

While the Cold Warriors used specious arguments against the defendants, Trumbo used classical rhetoric on their behalf. *The Devil in the Book* sets out to vindicate the California Fourteen, who in 1952 were sentenced to five years in prison and a fine of $10,000. That the United States Supreme Court dropped all charges against them five years later indicates that the 1952 convictions were not a local aberration but a manifestation of anti-Communist hysteria which, if unchecked, could have resulted in the denial of due process. The reversal of the convictions in 1957 did not invalidate Trumbo's 1956 argument; what he was refuting was the charge that the Fourteen were plotting revolution *because* they were following Marxist principles. Holding a contemporary Marxist to the letter of Marxism, he argued, is comparable to holding present-day Christians to the letter of the Bible, in which exhortations to murder and violence are by no means absent.

The Time of the Toad purports to be an attack on HUAC; on a deeper level, it is a criticism of American anti-Communism and the anti-Communist left—the latter a term that Trumbo finds contradictory. The exordium is an elaborate analogy between toadeating and toadyism: Dreyfus swallowed a live toad to fortify himself against the mendacity of the French press (to prove that ingesting what is thought to be poisonous is an antidote against poison); HUAC proclaimed toadmeat as the postwar diet (but without prescribing a remedy to counter its effects). Those who eat the toad became, in the vernacular, toadies; and since toadmeat is superior to any other kind, toadies are superior to noninformants. It is not the most felicitous of comparisons: to Dreyfus, the toad was a means of immunizing the righteous against meretricious journalism; to HUAC, toadyism was a means of immunizing the right against the left. Nevertheless, as Trumbo sees it, either one eats toadmeat and becomes a toady, or one refuses to answer HUAC's two-pronged question about membership in the Screen Writers Guild and the Communist Party and becomes an unfriendly witness. To answer is to be a toad; to decline is to maintain one's integrity. To answer even the first question is to violate a long-standing principle of trade unionism: secrecy of membership. Admitting SWG membership invites questions about the membership of others; disclosing membership in the Party does the same.

Trumbo always inhabited an either-or world. In the 1930s it was fascism or antifascism; during World War II it was the Allies or the Axis; during the Cold War it was anti-anti-Communism or anti-Communist liberalism. By Trumbo's logic, the non-Communist left was the non-antifascist left; by not being an anti-anti-Communist, the non-Communist left is the fascist right. Still clinging to the 1930s distinction between Communism and fascism, Trumbo could not accept the new liberals who were also anti-Communists. While he was never an apologist for the Soviet Union, he also never denounced it; his policy was to say nothing derogatory about it. Making the Soviet Union the arch-fiend would only aggravate anti-Communist paranoia and weaken the American left. As Trumbo rightly predicted, an obsession with Communism would make the Soviet Union "a moral yardstick by which we evaluate our national deeds and virtues."[41] Even as late as 1965, after he had been reinstated in his profession, Trumbo wrote that "the whole degrading process of politics-as-magic and incantation-as-intellect will continue until that terrible word, 'Communist,' is wrested from sorcerers and robbed of its necromaneous power to drive us mad" and until Americans accept "the rational probability that Communists, as individual human beings, have as many (although possibly different) virtues as ourselves" (152-53).

Because of his early conversion to the left, Trumbo never associated Communism with a lack of freedom. Freedom was a given; as such, it was something to be exercised, enjoyed, and defended. As he grew older, freedom began to take on mystical associations; it became a kind of cosmic liberation in which the individual would participate in the boundlessness of the universe. Even if this kind of freedom could never come to pass, it could at least be a goal. When he was preparing for an interview in conjunction with *Lonely Are the Brave*, he jotted down some notes on the film's theme: the kind of freedom that existed when the West was being settled but that was gradually lost as the garden encroached upon the desert: "But some men remember that other freedom that we've lost—and they prefer a horse to a truck—a mountain stream to a fountain in the city—and a fenced-in country wounds them—and they want to cling to that old concept of a free America standing in the midst of a boundless landscape. And of course it can't be done. So these people encounter tragedy . . . and the interesting thing is they accept that possibility."

To Trumbo, freedom and brotherhood were even more important than art. In "Confessional," Trumbo's poem (published in *Mainstream*, Winter 1947) from which Bessie quotes in *The un-Americans*, the speaker has renounced his membership in the Party but has not given up on the myth that brought him into it: the myth of the classless society, the terrestrial paradise, the New Jerusalem. He still looks forward to a time when Communists and non-Communists can greet one another if not as comrades, then as brothers and sisters: "On this pavilion we shall meet again / And I shall take my brother's hand and yours / And we shall sing together in the dawn / And we shall stand like angels in the sun / And hail the new Jerusalem!"

This is not the New Jerusalem in which Raskolnikov believes; it is one intended to exist on earth—not in Trumbo's lifetime, not in anyone's, yet that should not prevent its being envisaged and promoted as the ideal. That Trumbo did both in his films and, at the same time, was handsomely compensated for it is not inconsistent. His goal was the same as that of the speaker in his poem: "I wish to be both rich and holy too."

Dalton Trumbo found his holiness and his riches in film.

Epilogue

It is a truism of American film history that the blacklist which followed the 1947 hearings contributed to the decline of the movie industry after World War II. There were other factors of course, the most significant being the Supreme Court's "Paramount Decision," which required the vertically integrated majors—Paramount, MGM, Fox, Warner Brothers, and RKO—to divest themselves of their theater chains. Nevertheless, any standard history of film not only substantiates the role of the blacklist in the waning of Hollywood but also holds it accountable for the pall that enshrouded the movie world in the late 1940s; says David Cook, "As damaging to the American cinema as the loss of individual talent was the pervasive mood of fear, distrust, and self-loathing that settled over Hollywood in the wake of the hearings."[1]

The firing of the Ten was only a prologue to a tragedy with a cast not of ten but of hundreds. If only ten had been affected, the industry could easily have managed. The number was considerably higher; according to Adrian Scott's count:

The blacklist includes some 214 motion picture craftsmen and professionals who are now barred from employment in the motion picture industry. Among them are: 106 writers, 36 actors, 3 dancers, 11 directors, 4 producers, 6 musicians, 4 cartoonists, 44 other craftsmen and professionals. They became unemployable by failing in one or more of the following ways to "cooperate" with the House Committee on Un-American Activities: (a) by invoking the First Amendment to the Constitution, protecting freedom of speech and association; (b) by invoking the Fifth Amendment to the Constitution, protecting a witness from being required to testify against himself; (c) by not appearing before the Committee as an informer after being named as a Communist, or former Communist, by an informer.

The "greylist" includes hundreds of studio craftsmen and professionals who are partially unemployable; that is, whose employment in the studios is limited in varying degrees. They become "greylisted" by failing to repudiate (convincingly) activities such as the following: (a) support for New Deal or Independent political organizations such as the Hollywood Democratic Committee and Progressive Citizens of America; (b) support for anti-Fascist organizations such as the Hollywood Anti-Nazi League and the Committee to Aid Spanish Refugees; (c) support for organizations responsible for civilian war work in World War II, such as the Hollywood Writers Mobilization and the Actors Lab; (d) attending or teaching at schools such as the League of American

Writers School and the People's Educational Center; (e) subscribing to left-wing publications such as the National Guardian and the People's World, or being mentioned favorably in such publications; (f) opposing the Un-American Activities Committee by such actions as signing the Amicus Curiae brief in behalf of the Hollywood 10 and supporting the Committee for the First Amendment; (g) union activity, such as signing a nominating petition for a blacklisted person and contributing to a strike welfare fund; (h) expressing disapproval of informers, through word or deed.[2]

The view that "the talent swept out the door by the witch hunt was unimportant"[3] is dangerously naive as well as historically false. If Hollywood was "drained of creative vitality" and experiencing "intellectual stagnation and moral paralysis,"[4] the reason was that the source of much of its vitality and creativity had been shut off.

In a study devoted exclusively to the Hollywood Ten, it is impossible to address all the issues raised by the blacklist and reach conclusions applicable to several hundred individuals. However, two conclusions can be reached about the Ten—conclusions that some may find difficult to accept because they require an appreciation of the ironic as well as an ability to distinguish between a discriminatory action that prevented qualified personnel from working in their profession, and the unexpected revelation of talent that resulted from that action.

The witch-hunters failed to perceive that even without them, the ranks of the Hollywood radicals would have been diminished by events over which no one, much less HUAC, had control. History, as T.S. Eliot observed in "Gerontion," has "many cunning passages, contrived corridors." Even if the blacklist had not occurred, the events that intensified American anti-Communism (the fall of China to the Communists, the Korean War, atomic espionage cases) would have; even if the blacklist had not occurred, the same factors that changed the face of Hollywood over the next two decades (the Paramount Decision, television, inflation, the dissolution of the studio system, and the move toward corporate ownership) would have.

Although no one can be absolutely certain how the Ten would have fared in a Hollywood ruled by "the boys with beards and zoom lenses," as Billy Wilder dubbed the new breed in *Fedora* (1979), there is little likelihood that Dmytryk would have been without work. Able to adjust to any screen size or genre, Dmytryk applied his skills to whatever film he was directing, whether it was meant for the standard screen or the wide screen, whether it was about the War of 1812 or World War II. When his directing days ended in 1975, he embarked upon two new careers: university teaching and textbook writing.

With or without a blacklist, Lester Cole would probably not have lasted very long at MGM, despite his new contract and prospects of producing. MGM joined the anti-Communist crusade early in the Cold

War with *The Red Danube* (1949), which sanctioned a ballerina's decision to commit suicide rather than be repatriated to the Soviet Union. Cole might even have left a year earlier—in 1948, when Dore Schary became vice-president in charge of production. It is impossible to imagine Schary's waxing enthusiastic about Cole's plan to write the script of his dreams for MGM: the life of Emiliano Zapata. Cole was a survivor, but not of the Dmytryk variety; having neither the support nor the sympathy of an industry that welcomes the repentant and excludes the unshriven, he had to resort for a time to menial jobs that few of his colleagues could have performed: waiter, short-order cook, warehouse worker. Yet he ended his days doing something he might not have done if he had not been blacklisted: he taught screenwriting. That a high school dropout was so beloved by his students that they considered him a major influence on their lives, and that one of those students would establish in his memory the Lester Cole Scholarship in Dramatic Writing at New York University—these are more impressive than a two-page filmography.

There is no doubt that even before the blacklist the Hollywood careers of Ornitz, Bessie, and Biberman were about to end and that Lawson's was imperiled. By the beginning of the 1940s Ornitz had outlived his usefulness to the studios. His Hollywood period was not so much a strange interlude as an unreal one; it was a distraction from the kind of writing at which he excelled as well as an easy way of making a living while fighting fascism, whose defeat he considered more important than the novels he might have written. One would like to think Ornitz would have written *Bride of the Sabbath* even had he still been active as a screenwriter, yet the dates of his novels suggest otherwise: two appeared before he went to Hollywood, the best not until after the blacklist. At least he lived to see his last novel reach tenth place on the best-seller list in 1951 and to read reviews that vindicated his talent.

Hollywood also proved a distraction and an impediment to Bessie, whose career as a contract writer was also over before the hearings, when Warner Brothers let him go in 1945. Bessie wrote most of his short stories, the highly regarded *Men in Battle,* and his first two novels before going to Hollywood and began writing seriously again in 1957. He did his best work before and after the blacklist; it is difficult to imagine his pressing for the publication of his stories, for which he had a genuine talent, had he been able to go on writing screenplays.

The blacklist backfired in Biberman's case, too. With RKO's decision not to renew him in 1944, and with his unimpressive writing and directing record, he had two options: producing or directing for the independents. What Biberman directed in the 1950s was a film for a production company he had cofounded—a company that would never have existed if there had not been a blacklist. *Salt of the Earth*, an international success and a campus favorite, is the only film his company ever made; it also gave him the only real recognition he would ever know.

Lawson's studio connection ended shortly after Biberman's, in 1945, when Harry Cohn fired him from Columbia for supporting the Conference of Studio Unions strike (which even the Screen Writers Guild would not back). Yet screenwriting mattered less to Lawson than understanding the forces that shaped world history, as is clear from *The Hidden Heritage*. It was not the first time his interests had changed dramatically. In 1932 Harold Clurman thought Lawson was the hope of the New York theater; and it did seem for a time that he would at least be *a* hope. No one will ever know; within two weeks of *Gentlewoman's* closing in 1934, Lawson had answered Mike Gold's criticism of his political indecisiveness. From that point on, the movement took precedence over the theatre, just as for Ornitz the death of fascism took precedence over the writing of fiction. Lawson's ability to write the radical play, *Marching Song*, his last New York production, was less important than its acceptance by the Communist press. When he returned to the theater, it was not in New York but in East Germany in 1963, with a revision of his *Parlor Magic*, which in 1939 Harold Clurman had found unstageworthy. In the intervening decades the play had become worse; it seems to have been rewritten in a time warp. The curtain line—"It's not easy to stand up for what's right"—encapsulates its banality.

Though Lawson abandoned the New York stage, what he wrote for it was far more innovative than anything he wrote for Hollywood. Screenwriting was a livelihood, and Lawson's scripts resulted in good but not great films. Yet greatness is not even the issue; once Lawson embarked upon *The Hidden Heritage*, it was evident that what he really wanted to do was synthesize past and present. When Lawson appeared before HUAC on 27 October 1947 and announced in a voice tinged with contempt and pomposity, "It is unfortunate and tragic that I have to teach this Committee the basic principles of American—" (he was interrupted before he could say "democracy"), his choice of verb was appropriate. He would teach when he had no further prospects; but even before he turned to the classroom, a generation of students learned the essentials of play construction and the nature of film from his books.

Lawson's career is a study in incremental irony; the careers of Albert Maltz and Adrian Scott are studies in tragedy that has been denied the palliative of catharsis. Just as Maltz found a narrative form with which he was comfortable, revealing it in *The Journey of Simon McKeever*, and just as he was envisioning a new life in which he could alternate essays, reviews, fiction, and film, he discovered that life had ended before it began: "Funds I had accumulated to finance a three volume historical novel requiring much research have now gone into this [legal] fight. I can no longer finance the writing of this novel. It is indefinitely postponed. [There has been] a severe drain on time and energy away from creative and artistic pursuits into fighting an inquisition and fighting to stay out of jail. I am robbed of my ability to practice the art of screenwriting where my work had been previously sought. I am constantly faced by a spectre: if a blacklist in the films can be maintained, why not a blacklist in books? If today I am not permitted to write films, how do I know whether tomorrow I will be allowed to write novels."[5]

The blacklist handicapped Maltz psychologically and creatively. Although he had virtually stopped publishing fiction in the late 1960s, *A Tale of One January* and the 1968 *Saturday Evening Post* stories show that he finally understood that emotional control in the writer produces a greater emotional effect on the reader. But he did not act further on this knowledge. Likewise, after he proved he had not forgotten how to write a screenplay with *Two Mules for Sister Sara*, he wrote one failure, *Scalawag*, and then stopped. Maltz produced more during the two decades he was on the blacklist than he did afterward.

The fate of Adrian Scott goes beyond tragedy, which, as Jean Anouilh reminds us in *Antigone* (1944), is clean and restful; Scott's is an instance not of tragedy but of the tragic, which is messy and disquieting because it refuses to obey the rules. In classical tragedy the hero does not plunge from promise to oblivion without passing through the intermediate stage of misfortune. With Scott, misfortune was oblivion. Most of the Ten produced some significant work while they were blacklisted; Scott was never given the chance to show what he could have done. It is small comfort to Joan Scott to remember that in 1947 her husband was the industry's most promising producer, that he inspired adjectives like "decent" and "honorable," and that during the Ten's whistle-stop speaking tour he was the peacemaker when tempers flared. Carson McCullers once remarked that God had confused her with Job. A similar confusion seems to have occurred with Adrian Scott.

"Of all sad words flung through the Hollywood offices of the Screen Writers Guild, the saddest may indeed be Ring Lardner, Jr." One can imagine Lardner's reading Richard Corliss's lament and musing, "I think rather than 'saddest,' 'most incongruous.' " Lardner's screenwriting career spanned four decades (1937-77). Although he had no screen credits for almost two of those decades, he still managed to win two Oscars for films separated by almost three of them: *Woman of the Year* (1942) and *M*A*S*H* (1970). Philip Dunne was right in bemoaning the films Lardner was prevented from writing; given his track record, some might well have been Oscar winners. The final incongruity made Lardner's persecutors his footstool. Although Hollywood denied him work and the State Department a passport, Lardner succeeded in writing a satire, *The Ecstasy of Owen Muir,* that delineates the McCarthy era with a wit which never loses its buoyancy but also never becomes airborne; and although rendered nameless, he and Ian McLellan Hunter created a television series, *The Adventures of Robin Hood,* that for three seasons competed successfully in the same time slot with such shows as *Topper, Bold Journey, American Bandstand,* and *The Price Is Right.* Lardner may have written more unproduced than produced scripts, but he has had the last laugh.

While Dalton Trumbo seems to have been unique in the sense of being productive before, during, and after his blacklisting, his career also exhibits its share of incongruities. Trumbo not only survived the blacklist period; he also turned out some of his most interesting scripts during those years: *Gun Crazy, The Prowler, The Boss, Spartacus.* The screenplays he wrote afterward, except for *Exodus* and *Lonely Are the Brave,* are not even as good as some he turned out at RKO in the late 1930s.

The greatest irony of the blacklist, then, was the way it backfired on the industry that set it in motion: it weakened the industry that it was supposed to strengthen; it strengthened some whom it was supposed to destroy—by eliciting from them work that was often better than they had done previously. Yet some aspects of the blacklist transcend irony: the premature deaths and suicides it caused, the dull and sanctimonious films it spawned.

Its most demeaning aspect for writers was enforced anonymity. "Cashing a check made out to an imaginary person is not a simple matter when your own name cannot appear as an endorser," as Ring Lardner, Jr., explained. "You have to open a bank account under an alias, and my recommendation is that you start in the savings department, where no attempt is made to verify your identity."[6] Trumbo could vouch for this. He opened one checking account under the name of James Bonham (his protagonist in *Johnny Got His Gun*), then endorsed his checks twice—as James Bonham and as the payee (John Abbott, Sam Jackson or another pseudonym). When a check had cleared, James Bonham would write out a check to Dalton Trumbo for deposit in an account under the name of Dalton Trumbo in another bank.[7]

Worse than resorting to such ruses, for Trumbo, was having to relinquish rights to his black market scripts: "I am perfectly willing to sign any releases . . . necessary to protect . . . any relationship I may have had with that person and that corporation and those literary properties."[8] In those absurd times Trumbo behaved absurdly, pushing anonymity to the limit. Being a nonperson, he could say what he pleased, since he was speaking as the (nonexistent) Robert Rich or Sam Jackson. Since he had signed so many waivers, he could then cast doubt on screenplay authorship in general, infuriating Jerry Wald, who accused him of insulting the Screen Writers Guild by alerting the public to the existence of the black market, thereby causing speculation as to who was writing what scripts. While the Screen Writers Guild was ineffectual, the Academy of Motion Picture Arts and Sciences was malevolent; it cooperated with the blacklist by deliberately passing a resolution that blacklisted writers would not be eligible for Oscars, knowing full well that Michael Wilson would be for *Friendly Persuasion* (1956).

Billy Wilder was wrong; the Ten were talented—but their talent did not lie exclusively in film, as a study of their work shows. The best of what each of the Ten has produced requires no apology.

Chronologies, Bibliographies, and Filmographies

ABBREVIATIONS

AA = Academy Award	cos = coauthor, story
ad = adaptation	cosp = coauthor, screenplay
addl dial = additional dialogue	dial = dialogue
AN = Academy nomination	dir = director
coad = coauthor, adaptation	prod = producer
codial = coauthor, dialogue	s = story
contrib = contribution	sp = screenplay
coprod = coproducer	uncr = uncredited

Primary sources are listed in chronological order of publication; secondary sources, alphabetically by author.

ALVAH BESSIE (1904-85)

1904	born 4 June, New York City
1924	B.A., Columbia University
1924-28	actor and stage manager in New York and Massachusetts; begins brief career as translator of French literature
1928	joins *Paris-Times* for three months
1929	publishes first short story, "Redbird," in *Transition*; returns to America; works as freelance writer and proofreader for the *New Yorker*
1930-35	moves to Vermont, working first as cook and laborer, then buying a small farm; publishes short stories regularly and translates from the French
1935	awarded Guggenheim Fellowship; publishes first novel
1936-37	assistant editor of Sunday magazine, *Brooklyn Eagle*; leaves after quarrel with editor about Spanish Civil War pieces; joins New York office of Spanish Information Bureau as publicist
1938	volunteers in Abraham Lincoln Battalion to fight for Spanish republic
1939-43	drama and film editor, *New Masses*
1943	hired as screenwriter by Warner Brothers
1943-47	Hollywood period
1945	option dropped by Warner Brothers
1947	appears 28 October before HUAC

1950	sentenced 23 June to one year at Federal Correctional Institution at Texarkana, Texas, and fined $1,000; serves ten months
1951-56	assistant editor, ILWU *Dispatcher*
1954	gives up membership in Communist Party
1956-63	stage manager/light man/announcer at hungry i nightclub in San Francisco; reviews films under pseudonyms (e.g. David Ordway)
1957	resumes writing novels
1985	dies of heart attack 21 July in Terra Linda, California

Published Work

FICTION

Dwell in the Wilderness. New York: Covici, Friede, 1935.
Bread and a Stone. New York: Modern Age Books, 1941.
The un-Americans. New York: Cameron Associates, 1957.
The Symbol. New York: Random House, 1966.
One for My Baby. New York: Holt, Rinehart & Winston, 1980.
Alvah Bessie's Short Fictions. Novato, Calif.: Chandler & Sharp, 1982.

NONFICTION

Men in Battle: A Story of Americans in Spain. New York: Scribner, 1939.
This Is Your Enemy: A Documentary Record of Nazi Atrocities against Citizens and Soldiers of Our Soviet Ally [pamphlet]. New York: Front Line Fighters Fund, 1942.
Inquisition in Eden. New York: Macmillan, 1965.
Spain Again. San Francisco: Chandler & Sharp, 1975.
The Soviet People at War [pamphlet]. New York: American Council on Soviet Relations, n.d.

EDITION

The Heart of Spain: Anthology of Fiction, Non-Fiction, and Poetry. New York: Veterans of the Abraham Lincoln Brigade, 1952.

Films

1943	*Northern Pursuit* (Warner Brothers, cosp)
1944	*The Very Thought of You* (Warner Brothers,cosp)
1945	*Objective, Burma!* (Warner Brothers, s, AN)
	Hotel Berlin (Warner Brothers, cosp)
1948	*Smart Woman* (Allied Artists, cosp)
	Ruthless (Eagle-Lion, uncr, ad)
1968	*España otra vez* (Spanish, cosp, actor)

HERBERT BIBERMAN (1900-71)

1900	born 4 March, Philadelphia
1921	B.S. economics, University of Pennsylvania
1925	enrolls in Yale's drama school, studying under George Pierce Baker

1927	M.A. drama, Yale University
1927-28	travels in Europe with artist brother Edward
1928	joins Theatre Guild as assistant stage manager, then director
1929	cofounds Theatre Guild Studio; directs Soviet play *Red Rust*
1930	marries Gale Sondergaard; directs *Roar China* and *Green Grow the Lilacs* for Theatre Guild
1931	directs *Miracle at Verdun* for Theatre Guild
1933	writes *Legend of America* series for CBS radio
1934	hired by Columbia for two films; codirects *Valley Forge* for Theatre Guild
1935-47	Hollywood period
1947	appears 29 October before HUAC
1950	sentenced 29 June to six months in Federal Correctional Institution, Texarkana, Texas, and fined $1,000; serves five months
1951	cofounds Independent Productions Company (IPC)
1955	*Salt of the Earth* awarded International Grand Prize for best film
1956	works as land developer
1971	dies of bone cancer 30 June in New York

Published Work

NONFICTION

Salt of the Earth: The Story of a Film [includes screenplay]. Boston: Beacon Press, 1965.

Films

1935	*One Way Ticket* (Columbia, dir)
1936	*Meet Nero Wolfe* (Columbia, dir)
1938	*King of Chinatown* (Paramount, s)
1944	*Action in Arabia* (RKO, cos, cosp)
	The Master Race (RKO, s, cosp, dir)
	Together Again (Columbia, cos)
1946	*Abilene Town* (United Artists, assoc prod)
1947	*New Orleans* (United Artists, cos, coprod)
1954	*Salt of the Earth* (IPC, dir)
1969	*Slaves* (United Artists, cosp, dir)

LESTER COLE (1904-85)

1904	born 19 June, New York City
1920	drops out of high school; begins brief career in the theater
1925-26	assistant stage manager for Max Reinhardt's production of *The Miracle* in New York and on tour
1927	stage manager for opening of Grauman's (now Mann's) Chinese Theatre in Hollywood
1928-30	acts in west coast plays and a few films
1930	his play *Love Technique* performed in Chicago

1930-32   becomes freelance story analyst; continues to write plays
1932   hired by Paramount as screenwriter
1932-47   acquires over thirty screen credits
1934   joins Communist Party
1942-44;
1945-46   vice-president, Screen Writers Guild
1947   appears 30 October before HUAC; dismissed 2 December from
          MGM
1948   wins $74,250 suit against MGM; decision later reversed on appeal
1950   sentenced 29 June to one year at Federal Correctional Institution,
          Danbury, Connecticut, and fined $1,000; serves ten months
1961   moves briefly to London; tries unsuccessfully to write plays
1966-85   teaches screenwriting, mostly at San Francisco State University
1974-85   film reviewer for *People's World*
1985   dies of heart attack 15 August in San Francisco

Published Work

NONFICTION

Hollywood Red: The Autobiography of Lester Cole. Palo Alto, Calif.: Ramparts Press,
   1981.

Films

1932   *If I Had a Million* (Paramount, cosp)
1933   *Charlie Chan's Greatest Case* (Fox, ad)
1934   *Pursued* (Fox, cosp)
          Sleepers East (Fox, sp)
          Wild Gold (Fox, coad)
1935   *Under Pressure* (Fox, cosp)
          Hitch Hike Lady (Republic, cosp)
          Too Tough to Kill (Columbia, coad)
1936   *Follow Your Heart* (Republic, cosp)
          The President's Mystery (Republic, cosp)
1937   *The Affairs of Cappy Ricks* (Republic, sp)
          The Man in Blue (Universal, sp)
          Some Blondes Are Dangerous (Universal, sp)
1938   *The Crime of Dr. Hallett* (Universal, cosp)
          Midnight Intruder (Universal, cosp)
          The Jury's Secret (Universal, cosp)
          Secrets of a Nurse (Universal, cosp)
          Sinners in Paradise (Universal, cosp)
1939   *Winter Carnival* (United Artists, cosp)
          I Stole a Million (Universal, s)
          The Big Guy (Universal, sp)
1940   *The Invisible Man Returns* (Universal, cosp)
          The House of Seven Gables (Universal, sp)
1941   *Among the Living* (Paramount, cos, cosp)

Footsteps in the Dark (Warner Brothers, cosp)
1942   *Pacific Blackout* (Paramount, cosp)
        Night Plane from Chungking (Paramount, cosp)
1943   *Hostages* (Paramount, cosp)
1944   *None Shall Escape* (Columbia, sp)
1945   *Blood on the Sun* (United Artists, sp with "additional scenes" by
        Nathaniel Curtis)
        Objective, Burma! (Warner Brothers, cosp)
1946   *Strange Conquest* (Universal, cos)
1947   *Fiesta* (MGM, cosp)
        High Wall (MGM, cosp)
        The Romance of Rosy Ridge (MGM, sp)
1950   *Chain Lightning* (Warner Brothers, s under pseud J. Redmond Prior)
1957   *Pied Piper of Hamlin* (TV movie, uncr cosp)
1965   *Born Free* (Columbia, uncr sp)

EDWARD DMYTRYK (1908-)

1908   born 4 September, Grand Forks, British Columbia
1923   hired by Famous Players–Lasky (precursor of Paramount) as errand
            boy
1926   enrolls at California Institute of Technology for a year
1927   returns to studio, now Paramount, as projectionist
1929   becomes film editor
1932   marries Madeleine Robinson
1935   directs first film
1939-47   directs twenty-four films
1944   joins Communist Party
1945   leaves Party
1947   divorced; appears 29 October before HUAC
1948   marries Jean Porter; goes to England to direct two films
1950   sentenced 29 June to six months in Mill Point Prison Camp, West
            Virginia, and fined $1,000; serves 4½ months
1951   recants before HUAC 25 April, naming twenty-six names; resumes
            directing
1951-75   directs twenty-five films
1976   retires from directing to teach and write film texts

Published Work

NONFICTION

It's a Hell of a Life but Not a Bad Living: A Hollywood Memoir. New York: Times
    Books, 1978.
On Screen Directing. Boston: Focal Press, 1983.
On Screen Writing. Boston: Focal Press, 1984.
On Film Editing: An Introduction to the Art of Film Construction. Boston: Focal
    Press, 1984.

On Screen Acting: An Introduction to the Art of Acting for the Screen, with Jean
    Porter Dmytryk. Boston: Focal Press, 1984.
On Filmmaking (one-volume edition of previous text books). Boston: Focal
    Press, 1986.

Films

1935   The Hawk (Independent, dir)
1939   Television Spy (Paramount, dir)
        Emergency Squad (Paramount, dir)
        Golden Gloves (Paramount, dir)
1940   Mystery Sea Raider (Paramount, dir)
        Her First Romance (I.E. Chadwick, dir)
1941   The Devil Commands (Columbia, dir)
        Under Age (Columbia, dir)
        Sweetheart of the Campus (Columbia, dir)
        The Blonde from Singapore (Columbia, dir)
        Secrets of the Lone Wolf (Columbia, dir)
        Confessions of Boston Blackie (Columbia, dir)
1942   Counter-Espionage (Columbia, dir)
        Seven Miles from Alcatraz (RKO, dir)
1943   Hitler's Children (RKO, dir)
        The Falcon Strikes Back (RKO, dir)
        Captive Wild Woman (Universal, dir)
        Behind the Rising Sun (RKO, dir)
        Tender Comrade (RKO, dir)
1944   Murder, My Sweet (RKO, dir)
1945   Back to Bataan (RKO, dir)
        Cornered (RKO, dir)
1946   Till the End of Time (RKO, dir)
1947   So Well Remembered (RKO-Rank, dir)
        Crossfire (RKO, dir)
1949   The Hidden Room (English Independent, dir)
        Give Us This Day/Salt to the Devil (Eagle-Lion, dir)
1952   Mutiny (United Artists, dir)
        The Sniper (Columbia, dir)
        Eight Iron Men (Columbia, dir)
1953   The Juggler (Columbia, dir)
1954   The Caine Mutiny (Columbia, dir)
        Broken Lance (Fox, dir)
1955   The End of the Affair (Columbia, dir)
        Soldier of Fortune (Fox, dir)
        The Left Hand of God (Fox, dir)
1956   The Mountain (Paramount, prod, dir)
1957   Raintree County (MGM, dir)
1958   The Young Lions (Fox, dir)
1959   Warlock (Fox, prod, dir)
        The Blue Angel (Fox, dir)

1962   *Walk on the Wild Side* (Columbia, dir)
        The Reluctant Saint (Columbia, prod, dir)
1964   *The Carpetbaggers* (Paramount, dir)
        Where Love Has Gone (Paramount, dir)
1965   *Mirage* (Universal, dir)
1966   *Alvarez Kelly* (Columbia, dir)
1968   *Anzio* (Columbia, dir)
        Shalako (Columbia, dir)
1972   *Bluebeard* (Cinerama, cos, prod, dir)
1974   *He Is My Brother* (Independent, dir)
1975   *The Human Factor* (Bryanston, dir)

RING LARDNER, JR. (1915-)

1915   born 19 August, Chicago
1932-34   attends Princeton
1934   sails for Europe, travels in Germany and Russia
1935   reporter, *New York Daily Mirror*
1936   begins Hollywood career, first as publicist for Selznick and later as uncredited contributor to two Selznick films
1937-47   works regularly as screenwriter
1943   wins Oscar for *Woman of the Year*
1947   signs contract with Fox at $2,000 a week; appears 30 October before HUAC
1950   sentenced 29 June to one year at Federal Correctional Institution, Danbury, Connecticut, and fined $1,000; serves 9½ months
1954   publishes first novel
1955   collaborates with Ian McLellan Hunter on *Robin Hood* teleplays
1964   *Foxy*, book by Lardner and Hunter, opens on Broadway; blacklisting ends for Lardner
1971   wins second Oscar for *M*A*S*H*
1986   writes script for program 7 April at Avery Fisher Hall, New York, commemorating fiftieth anniversary of Spanish Civil War

Published Work

FICTION

The Ecstasy of Owen Muir. London: Jonathan Cape, 1954; New York: New American Library, 1972.
All For Love. New York: Franklin Watts, 1985.

NONFICTION

"My Life on the Blacklist." *Saturday Evening Post*, 14 Oct. 1961, pp. 38-44.
The Lardners: My Family Remembered. New York: Harper & Row, 1976.

Films

1937   *A Star Is Born* (United Artists, addl dial, uncr)

	Nothing Sacred (United Artists, addl dial, uncr)
1939	*Meet Dr. Christian* (RKO, cosp)
1940	*The Courageous Dr. Christian* (RKO, cosp)
1941	*Arkansas Judge* (Republic, coad)
1942	*Woman of the Year* (MGM, cos, cosp, AA)
1943	*The Cross of Lorraine* (MGM, cosp)
1944	*Tomorrow the World* (United Artists, cosp)
	Marriage Is a Private Affair (MGM, sp contrib, uncr)
	Laura (Fox, sp contrib, uncr)
1946	*Cloak and Dagger* (Warner Brothers, cosp)
1947	*Forever Amber* (Fox, cosp)
1949	*Forbidden Street* (Fox, sp)
1950	*Four Days Leave* (Swiss, Film Classics, uncr dial)
1951	*The Big Night* (United Artists, sp contrib, uncr)
1959	*Virgin Island* (Films-Around-the-World, cosp with Hunter under joint pseud "Phillip Rush")
1960	*A Breath of Scandal* (Paramount, uncr cosp)
1965	*The Cincinnati Kid* (MGM, cosp)
1970	*M*A*S*H* (Fox, sp, AA)
1972	*The Deadly Trap* (National General Pictures, sp contrib, uncr)
1977	*The Greatest* (Columbia, sp)

Interviews and Criticism

Bruccoli, Matthew J., and C.E. Frazer Clark, Jr., eds. *Conversations with Writers*, vol. 1. Detroit: Gale Research, 1977.

Corliss, Richard, ed. *The Hollywood Screenwriters: A Film Comment Book*. New York: Avon Books, 1972.

Corliss, Richard. *Talking Pictures: Screenwriters in the American Cinema*. New York: Penguin Books, 1974.

Sorkin, Adam J. "Politics, Privatism and the Fifties: Ring Lardner, Jr.'s 'The Ecstasy of Owen Muir.' " *Journal of American Culture* 8 (1985): 59-73.

JOHN HOWARD LAWSON (1894-1977)

1894	born 25 September, New York City
1906	sent by father on tour of Europe with sister
1908	writes first play, *Savitri*
1910	enrolls in Williams College, youngest member of his class
1914	graduates with B.A. in English
1914-15	cable editor, Reuters New York; sells play, *Standards*, to Sam Harris and George M. Cohan
1916	*Standards* produced in Albany; *Servant-Master-Lover* produced in Los Angeles
1917	serves with American Red Cross Volunteer Ambulance Service during World War I; meets John Dos Passos
1920	early play *The Spice of Life* sold to Paramount but never filmed

1923-28	has five plays produced in New York (including unpublished *Nirvana*)
1927	becomes one of founding directors of New Playwrights
1928	begins screenwriting career with three-month MGM contract
1928-47	writes for films without totally giving up theater
1932-37	has four more plays produced in New York
1933	becomes first president of Screen Writers Guild
1934	formally identifies with Communist Party after Mike Gold accuses him of indecisiveness
1938	begins history research
1942	returns to screenwriting after two-year hiatus
1945	fired from Columbia for supporting CSU strike
1947	appears 27 October before HUAC
1950	sentenced 9 June to one year at Ashland, Kentucky, Federal Correctional Institution and fined $1,000; serves ten months
1960	begins intermittent teaching career
1961-63	spends time in Soviet Union; revised *Parlor Magic* performed in East Germany and Soviet Union
1977	dies in San Francisco, 14 August

Published Work

DRAMA

Roger Bloomer. New York: Thomas Seltzer, 1923.
Processional. New York: Thomas Seltzer, 1925.
Loud Speaker. New York: Macaulay, 1927.
The International. New York: Macaulay, 1927.
Success Story. New York: Farrar & Rinehart, 1932.
With a Reckless Preface: Two Plays [The Pure in Heart; Gentlewoman]. New York: Farrar & Rinehart, 1934.
Marching Song. New York: Dramatists Play Service, 1937.

NONFICTION

A Southern Welcome: A Report. New York: National Committee for the Defense of Political Prisoners, 1934.
"Inner Conflict and Proletarian Art, A Reply to Michael Gold," *New Masses,* 17 April 1934, pp. 29-30.
Theory and Technique of Playwriting. New York: Putnam, 1936.
Theory and Technique of Playwriting and Screenwriting. New York; Putnam, 1949.
The Hidden Heritage: A Rediscovery of the Ideas and Forces That Link the Thought of Our Time with the Culture of the Past. New York: Citadel, 1950; rev. ed., 1968.
Film in the Battle of Ideas. New York: Masses and Mainstream, 1953.
Film, the Creative Process: The Search for an Audio-Visual Language and Structure. New York: Hill & Wang, 1964; 2d ed., 1967.

Films

1928	*Dream of Love* (MGM, co-titles)
1929	*The Pagan* (MGM, titles)

Dynamite (MGM, codial)
1930   *The Ship from Shanghai* (MGM, sp)
        The Sea Bat (MGM, cosp)
        Our Blushing Brides (MGM, cosp)
1931   *Bachelor Apartment* (RKO, s, uncr sp)
1933   *Goodbye Love* (RKO, addl dial)
1934   *Success at Any Price* (RKO, cosp)
1935   *Party Wire* (Columbia, coad)
1937   *The Heart of Spain* (uncr co-commentary)
1938   *Blockade* (United Artists, sp)
        Algiers (United Artists, sp)
1939   *They Shall Have Music* (United Artists, sp)
1940   *Earthbound* (Fox, cosp)
        Four Sons (Fox, sp)
1943   *Action in the North Atlantic* (Warner Brothers, sp)
        Sahara (Columbia, cosp)
1945   *Counter-Attack* (Columbia, sp)
1946   *The Jolson Story* (Columbia, uncr cosp by request)
1947   *Smash-Up* (Universal, sp)
1951   *Cry the Beloved Country* (Korda, uncr sp)

Criticism

Bigsby, C.W.E. *A Critical Introduction to Twentieth Century American Drama, 1900-1940.* New York: Cambridge Univ. Press, 1982.

Clurman, Harold. *The Fervent Years: The Story of the Group Theatre and the Thirties.* New York: Hill & Wang, 1957.

Carr, Garry. *The Left Side of Paradise: The Screenwriting of John Howard Lawson.* Ann Arbor, Mich.: UMI Research Press, 1984.

Goldstein, Malcolm. *The Political Stage: American Drama and Theater of the Great Depression.* New York: Oxford Univ. Press, 1974.

Levine, Ira A. *Left-Wing Dramatic Theory in the American Theatre.* Ann Arbor: UMI Research Press, 1985.

Lowenfish, Lee Elihu. "John Howard Lawson's 'A Calendar of Commitment.' " *ICarbS* 3 (Summer-Fall, 1976): 25-36.

Rabkin, Gerald. *Drama and Commitment: Politics in the American Theatre of the Thirties.* Bloomington: Indiana Univ. Press, 1964.

Smiley, Sam. *The Drama of Attack: Didactic Plays of the American Depression.* Columbia: Univ. of Missouri Press, 1972.

ALBERT MALTZ (1908-85)

1908   born 28 October, Brooklyn, New York
1930   B.A. (Phi Beta Kappa) philosophy, Columbia University
1931   enrolls at Yale's school of drama, meets George Sklar
1932   collaborates with Sklar on *Merry-Go-Round*
1933   first Theatre Union production (*Peace on Earth*, also with Sklar)

1935   continues playwriting, begins publishing short stories with "Man
          on the Road"
1936-37   publishes five more stories
1937-41   teaches playwriting at New York University's School of Adult Educa-
          tion
1938   "The Happiest Man on Earth" wins first prize in O. Henry Memorial
          Awards
1940   begins publishing novels
1941   hired by Paramount as screenwriter
1942-47   acquires seven screen credits
1947   appears 28 October before HUAC
1949   *The Journey of Simon McKeever* rights sold to Fox, which then declines
          to make film version because of blacklist
1950   sentenced 29 June to one year at Mill Point Prison Camp, West
          Virginia, and fined $1,000; serves ten months
1952-62   lives in Mexico
1957   resumes publishing novels
1960   Frank Sinatra announces hiring of Maltz to write screenplay for *The
          Execution of Private Slovik*, then reneges
1968   publishes two stories in the *Saturday Evening Post* under his own
          name
1970-73   writes two films after blacklist
1985   dies 26 April in Los Angeles

Published Work

DRAMA AND SCREENPLAY

Peace on Earth. New York: Samuel French, 1934.
The Black Pit. New York: G.P. Putnam's Sons, 1935.
Private Hicks. In William Kozlenko, ed., *The Best Short Plays of the Social Theatre*.
     New York: Random House, 1939.
Rehearsal. *One-Act Play Magazine* 1 (March 1938): 994-1020.
Red Head Baker. In William Kozlenko, ed., *One Hundred Non-Royalty Radio Plays*.
     New York: Greenberg, 1941.
The Naked City: A Screenplay by Malvin Wald and Albert Maltz. Carbondale:
     Southern Illinois Univ. Press, 1979.

FICTION

The Ways Things Are. New York: International Publishers, 1938.
The Underground Stream. Boston: Little, Brown, 1940.
The Cross and the Arrow. Boston: Little, Brown, 1944.
The Journey of Simon McKeever. Boston: Little, Brown, 1949.
A Long Day in a Short Life. New York: International Publishers, 1957.
A Tale of One January. London: Calder & Boyers, 1966.
Afternoon in the Jungle: The Selected Short Stories of Albert Maltz. New York:
     Liveright, 1971.

NONFICTION

"What Shall We Ask of Writers?" *New Masses*, 12 Feb. 1946, pp. 19-22.
The Citizen Writer: Essays in Defense of American Culture. New York: International Publishers, 1950.

Films

1942	*This Gun for Hire* (Paramount, cosp)
	Moscow Strikes Back (American version of Russian documentary *Defeat of the German Armies near Moscow*, commentary, AA)
1944	*Destination, Tokyo* (Warner Brothers, cosp)
1945	*The House I Live In* (RKO, sp, AA)
	Pride of the Marines (Warner Brothers, sp, AN)
1946	*Cloak and Dagger* (Warner Brothers, cosp)
1948	*The Naked City* (Universal, cosp, AN)
1953	*The Robe* (Fox, uncr cosp)
1970	*Two Mules for Sister Sara* (Universal, sp)
1971	*The Beguiled* (Universal, uncr cosp)
1973	*Scalawag* (Paramount, cosp)

Criticism

Goldstein, Malcolm. *The Political Stage: American Drama and Theater of the Great Depression*. New York: Oxford Univ. Press, 1974.
Rabkin, Gerald. *Drama and Commitment: Politics in the American Theatre of the Thirties*. Bloomington: Indiana Univ. Press, 1964.
Rideout, Walter B. *The Radical Novel in the United States, 1900-1954: Some Interrelations of Literature and Society*. Cambridge, Mass.: Harvard Univ. Press, 1955.
Salzman, Jack. *Albert Maltz*. Boston: Twayne, 1978.

SAMUEL ORNITZ (1890-1957)

1890	born 15 November, New York City
1909-14	does penal research, probation and parole work for Prison Association of New York City
1914-20	associate superintendent of Brooklyn Society for the Prevention of Cruelty to Children
1918	publishes one-act play, *The Sock*, under pseudonym of Don Orno
1919	*Deficit* performed at the People's Playhouse, New York
1923	publishes first novel anonymously
1925-28	editor-in-chief, Macaulay Company
1928	sells two stories to Paramount
1928-45	Hollywood period
1931	travels to Harlan County, Kentucky, with committee headed by Theodore Dreiser in support of National Miners Union strike

1934   *Geraniums in My Window*, coauthored with Vera Caspary, opens in
        New York 26 October
1947   appears 29 October before HUAC
1950   sentenced 30 June to one year at Medical Center for Federal Pris-
        oners, Springfield, Missouri, and fined $1,000; released after nine
        months for good behavior
1951   *Bride of the Sabbath* reaches tenth place on best-seller list
1957   dies of cancer 10 March at Motion Picture Country Home, Los
        Angeles

Published Work

FICTION

Haunch Paunch and Jowl: An Anonymous Biography. New York: Boni & Liveright,
    1923.
Round the World with Jocko the Great. New York: Macaulay, 1925.
A Yankee Passional: The Biography of a Synthetic Self. New York: Boni & Liveright,
    1927.
Bride of the Sabbath. New York: Rinehart, 1951.

DRAMA

Don Orno [pseud.], *The Sock: A Play of Protest.* Brooklyn: The Three Pam-
    phleteers, 1918.
In New Kentucky. New Masses, 3 April 1934, pp. 17-28.

Films

1929   *The Case of Lena Smith* (Paramount, s)
        Chinatown Nights (Paramount, s)
1930   *Sins of the Children* (MGM, ad)
1932   *Hell's Highway* (RKO, cosp)
        Secrets of the French Police (RKO, cosp)
        Men of America (RKO, cosp)
1933   *One Man's Journey* (RKO, cosp)
1934   *One Exciting Adventure* (Universal, cosp)
1935   *The Man Who Reclaimed His Head* (Universal, cosp)
        Three Kids and a Queen (Universal, cosp)
1936   *Fatal Lady* (Paramount, sp)
        Follow Your Heart (Republic, cosp)
1937   *A Doctor's Diary* (Paramount, cos)
        The Hit Parade (Republic, cosp)
        Portia on Trial (Republic, sp)
        It Could Happen to You (Republic, cosp)
        Two Wise Maids (Republic, sp)
1938   *Army Girl* (Republic, cosp)
        Little Orphan Annie (Paramount, cosp)
1940   *Three Faces West* (Republic, cosp)
1944   *They Live in Fear* (Columbia, cosp)

1945   *China's Little Devils* (Monogram, sp)
         Circumstantial Evidence (Fox, ad)

Criticism

Liptzin, Solomon. *The Jew in American Literature*. New York: Bloch, 1966.

ROBERT ADRIAN SCOTT (1911-72)

1911   born 6 February, Arlington, New Jersey
1934   B.A., English and History, Amherst College; works briefly at RKO
          where playwright-brother Allan is employed as screenwriter
1937-38   associate editor and assistant editor for film, *Stage* magazine
1938   returns to Hollywood, tries unsuccessfully to write socially signifi-
          cant documentaries
1940   first screen credit
1942   hired 20 July as screenwriter by RKO
1943-47   produces six films for RKO
1947   *Mr. Lincoln's Whiskers* performed 30 June at Actor's Lab in Los An-
          geles; appears 29 October before HUAC; terminated by RKO 26
          November
1948   sues RKO for wrongful discharge and compensation due on re-
          mainder of contract; case continues until 1957, when Supreme Court
          refuses to hear it
1949   divorced by Anne Shirley because of his stand against HUAC
1950   found guilty of contempt 20 June; sentenced 27 September (delay
          caused by ill health), to one year at Federal Correctional Institution,
          Ashland, Kentucky, and $1,000 fine; serves nine months
1954-61   writes for television series (*Ironside; The Bold Ones; Lassie*) with Joan
          La Cour first as front, then as collaborator
1955   marries Joan La Cour 5 Sept.
1961   works as production executive for MGM in London but acquires no
          credits
1968   returns to Hollywood
1969   produces TV movie of *Mr. Lincoln's Whiskers*, retitled *The Great Man's
          Whiskers*, at Universal
1972   dies 25 December of lung cancer in Los Angeles
1973   *The Great Man's Whiskers* telecast 13 February

Published Work

DRAMA

Mr. Lincoln's Whiskers. New York: Greenberg, 1948.

NONFICTION

"You Can't Do That." In *Thought Control in the United States of America: The
Collected Proceedings of the Conference on the Subject of Thought Control in the*

United States, Called by the Hollywood Arts, Sciences & Professions Council, Progressive Citizens of America, July 9-13, 1947. Los Angeles, 1947. "Blacklist: The Liberal's Straightjacket and Its Effect on Content." *Hollywood Review* 2 (Sept.-Oct. 1955): 1-6.

Films

1940	*Keeping Company* (MGM, cosp)
1941	*We Go Fast* (Fox, cosp)
	The Parson of Panamint (Paramount, cosp)
1943	*Mr. Lucky* (RKO, cosp)
1944	*My Pal Wolf* (RKO, prod)
	Murder, My Sweet (RKO, prod)
1945	*Cornered* (RKO, prod)
1946	*Miss Susie Slagle's* (Paramount, coad)
	Deadline at Dawn (RKO, prod)
1947	*Crossfire* (RKO, prod)
	So Well Remembered (RKO-Rank, prod)
1960	*Conspiracy of Hearts* (Paramount, "based on original material by Dale Pitt," Scott's front for 1956 teleplay)

DALTON TRUMBO (1905-76)

1905	born 5 December, Montrose, Colorado
1906	family moves to Grand Junction, Colorado (fictionalized by Trumbo as Shale City)
1923-24	begins writing short stories while attending Grand Junction High School
1924-25	attends University of Colorado
1925	family moves to Los Angeles
1925-33	works at bakery; writes fiction regularly
1928-29	studies writing, criticism, and psychology at University of Southern California
1931	publishes first story; writes mock defense of movies in *Film Spectator*, rebutting George Jean Nathan
1932-37	publishes short stories and articles in *Vanity Fair, Liberty, Saturday Evening Post, McCall's, North American Review*
1933	leaves bakery to become associate editor of *Hollywood Spectator*
1934-36	becomes story analyst at Warner Brothers; starts writing novels
1936-73	screenwriting period with about forty credits
1938	marries Cleo Fincher
1939	first child, Nikola, born
1943	joins Communist Party
1945	tours Pacific combat zone as war correspondent; founding editor, *Screen Writer*; member of American delegation to United Nations Founding Conference in San Francisco to write speech on the admis-

sion of Argentina for delivery by Secretary of State Edward Stettinius (pro-Peron speech ultimately written by Nelson Rockefeller's speech writer)

1947	appears before HUAC 28 October
1948	leaves Party; convicted of contempt 5 May
1949	27 briefs filed in support of Trumbo and Lawson between 1 February and 1 October; *The Biggest Thief in Town* opens on Broadway 30 March; starts writing for black market
1950	petition of Lawson and Trumbo for rehearing denied by Supreme Court; fined $1,000 and begins serving sentence 21 June at Federal Correctional Institution, Ashland, Kentucky; serves ten months
1951-53	lives in Mexico with other blacklistees including Ian McLellan Hunter, Ring Lardner, Jr., Hugo Butler, and Albert Maltz
1954	rejoins Party as gesture of support for California Fourteen; leaves again when convictions are reversed
1957	"Robert Rich" (Dalton Trumbo) wins Oscar for *The Brave One* (Best Motion Picture Story)
1958	begins association with Kirk Douglas's Bryna Productions
1960	comes off blacklist with Otto Preminger announcement 19 January of assignment to adapt *Exodus*; begins writing but never finishes posthumously published last novel
1970	delivers "only victims" speech at Laurel Award dinner 13 March
1973	undergoes surgery for lung cancer
1975	receives Oscar for *The Brave One*, personally presented by Academy president, Walter Mirisch
1976	dies of heart attack 10 September in Los Angeles

Published Work

FICTION: NOVELS AND SELECTED SHORT STORIES

"The Governor Enters Heaven." *Topics of the Town*, November 1931, pp. 8-9, 28-29.

"Kidnapped," *International Detective Magazine*, October 1933, pp. 14-27.

"Darling Bill." *Saturday Evening Post*, 20 April 1935, pp. 8, 94.

"Five C's for Fever the Five." *Saturday Evening Post*, 30 November 1935, pp. 10, 11, 36, 38.

Eclipse. New York: Dickson, 1935.

Washington Jitters. New York: Knopf, 1936.

"The World and All." *McCall's*, July 1937, pp. 12, 57, 58.

Johnny Got His Gun. Philadelphia: Lippincott, 1939.

The Remarkable Andrew. Philadelphia: Lippincott, 1940.

Night of the Aurochs. Edited with an introduction by Robert Kirsch. New York: Viking, 1979.

DRAMA

The Biggest Thief in Town. New York: Dramatists Play Service, 1949.

NONFICTION: LETTERS, PAMPHLETS, AND SELECTED ARTICLES
"The Fall of Hollywood." *North American Review*, August 1933, pp. 140-47.
"Back to Smut!" *Hollywood Reporter*, 31 March 1936, pp. 25-26.
Harry Bridges: A Discussion of the Latest Effort to Deport Civil Liberties and the Rights of American Labor. Hollywood: League of American Writers, 1941.
"The Graven Image." *Theatre Arts*, July 1950, pp. 32-35.
"Blacklist = Black Market." *Nation*, 4 May 1957, pp. 383-87.
"The Oscar Syndrome." *Playboy*, April 1960, pp. 33, 36, 78, 86-87.
"The Secret of Freedom." *National Guardian*, 23 May 1960, p. 11.
Additional Dialogue: Letters of Dalton Trumbo, 1942-1962. Edited by Helen Manfull. New York: M. Evans, 1970.
The Time of the Toad: A Study of the Inquisition in America and Two Related Pamphlets. New York: Perennial Library/Harper & Row, 1972.

POETRY
"Confessional." *Mainstream* 1 (Winter 1947): 16-22.
"Poems on Parting." *Masses and Mainstream* 3 (1950): 14-22.
"Portrait of the Artist as Middle-Aged Man." *Masses and Mainstream* 5 (1952): 10-16.
"Korean Christmas." *Unity* 2 (1953): 19-20.
"Syncopation for a 'Patriot.' " *Masses and Mainstream* 7 (1954): 15.

Films

1936	*Road Gang* (Warner Brothers, sp)
	Love Begins at Twenty (Warner Brothers, cosp)
	Tugboat Princess (Columbia, cos)
1937	*Devil's Playground* (Columbia, cosp)
	That Man's Here Again (Warner Brothers, coad)
1938	*A Man to Remember* (RKO, sp)
	Fugitives for a Night (RKO, sp)
1939	*The Flying Irishman* (RKO, cos, cosp)
	Sorority House (RKO, sp)
	The Kid from Kokomo (Warner Brothers, s)
	Five Came Back (RKO, cosp)
	Heaven with a Barbed Wire Fence (RKO, cosp)
	Career (RKO, sp)
1940	*Half a Sinner* (Universal, s)
	Never to Love (RKO, sp)
	Kitty Foyle (RKO, sp, AN)
	Curtain Call (RKO, sp)
	The Lone Wolf Strikes (Columbia, s)
	We Who Are Young (MGM, s, sp)
1941	*You Belong to Me* (Columbia, s)
	Accent on Love (Fox, s)
1942	*The Remarkable Andrew* (Paramount, sp from his novel)
1943	*Tender Comrade* (RKO, s, sp)
	A Guy Named Joe (MGM, sp)

1944   *Thirty Seconds over Tokyo* (MGM, sp)
1945   *Our Vines Have Tender Grapes* (MGM, sp)
        Jealousy (Republic, original idea)
1949   *The Beautiful Blonde from Bashful Bend* (Fox, s under Earl Felton's name)
1950   *Gun Crazy* (United Artists, cosp with Millard Kaufman as front)
1951   *The Prowler* (United Artists, uncr cosp)
        He Ran All the Way (United Artists, uncr cosp)
1953   *Roman Holiday* (Paramount, s with Ian McLellan Hunter as front, AA)
1954   *Carnival Story* (RKO, s under pseud Marcel Klauber, uncr sp)
1956   *The Boss* (United Artists, sp under pseud Ben L. Perry)
        The Brave One (RKO, s under pseud Robert Rich, uncr sp, AA)
1957   *The Green-Eyed Blonde* (Warner Brothers, sp with Sally Stubblefield as front)
1958   *Terror in a Texas Town* (United Artists, sp under pseud Ben L. Perry, rewrite of Lawson script)
        Cowboy (Columbia, uncr cosp)
1959   *Last Train from Gun Hill* (Paramount, s under pseud Les Crutchfield)
1960   *Conspiracy of Hearts* (Paramount, sp with Robert Presnell, Jr., as front)
        Spartacus (Universal, sp)
        Exodus (United Artists, sp)
1961   *The Last Sunset* (Universal, sp)
1962   *Lonely Are the Brave* (Universal, sp)
1965   *The Sandpiper* (MGM, cosp)
1966   *The Cavern* (Fox, uncr sp)
        Hawaii (United Artists, cosp)
1968   *The Fixer* (MGM, sp)
1971   *The Horsemen* (Columbia, sp)
        Johnny Got His Gun (Cinemation, sp, dir)
1972   *F.T.A.* (American International, cosp apparently for excerpt from *Johnny Got His Gun*)
1973   *Executive Action* (Warner Brothers, sp)
        Papillion (Allied Artists, cosp)

Criticism

Cook, Bruce. *Dalton Trumbo*. New York: Scribner, 1977.
Corliss, Richard. *Talking Pictures: Screenwriters in the American Cinema*. New York: Penguin Books, 1975.
Corliss, Richard, ed. *The Hollywood Screenwriters: A Film Comment Book*. New York: Avon Books, 1972.

Notes

INTRODUCTION

1. House of Representatives, Committee on Un-American Activities, 80th Cong., 1st sess., 20-24, 27-30 October 1947, *Hearings regarding the Communist Infiltration of the Motion Picture Industry* (Washington, D.C.: Government Printing Office, 1947), p. 522 (hereafter cited by page references to this transcript).
2. Larry Ceplair and Steven Englund, *The Inquisition in Hollywood: Politics in the Film Community, 1930-1960* (Garden City, N.Y.: Anchor Press/Doubleday, 1980).
3. The number is sometimes given as forty-five. There is a slight discrepancy between the names of the subpoenaed printed in the *Hollywood Reporter*, 22 September 1947, and those on HUAC's schedule of witnesses. Charlie Chaplin was subpoenaed but never had to appear; as he states in *My Autobiography* (New York: Simon & Schuster, 1964), pp. 447, 449, he informed the committee that he was not a Communist and was told that he "could consider the matter closed." Clifford Odets, also subpoenaed, was apparently not on HUAC's schedule; although the committee's chief investigator said Odets would be called the week of 27 October, he never was. Samuel Goldwyn was listed in the *Hollywood Reporter*, as were Donald Ogden Stewart, William Pomerance, Cedric Gibbons, and Joseph E. Davies; none appeared on HUAC's roster.
4. The story is vividly told in Nancy Lynn Schwartz, *The Hollywood Writers' Wars*, completed by Sheila Schwartz (New York: Knopf, 1982); see also Ceplair and Englund, *Inquisition in Hollywood*, pp. 1-46.
5. Lardner has always maintained that he might never have been called if Stripling had not seen a picture of him and his wife in the newspapers and concluded that he was a famous author's son and thus publicity fodder.

1. SAMUEL ORNITZ

1. *Additional Dialogue: Letters of Dalton Trumbo, 1942-1962*, ed. Helen Manfull (New York: M. Evans, 1970), p. 386.
2. The pamphlet in which *The Sock* is printed can be read at the New York Public Library.
3. Samuel Ornitz, *Haunch Paunch and Jowl: An Anonymous Biography* (New York: Boni & Liveright, 1923), p. 69.
4. Ibid., p. 224.
5. *Encyclopedia Judaica* (New York: Macmillan, 1971), 12:1474.
6. Box 1, Samuel Ornitz Collection, State Historical Society of Wisconsin, Madison (hereafter cited as SHSW).
7. Samuel Ornitz, *Round the World with Jocko the Great* (New York: Macaulay, 1925), pp. 177, 191.
8. Samuel Ornitz, *A Yankee Passional: The Biography of a Synthetic Self* (New York: Boni & Liveright, 1927), p. 120 (hereafter cited in the text by page number).
9. Box 1, Ornitz Collection.
10. Samuel Ornitz, *Bride of the Sabbath* (New York: Rinehart, 1951), p. 410.
11. Production information is taken from the *Hell's Highway* production file, RKO archives, Los Angeles.
12. Production information is taken from the *Secrets of the French Police* production file, RKO archives.
13. The play can be read in manuscript at the Lincoln Center Library for the Performing Arts in New York.

14. Production information is taken from the *Circumstantial Evidence* production file, Fox Collection, University of Southern California, (hereafter cited as Fox-USC).

15. Written on second treatment (31 Jan. 1939), Fox-USC.

16. "Conference with Mr. Zanuck on Revised Treatment of February 16, 1939" (20 Feb. 1939), Fox-USC.

2. LESTER COLE

1. Production information is taken from the *If I Had a Million* production file, Paramount Collection, Margaret Herrick Library of the Academy of Motion Picture Arts and Sciences (hereafter cited as Paramount-Herrick).

2. Production details are derived from the *Sleepers East* production file, Twentieth Century–Fox Archive, Theater Arts Library, University of California at Los Angeles (hereafter cited as Fox-UCLA).

3. Production information comes from the *Under Pressure* production file, Fox-UCLA.

4. Cole's Republic scripts can be read in the Republic Collection, Department of Special Collections, UCLA.

5. Production information comes from the *Among the Living* production file, Paramount-Herrick.

6. *Film Noir: An Encyclopedic Reference to the American Style*, ed. Alain Silver and Elizabeth Ward (Woodstock, N.Y.: Overlook Press, 1979), p. 10.

7. Production information comes from the *Pacific Blackout* production file, Paramount-Herrick.

8. Production information comes from the *Night Plane from Chunking* production file, Paramount-Herrick.

9. Production information comes from the *Hostages* production file, Paramount-Herrick.

10. Other perpetrators of this error include Murray Kempton, *Part of Our Time: Some Ruins and Monuments of the Thirties* (New York: Simon & Schuster, 1955), p. 195; Walter Goodman, *The Committee: The Extraordinary Career of the House Committee on Un-American Activities* (New York: Farrar, Straus & Giroux, 1968), p. 215; Stefan Kander, *A Journal of the Plague Years* (New York: Atheneum, 1973), p. 84.

11. Tom Dardis, *Some Time in the Sun: The Hollywood Years of Fitzgerald, Faulkner, Nathanael West, Aldous Huxley, and James Agee* (New York: Scribner, 1976), p. 158.

12. *Hollywood Red: The Autobiography of Lester Cole* (Palo Alto, Calif.: Ramparts Press, 1981), pp. 219-20.

13. *Thirty Years of Treason: Excerpts from Hearings before the House Committee on Un-American Activities, 1938-1968,* ed. Eric Bentley (New York: Viking, 1971), p. 139.

14. The *Born Free* screenplay is in the Lester Cole Collection at The University of Wyoming in Laramie.

3. JOHN HOWARD LAWSON

1. Garry Carr, *The Left Side of Paradise: The Screenwriting of John Howard Lawson* (Ann Arbor, Mich.: UMI Research Press, 1984); Carr draws on Lawson's unpublished auto-biography in the Lawson Papers, Southern Illinois University at Carbondale.

2. John Howard Lawson, *Roger Bloomer: A Play in Three Acts* (New York: Thomas Seltzer, 1923), p. 225.

3. Lawson revised the play in 1937, changing the black character from Rastus Jolly to Joe Green and making him a militant. Lawson was by then a Communist and had become more conscious of racial stereotypes.

4. John Howard Lawson, *Loud Speaker* (New York: Macaulay, 1927), p. 108.

5. Malcolm Goldstein, *The Political Stage: American Drama and Theater of the Great Depression* (New York: Oxford University Press, 1974), p. 18, claims that the play is "virtually impossible to follow on the printed page."

6. John Howard Lawson, *The International* (New York: Macaulay, 1927), pp. 144-45.

7. Carr, *Left Side of Paradise*, p. 12.

8. The DeMille Collection at Brigham Young University contains a copy of an unsigned letter to Lawson of 26 July 1929, prepared by DeMille's publicist Barrett Kiesling: "Mr. DeMille desires me to express to you his very deep regret over the error in the opening ads for "Dynamite" which credited both "story and dialog" to Jeanie Macpherson. This matter has been taken up with West Coast Theatres and dialog credit to Miss Macpherson removed, as you will notice in the Los Angeles Times for July 26." The fact that the same letter was sent to Gladys Unger, who was also involved in the script, suggests that Macpherson's contribution was minor; still, she got the story credit.

9. Foreword to John Howard Lawson, *With a Reckless Preface: Two Plays* (New York: Farrar & Rinehart, 1934), p. xxv (page references in the text for *The Pure in Heart* and *Gentlewoman* are to this edition).

10. *Golden Boy*, in *Six Plays of Clifford Odets*, introd. Harold Clurman (New York: Grove Press, 1979), p. 316.

11. Gold had the last word; in his rebuttal of 24 April he wondered how Lawson "could sit on the fence as long as he has."

12. For *Blockade*'s production history, see Larry S. Ceplair, "The Politics of Compromise in Hollywood: A Case History," *Cineaste* 8, no. 4 (1970): 2-7.

13. From an undated outline in the *Earthbound* production file, Fox-UCLA.

14. Robert T. Elson and the Editors of Time-Life Books, *World War II: Prelude to War* (Alexandria: Time-Life Books, 1977), p. 202.

15. Darryl Zanuck, "Notes on a Conference on Treatment" (11 Nov. 1939), *Four Sons* production file, Fox-UCLA.

16. It was also financially advantageous to make such films; see Nick Roddick, *A New Deal in Entertainment: Warner Brothers in the 1930s* (London: British Film Institute, 1983).

17. John Howard Lawson, *Film, the Creative Process: The Search for an Audio-Visual Language and Structure*, 2d ed. (New York: Hill & Wang, 1967); hereafter cited as FCP.

18. Production details have been taken from box 91 of the Walter Wanger Papers, SHSW.

19. Carr, *Left Side of Paradise*, p. 87.

20. Bob Thomas, *King Cohn: The Life and Times of Harry Cohn* (New York: Putnam, 1967), p. 226; on Buchman's contribution see also Doug McClelland, *Blackface to Blacklist: Al Jolson, Larry Parks, and "The Jolson Story"* (Metuchen, N.J.: Scarecrow Press, 1987), p. 189.

21. Thomas, *King Cohn*, p. 228.

22. John Howard Lawson, *Theory and Technique of Playwriting and Screenwriting* (New York: Putnam, 1949), p. 407; hereafter cited as TTPS.

23. Longstreet regarded himself as the film's writer; in a letter to *Time* (28 Oct. 1946) he chastized the film reviewer for ignoring his contribution: "Remember a motion picture is only as good as its story and dramatic content. Every producer in town will tell you a director can't shoot a bad script and get a great picture." *Time* apologized.

24. Letter to Edward Lewis, 8 June 1959, in box 11, Kirk Douglas Papers, SHSW.

25. Letter from Jefferson W. Asher, Jr., to Leon Kaplan, 27 May 1959, box 11, Douglas Papers. Supposedly, the $2,500 was an unspecified loan to "James Howard." As intermediary, Lewis claimed that it was in payment for a writing project but could not specify which one; Lawson was involved in several.

26. Letter to Edward Lewis, 8 June 1959, box 11, Douglas Papers.

27. Sergei Eisenstein, *Film Form: Essays in Film Theory*, ed. and trans. Jay Leyda (New York: Harcourt, Brace & World/Harvest Books, 1949), p. 238.

28. John Howard Lawson, *Film in the Battle of Ideas* (New York: Masses and Mainstream, 1953), pp. 20-21.

29. Ibid., p. 55.

30. John Howard Lawson, *The Hidden Heritage: A Rediscovery of the Ideas and Forces That Link the Thought of Our Time with the Culture of the Past* (New York: Citadel Press, 1950), p. 17.

4. HERBERT BIBERMAN

1. George Freedley and John A. Reeves, *A History of the Theatre*, rev. ed. (New York: Crown, 1955), pp. 550-51.
2. Box 8, Biberman-Sondergaard Collection, SHSW.
3. Ibid., box 9.
4. Larry Swindell, *Body and Soul: The Story of John Garfield* (New York: William Morrow, 1975), p. 32; for the Theatre Guild's impressions of Biberman, see Lawrence Langer, *The Magic Curtain* (New York: Dutton, 1951), pp. 248-49.
5. The stories are in box 15, Biberman-Sondergaard Collection.
6. Undated essay, ibid., box 15.
7. From an undated address, "The Politics of the Artist, Scientist and Professional," ibid., box 21.
8. Ibid., box 8.
9. The extensive *New Orleans* material in ibid., box 10, includes some of the music used in the film.
10. Herbert Biberman, *Salt of the Earth: The Story of a Film* (Boston: Beacon Press, 1965). This account of the filming should be supplemented by the account of the actual strike in *Salt of the Earth: Screenplay by Michael Wilson, Commentary by Deborah Silverton Rosenfelt* (Old Westbury, N.Y.: Feminist Press, 1978), pp. 93-126.
11. Box 35, Dalton Trumbo Collection, SHSW.
12. From an IPC meeting report, 22 March 1952, in Biberman-Sondergaard Collection, box 19.

5. ALBERT MALTZ

1. *The Best Short Plays of the Social Theatre*, ed. William Kozlenko (New York: Random House, 1939).
2. Albert Maltz, *Rehearsal, One-Act Play Magazine* 1 (March 1938): 1019.
3. For Theater Union's manifesto, see Goldstein, *The Political Stage*, p. 59.
4. George Sklar and Albert Maltz, *Peace on Earth: An Anti-War Play in 3 Acts* (New York: Samuel French, 1934).
5. Albert Maltz, *The Way Things Are* (New York: International Publishers, 1938), p. 218 (page references in the text are to this edition).
6. *Afternoon in the Jungle: The Selected Short Stories of Albert Maltz* (New York: Liveright, 1971), p. 218.
7. The production history of *This Gun for Hire* is based on material in Paramount-Herrick, and in box 4, folders 8-12, Albert Maltz Collection, SHSW.
8. Robert Vaughn, *Only Victims: A Study of Show Business Blacklisting* (New York: Putnam, 1972), p. 291.
9. Graham Greene, *A Gun for Sale: An Entertainment* (New York: Penguin Books, 1983), p. 170.
10. Production history is based on material in the *Destination, Tokyo* production file, Warner Archive, Archives of Performing Arts, University of Southern California (hereafter Warner-USC), and in box 5, folders 1-6, Maltz Collection.
11. Production history is based on material in the *Pride of the Marines* production file, Warner-USC, and in box 5, folders 7-8, Maltz Collection.
12. "Suggestions for *Al Schmid-Marine*," 9 September 1943, Warner-USC.
13. Ibid.
14. Letter from Gassner to Maltz, 19 Feb. 1946, box 5, folder 7, Maltz Collection.
15. Sinatra to Maltz, 11 Aug. 1945, ibid., box 5, folder 7.
16. For the film's background, see Bernard F. Dick, *The Star-Spangled Screen: The American World War II Film* (Lexington: Univ. Press of Kentucky, 1985), pp. 122-23.
17. Keith Wheeler and the Editors of Time-Life Books, *World War II: The Fall of Japan* (Alexandria, Va.: Time-Life Books, 1983), p. 62.

18. From detailed production notes for producer Mark Hellinger (who also narrated the film) in box 6, folder 3, Maltz Collection.

19. Ibid.

20. Box 6, folder 5, Maltz Collection. *The Robe* material includes notes, revisions, and three scripts written between Dec. 1945 and Dec. 1946.

21. Philip Dunne, *Take Two: A Life in Movies and Politics* (New York: McGraw-Hill, 1980), p. 254.

22. "Conference Notes on First Draft Continuity" (25 July 1952), *The Robe* production file, Fox-UCLA.

23. Undated notes in box 15, folder 1, Maltz Collection.

24. Sinatra to Maltz, 11 Aug. 1945.

25. Box 14, folder 9, Maltz Collection.

26. The script is in USC's screenplay collection.

27. Siegel to Eastwood, 19 September 1969, quoted in Stuart M. Kaminsky, *Don Siegel: Director* (New York: Curtis Books, 1974), p. 253.

28. The story, originally published in *Harper's*, is included in *Afternoon in the Jungle*.

29. Jack Salzman, *Albert Maltz* (Boston: Twayne, 1978), p. 140.

30. Albert Maltz, *The Journey of Simon McKeever* (Boston: Little, Brown, 1949), p. 200.

31. Albert Maltz, *A Long Day in a Short Life* (New York: International Publishers, 1957), p. 11 (page references in the text are to this edition).

32. *Saturday Evening Post*, 13 July 1968, pp. 43-53; 5 October 1968, pp. 65-66, 70-72.

6. ALVAH BESSIE

1. "A Night Call" (1934), in *Alvah Bessie's Short Fictions* (Novato, Calif.: Chandler & Sharp, 1982), p. 101 (references to Bessie's stories in the text cite this edition).

2. Alvah Bessie, *Dwell in the Wilderness* (New York: Covici, Friede, 1935), pp. 180-81 (page references in the text are to this edition).

3. Alvah Bessie, *Men in Battle: A Story of Americans in Spain* (New York: Scribner, 1939), p. 182 (page references in the text are to this edition).

4. As quoted in *Contemporary Authors*, n.s. 2:59.

5. Alvah Bessie, *Inquisition in Eden* (New York: Macmillan, 1965), p. 19.

6. Raoul Walsh, *Each Man in His Time: The Life Story of a Director* (New York: Farrar, Straus & Giroux, 1974), p. 335.

7. The script and other production material are in the *Northern Pursuit* production file, Warner-USC.

8. The original story (12 Jan. 1944) is in box 26, folder 4, Alvah Bessie Collection, SHSW.

9. *Objective, Burma!* production file, Warner-USC.

10. Box 26, folder 4, Bessie Collection.

11. Production information comes from box 26, folders 2-3, Bessie Collection, and *The Very Thought of You* production file, Warner-USC.

12. Eric Stacey to T.S. Wright, 28 Dec. 1944, *Hotel Berlin* production file, Warner-USC. "Tenny" Wright was production manager at Warner Brothers.

13. Bessie, *Inquisition in Eden*, p. 100.

14. Ibid., p. 163.

15. Peter Bogdanovich, "Interview with Edgar G. Ulmer," in *King of the Bs: Working within the Hollywood System*, ed. Todd McCarthy and Charles Flynn (New York: Dutton, 1975), p. 406.

16. *Ruthless* treatment and scripts are in box 27, folders 5- 6, Bessie Collection.

17. *Smart Woman* drafts are in ibid., folders 7-8.

18. Cameron to Bessie, 9 Dec. 1957, ibid., box 4, folder 3.

19. Bessie to Cameron, 13 Dec. 1957, ibid.

7. ADRIAN SCOTT

1. For a sample, see Don Miller, "*B*" *Movies: An Informal Survey of the American Low-Budget Film, 1933-1945* (New York: Curtis Books, 1973), p. 248.
2. Information about Adrian Scott's RKO period comes from the RKO archives.
3. Paul de Kruif, *The Fight for Life* (New York: Harcourt, Brace, 1938), p. 338.
4. Ullman had produced *This Is America* (1933) with commentary by Gilbert Seldes, a compilation of newsreel material from World War I to the beginning of the Great Depression.
5. Production information comes from *The Parson of Panamint* production file, Paramount-Herrick.
6. David Hempstead to Commanding Officer, Induction Center, Los Angeles, 12 Aug., 1942, RKO archives. Hempstead was very much a liberal, having produced two Dalton Trumbo films (*Kitty Foyle*, 1940; *Tender Comrade*, 1943), the anti-Nazi *Joan of Paris* (1942), and Clifford Odets's *None but the Lonely Heart* (1944).
7. Bruce Cook, *Dalton Trumbo* (New York: Scribner, 1977), p. 281.
8. Production information comes from the *Mr. Lucky* production file, RKO archives.
9. Production information comes from the *Miss Susie Slagle's* production file, Paramount-Herrick.
10. *Crossfire* production file, RKO archives.
11. Stephen Pendo, *Raymond Chandler on Screen: His Novels into Film* (Metuchen, N.J.: Scarecrow Press, 1976), p. 31, quoting from personal correspondence with Paxton.
12. From legal files, RKO archives.
13. Production information derives from *Crossfire* production file, RKO archives.
14. Myron C. Fagan, *Documentation of the Red Stars in Hollywood* (Hollywood, Calif.: Cinema Education Guild, 1950), p. 56.
15. Legal files, RKO archives.
16. Facsimiles of Grace Bedell's letter to Lincoln and his reply appear in Adrian Scott, *Mr. Lincoln's Whiskers* (New York: Greenberg, 1948), pp. 10-12.
17. Scott, "Some of My Worst Friends," *Crossfire* production file.

8. EDWARD DMYTRYK

1. Edward Dmytryk, *It's a Hell of a Life but Not a Bad Living: A Hollywood Memoir* (New York: Times Books, 1978), p. 3. Biographical details are taken primarily from this source.
2. The literature on *film noir* is enormous. The best sources are Foster Hirsch, *The Dark Side of the Screen: Film Noir* (New York: Barnes, 1981); Amir M. Karim, *Toward a Definition of Film Noir* (1941-1949) (New York: Arno Press, 1976); Paul Schrader, "Notes on Film Noir," in *Awake in the Dark*, ed. David Denby (New York: Random House, 1977), pp. 278-90; J.P. Telotte, "Film Noir and the Dangers of Discourse," *Quarterly Review of Film Studies* 9 (Spring 1984): 101-12. The most concise summary of *film noir*'s conventions is in Jeanine Basinger, *Anthony Mann* (Boston: Twayne, 1979), pp. 48-49. In an attempt at comprehensiveness, Silver and Ward's encyclopedia, *Film Noir*, covers so many different kinds of films that its usefulness is restricted to analyses of individual films and production credits.
3. William Luhr, *Raymond Chandler and Film* (New York: Ungar, 1982), pp. 116-17.
4. Lotte H. Eisner, *The Haunted Screen: Expressionism in the German Cinema and the Influence of Max Reinhardt*, trans. Roger Greaves (Berkeley: Univ. of California Press, 1969), pp. 129-37, is esp. good on the expressionistic use of the mirror and other reflectors as symbols of the double.
5. Pendo, *Raymond Chandler on Screen*, p. 18, quoting from correspondence with Paxton.
6. Bentley, *Thirty Years of Treason*, p. 384.
7. Production information comes from the *Cornered* production file, RKO archives.

8. Four years later, Lawson was behaving the same way toward Robert Rossen who, like Dmytryk, had also been a Party member but recanted and informed. Rossen had just made *All the King's Men* (1949) in which a populist figure, modeled after Huey Long, evolves into a fascist demagogue. Lawson castigated Rossen for making Willie Stark, the Long figure, a poor spokesman for Communism.

9. Perhaps so, in 1941. But according to RKO's legal files, Dmytryk was classified 1-A in 1944, and the studio wrote his draft board to claim that he was needed in his job.

10. Maltz was reacting to Richard English, "What Makes a Hollywood Communist," *Saturday Evening Post*, 19 May 1951, pp. 31, 147-50. Maltz's letter to the editor was dated 28 May 1951.

11. Personal interview with Ring Lardner, Jr., 11 Oct. 1986.

12. Gene D. Phillips, *Graham Greene: The Films of His Fiction* (New York: Columbia Univ. Teachers College Press, 1974), p. 130, quotes Dmytryk's claim that Columbia thought a preponderance of flashbacks would confuse the audience.

13. It was well known from reports in *Variety* (30 April 1974) and *Boxoffice* (19 May 1975) that Dmytryk was directing *He Is My Brother*; that it was filmed on Kauai; that it was based on the life of Father Damien's friend Joseph Dutton (played by Keenan Wynn); and that singer Bobby Sherman accepted a leading role because of Dmytryk's "track record."

9. RING LARDNER, JR.

1. Kenneth Geist, "Trials and Traumas: Ring Lardner, Jr." in *The Hollywood Screenwriters*, ed. Richard Corliss (New York: Avon Books, 1972), p. 134.

2. Ibid., p. 135. Geist gives the scene as follows: "A woman . . . inquires 'Has anyone ever mentioned your resemblance to Hazel Flagg?' to which Lombard replies, 'That phony!' and indignantly walks away."

3. Bentley, *Thirty Years of Treason*, p. 187.

4. Craig Thompson, "The Tragedy of Ring Lardner, Jr.," *Coronet*, March 1951, p. 40.

5. Biographical details are taken from Ring Lardner, Jr., *The Lardners: My Family Remembered* (New York: Harper & Row, 1976).

6. Lardner did a script for *The Kid from Kokomo* (1939), based on a Dalton Trumbo story, but it was not used. The Warner Bros. Archive of Historical Papers (USC) lists three other Lardner scripts: "Hollywood Studio Club"; "Don Juan"; and "Forgive Us Our Trespasses." The Jerry Wald Collection at USC also contains a treatment that Wald and Lardner did at Warner's, "Heart Grows Fonder," about an acting team, a husband and wife who retire to Maine and are lured back to Broadway. It never went beyond the treatment stage.

7. Production information is taken from the *Woman of the Year* production file at MGM, Culver City, Calif.

8. Kenneth L. Geist, *Pictures Will Talk: The Life and Films of Joseph L. Mankiewicz* (New York: Scribner, 1978), p. 107.

9. Richard Corliss, *Talking Pictures: Screenwriters in the American Cinema* (New York: Penguin Books, 1975), p. 346, calls Lardner's career "the most frustrating" among those of major screenwriters.

10. Production information is taken from the *Laura* production file, Fox-UCLA. For a more detailed account, see Rudy Behlmer, *America's Favorite Movies: Behind the Scenes* (New York: Ungar, 1982), pp. 177-99.

11. Zanuck, "Notes on First Draft, 1 November 1943," Fox-UCLA.

12. Rouben Mamoulian was; see Behlmer, *America's Favorite Movies*, p. 184.

13. Production information is taken from the *Forever Amber* production file, Fox-UCLA.

14. Production information is taken from the *Forbidden Street* production file, Fox-UCLA.

15. Zanuck, "Memo on Lardner's First Draft Continuity," 19 July 1947, *Forbidden Street* production file, Fox-UCLA.

16. *Inquisition: The Case of the Hollywood Ten* (Hollywood, Calif.: Committee for the Hollywood Ten Arts, Sciences, and Professional Council, n.d.), p. 5.

17. Victor S. Navasky, *Naming Names* (New York: Viking, 1980), p. 377.

18. See, e.g., Adam J. Sorkin, "Politics, Privatism, and the Fifties: Ring Lardner, Jr.'s, 'The Ecstasy of Owen Muir'," *Journal of American Culture* 8 (1985): 59-73.

19. From Hunter's reply to a Finnish archivist (29 Oct. 1984) seeking information about the authorship of the *Robin Hood* scripts. I am grateful to Mr. Hunter for a copy of this letter.

20. Gerald Boardman, *American Musical Theatre: A Chronicle* (New York: Oxford Univ. Press, 1977), p. 634.

21. For the text of the letter, see Lardner, *The Lardners*, pp. 268-69.

22. Dunne, *Take Two*, p. 246.

10. DALTON TRUMBO

1. Whether United Artists, which distributed *Exodus*, should be given credit as well is dubious. As Ring Lardner, Jr., noted in "My Life on the Blacklist," *Saturday Evening Post*, 14 Oct. 1961, p. 42, "United Artists . . . was not a member of the association that formulated the blacklist"; moreover, Preminger's decision to hire Trumbo, courageous as it seems, was not without publicity value.

2. Cook, *Dalton Trumbo*, p. 39.

3. Box 11, Trumbo Collection.

4. The stories are in ibid, boxes 11-12.

5. Ibid., box 15.

6. Cook, *Dalton Trumbo*, p. 67.

7. Dalton Trumbo, *Washington Jitters* (New York: Knopf, 1936), p. 170.

8. Dalton Trumbo, *Johnny Got His Gun* (New York: Bantam Books, 1983), p. 36; subsequent page references are to this edition.

9. Production information comes from the *Road Gang* production file, Warner-USC.

10. Richard B. Jewell, with Vernon Harbin, *The RKO Story* (New York: Arlington House, 1982), p. 116.

11. The drafts are in the *Fugitives for a Night* production file, RKO archives.

12. Production information comes from the *Five Came Back* production file, RKO archives.

13. Production information comes from the *Kitty Foyle* production file, RKO archives.

14. According to Robert L. Carringer, *The Making of Citizen Kane* (Berkeley: Univ. of California Press, 1985), p. 19, the glass globes for both were constructed in the RKO property department.

15. Christopher Morley, *Kitty Foyle* (Philadelphia: Lippincott, 1939), pp. 29-30.

16. From Trumbo's 1938 story "The General Came to Stay" (which became the basis of the novel and the film) in *The Remarkable Andrew* production file, Paramount-Herrick.

17. The drafts are in the *Tender Comrade* production file, RKO archives.

18. In the *Our Vines Have Tender Grapes* production file at MGM, Culver City. Margulies's same-day reply admits that the charge can be made of *Song of Russia*, but as for *Vines*, "the only possible connection is . . . that it points out the hardships of making a living from the earth and they [critics] compared it to . . . 'The Southerner' which was supposed indirectly to have some social significance." *Ergo*, if a film is about farmers and is socially significant, it may be Communistic.

19. Cook, *Dalton Trumbo*, p. 243.

20. From the *Wild Is the Wind* production file, Paramount-Herrick.

21. From *The Green-Eyed Blonde* production file, Warner-USC.

22. In box 32, Douglas Papers, which also includes the scripts but not "Les Crutchfield's" story. It should be noted that *Last Train from Gun Hill* was not Trumbo's first involvement with Douglas; in Jan. 1958, Eddie Lewis paid "Sam Jackson" a $2,500 advance

against a contract to write a script for the film that became *Lonely Are the Brave*. Since the latter did not come out for four more years, however, *Last Train* might be considered Trumbo's first attempt at writing for Douglas.

23. I am indebted to Joan Scott for this information.

24. Box 28, Trumbo Collection.

25. Interview with Ian McClellan Hunter, 13 Dec. 1986.

26. Wyler claimed that out of sympathy for Sturges, whose Hollywood career was ruined by *The Beautiful Blonde from Bashful Bend* (ironically, a Trumbo original), he told Paramount that *Roman Holiday* needed additional rewriting, which it did not; Sturges rewrote it, but his script was unusable, according to James Curtis, *Between Flops: A Biography of Preston Sturges* (New York: Harcourt Brace Jovanovich, 1982), p. 263.

27. In the *Roman Holiday* production file, Paramount-Herrick.

28. Originally, Trumbo was to have written *Terror*; unable to do so at the time, he recommended Lawson, whose script proved unsatisfactory. Since Trumbo had guaranteed rewrites, he rewrote Lawson's script. See Cook, *Dalton Trumbo*, p. 242.

29. Jesse L. Lasky, Jr., *Whatever Happened to Hollywood?* (New York: Funk & Wagnalls, 1975), p. 269.

30. In box 26, Trumbo Collection.

31. Charles Higham, *The Films of Orson Welles* (Berkeley: Univ. of California Press, 1971), pp. 84-99; see also Barbara Leaming, *Orson Welles: A Biography* (New York: Viking, 1985), pp. 246-56.

32. The most detailed account thus far is by Todd McCarthy, "Some 18-20 Hours from 1942 'True' Are Salvaged," *Variety*, 27 Aug. 1986, pp. 1, 106.

33. Details of the Rader and Duval claims (see below) are from accounts in *Daily Variety*, 8 April 1957; *Hollywood Reporter*, 25 July 1958; and *Variety*, 2 July 1962.

34. In an undated memo in box 9, Trumbo Collection. The tone is quite different from the 6 Aug. 1958 letter to Eddie Lewis (Trumbo, *Additional Dialogue*, pp. 439-40), in which he assumes that the Duval claim is a "shakedown."

35. Production details are taken from boxes 38-42, Trumbo Collection.

36. "Second After-Thought: Directors and Their Delusions," ibid., box 40.

37. "Report on Spartacus," p. 13, ibid.

38. Ibid.

39. Dalton Trumbo, *Night of the Aurochs*, ed. and introd. Robert Kirsch (New York: Viking, 1979), pp. 133-34 (page references in the text are to this edition).

40. Trumbo, *Additional Dialogue*, pp. 444-45.

41. Dalton Trumbo, *The Time of the Toad: A Study of the Inquisition in America and Two Related Pamphlets* (New York: Perennial Library/Harper & Row, 1972), p. 35 (page references to the pamphlets cite this edition).

EPILOGUE

1. David A. Cook, *A History of the Narrative Film* (New York: Norton, 1981), p. 410.

2. Editorial insert in Adrian Scott, "Blacklist: The Liberal's Straightjacket and Its Effect on Content," *Hollywood Review* 2 (Sept.-Oct. 1955): 3.

3. Charles Higham, *Hollywood at Sunset* (New York: Saturday Review Press, 1972), p. 65.

4. Cook, *Narrative Film*, p. 410.

5. Box 15, folder 1, Maltz Collection.

6. Lardner, "My Life on the Blacklist," p. 42.

7. Trumbo, *Additional Dialogue*, p. 489.

8. Letter from "Sam Jackson" to J.W. Asher, Jr., 9 June 1959, in box 11, Douglas Papers.

Index